CATHOLIC BELFAST AND NATIONALIST IRELAND IN THE ERA OF JOE DEVLIN, 1871–1934

Catholic Belfast and Nationalist Ireland in the Era of Joe Devlin, 1871–1934

A. C. HEPBURN

OXFORD
UNIVERSITY PRESS

OXFORD

UNIVERSITY PRESS

Great Clarendon Street, Oxford OX2 6DP

Oxford University Press is a department of the University of Oxford.
It furthers the University's objective of excellence in research, scholarship,
and education by publishing worldwide in

Oxford New York

Auckland Cape Town Dar es Salaam Hong Kong Karachi
Kuala Lumpur Madrid Melbourne Mexico City Nairobi
New Delhi Shanghai Taipei Toronto

With offices in

Argentina Austria Brazil Chile Czech Republic France Greece
Guatemala Hungary Italy Japan Poland Portugal Singapore
South Korea Switzerland Thailand Turkey Ukraine Vietnam

Oxford is a registered trade mark of Oxford University Press
in the UK and in certain other countries

Published in the United States
by Oxford University Press Inc., New York

British Library Cataloguing in Publication Data

Data available

Library of Congress Cataloging in Publication Data

Hepburn, A. C. (Anthony C.)
Catholic Belfast and Nationalist Ireland in the era of Joe Devlin, 1871–1934 / A.C.
Hepburn.
p. cm.
Includes bibliographical references and index.
ISBN-13: 978–0–19–929884–6 (acid-free paper) 1. Belfast (Northern Ireland)–History.
2. Catholics–Northern Ireland–Belfast–History–19th century. 3. Catholics–Northern
Ireland–Belfast–History–20th century. 4. Nationalism–Northern Ireland–Belfast–
History. 5. Religion and politics–Northern Ireland–Belfast–History. 6. Northern
Ireland–Politics and government. 7. Devlin, Joseph, 1871–1934. I. Title.
DA995.B5H45 2008
941.608–dc22
2008020967

Typeset by Laserwords Private Limited, Chennai, India
Printed in Great Britain
on acid-free paper by
CPI Antony Rowe, Chippenham, Wiltshire

ISBN 978–0–19–929884–6

1 3 5 7 9 10 8 6 4 2

For Ethan and Freya

and in memory of my teachers
Maurice Cowling (1926–2005)
F. S. L. Lyons (1923–1983)
Nicholas Mansergh (1910–1991)
E. N. Williams (1917–1993)

Acknowledgements

This book has been a long time in the making, and draws on a career's length of research. Its subject is both a politician who destroyed his papers and the urban community that supported him. It is appropriate, therefore, to begin by thanking the archivists and librarians whose collections have made such a study possible. Thanks especially to Dr Gerry Slater and his staff at the Public Record Office of Northern Ireland for the range of collections that they have gathered over the years to compensate for the lack of a Devlin archive; to the grandson of Cahir Healy for permission to quote from his papers; to Captain Robert Lowry for permission to quote from the H. de F. Montgomery Papers; and to the descendants of Matthew and Hannah Keating for depositing their collection of letters and photographs of Joe Devlin. Likewise Seamus Helferty and the staff of the University College Dublin Archives Department made a number of large collections available, including the papers of Ernest Blythe, T. M. Kettle, Michael McCartan, Dennis McCullough, Seán MacEntee, and Eoin MacNeill, and also the Eamon de Valera Papers, which they hold as part of the UCD–OFM Partnership with the Order of Friars Minor. I am grateful also to the staff of the Department of Manuscripts, Trinity College, Dublin, for their assistance, and to the Board of Trinity College, Dublin, for permission to quote from the papers of John Dillon and of Michael Davitt. Quotations from the papers of G. F. H. Berkeley, Edward Blake, Eamon Ceannt, W. G. Fallon, T. P. Gill, Maurice Moore, William O'Brien (of Cork), Thomas O'Donnell, John Redmond, and Francis and Hannah Sheehy-Skeffington are with the permission of the Board of the National Library of Ireland. Further collections of the G. F. H. Berkeley Papers are quoted with the permission of Cork City and County Archives and of the William O'Brien Papers with the permission of Special Collections, the Boole Library, University College, Cork. I am grateful to the Parliamentary Archives, Westminster, for permission to quote from the papers of David Lloyd George and Andrew Bonar Law. The Churchill Archives Centre at Churchill College, Cambridge, kindly granted access to the Chartwell Papers, as did the Bodleian Library, Oxford, to the papers of H. H. Asquith, Augustine Birrell, Matthew Nathan, and F. A. Hemming (the latter with the permission of Corpus Christi College, Oxford). The British Library granted access to the papers of J. H. Bernard and Charles Dilke, and also to another collection of Augustine Birrell Papers. I am grateful also for Crown Copyright permission to quote from papers by government ministers in various collections and from public records in The National Archives. The Cardinal Tomás Ó Fiaich Memorial Library and Archive, which houses the Armagh diocesan archives, kindly granted access to the papers of Archbishop Joseph

Dixon and Cardinals Michael Logue, Patrick O'Donnell, Joseph MacRory, and W. J. Walsh. The correspondence of Sir Horace Plunkett was consulted with the permission of the Plunkett Foundation, Woodstock, Oxon., and the Horace Plunkett Diary with the permission of the Golden Jubilee Trust Ltd., Plunkett House, Dublin. Brother Peter Fogarty of the Christian Brothers' Generalate, Rome, was very helpful to me many years ago, as was the Revd George O'Hanlon of the Down and Connor Archives, who kindly provided Figure 3.3. My thanks also to the staff of the Irish Military Archives, Dublin, who provided copies of the Belfast witness statements gathered by the Bureau of Military History. I am especially grateful to successive Rectors of the Pontifical Irish College, Rome, for access to the papers of their predecessors and for providing accommodation on a number of occasions. More recently the College Archivist, Vera Orschel, has been especially generous with support and assistance in tracing and verifying items. I have also received help from the Linenhall Library, Belfast; Surrey County Libraries; and the libraries of the Universities of Sunderland, Ulster, Cambridge, Newcastle upon Tyne, and Durham.

I am grateful also to colleagues who helped with research at different stages, including Margaret Pearson and Mervyn Hall, who long ago followed Joe Devlin through a maze of archives and newspapers; Brenda Collins, who worked on the census data used in Chapter 2; and more recently John Flanagan, Angela Long, and Marianne Rogowski at the University of Sunderland. Ludmilla Jordanova and John Morrill kindly granted me a Visiting Fellowship at the Centre for Research in Arts, Social Sciences, and Humanities (CRASSH) in 2004, during which time I also benefited from the support of the Master and Fellows of Downing College. Roy Foster's Irish History Seminar at Hertford College, Oxford, provided an opportunity for wide-ranging discussion and a number of fresh insights. The Arts and Humanities Research Council and the University of Sunderland provided generous periods of research leave, without which the work would not have been completed. Christopher Wheeler and his colleagues at Oxford University Press were most supportive and helpful during the publication stage of the project, including Matthew Cotton, Kate Hind, Rachel Kemp, Natasha Knight, and Hilary Walford.

Many colleagues and friends have made helpful suggestions, engaged in discussions, or read parts of drafts, including Joan Allen, Paul Bew, Fergus Campbell, Sean Connolly, Marianne Elliott, Tom Fraser, Neal Garnham, Michael Hopkinson, Keith Jeffery, Michael Keating, Jim MacPherson, Donald MacRaild, Chris Manson, Patrick Maume, John O'Kane, Terry O'Keeffe, Eamon Phoenix, Malcolm Smith, Richard M. Smith, Jim Smyth, Brian Trainor, Sally Warwick-Haller, and Michael Wheatley. Simon Veit-Wilson helped to improve the quality of some of the newspaper photographs. I am especially grateful to friends who shared dinner tables, holidays, and country rambles with Joe Devlin above and beyond the call of friendship: Sheila Bone and Hugh Keegan, Ginny Burnett and Fred Hepburn, John and Marie Darby, Steve and

Jane Ickringill, Sandra and Tony Pollard, Cherrie and Derek Stubbs, and most of all Felicity Hepburn, who has lived with Joe Devlin for far too long. Inspiration came also from the memory of two bartenders who went on to greater things, Wee Joe Devlin (1871–1934) and Big Joe Turner (1911–85).

A. C. HEPBURN

Newcastle upon Tyne
March 2008

Contents

List of Illustrations

List of Tables

Abbreviations

ACBGR	Archives of the Christian Brothers' Generalate, Rome
ADA	Armagh Diocesan Archives
AfIL	All-for-Ireland League
AMCOMRI	American Committee for Relief in Ireland
AOH	Ancient Order of Hibernians
ASE	Amalgamated Society of Engineers
ASU	Active Service Unit
BL	British Library
BLP	Bonar Law Papers
BLUCC	Boole Library, University College, Cork
BMH	Bureau of Military History
BOD	Bodleian Library, Oxford
CA	Catholic Association
CCA	Churchill College Archives, Cambridge
CCCA	Cork City & County Archives
CDS	Catholic Defence Society
CHP	Cahir Healy Papers
CIGS	Chief of the Imperial General Staff
CP	Chartwell Papers
CUL	Cambridge University Library
DATI	Department of Agriculture & Technical Instruction
deVP	Eamon de Valera Papers
DMP	Dublin Metropolitan Police
DORA	Defence of the Realm Act
DP	John Dillon Papers

FJ	*Freeman's Journal*
GAA	Gaelic Athletic Association
GL	Gaelic League
HC	House of Commons
HLRO	House of Lords Record Office
IAOS	Irish Agricultural Organization Society
ICA	Irish Citizen Army
ILP	Independent Labour Party
IN	*Irish News*
INA	Irish National Archives
INF	Irish National Foresters
INFed.	Irish National Federation
INL	Irish National League (to 1900)
INL	Irish Nation League (1916–17)
INTO	Irish National Teachers' Organization
IPP	Irish Parliamentary Party
IRA	Irish Republican Army
IRB	Irish Republican Brotherhood
IFS	Irish Free State
ISDL	Irish Self-Determination League
ITGWU	Irish Transport and General Workers' Union
ITUC	Irish Trades Union Congress
JHP	John Hagan Papers
JP	Justice of the Peace
KIR	Tobias Kirby Papers
LCC	London County Council
LGP	Lloyd George Papers
LHL	Linen Hall Library, Belfast
LRC	Labour Representation Committee

LRO	Liverpool City Record Office
LVA	Licensed Vintners' Association
MC	Military Cross
McCP	Denis McCullough Papers
MMP	Maurice Moore Papers
MOR	Michael O'Riordan Papers
NEBB	North Eastern Boundary Bureau
NILP	Northern Ireland Labour Party
NLI	National Library of Ireland
NLS	National Library of Scotland
NRU	National Registration Union
NS	*Northern Star*
NUDL	National Union of Dock Labourers
OBP	William O'Brien (of Cork) Papers
PF	Plunkett Foundation
PICR	Pontifical Irish College, Rome
PP	parish priest
PPS	Parliamentary Private Secretary
PR	Proportional Representation
PRONI	Public Record Office of Northern Ireland
QUB	Queen's University of Belfast
RIC	Royal Irish Constabulary
RP	Redmond Papers
RUC	Royal Ulster Constabulary
SDLP	Social Democratic and Labour Party
TCDA	Trinity College Dublin Archives
TD	Teachta Dála (Member of the Dáil)
TNA	The National Archives, London

UCDA	University College Dublin Archives
UDC	Urban District Council
UIL	United Irish League
UILGB	United Irish League of Great Britain
UVF	Ulster Volunteer Force
VA	Vatican Archives
VF	Vicar Forane
VG	Vicar General
WFJ	*Weekly Freeman's Journal*
WSPU	Women's Social and Political Union
YIB	Young Ireland Branch of the United Irish League

Note on the Text

The capitalized term 'Nationalist' is used to refer to the Irish Parliamentary Party and its supporters, and to supporters of Joe Devlin in Northern Ireland after 1921. In its non-capitalized form, 'nationalist' is used as a general term to embrace all supporters of Irish home rule and independence, including Sinn Féiners and republicans.

What excellent fools Religion makes of men.

> (Ben Johnson, *Sejanus: His Fall* (London, 1605; The World's Classics edn., Oxford, 1953), 181)

TOM: A'll go til Glasgow after this is over, or mebbe til Englan'. They don't make a lot of damned fools o' themselves about religion over there.

MRS RAINEY: Aw, but mebbe they have their own way o' being' foolish! Ye nivir know.

> (St John Ervine, *Mixed Marriage*, in *Four Irish Plays* (Dublin, 1914), 48)

It has been said that though God cannot alter the past, historians can. It is perhaps because they can be useful to him in this respect that He tolerates their existence.

> (Samuel Butler, *Erewhon* (1872), ch. 14)

George is bogged down in the History Department. He's an old bog in the History department, that's what George is . . .

> (Edward Albee, *Who's Afraid of Virginia Woolf?* (London: Jonathan Cape, 1964), 50)

1

North and South

Het þa hyssa hwæne   hors forlætan,
feor afysan,   and forð gangan,
hicgan to handum   and to hige godum.

(*The Battle of Maldon, c.* tenth century AD[1])

tri choicait mac do maccaib ríg Ulad im Follomain mac Conchobair, &
dos-bertsat teora catha dona slúagaib, co torchratar a trí comlín & torchratar
in macrad dana . . .

(*The Cattle-Raid of Cooley, c.* seventh century AD[2])

Both the cultures represented above, the Anglo-Saxon and the Gaelic, were
destroyed by Norman French invaders, the first quickly and totally, the other
slowly and partially. It is often said that 'England' invaded 'Ireland' in the
twelfth century, but this is to read history backwards. The dividing line between
state-building and colonization is not an absolute one. The incorporation of
Languedoc and other areas of southern France into the French state was a
slow and sometimes bloody business, but now appears to have been entirely
successful. Less than a century ago the same might have been said of the
place of Scotland and Wales within the United Kingdom; now the future is
less easy to predict. Ireland's relationship with Britain was clearly a case of
failed state-building, a fact that has been indisputable since 1916–22, hard
to gainsay since the 1790s, and arguably on the cards since the Reformation.
Yet Irishmen were over-represented in the British Army for much of modern
history, and, as the economic failure of Ireland's union with nineteenth-century

---

[1] Then he commanded each young man
To leave his horse, to drive it far off,
and to go forth, with mind turned
to strong hands and good thoughts . . .

[2] Thrice fifty boys of the sons of the kings of Ulster, accompanying Follomain, Conchobar's
son, and three battles they offered to the hosts, so that thrice their number fell and the youths
also fell . . .

Britain intensified popular antagonism towards the larger island, so more and more Irish people settled in the country that they regarded as the cause of their problems. But we know that increased contact between rival ethnic groups can have a negative effect on relationships. A group, however dominant, that is over the horizon is less likely to provoke direct hostility than one that is highly visible, whether in the form of British soldiers in Cork farmhouses and West Belfast streets, or in the form of 'host' to an immigrant Irish 'community'. It is, for instance, quite noticeable how many of those prominent in the Irish revolution had previously lived and worked—sometimes quite successfully, as in the case of Michael Collins—in Britain. A similar pattern is apparent within the ethnically mixed area of north-east Ulster. Catholic–Protestant conflict, though its modern phase began in the late eighteenth century with land competition in congested areas such as north Armagh, became much more bitter and intense as two distinct working-class communities developed in nineteenth-century Belfast. Any significant vestige of Presbyterian sympathy with Irish republicanism withered as quickly as the French revolutionary ideology that had given it life.

The Irish revolution of 1916–23 is generally regarded as a success. Notwithstanding unease about the 'blood sacrifice' mentality of 1916, the violence and reprisals of the War of Independence and the savagery of the Civil War, the overall assessment of the struggle has been a positive one, for the ultimate outcome was a stable and civilized state. But for the Catholic and nationalist minority in what became Northern Ireland the revolution was a disastrous failure—producing partition, a discriminatory majoritarian regime, and, more recently, a generation of renewed violence and a decade of political impasse. It is frequently suggested by supporters of the republican tradition and others that the blame for this outcome lies not only with 'perfidious Albion' and the 'bigotry' of Ulster Unionism but also in large measure with the representatives of the constitutional nationalist tradition—John Redmond, John Dillon, and Joe Devlin—for persuading Ulster Nationalists into provisional acceptance of temporary partition in 1916, and with Joe Devlin more generally for the alleged sectarianization of nationalism through his use of the exclusively Catholic Ancient Order of Hibernians as a national political machine. But too much modern Irish history has been written from the standpoint of the winners. This book will seek to redress the balance by taking the Catholic and nationalist minority of Belfast as the prism through which the years from the fall of Parnell in 1891 to the confirmation of the two-state solution during the inter-war period is studied. It will be argued that the views referred to above are less a historical analysis than a foundation myth for the successful twenty-six-county state. Violent revolution did lead to sovereign independence for three-quarters of the country more rapidly than a continuation of constitutional nationalism would have done, but at very heavy cost to the Catholic minority in the remaining quarter.

The framework for the book is the history of Catholic and nationalist Belfast during the years from the late nineteenth century to the early years of partition, interwoven with the career of the Belfast-born Irish Nationalist leader Joseph Devlin. Because Devlin was at the centre of Irish national politics for twenty years, and then became the effective leader of constitutional nationalism in the North through and beyond the period of revolution that followed, the book will also offer a general reinterpretation of Irish nationalist strategy during these crucial years. A study in which Devlin and Catholic Belfast are more closely considered will permit a needed reassessment of the politics of the Irish Party in the post-Parnell era, and of Sinn Féin's Ulster policy after 1918. Partition came about primarily because the Ulster Unionists were able to press effectively for it, inside and outside Parliament, between 1912 and 1921. But, so far as the nationalist side is concerned, it will be argued here that the main cause of the total and apparently permanent partition between sovereign states that emerged in 1921–2 was not the provisional and temporary concession made by Devlin and his colleagues in 1916 but the era of violence provoked by Sinn Féin's 1918 general-election victory. It will also be suggested that the Catholic Church, in its anxiety to keep up with the sudden popular surge of extreme nationalism, and to avoid any part of its territory coming under a Belfast Protestant administration, inadvertently helped to turn its nightmare scenario into reality.

The question of whether or not the conflict in the north of Ireland is 'about religion' is a misleading one. It is about ethnic difference and rivalry between two communities, of 'native' and 'settler' origins respectively, where a Catholic–Protestant religious divide matches the other divisions. Historical folk memories (including that of language difference) gave the divide much of its salience, but religious difference was the vital factor that could not easily be eroded by the passage of time, or by long spells of relative harmony, or by cheek-by-jowl living in cramped urban circumstances. Because this situation made religious leaders into community leaders to a considerable extent, the communities were led by people for whom specifically religious concerns, most notably education, were of central importance. The 'native Irish' of the early seventeenth century became the 'Catholic community' of the late eighteenth century. The 'Scots' and 'English' settlers were differentiated as 'Presbyterians' and 'Episcopalians', another divide that had great importance in parts of Ulster, especially during the 1790s. But the common sense of settler origins and the narrower intra-Protestant theological differences meant that this particular ethnic division declined in salience during the nineteenth century. By the late 1880s Ireland contained a large Catholic community that, with few exceptions, regarded itself as 'Irish' and was coming, in the mode of the times, to see itself as a separate nation with a right to statehood. It also contained a much smaller but more concentrated 'Protestant community' that, though less clear about the precise details of its ethnic identity, was coming to regard the maintenance of the British link as an important part of its heritage.

Joe Devlin's personal background was typical of Catholic West Belfast in the mid-nineteenth century. His parents had both migrated to the city in the post-famine years, and lived in working-class neighbourhoods in more-or-less exclusively Catholic streets. Devlin retained his appeal to the ordinary people of these neighbourhoods throughout his life, and indeed beyond it. Increasingly his personal friends were members of the rising Catholic business class and—surprisingly in view of his earlier career—priests. His parliamentary skills drew praise from his contemporary Winston Churchill, both before the First World War and in the post-Treaty period. But he also remained the idol of the Belfast mill girls. In public life his forceful oratory and his formidable organizing skills made him enemies as well as friends. Tim Healy famously dismissed him as the 'duodecimo Demosthenes'. William O'Brien preferred to characterize him as Frankenstein, creator of the Ancient Order of Hibernians' Board of Erin, which in O'Brien's view was 'the real dispenser of all power and offices and titles' in Ireland between 1906 and 1916. James Connolly thought that 'the Orange Society would long since have ceased to exist' has it not been for the Board of Erin, and that 'to Brother Devlin, and not to brother Carson, is mainly due the progress of the Covenanter movement in Ulster'.[3] Academic writers have been less harsh, but until recently have not given Devlin sufficient attention. In part this may be due to his personal circumstances. He never married, and he had few indirect descendants. More important, probably, is the fact that Devlin instructed his secretary to destroy his papers on his death. Furthermore, he also advised Bishop MacRory, on his translation to the Archdiocese of Armagh in 1928, to destroy the previous forty years of the Down & Connor Archives. So Devlin does not really *deserve* a biography! On the other hand, his role in both the mainstream Nationalist movement and in the particular problem of Belfast and Ulster, together with the fact that his active career—uniquely among leading figures—spans the home rule, partition, and post-partition eras, makes the absence of such a study a serious gap in the literature. Individually he was a remarkable character, and his public life includes formidable achievements as well as great disappointments.

Devlin's only biographer to date has been F. J. Whitford, formerly of Queen's University, Belfast, who wrote a London University thesis in the 1950s, 'Joseph Devlin: Ulsterman and Irishman'. The results of his research were serialized over fourteen weeks in the *Sunday Independent* during 1959. Whitford was able to gather material from some of Devlin's then-surviving contemporaries. Several small collections now in the Public Record Office of Northern Ireland are the direct result of his work. Whitford's assessment of Devlin is generally a positive one, but he sets his analysis in a framework reminiscent of Denis Gwynn's *History of Partition* (1950). Ulster Unionists, he suggests, destroyed the Irish Party through their use of 'methods which shattered the faith of Irishmen in

---

[3] W. O'Brien, *The Irish Revolution and how it Came about* (London, 1923), 31–2.

constitutionalism', professing 'a loyalty to Ulster and the Empire which lacks any sense of responsibility *to* or any sense of responsibility *for* Ireland as a whole'. He adds that the Irish Party 'went into that last fight during which Ireland was torn asunder with its organization in poor shape. For this Devlin must be held partly responsible. He . . . relied too much on safe, orthodox men, on his skill in managing and . . . on his . . . oratory.'[4]

For F. S. L. Lyons, the leading historian of the home-rule movement, Devlin was 'an able newcomer', 'loved and respected by Northern Catholics', and 'a first-class organizer, who took from Redmond's shoulders the business of local and sometimes grubby negotiation which the Chairman found repugnant'.[5] In similar vein T. W. Moody admired, in the words of Roy Foster, 'the integrity and commitment of the nineteenth-century Fenian movement, which he constantly emphasized, at the expense, perhaps, of the openly sectarian Ancient Order of Hibernians, who, it could be argued, were far more influential in shaping Irish politics in the early twentieth century . . . Joe Devlin might tactfully be left for later.'[6] In A. T. Q. Stewart's *The Narrow Ground* (1977), a specialist study of the history of community relations in the North, Devlin received no mention. Again, the name of the leader of Northern Nationalism does not appear in the index of one of the major studies of the period, J. J. Lee's 750-page volume *Ireland, 1912–85* (1989). Emmet Larkin, in his biography of *James Larkin* (1965), had Devlin attempting to ride on the back of the Belfast labour agitation of 1907 but not otherwise appearing. In Arthur Mitchell's *Labour in Irish Politics* (1974) Devlin appeared only as a sporadic opponent or deflector of the advance of labour. John Gray's study of the Belfast strike of 1907, *City in Revolt* (1985), includes what is in many ways a shrewd assessment of Devlin's politics, but declared that his weekly paper, the *Northern Star*, 'represented the worst of the gut politics on which Devlin depended in his West Belfast base'. For Richard English, Devlin 'was both a sentimental Irish nationalist . . . and a deeply Catholic patriot'.[7] Patrick Maume comments that Devlin's 'advocacy of social reform sat uneasily with his alliance with nationalist business interests'.[8] For Paul Bew, Devlin is 'a spectacular example of upward social mobility', and 'a complex figure, sectarian in so far as his role in the AOH went but also socially progressive, and able even to attract some Belfast Protestant working-class votes'.[9] Until the 1990s there was very little archivally based work on Devlin's later career in the post-partition era. Since then Eamon Phoenix and Enda Staunton have published detailed research studies of what I suppose we should call the 'high politics' (though not very

---

[4] F. J. Whitford, *Sunday Independent*, 3 May 1959.

[5] F. S. L. Lyons, *Ireland since the Famine* (London, 1971), 258.

[6] R. F. Foster, *The Irish Story: Telling Tales and Making it up in Ireland* (London, 2001), 47.

[7] R. English, *Irish Freedom: The History of Nationalism in Ireland* (London, 2006), 344.

[8] P. Maume, *The Long Gestation: Irish Nationalist Life, 1891–1918* (Dublin, 1999), 225.

[9] P. Bew, *Ideology & the Irish Question: Ulster Unionism & Irish Nationalism, 1912–1916* (Oxford, 1994), 19, 78.

high) of these years, which focus specifically on Northern nationalism for the first time. Phoenix, in particular, picks up the story from the third Home Rule Bill onwards, and so has begun to bridge the partition and home-rule era/Sinn Féin era divide that characterized so much previous work.[10] Finally, Marianne Elliott comments that after 1922, 'sick and disillusioned, Devlin saw himself going in directions which his whole career had fought against . . . the constant need to pursue Catholic issues made him realize that he was leading a Catholic party (and this when he had always been cold-shouldered by the local bishop and cardinal).'[11]

Consistency is scarcely the quality most commonly associated with politicians. In his loyalty to John Dillon and to what he saw as the mainstream of Irish nationalist politics, Joe Devlin was probably more consistent than most. Yet his career was permeated by paradox. A relatively uncomplicated man, at least in his public life, he is nevertheless something of an enigma. He entered politics as a vigorous and outspoken campaigner for independent lay leadership in politics against episcopal domination, yet his later years were devoted to the defence of Catholic Church interests. From a working-class background, he worked effectively to improve the condition of the working masses of his native city, but the ethos of his own circle was characterized by an essentially individualist drive for upward social mobility. A proponent of working-class unity for Catholics and Protestants in Belfast, he made an exclusively Catholic association, the Ancient Order of Hibernians, his lifelong political machine. A forthright opponent of Orangeism and a believer in advancing the interests of Ulster's Catholics through participation in a wider all-Ireland Nationalist movement, his toughest organizational achievement was to persuade his followers to accept the principle of temporary partition. A man who appeared to be destined by his organizational and rhetorical abilities to progress from the back streets of Belfast to the leadership of Ireland under home rule was instead displaced by revolutionary Sinn Féin. His public life came nearly full circle as he returned in the 1920s to the narrower world of politics in Northern Ireland. He thus failed to break out of the sectarian straitjacket, and was in that sense a 'prisoner of the city'.

---

[10] E. Phoenix, *Northern Nationalism: Nationalist Politics, Partition & the Catholic Minority in Northern Ireland, 1890–1940* (Belfast, 1994); E. Staunton, *The Nationalists of Northern Ireland, 1918–1973* (Dublin, 2001).

[11] M. Elliott, *The Catholics of Ulster: A History* (London, 2000), 296, 397.

2

'Prisoners of the City': Catholic Belfast in the Late Nineteenth Century

> We are all prisoners of this city.
> (BBC Radio Ulster, vox
> pop., 1987)

The position of ethnic minorities in contested cities and regions is an unenviable one. They have the same need for communal cultural and economic support as do migrants in confident monolithic states, yet the manifestation of these needs in disputed territories provokes an opposition from the dominant community that makes assimilation difficult on any terms. Where political circumstances permit, such minorities respond by seeking help outside the region, whether from the benign liberal blanket of a metropolitan or imperial regime, or from the more heady inspiration of a secessionist movement, or from the seductive lure of a neighbouring state with its own unchallenged homeland. In such circumstances there is no long-term trend towards assimilation. Segregation and cultural separation continue indefinitely.

The Catholics of Belfast constituted a distinct community within the city by the beginning of the nineteenth century. By mid-century they were identified with a broad political viewpoint, and by the 1880s they had attached themselves to a specific political programme. Individual Catholics, especially those few who lived in predominantly Protestant local environments, might continue to hold whatever political views they liked, but in the decades after 1850 the terms 'Catholic community' and 'Nationalist community' became increasingly interchangeable. Joe Devlin was born in 1871 and grew up in that community. His early social aspirations, as we shall see, reflected its horizons and realities, and his subsequent career development epitomized its reaching out to other Irish Catholic urban communities and, most of all, to the wider political horizons of Dublin and London, where levers of power might be grasped that were beyond the reach of those who confined themselves to the constrained political world of Catholic Belfast.

ETHNIC ARITHMETIC: THE POPULATION OF BELFAST

Belfast was first incorporated as a town in 1613. As with so many cities on Europe's ethnic frontiers, it was in origin a settler town. Its population in 1659 was estimated at 589, of which 38 per cent were said to be 'Irish'. But, as it grew, the 'Irish' or 'Catholic' population increased very little. It remained a Protestant town, no more than about 6 per cent Catholic, until the 1780s, when the introduction of cotton manufacturing drew a new industrial workforce from the surrounding countryside. The next two generations saw Catholics coming into the town at a faster rate than Protestants.[1] Throughout the nineteenth century Belfast's economic and demographic development, though typical of British industrial cities of the period, was more or less unique in Ireland. In 1800 it was a linen-marketing centre and small port, comparable to Derry or Newry. The growth of textile manufacturing—first cotton, then its replacement by linen from the 1820s—and later shipbuilding, heavy engineering and general port development, were on such a scale that, measured across the period 1841–1901, Belfast was the fastest growing of all the major cities of the United Kingdom. At the time of the first Census of Ireland in 1821 Belfast's population was a mere fifth of that of Dublin; in 1911 it was a fifth larger than the southern capital. Few other towns in Ireland grew dramatically in the nineteenth century, and indeed many actually shrank. The only exceptions were the smaller linen-manufacturing towns within Belfast's industrial orbit, together with the shirt-making and port city of Derry. In another way, also, Belfast's pattern of population growth was distinctive in nineteenth-century Ireland. The nine Irish centres that had attained city status by 1900 all showed a moderate increase in the Catholic proportion of their population except Belfast, which showed a somewhat more pronounced decline from the Catholics' relative high point in 1861 (Table 2.1). Unlike the other Irish cities, however (with the limited exception of Derry), Belfast was growing rapidly, so that, notwithstanding its relative decline, the Catholic population actually increased substantially in absolute terms from about 1,000 in the 1780s to 55,000 in the year of Devlin's birth and over 100,000 at the time of his death.

The Belfast Catholic experience, as a rapidly growing industrial community in the midst of an even more rapidly growing Protestant population, was therefore unique in Ireland. For a comparable experience we have to look beyond Ireland, to cities such as Glasgow, Liverpool, London, Boston, Chicago, and New York. Such cities, beginning with Belfast, were the focus for Joe Devlin's particular style of nationalist appeal, an appeal to communities that, on the one hand, were growing and developing a more complex internal social structure, but that

---

[1] I. Budge and C. O'Leary, *Belfast: Approach to Crisis* (London, 1973), 32.

Table 2.1. Population and religion in Irish cities, 1861–1911

City	1861	1871	1881	1891	1901	1911
Belfast No.	121,602	174,412	208,122	255,950	349,180	386,947
% RC	*34.1*	*31.9*	*28.8*	*26.3*	*24.3*	*24.1*
Londonderry City No.	20,519	25,242	29,162	33,200	39,892	40,780
% RC					*55.2*	*56.2*
Dublin City No.	246,465	246,326	249,602	245,001	290,638	304,802
% RC	*77.1*	*79.2*	*80.4*	*82.2*	*81.8*	*83.1*
Cork City No.	79,594	78,642	80,124	75,345	76,122	76,673
% RC	*83.9*	*84.8*	*85.7*	*85.7*	*86.4*	*88.4*
Limerick City No.	43,924	39,353	38,562	37,155	38,151	38,518
% RC	*87.9*	*88.5*	*87.9*	*88.5*	*89.1*	*90.5*
Galway City No.	16,448	15,597	5,471	13,800	13,426	13,255
% RC	*96.8*	*93.6*	*91.0*	*91.3*		
Waterford City No.	22,869	23,349	22,457	20,852	26,769	27,464
% RC	*87.7*	*88.2*	*90.3*	*90.2*	*91.8*	*92.2*
Kilkenny City No.	13,235	12,710	12,299	11,048	10,609	10,514
% RC	*89.7*	*89.5*	*89.0*	*89.6*		

Note: Blank cells indicate that no data are available.
Sources: W. E. Vaughan and A. J. Fitzpatrick (eds.), *Irish Historical Statistics: Population, 1821–1971* (Dublin, 1978); *Census of Ireland*, 1861–1911.

also still saw themselves as embattled minorities needing to band together in order to assert themselves. Belfast was the only one of these cities where ethnic demography impacted not only on jobs and housing, but also on the political status of the territory. Indeed, the struggle in Belfast was crucial to the future political status of north-eastern Ireland. In 1861 only 8 per cent of the six-county population lived in Belfast, whereas the figure in 1911 was 31 per cent and in 1937 34 per cent. In this specific sense Belfast truly became the cockpit of conflict in Ulster, control of the city deciding the destiny of the region.

Nineteenth-century Belfast was a city of migrants. In 1901 only an estimated 39 per cent of the population had been born in the city, rising to 69 per cent in 1937 (see Table 2.2). Like most British industrial cities, Belfast drew its nineteenth-century migrants from nearby. Only in 1851, in the aftermath of the famine, did the proportion born outside Belfast, Antrim, and Down fall below 75 per cent. By 1901 Belfast Catholics were slightly more likely than Protestants to have been born in western Ulster or in the south of Ireland, but they were also more likely than Protestants to have been born in Belfast itself. The relative decline of the Catholic population in the city after 1861 had a number of causes. One was the surge of migration from the immediate hinterlands, which were predominantly Protestant. But, as late as 1901, an estimated 31 per cent of Catholic children under the age of 9 had been born outside the city, compared to 35 per cent of Protestant children, which suggests that recent

Catholic Belfast and Nationalist Ireland

Table 2.2. Birthplaces of the Belfast population, 1841–1937 (%)

Year	Belfast, Counties Antrim and Down	Belfast County Borough	Rest of Ulster	Leinster, Munster, and Connacht	Great Britain	Other
1841	84.9		10.5	2.1	2.4	0.2
1851	72.6		19.3	3.3	4.4	0.4
1861	75.2		15.8	3.3	5.1	0.6
1871	77.1		14.4	3.2	5.2	0.6
1881	77.3		13.7	3.0	5.2	0.7
1891	76.9		12.6	3.1	6.7	0.8
1901	76.7		12.6	3.2	6.6	0.8
RC*	72.4	42.9 (25.0)	16.2	5.8	4.4	1.1
OD*	77.8	38.1 (20.5)	11.7	2.2	7.2	1.1
1911	77.8		10.9	3.3	7.2	0.8
			Rest of NI	Rest of Ireland		
1926	79.5	63.8	8.1	5.4	6.1	0.5
1937	82.2	69.1	7.1	4.6	5.3	0.4

Note: Blank cells indicate that no data are available. RC = Roman Catholic and OD = Other Denominations. *Heads of households only.

Sources: Census of Ireland Reports, 1841–1911; Census of NI Reports, 1926–37; 1901 Census schedules (sample sizes RC = 6,483, OD = 19,852).

Catholic in-migration was still considerable.[2] The other side of the demographic picture, therefore, was a high level of Catholic out-migration. Some of this may have been seasonal, temporary, or recurrent, which is suggested by the low ratio of adult Catholic males to females in 1901. Whereas the numbers of males and females under the age of 20 were about the same, among Catholics aged 20 and over there were only 64 males per 100 females, against a Protestant ratio of 79 per 100. By 1937 these ratios had improved only to 73 for Catholics and 85 for Protestants. This is mainly explained by the fact that Belfast was a textile city with far more work for women than for men. A further factor, surprising to students of more recent patterns of behaviour, is what appears to have been a Catholic reproduction rate that was considerably lower than that of Protestants, as measured by crude fertility ratios in both 1871 and 1901.[3] Thus the relative growth of the Catholic population in the first half of the nineteenth century was dramatically reversed in the half-century to 1911, the period in which Nationalist politics came to take a hold on the Catholic community. The era of massive inter-communal rioting that coincided with the reversal was not the only—and probably not even the dominant—factor in reversing ethnic population trends.

[2] 1901 Census sample, based on an analysis of 1,270 Catholic children and 4,066 Protestant children.

[3] A. C. Hepburn, *A Past Apart: Studies in the History of Catholic Belfast, 1850–1950* (Belfast, 1996), 114, 116.

THE CATHOLIC ELITE AND MIDDLE CLASS

The novelist Joseph Tomelty wrote in the 1950s of the sense of victimhood and the 'awful fatalism of the Falls Road'.[4] A century earlier the master baker Bernard Hughes (1808–78) had told a royal commission, that although the Catholics of Belfast were regarded as 'the hewers of wood and the drawers of water . . . the bone and sinew of the town is Roman Catholic . . . [but] . . . it is governed by Protestants in every department'.[5] This claim aroused considerable hostility in the Protestant community, and lost the Liberal Hughes his place as the only Catholic on the town council. Four years later the first Census of Ireland to take account of religious denomination demonstrated that, although Hughes had overstated the demographic case, Catholics were grossly under-represented in the public life of the growing town. In 1857 a survey by the 'United Protestant Committee' for the Conservative *Belfast Newsletter* which had been produced, curiously enough, as an intended riposte to Hughes's claim, in fact confirmed 'that there is a vast preponderance of Protestants in all the public bodies and in every trade and profession to which Belfast owes its commercial importance and distinguished position'.[6] Catholics, who made up 34 per cent of the population, comprised 20 per cent of the parliamentary electorate, 17 per cent of the municipal electorate, 9 per cent of those engaged in professions and trades, and 4 per cent of Chamber of Commerce membership. The free professions and the liquor trade constituted a somewhat larger proportion of the Catholic professional and merchant class than was the case among Protestants, but the strong Protestant predominance in textile and metal manufacturing and shipbuilding was already beginning to emerge.

On the other hand, there were some opportunities for Catholic career success in Belfast. The first grand Catholic church in Belfast, St Patrick's, Donegall Street, had been built in 1815 with substantial help from Protestant subscriptions. Half a century later support from this quarter was less in evidence, deterred by such militant polemics as 'there are men who bear the Protestant name, and are members of Protestant churches, who think it is no crime to subscribe funds for Popish mass-houses—who think it no shame to forge fetters for their own slavery'.[7] Catholic church-building nonetheless entered a period of formidable growth. Bishop Patrick Dorrian told a royal commission in 1864 that there were perhaps seventy or ninety Catholics in Belfast with sufficient capital to donate £100 per year from their incomes. These included a few Catholic Conservatives

---

[4] Cited in E. Longley, *The Living Stream: Literature and Revisionism in Ireland* (Newcastle upon Tyne, 1994), 92.

[5] J. Magee, *Barney: Bernard Hughes of Belfast, 1808–1878* (Belfast, 2001), 89–90.

[6] United Protestant Committee, *Statistics of Protestantism and Romanism* (Belfast, 1857), 4–5.

[7] C. Kinealy and G. MacAtasney, *The Hidden Famine: Hunger, Poverty and Sectarianism in Belfast* (London, 2000), 105.

such as the urban landowner John Hamill, a long-serving member of the town council, who gave his name to the street in which Joseph Devlin was born. Bernard Hughes, a Liberal councillor, came to Belfast as a young baker and by the 1840s had established a bakery that employed 150 people. Peter Keegan founded a whiskey distillery during the early nineteenth century, which, again, was to thrive as a family concern for more than a century. William Watson, a Liberal and a Poor Law Guardian, had made a fortune as a merchant in London, much of which he invested in housing development in Belfast. In the same era William Ross was the only Catholic member of the 'millocracy', proprietor of a flax mill in west Belfast that employed 600 people.[8] There was also a small professional class of lawyers, doctors, and journalists whose custom came mainly from their fellow Catholics. But the majority of those Catholics who lived above the level of the working class were employed in retail trades, most notably in butchery, a trade in which their predominance over Protestants gradually decreased, and the liquor trade, where it increased dramatically.

The Catholic middle class continued to develop in Belfast during the so-called age of riots that characterized the second half of the nineteenth century. Table 2.3 indicates the pattern of development of many of the major categories of middle- and lower-middle-class employment. Some important areas of employment, including all manufacturing and many areas of trading, cannot be included, because the tables in the published census do not make it possible to distinguish between grades of work in these areas, nor, in many cases, do they distinguish between manufacturing a product and trading in it. Nonetheless, the data available provide reasonably precise categorization for a large proportion of this class. The most striking imbalance is in the retailing of liquor, where Catholic predominance increased enormously, during a period when the Catholic proportion of the population was declining. Writing at the time of a threatened closure of pubs during the First World War, Joe Devlin told a colleague that such a change for Belfast would mean 'the complete destruction of the business of over 1,300 publicans and their families—men who have invested from one to ten thousand pounds in their business . . . [This would] . . . ruin them in the only business they have been allowed to enter for, as you know, no Catholic has ever had, or has now a chance of getting into any other business in Belfast.'[9] While the term 'publican' could describe anything from a shebeen-keeper to the owner of several substantial establishments, many educated Belfast Catholics in the later twentieth century could point to the pub in the family background as their stepping stone into the professional or business middle class. Patrick Darby, for instance, who became one of Joe Devlin's leading fundraisers and an organizer of the 'days of delight', came from the village of Kilcoo, Co. Down, during the 1890s to work in a bar. After a few years he was able to get security for a

---

[8] A. Macaulay, *Patrick Dorrian: Bishop of Down & Connor, 1865–1885* (Dublin, 1987), 80, 122.
[9] Devlin to O'Connor, 20 Mar. 1915 (LGP, C/6/10/13).

Table 2.3. Middle- and lower-middle-class male occupations, Belfast, 1871–1911

Occupation	1871	1881	1891	1901	1911
Publicans, wine merchants No.	446	779	989	1,103	1,105
% RC	*52.2*	*53.0*	*68.4*	*77.2*	*80.1*
Police officers, all ranks No.	389	642	731	932	1,061
% RC	*34.4*	*44.1*	*43.4*	*46.1*	*47.2*
Teachers No.	219	337	396	522	567
% RC	*22.4*	*24.6*	*23.0*	*24.3*	*32.5*
Civil servants: officers and clerks No.	225	290	379	471	520
% RC	*36.9*	*29.7*	*25.9*	*28.2*	*30.0*
Lawyers, law clerks No.	175	228	293	405	421
% RC	*20.6*	*24.6*	*23.5*	*22.2*	*18.3*
Physicians, dentists No.	99	157	195	269	402
% RC	*10.0*	*12.1*	*9.7*	*10.8*	*14.4*
Commercial clerks and commercial travellers No.	1,956	2,412	3,985	5,745	6,305
% RC	*13.4*	*14.7*	*12.5*	*13.3*	*14.0*
Merchants, bankers, insurance, auctioneers, accountants No.	608	691	841	1,628	1,977
% RC	*14.0*	*14.8*	*11.1*	*10.0*	*10.6*
Municipal officers No.	59	106	146	274	344
% RC	*15.3*	*11.3*	*8.9*	*8.4*	*9.0*
Male workforce accounted for by above groups No.	4,176	5,642	7,955	11,349	12,702
% RC	*8.4*	*9.6*	*10.3*	*11.1*	*11.4*
Total male workforce	49,868	58,516	77,138	101,789	111,580
Total male Catholic workforce No.	15,464	16,727	20,007	23,869	25,920
% RC	*31.0*	*28.6*	*25.9*	*23.4*	*23.2*

Source: Census of Ireland Reports, 1871–1911.

loan from Dunville's Distillery—a large Protestant concern—to begin his own business. He soon had two pubs, and in due course he and his family moved to a spacious house near the city boundary at the top of the Falls, which by the 1920s had become the first predominantly Catholic middle-class neighbourhood in the city.[10] The rise of the temperance movement within the Protestant churches is the main reason why this valuable ethnic niche remained open to the Catholic minority. The other area of significant Catholic over-representation, the police service, though important, is explained mainly by the recruiting and employment practice of the Royal Irish Constabulary (RIC), under which recruits were not allowed to be stationed in their home counties. After the abolition of the Town Police in 1865 it was government policy to achieve an approximate ethnic balance in the RIC in Belfast. Teaching was a third area in which, by 1911, Catholics had become over-represented. This is only partly explained by the fact that Catholics

---

[10] Interview with his son Patrick Darby.

(in 1901) made up 24.1 per cent of the male population aged 12 and under, as against 23.0 per cent of the post-compulsory schooling age group.

The sharpest contrast displayed in Table 2.3 is that between employment in the civil service, under the control of government departments in London or Dublin, where Catholics were slightly over-represented, and municipal employment, which was the category of white-collar work in which Catholics were least likely to be found. The under-representation, both in financial areas and in the large area of white-collar commercial employment, reflects the generally weak Catholic position in the large sector of modern manufacturing industry. An important part of this was the gradual acceptance by most major employers of the harsh fact that in many areas of skilled employment it was easier to avoid conflict in the workplace by bowing to Protestant pressure from below and employing few, if any, Catholics in such posts, rather than have to use employer muscle and threats to keep warring factions apart.[11] An important additional factor, of course, was the fact that—as in Britain—it was quite customary in this period for industrial workers to vote their employers into Parliament. This gave politically ambitious employers a further reason to play the sectarian card.

As well as skilled manual work, which will be discussed below, we know that white-collar work in the linen industry, together with shipbuilding and engineering, were areas where Catholics were much under-represented, and where Catholic public figures, from Bernard Hughes to Joe Devlin, made allegations of systematic Catholic exclusion. The ethnic balance in shopkeeping, the other main area of non-manual employment not included in Table 2.3, was more mixed. Table 2.4, using sample data from 1901, attempts to identify the elite of the two communities by taking the top 10 per cent of householders—male and female—from a sample of the 1901 census schedules, as measured by the rateable value of the property in which they lived. In the case of Protestants this produced a list of householders with a rateable valuation of £19 and above, while on the Catholic side ten per cent of the population had valuations of £13.50 and above. The patterns previously observed are reinforced. This table includes all household heads in the sample whose rateable valuations meet the criterion, and areas of employment are listed in order of their relative size within each of the two elites. The liquor trade accounted for almost a quarter of the Catholic elite, while the grocery business was of considerable importance to both sides. This suggests that each side literally catered for its own in food supply, whereas the supply of liquor to both communities was left increasingly to Catholic publicans. In 1909 the number of pubs in Belfast was 617.[12]

Table 2.4 also brings out sharply, as Table 2.3 was unable to do, the importance to the Protestant middle class of employment in the textile manufacturing sector and its complete absence from the profile of the Catholic middle class. From

---

[11] Hepburn, *Past Apart*, 38.
[12] Peter Connery, Chairman of Belfast and Ulster LVA, to Dillon, 17 July 1909 (DP 6782/1196).

Table 2.4. Industrial distribution of top 10% of ratepayers by religion, Belfast, 1901 (%)

Protestants		Catholics	
Grocery, food dealing	13.2	Publicans, liquor sales	22.6
Legal, medical, clergy	8.0	Grocery, food dealing	12.0
Textile manufacturing	7.5	Public officials, police, military	8.3
Drapery, clothes dealers	7.3	Food production	8.3
Unspecified managers, agents, and		Garment manufacturing	5.3
commercial travellers	7.3		
Construction	5.3	Other dealers	5.3
Food production	5.0	Construction	3.8
Garment manufacturing	4.8	Drapery, clothes dealers	3.8
Other dealers	4.8	Other manufacturing	3.0
Financial services	4.3	Arts, journalism, teaching	3.0
Other manufacturing	3.9	Financial services	3.0
Metal/ship manufacturing	3.4	Metal/ship manufacturing	2.3
Publicans, liquor sales	3.2	Legal, medical, clergy	2.3
Public officials, police, military	3.2	Unspecified managers, agents, and	
		commercial travellers	1.5
Arts, journalism, teaching	2.7	Transport	0.0
Transport	2.7	Textile manufacturing	0.0
Independent, not working	13.2	Independent, not working	15.8
Female ratepayers	21.6	Female ratepayers	25.0
TOTAL NUMBER IN SAMPLE	438	TOTAL NUMBER IN SAMPLE	133

Note: Protestant ratepayers include householders with a rateable valuation of £19 or more; Catholic ratepayers include householders with a rateable valuation of £13.50 or more.
Source: Sample from Census of Ireland, 1901.

the almost equally large discrepancy in the category of unspecified managers, agents, and commercial travellers, it seems likely that this category also included many who worked in the modern industrial sector. Finally it should be noted that the property valuations on which inclusion in Table 2.4 is based are the valuations of the property in which the householders lived. There is no division in the valuation records between the residential part of a property and any part of it that may have been used for commercial purposes. It was, however, noted in the records when the valuation included a shop or other business premises. In the case of those householders included in this table, 52 per cent of Catholics did indeed have a commercial element included in their valuation (that is, they lived 'above the shop') as against only 25 per cent of this class of Protestant householder. In this sense, therefore, the Catholic middle class was very much a retail commercial community. It was also a somewhat less well-off community, even within the middle and lower-middle classes. Although about 10 per cent of both Catholic and Protestant employed males in 1901 could be assigned to Classes I and II of the Registrar-General's system of occupational classification, the mean average valuation of the property in which these people lived varied significantly, with the Protestants in the class valued at £24.47 as against a mean Catholic valuation of £15.28. Likewise, for males employed in the clerical and supervisory category of Class III (non-manual), the average Protestant valuation was £12.90 as against £9.13 for Catholics.[13]

In cases of urban ethnic conflict it is quite normal to find a middle class —restricted, perhaps, but not insignificant—within a non-dominant group. A number of explanations have been offered for this. A century ago the Black American writer W. E. B. DuBois identified a 'talented tenth', the college-educated elite of the black minority in American society which, he suggested, had the capacity and the duty to assist others 'up to their vantage ground'.[14] There have also been racist twists on this: white racism has tended to explain such success by the presence of 'white blood' in such people, while black racism suggested that a less 'black' appearance gave such people more of a chance to succeed in a white-dominated society. A more likely line of explanation is the economic one, where—except in cases of extreme domination such as apartheid in South Africa—a non-dominant community is able to draw at least some advantage from segregation by developing its own retail, professional and personal services. In American history such opportunity was long limited to 'teachers and preachers', although Dubois believed that even this was a crucial foothold. The struggle to establish 'black capitalism' in the ghettoes took until the 1960s. In Belfast this was happening a century earlier.

THE CATHOLIC WORKING CLASS

Like all late Victorian manufacturing cities, Belfast was populated predominantly by an industrial working class, most of whom were employed in large factories from an early age and for long hours. Linen production, once it supplanted cotton in the 1820s, quickly became and remained the largest employer of labour. By the 1870s this was a predominantly female workforce, only the early stages of preparing the flax for spinning continuing to be men's work. Converting Belfast's swampy river mouth into a first-class port, and establishing it as the centre of a railway network, brought much unskilled heavy manual labour into the town, while the town's very rapid growth in the second half of the nineteenth century brought big opportunities for both skilled and unskilled labour in the building industry. These developments in turn provided the basis for one of the world's leading shipbuilding industries to emerge in the late 1850s, followed by heavy engineering, which specialized initially in the building of textile machinery. It was in these latter areas, where a high proportion of the workforce was skilled

    [13] Hepburn, *Past Apart*, 95.
    [14] W. E. B. DuBois, 'The Talented Tenth', in B. T. Washington (ed.), *The Negro Problem: A Series of Articles by Representative Negroes of To-day* (New York, 1903).

Table 2.5. Selected male manual occupations by religion, Belfast, 1857–1911

Occupation	1857	1871	1881	1891	1901	1911
Shipbuilding trades No.	276	758	1,327	2,773	4,986	6,809
% RC	14.5	9.4	10.5	9.0	7.1	7.6
Engineering, machine manufacture, etc. No.	465	1,182	1,245	2,771	3,900	5,845
% RC	14.6	25.4	17.8	14.9	8.2	11.4
Printing No.	41	634	763	1,149	1,278	1,342
% RC	29.3	24.8	24.4	21.4	17.6	15.2
Linen manufacture No.	594*	3,881	5,163	6,751	6,363	6,253
% RC	14.6	34.8	27.6	27.0	23.2	23.4
Bricklaying, masonry No.	170	737	881	1,388	1,513	981
% RC	38.8	30.8	32.2	29.8	27.8	23.6
Plastering, whitewashing No.	?	238	284	348	477	339
% RC		39.9	43.3	40.2	36.1	35.4
Housepainting No.	182	?	768	998	1,589	1,909
% RC	19.2		22.8	26.0	21.4	20.0
Carpentry, joinery No.	415	1,797	2,295	2,669	3,947	3,520
% RC	21.7	20.6	15.9	16.8	15.6	12.6
Plumbing No.	19	?	283	463	830	1063
% RC	10.5		14.8	12.1	11.6	11.9
Carting No.	?	1,259	1,473	1,584	2,915	3,244
% RC		35.3	30.6	23.7	25.0	27.9
Dock work No.	?	366	655	1,224	1,456	1,565
% RC		42.1	48.7	42.5	42.0	39.6
General labouring No.	?	7,639	8,327	10,304	15,253	18,958
% RC		42.8	36.9	37.0	32.1	33.1
Catholic % of total male workforce	33.0 est.	31.0	28.6	25.9	23.4	23.2
Total number in above occupations as % of male workforce	—	38.6	40.1	42.0	43.7	46.1

* Figure for linen lappers only.

Source: Census of Ireland, Reports, 1871–1911; *Statistics of Protestantism and Romanism* (Belfast, 1857).

and their wages relatively high, and where the apprenticeship system was firmly in place, that Protestants became well established from the outset, and where few Catholics were able to gain positions at any level.

Table 2.5 gives an indication of the ethnic distribution within most of the main categories of male manual employment. Again the limitations of the census reports mean that it is not always possible to distinguish within particular industries between manufacturers and dealers, and between non-manual and manual categories of work. Categories have been selected where we may be reasonably confident that the numbers are exclusively or very predominantly made up of manual workers, and where numbers in the category are large. Table 2.5, together with its middle-class counterpart, Table 2.3, accounts for more than two-thirds of the male workforce in each census column. Table 2.5 also includes a growing proportion of the manual workforce across the period. As well as data from the five usable censuses, the 1857 survey by the *Belfast Newsletter* is used here, as it includes an analysis of 'skilled labour operatives', based on data supplied by craft unions and other bodies. Even at this early stage in the development of Belfast industry Protestants predominated, with Catholics accounting for only 22 per cent of skilled manual workers at a time when they comprised about 34 per cent of the town's population. The patterns changed little over the following half-century. Among the skilled manufacturing trades, shipbuilding and engineering grew most rapidly, a fact that consolidated Protestant advantage. Manual linen work for men, even that classified as skilled, attracted wage levels very much lower than those that obtained in shipbuilding and engineering. Thus Catholic men were able to maintain their relative position in this corner of the labour market.

The other skilled group of trades in Table 2.5 are those connected with building. Belfast, of course, grew very rapidly during these years, although manifesting the uneven pattern of growth typical of building cycles in the industrial era. During the 1890s, for instance, there was overproduction of housing, which brought about an absolute decline in the number of joiners, bricklayers and plasterers during the Edwardian decade. Here there was a substantial Catholic presence, especially among bricklayers, and the less strictly apprenticeship-based trades of plastering/whitewashing and house painting, while among the best-paid categories of joinery and plumbing Catholic proportions were lower and, in the case of joinery, declining quite steeply. The other main categories in the table—carters, dockers, and labourers—were jobs that required strength and stamina, but not apprenticeship-based skills. Here the Catholic side was over-represented to a significant extent. This fact is of some significance in the widespread extension of communal conflict, which will be discussed below. Although there were clear differences in the occupational profiles of Catholics and Protestants, much of the bitterest opposition to Catholics came not from those Protestants who benefited from their community's hegemonic position, but from those who did not. As Table 2.5 indicates, in absolute terms there were twice as many Protestant unskilled labourers as Catholics. Thus something akin to the 'poor white syndrome' operated. The material condition of unskilled workers and their families, Catholic and Protestant, though better than in Dublin, was poorer than in most British industrial cities. While skilled wages in most trades in Belfast compared quite favourably with wages in Britain, the over-supply of unskilled labour in Ireland meant that labourers' wages were significantly lower.[15] In mid-century, the housing of the poor was also very bad.[16] After

[15] A. L. Bowley, *Wages in the United Kingdom in the Nineteenth Century* (Cambridge, 1900).
[16] W. M. O'Hanlon, *Walks among the Poor of Belfast* (Belfast, 1853; new edn., Wakefield, 1971), 49–50.

legislation in 1878, the new and purpose-built working-class housing of Belfast compared favourably with the converted multi-occupancy slums and tenements characteristic of the poorer parts of Dublin and many British cities. By 1914, however, this position was being eroded. The financial restrictions imposed by the 1910 budget, the inevitable disruption of housing provision caused by the war, and the relative lateness of Belfast Corporation's entry into the business of building council houses (in 1917) led to a situation where the Corporation's Housing Committee estimated a shortage of 3,000 houses, of which 1,600 were urgent, while the city's chief health officer estimated the number needed at 10,000.[17]

Unlike areas of the United Kingdom dominated by mining and other heavy industries, the workforce of textile towns included a large proportion of female workers. In Belfast, women and girls made up 45 per cent of the workforce in 1871, falling to 36 per cent—but nonetheless more than doubling in absolute terms—by 1911. Women were employed in a much narrower range of occupations than men. For most of the half-century to 1914, the majority were employed in textile manufacture or finishing; the other large group were domestic servants of various kinds. The occupations listed in Table 2.6 account for between 80 and 90 per cent of the entire female workforce at different dates. Wages were very low, spinners and weavers earning around 10s. per week at a time when male labourers earned about £1. Across the period shopkeeping was the only sizeable category of female employment where opportunities were slightly better, though no doubt most of such business concerns were small and marginal. Only at the very end of the period did women begin to work in significant numbers as commercial clerks, although even in 1911 they made up less than 4 per cent of the female workforce, while female schoolteachers made up an even smaller proportion. The number of nuns has also been recorded here, on the assumption that a significant number would have been engaged in teaching children: if, for instance, fifty nuns were teaching in Belfast in 1911, the Catholic proportion of the female teaching profession in that year would rise from 14 to 18 per cent.

Whether or not women worked at all in this era was a matter determined primarily by class. The decline in the relative number of women workers between 1871 and 1911, in a city where the chronic lack of employment opportunities and pressures for outward labour migration fell more heavily on men, is evidence of this. There were more Protestant women workers than Catholic women workers in absolute terms, but the proportion of Catholic women who worked was substantially greater. Ethnic differentiation within the female workforce existed, but at a more marginal level than was the case for men. Catholic women and girls were heavily over-represented among the low-paid and low-status domestic workers, and also among shopkeepers. In the textile trades the more detailed

Table 2.6. Selected female occupations by religion, Belfast, 1871–1911

Occupation	1871	1881	1891	1901	1911
Teachers, governesses No.	475	821	1,082	1,435	1,396
% RC	*16.2*	*16.2*	*16.3*	*13.7*	*14.2*
Nuns No.	21	79	89	114	162
% RC	*100.0*	*100.0*	*100.0*	*100.0*	*100.0*
Commercial clerks No.	9	12	234	1,122	2,478
% RC	*22.2*	*8.3*	*11.1*	*11.6*	*13.9*
Civil servants No.	6	25	49	159	151
% RC	*50.0*	*32.0*	*16.3*	*23.3*	*20.5*
Shopkeepers, general dealers, grocers, greengrocers, drapers No.	887	1,396	1,938	2,587	2,235
% RC	*48.1*	*39.5*	*38.1*	*32.9*	*31.9*
Flax and Linen workers *All* No.	8,041	17,489	23,195	23,158	23,485
% RC	*44.0*	*40.9*	*38.7*	*35.1*	*37.2*
Spinning processes No.				10,254	11,313
% RC				*45.7*	*46.4*
Weaving processes No.				9,796	9,264
% RC				*26.1*	*28.6*
Dressmakers, shirtmakers, seamstresses, tailoresses, machinists No.	4,493	7,215	9,468	12,993	12,767
% RC	*24.5*	*25.5*	*24.0*	*23.9*	*26.4*
Bookbinders No.	121	132	241	309	251
% RC	*29.8*	*24.2*	*22.8*	*21.0*	*15.1*
Domestic servants, housekeepers, maids, cooks, laundry workers No.	8,498	15,673	8,638	10,480	9,328
% RC	*38.9*	*35.8*	*39.1*	*39.7*	*39.8*
Paper bag/box makers No.	6	197	661	797	882
% RC	*33.3*	*34.5*	*28.9*	*25.6*	*26.3*
Factory/general labourers No.	9,754	3,204	1,913	2,041	1,563
% RC	*43.6*	*41.1*	*43.8*	*37.1*	*34.0*
Above occupations as % of female workforce	*80.6*	*89.9*	*88.0*	*88.4*	*85.7*
Total female workforce No.	40,043	51,370	53,938	62,525	63,914
% RC	*40.3*	*35.6*	*34.8*	*31.6*	*32.0*
% RC in female population	*33.2*	*30.1*	*27.5*	*25.3*	*24.9*
Female workforce as % of all females aged 15 and over	*61.6*	*65.9*	*56.1*	*47.8*	*44.5*

Source: Census of Ireland, Reports, 1871–1911.

data available for 1901 and 1911 indicate the high level of separation between Catholic and Protestant even within the industry. Catholics were much more heavily over-represented in the spinning processes than in the weaving and finishing trades. Spinners' wages tended to be fractionally lower than those of weavers, while their working conditions were less pleasant and more unhealthy. There was also the simple fact of separation: management of workers was a lot easier in mills and factories if Catholic and Protestant women worked in separate rooms or at separate processes.

SEGREGATION AND CONFLICT

As the scale of ethnic rivalry grew during the nineteenth century, so segregation in employment increased. In part it took the form of spatial segregation within a workplace. In other cases it took the form of segregation between whole industries. Either way, Protestants tended to hold the more attractive or, at least, the less unattractive categories of work. In high-wage industries such as shipbuilding and engineering, few Catholics were found. In dock work there was an ethnic division of labour between the more regular work provided by the cross-channel docks, which was a Protestant preserve, and the less regular employment in the deep-sea docks, where Catholics predominated. The growth of workplace segregation coincided with three important developments in the town: increased social tension arising from the famine immigration, increased political tension following the nationalist uprising of the Young Irelanders in the south, and—perhaps most significant—the emergence of a major new skilled sector in shipbuilding and engineering.

In 1857 the owner of a Sandy Row linen mill told the riots commissioners that he believed that the widespread attacks on Catholics at the Blackstaff crossing, at the northern end of Sandy Row, had arisen out of a combination at the mill to exclude Catholics.[18] In future riots this phenomenon became more widespread, as the workplace became a more important site of conflict. In 1864 Bernard Hughes stated that 'there are four large Catholic employers in the town and the others will not take Catholic apprentices, for the workers will not work with them as either apprentices or journeymen'.[19] In general terms, the interest of employers lies in an undivided labour market, providing the largest possible pool of labour to compete for jobs. But, when faced with massive, ongoing, and systematic conflict in the workplace, most employers seek the easy way out, which in Belfast tended to mean giving way to popular Protestant pressure. Thus the shipbuilding magnate Sir Edward Harland, for instance, closed his gates against sectarian rioters in 1864, but in 1886 declined to lock out the Protestant mob that was driving the remaining Catholic employees from the yard. Likewise, in 1886 the manager of Ewart's linen mill on the Crumlin Road refused to allow a police patrol into his factory to quell Protestant rioters. A similar trend is detectable on the Catholic side, inevitably on a smaller scale: Bernard Hughes's bakery workforce was about one-third Protestant in 1857, but

---

[18] Hepburn, *Past Apart*, 38.
[19] H. Patterson, *Class Conflict and Sectarianism: The Protestant Working Class and the Belfast Labour Movement, 1868–1920* (Belfast, 1980), p. xiv.

almost exclusively Catholic in 1886; the same appears to have been true of Ross's, the only large Catholic-owned mill, in the latter year. In most cases the ejected minorities were able to return to work once things had calmed down, but, in the shipyards especially, the long-term trend was to reduce the levels of Catholic employment.[20]

As segregation grew in the workplace, so it also imposed a distinctive residential pattern on the town. A certain degree of residential concentration is typical of multi-ethnic cities, determined by kinship and a wish to be close to particular cultural facilities. But where, as in Belfast, the threat of violence is never far away, these concentrations become denser, with fear emerging as an additional factor influencing residential choice. Even in Belfast, however, this developed slowly. By 1830 'the Pound' and 'Sandy Row', industrial suburbs to the west and south-west of the growing town, had acquired reputations as Catholic and Protestant neighbourhoods respectively, but there is no evidence of comparable divisions affecting other districts or other social classes. Even in these two neighbourhoods a further generation had to pass before segregation became anything like complete. Some Catholic homes in Sandy Row were burned out in 1843, and during the more serious riots of 1857 the remaining Catholics and mixed marriages were driven out, making the neighbourhood more or less exclusively Protestant.[21] To the north lay the main Catholic Pound area, which later expanded westwards as the Falls, spreading out from Smithfield market. There were probably more Protestants in this neighbourhood than there were Catholics in Sandy Row, at least until the riots of 1857.[22] Scotch Street, in the heart of the Pound, was said to be half-Protestant and half-Catholic at this time.[23] At the frontier between the two districts, shortly to become virtually a war zone, W. M. O'Hanlon found in 1853 that one of the court developments occupied by poor people was so well managed by its proprietor that it contained twenty-eight households 'of Protestants and Roman Catholics living in perfect harmony'.[24] This was not to last. After 1857 segregation became increasingly sharp in working-class districts, and spread more widely as the city entered its period of most rapid growth. Mixed marriages, regarded as betrayals and grounds for expulsion from Protestant neighbourhoods, were more often looked on as victories in Catholic neighbourhoods, especially as the children were almost always raised as Catholics and the non-Catholic partner frequently converted.

During the second half of the nineteenth century a sectarian residential framework developed steadily, accommodating the majority of new migrants and

---

[20] Hepburn, *Past Apart*, 37–8, 127.

[21] C. Hirst, *Religion, Politics and Violence in Nineteenth-Century Belfast: The Pound and Sandy Row* (Dublin, 2002), 17.

[22] Ibid. 15.

[23] *Report into the Origins and Character of the Riots in Belfast in July and September 1857*, HC, 1857–8, xxvi, Evidence, 135.

[24] O'Hanlon, *Walks among the Poor*, 31.

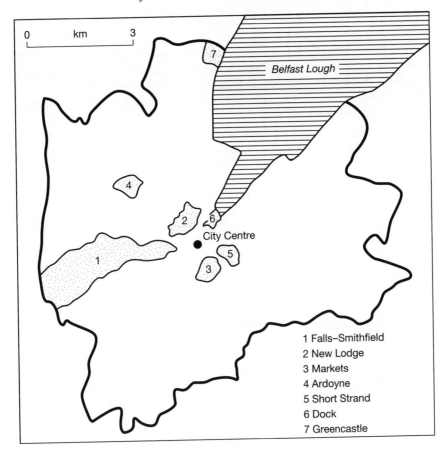

Fig. 2.1. The Catholic Districts of Belfast, 1901.

drawing in newly built neighbourhoods. By 1901 69 per cent of the Catholic population lived in neighbourhoods that were more or less exclusively Catholic. Manual workers, at 76 per cent, were more likely to live in these neighbourhoods than shopkeepers and business people at 60 per cent, or professionals and clerical workers at 49 per cent.[25] There were two categories of mixed areas: the 'twilight zones' of the transient poor, which were too run-down in both physical and human terms to establish any sort of ethnic identity; and a much larger category of middle-class neighbourhoods, which were predominantly Protestant but within which sizeable Catholic minorities also resided. It was only during the course of the twentieth century that the Catholic middle class became large enough and less heavily based on the live-in shop or pub, to develop sizeable middle-class

[25] Hepburn, *Past Apart*, 118–19.

neighbourhoods of its own. Thus, increased prosperity, as well as the violent troubles of 1920–2 and 1969–94, contributed to the rise in segregation levels that the twentieth century witnessed.[26] In a city where Catholics have been in a minority of two or three to one, they were statistically more likely to come into frequent contact with Protestants than the other way round. Catholics lived effectively in a Protestant city, whereas most Protestants were less likely to have any reason to enter Catholic neighbourhoods.

By 1901 there were seven identifiable Catholic neighbourhoods within the city boundary. One of these, Greencastle, a small mill village, was still outside the main urban area. Five of the others, accounting in all for just over a quarter of the Catholic population, were surrounded by Protestant territory and had in effect been closed off to further Catholic growth. These were: Short Strand, on the Co. Down bank of the Lagan; the Markets, on the opposite bank, in the south-east corner of the city centre; Dock, immediately to the north of the city centre beside the quays; Ardoyne and 'the Bone', close to the mills on the Crumlin Road in the north-west sector; and a slightly larger area, the New Lodge, to the north of the city centre. Larger than all the other Catholic districts combined was the Falls area, which by 1901 housed 41 per cent of the city's Catholic population and ran south-westwards from the city centre to the boundary of the urban area. Like the other neighbourhoods, the Falls had begun as a city-centre enclave, consisting of the animal pound, Smithfield market, and the old butchers' quarter of Hercules Street. Unlike the other neighbourhoods, however, it had succeeded in expanding outwards alongside the Farset stream, where many of the mills sprang up. This was to form the neutral borderland between the Falls district and the new Shankill district to the north, which from the 1870s began to succeed Sandy Row as the main centre of militant working-class Protestantism. The key factor in the expansion of the Falls was successful rioting. In the first great riots of 1857 the southern boundary of the Pound, at Albert Street, was held against challenges from Sandy Row, while in the riots of 1872 victory in 'the battle for Leeson Street', a new development that at that time marked the south-western boundary of the city, confirmed that further expansion along both sides of the Falls Road would be Catholic.[27] The line of mills and, further out, the Black Mountain to the north, and the Blackstaff river and surrounding Bog Meadows (reinforced in modern times by the M1 motorway) to the south, provided natural boundaries for a pattern of segregated development that has continued to the present day.

Rioting, therefore, was central to the town's pattern of development. The first recorded mortal clash was on 12 July 1813, when members of an Orange

---

[26] Hepburn, *Past Apart*, 49–50; D. J. Smith and G. Chambers, *Inequality in Northern Ireland* (Oxford, 1991), 105–10.
[27] F. Wright, *Two Lands on One Soil* (Dublin, 1996), 373.

procession, having been subject to abuse in Hercules Street, replied with gunfire. Soon Catholic–Protestant clashes lasting a day or two became common around 12 July and election days. But it was not until the second half of the century that conflict developed on a grand scale. In 1857 rioting remained serious and uncontrolled throughout the summer months, and in 1864 and 1872 it attained similar proportions. The immediate causes were of limited importance. The outcomes almost always involved attempts, mainly on the part of Protestants, to exclude Catholics from employment and from their neighbourhoods and attempts, mainly on the part of Catholics, to secure access to new housing developments. These social and economic issues were seldom if ever stated as grievances or causes of the riots, but, once rioting was under way, they inevitably emerged, indicating that such matters were of close concern to many members of the working class, and that riots offered appropriate opportunities for resolving them.

Inadequate, incompetent, or partisan policing was identified as a problem by the Commissions of Inquiry in 1857 and 1864, as a result of which the municipally controlled Town Police force was abolished and the Royal Irish Constabulary (RIC) took over.[28] The RIC was able to put a force into the town that had a better ethnic balance, and that was better trained and equipped.[29] But it was still unable to control rioting in the city in 1872, let alone the far more savage outbreaks, instigated mainly on the Protestant side, to celebrate the defeat of Gladstone's first Home Rule Bill in 1886. Provocative politico-religious parading was clearly a proximate cause of the majority of riots. The government made various efforts to ban such processions from 1835 onwards, most notably the Party Processions Act of 1850. But by 1868 it was clear that the ban was no longer enforceable, and in 1872 the government gave way, abolished the Act, and reverted to a policy of 'equal marching rights'. This in effect meant paying careful attention to local ethnic boundaries and symbols, and restricting marches to routes that were least likely to bring the two sides into conflict.[30] Marching thus came to assume the role in Ulster that it has retained ever since, which is the marking-out and maintenance of territory. Because marching, or 'walking', was so central to the Orange Order's activities, Orangeism has tended to be seen as the primary provocation and cause. On the other hand, recent research has suggested that, within the Catholic community, certain associational elements did not exist entirely for the purpose of communal defence. The Ribbon societies, very localized secret groupings, ethnically Catholic and descended in a general way from the eighteenth-century agrarian Defenders, were active in urban as well as rural areas, at least until the 1860s. Ribbonism in urban Ulster has been described as 'in reality a fighting organization directed at Orange parades and

28 A. C. Hepburn (ed.), *The Conflict of Nationality in Modern Ireland* (London, 1980), 34–6.
29 B. Griffin, *The Bulkies: Police and Crime in Belfast, 1800–1865* (Dublin, 1997).
30 Wright, *Two Lands*, 503.

individuals suspected of Orange sympathies'.[31] Rioting therefore played a crucial role in the social and spatial development of Belfast. It established boundaries, built a community spirit—albeit a negative and destructive one—behind those boundaries, and influenced the development of the labour market. The overt subject matter of the conflicts was ethno-religious, but the important outcomes at the local level, in these and in later riots, were to do with access to housing and jobs.

PRIESTS, PRESS, AND POLITICS

As was the case in early industrial Britain, the churches in Ireland were ill prepared for coping with rapid population growth and mass urbanization. The Catholic Church was no exception. St Mary's, near Smithfield, founded in 1784, was Belfast's first Catholic church, and was followed by the larger St Patrick's, Donegall Street, in 1815. But as late as 1853 O'Hanlon found that even in a central working-class district close to St Patrick's, such as the quarter between High Street and York Street, 'by no means the worst quarter of the town . . . we did not find that either Protestant or Roman Catholic clergy penetrate these haunts'. Likewise in the equally central Catholic area around Hamill Street 'we were given to understand that the face of a Christian instructor is never seen'.[32] In 1844 Cornelius Denvir, Bishop of Down and Connor in 1835–65, built a third Catholic church in Belfast, St Malachy's in the Markets area, and ten years later established a Convent of the Sisters of Mercy. But he became increasingly out of tune with most of his fellow bishops, especially after Paul Cullen returned to Ireland in 1850, as Archbishop and later Cardinal. In 1852 Denvir accepted appointment as a Commissioner of National Education, although Cullen 'did my best to dissuade him', and also 'drew the attention of Propaganda to Denvir's neglect of his duties'.[33] By 1854 Denvir felt obliged to send a defence of his administration of Belfast to Monsignor Tobias Kirby, Rector of the Irish College in Rome, claiming that 'Orange bigotry is a great obstacle', and that since 1848 'every Protestant is an Orangeman'.[34] Under pressure from Rome, Denvir brought an order of nuns into Belfast in 1854, but his arrangements for funding the project had been somewhat over-optimistic and in 1862 Archbishop Dixon of Armagh reported that 'the Sisters of Mercy have been turned out of their Convent for want of money to pay the contractor who built it'.[35] Of an estimated 12,000 children of school age, no more than 2,370 were receiving education

---

[31] M. Ó. Catháin, in R. J. Morris and L. Kennedy (eds.), *Ireland and Scotland: Order and Disorder, 1600–2000* (Edinburgh, 2005).

[32] O'Hanlon, *Walks among the Poor*, 3, 10, 27.

[33] Cullen to Kirby, 17 Mar. 1853, in Patrick J. Corish, 'Irish College, Rome: Kirby Papers, Part 2', *Archivium Hibernicum*, 31 (1973), 45; Macaulay, *Dorrian*, 87.

[34] Denvir to Kirby, 12 June 1854, in Corish, 'Kirby Papers, Pt. 2', 17.

[35] Dixon to Kirby, 8 Mar. 1862 (KIR/1862/36).

from the Sisters of Mercy and the Catholic-managed national schools. Only one Catholic in three was estimated to attend Sunday mass, and in Dixon's view Denvir's *'spiritus timoris* as regards the Orangemen among whom he lives so predominates in him that he is utterly unfit'.[36]

By June 1858 Dixon reached the conclusion that, 'if Dr Denvir had a coadjutor of courage and energy, Belfast would make progress such as it shall never make during his administration'. In 1860 Patrick Dorrian was appointed to this role.[37] Although Cullen initially regarded him as no more than 'a good parish priest' who would not be 'up to the mark', Dorrian proved to be a formidable figure who exercised a powerful influence over Catholic Belfast until his death in 1885.[38] He was at last given a free hand in May 1865, and moved rapidly to implement changes. During his first month 20,000 confessions, accounting almost half of the Catholic population aged 10 years and over, had been heard. Within a year he had 'increased the permanent staff in town by eight priests', and during his tenure the priest:people ratio in the town improved from 1:5,000 to 1:1,600. In 1866 the new pro-cathedral of St Peter's was opened with accommodation for 3,000, becoming the first church in the Pound/Lower Falls area, already long established as Belfast's largest Catholic neighbourhood.[39] Shortly afterwards Dorrian invited the lay teaching order, the Irish Christian Brothers, into the town. Two monastic orders, the Redemptorists at Clonard and the Passionist Fathers at Crumlin Road, and four further orders of nuns, were also brought in.[40] During Dorrian's time the working-class Catholic neighbourhoods of Belfast became intensely Catholic for the first time in terms of institutionalized religion as well as ethnicity. Rules and procedures regarding mixed marriages became strict, discouraging, and effective. Confraternities, missions, religious pageantry, Catholic schools, and churches all expanded to accommodate the numbers in the growing town. Similar missionary work proceeded apace on the Protestant side. Catholic and Protestant Belfast both grew stronger in terms of education, moral fibre, and self-esteem during these years, but they also grew further apart, religious belief emphasizing their differences in a way that was typical of western Christianity in the non-ecumenical ethos of the industrial era.

Dorrian became one of the first bishops to declare his support for Parnell and the Land League, arguing that 'religion will suffer if the bishops and priests show no sympathy with the people'.[41] Earlier, the rise of Fenianism had coincided with his appointment. Like most of the Catholic clergy he regarded this revolutionary secret society as 'valueless but to do harm'.[42] After Dublin,

36 Dixon to Kirby, 16 Sept., 31 Oct., and 21 Dec. 1863 (KIR/1863/235, 280, 334).
37 Dixon to Kirby, 2 June 1858 (KIR/1836–1861/2148).
38 Cullen to Kirby, 3 Dec. 1859, in Corish, 'Kirby Papers, Pt. 2', 73.
39 Dorrian to Kirby, 10 Dec. 1866 (KIR/1866/341); Hirst, *Religion, Politics & Violence*, 87.
40 Dorrian to Kirby, 10 Dec. 1866 (KIR/1866/341).
41 Dorrian to Kirby, 24 Nov. 1879, in Corish, 'Kirby Papers, Pt. 1', 89.
42 Dorrian to Kirby, 16 Nov. 1865 (KIR/1865/263).

Belfast was one of Fenianism's strongest centres, with up to 1,000 members. Clerks and artisans were everywhere prominent in the movement, but, given the social structure of Catholic Belfast at that time, it is not surprising to find that a majority of the thirty-four Belfast Fenians charged with offences were in fact from the labouring class.[43] An aid to Fenian recruitment, more important in Belfast than in many other places, was the existence of the older and more overtly sectarian Ribbon societies. The rhetoric of Fenianism was certainly less sectarian, and the movement, even in Belfast, did include some Protestants, but it was in essence a revolutionary movement appealing to ethnic Catholics. It was strongly and fairly effectively opposed by Dorrian and his clergy. 'The Fenians', he told Kirby, 'surrendered *en masse*, and have gone to the Sacraments'.[44] But, like the rebels of 1916 and the IRA of the late-twentieth-century hunger-strike era, the atmosphere of 'martyrdom' that followed the violence created popular sympathy and support that the clergy were less inclined to oppose. The funeral of local Fenian William Harbison, in 1867, brought more than 30,000 people on to the streets, while a Fenian amnesty procession in 1869 attracted almost 10,000 marchers as well as the support of the clergy and many middle-class Catholics.[45]

But while Dorrian gave support to the amnesty campaign, he took a much tougher and more ultramontane line with what he called 'presbyterian' tendencies among the local Catholic elite. A Catholic Institute had been established in the town in 1859. Founded mainly by members of the commercial and business elite to provide facilities for education, study, and recreation, it was effectively under lay control, and Dorrian did not like it. In 1864 he took advantage of a financial crisis to demand full episcopal control of its affairs. He may to some extent have been concerned about the potential danger of a lay-controlled body being manipulated in the interests of Fenianism, although Dorrian's biographer places more emphasis on his strict Cullenite view of episcopal authority.[46] Certainly those whom Dorrian regarded as his principal opponents in this matter included two of Catholic Belfast's richest businessmen, the baker Bernard Hughes and the mill-owner William Ross, both of whom were very far from being Fenians. Faced with Dorrian's challenge, the Catholic Institute decided in 1866 to dissolve itself and make over its property to the bishop.

More challenging to Dorrian was the dispute over control of the press. The *Belfast Morning News* had been founded in 1855 as a daily newspaper aimed at the Catholic community. But some Catholics, including Dorrian, did not like its Whiggish tone, and set about creating a rival, the *Ulster Observer*, which appeared in July 1862. But its editor, Andrew McKenna, soon became obnoxious to the new bishop through his close involvement in the Catholic Institute, his

---

[43] Hirst, *Religion, Politics & Violence*, 94, 96–7.
[44] Dorrian to Kirby, 31 May 1865 (KIR/1865/116).
[45] Hirst, *Religion, Politics & Violence*, 99–103.   [46] Macaulay, *Dorrian*, 163–92.

alleged anti-clericalism, and his emerging sympathy with the Fenian movement. By 1865 Dorrian had reached the conclusion that McKenna was 'a clever but troublesome and dangerous man'.[47] In 1867 the *Ulster Observer* was wound up.[48] McKenna then set up his own paper, the *Northern Star*, while Dorrian founded the *Ulster Examiner*. This was a much more explicitly Catholic paper, though it balanced its religious orthodoxies with savage attacks on 'Whiggery'. It adhered to a constitutional nationalist line, welcoming the new home-rule movement and denouncing the Catholic-owned, pro-Liberal *Belfast Morning News*. McKenna's *Northern Star* welcomed the home-rule movement, but also declared that 'home rule means separation; and for that separation we must be prepared to draw the sword'. His early death in 1872 led to the takeover of his paper by the *Examiner*. The merged paper became a financial drain on the diocese and in 1877 it was sold to Charles J. Dempsey, a Catholic home ruler and member of a prosperous family of Belfast publicans who will appear again in this story. In 1882, as Ulster Liberalism continued to contract and as Catholics sided overwhelmingly with home-rule politics, Dempsey also took over the *Belfast Morning News* and merged the two papers under the latter name.[49]

'WEE JOE' AND THE BROTHERS

Hamill Street in 1871 consisted of forty-seven small houses just west of the town centre. Its inhabitants were almost all manual workers and their families. It ranked above the poorest streets of the town, only about half of its householders being labourers or textile workers. Many others were employed in traditional crafts such as shoemaking and tailoring, or in petty dealing. The distinctive width of the street made it suitable for those who, like Devlin's father, operated a horse and cart from their homes. Its western end abutted on to Anglican Christ Church, while a few steps to the south lay the grand town houses of College Square North and the side wall of the Royal Belfast Academical Institution, the leading centre for Presbyterian education in Ireland. Yet, bordered on two sides as they were by these symbols of Protestant achievement, the householders of Hamill Street were Catholics almost to every last man, woman, and child.[50] Joseph Devlin was born at 10 Hamill Street on 13 February 1871. His parents, Charles Devlin, from east Tyrone, and Elizabeth King, from Faughart, near Dundalk, Co. Louth, were both from small-farm backgrounds and had moved to Belfast during the post-famine decade. They married at St Malachy's, Belfast,

---

[47] Dorrian to Kirby, 16 Nov. 1865, Cullen to Kirby, 22 Nov. 1867 (KIR/1865/263, 1867/423).
[48] Macaulay, *Dorrian*, 194–202.   [49] Ibid. 202–18.
[50] The names of 1,871 householders suggest a street that was predominantly, if not exclusively, Catholic; in 1901 there were 241 Catholic residents and a single family of 4 Protestant lodgers. *Belfast & Province of Ulster Directory*, 1871; Census of Ireland 1901, manuscript records (INA).

on 13 December 1858. Joe was their fourth son, the fifth child of the marriage.[51] At the time of his birth both parents were illiterate. The family moved into the house shortly before his birth.[52] His father was a jarvey who owned his horse and cab. His mother, who ran a small business selling bread and vegetables from the house, passed down to Joe an obsession with cleanliness and tidiness. She kept the boy at home quite a lot, as he suffered from the minor colds and chest complaints that were sometimes to preoccupy him in later life. As a young child he does not seem to have been very gregarious, though he was regarded as more than sufficiently loquacious by the members of his own family.[53] It may have been a relief for some of them when the chattering 4-year-old was enrolled at the nearby Barrack Street National School, where his vocal energies were quickly diverted into poetry recitation. By the time he was 7 he had transferred to the junior department of the Christian Brothers' School at the foot of the Falls Road, St Mary's, Barrack Street.[54]

The Christian Brothers had come to Belfast in 1866 at the invitation of Bishop Dorrian.[55] At that time, seventy of the eighty National schools in Belfast were Presbyterian-managed. Many of them included large numbers of Catholic pupils. Dorrian, a loyal Cullenite, viewed 'mixed education' as a serious danger to the faith. He thus provided residential accommodation and school premises for the Christian Brothers.[56] Soon the Brothers had 800 pupils, and by the 1880s they were responsible for the education of more than a quarter of all Catholic boys in the town.[57] Their schools quickly achieved 'a soldier-like precision of discipline' that greatly impressed the area schools inspector, though he feared that 'true and earnest adherents of the Church' were formed at the expense of 'that robustness and independence of character which a greater freedom tends to promote'.[58] The Congregation of the Christian Brothers of Ireland was a lay teaching order, founded in 1802. Since mid-century it had expanded massively as a provider of low-cost schooling outside the state system, funded mainly by small donations. Its main strength was in urban areas.[59] The Brothers produced their own textbooks and readers, concerning which one hostile critic commented that professing to cultivate a spirit of Irish nationality, the Christian Brothers have compiled for their more advanced pupils reading books abounding in narratives

---

[51] Devlin is an east Tyrone name, and the general understanding is that Devlin's father hailed from there, although the marriage register gives his birthplace as Co. Down (PRONI, copy of St Malachy's Church Parish Register); F. J. Whitford, 'Joseph Devlin: Ulsterman and Irishman', MA thesis (London, 1959), 1.

[52] *Belfast & Province of Ulster Directory* (1871), 296.

[53] Bro. S. B. MacSweeney, Memoir of Devlin (PRONI, David Kennedy Papers, T2420/1).

[54] Whitford, 'Devlin', 5.

[55] Dorrian to Bro. J. A. Hoare, Superior-General, 2 Aug. 1866 (ACBGR, 1949/001).

[56] Macaulay, *Dorrian*, 116, 167.

[57] Census of Ireland 1871, Borough of Belfast, app. X; Census of Ireland 1881, Borough of Belfast, Table U; Macaulay, *Dorrian*, 299; Bro. J. A. Caton, Belfast Superior, to Dorrian, 29 Mar. 1872 (ACBGR, 1949/007).

[58] Macaulay, *Dorrian*, 284.   [59] B. M. Coldrey, *Faith and Fatherland* (Dublin, 1988), 31.

of English perfidy and cruelty'.[60] Whatever the fairness of this assessment, the Brothers' curriculum differed sharply from that of the Commissioners of National Education, which sought to avoid offending any religious group by deliberately omitting 'any mention of Catholicism, or of Irish culture, geography, history or mythology'. The Brothers' texts were mostly compiled by the community of the North Monastery, Cork. Munster, most strongly nationalist of all the Irish regions in this era, contributed more than half of the 3,018 men who joined the order between 1851 and 1921.[61] All six of the Brothers who taught at St Mary's during Devlin's time as a pupil, 1878–83, were from the south of Ireland, a fact that contrasted sharply with the Ulster origins of most of the diocesan clergy and that no doubt contributed to the differences that soon emerged between the Brothers and the clergy in the town.[62]

The academic quality of Christian Brothers' education was generally high. Brothers were more likely to have received formal training than Catholic teachers working in National schools. From the 1870s onwards 'there was a considerable drift in Brothers' schools away from teaching the very poor to teaching boys who were in a position to play a more prominent role in national life'.[63] After 1878 they began to develop intermediate (that is, secondary) departments, providing for bright pupils whose parents could not or would not pay the high fees charged by the diocesan Catholic colleges, while attracting income from the new Board of Intermediate Education on the 'payment-by-results' system. Several commentators have noted that the Christian Brothers 'passed an exceptionally large proportion of the future leaders of the Irish revolution through their hands'.[64] Certainly their schools had a nationalist ethos and curriculum, at a time when the more prestigious middle-class Catholic schools were 'geared to English cultural and political norms' and 'highlighted the success of their students in the service of the Empire'.[65] But even the Brothers came to place a strong emphasis on training their pupils for the civil-service examinations, in part because the new meritocracy of the expanding public sector offered the best avenue of upward mobility for those without business advantages or connections, and in part because the payment-by-results system made such an approach financially attractive.

Although Dorrian had brought the Christian Brothers into Belfast, the order was responsible for the only serious internal challenge to episcopal authority that he ever experienced, a challenge that began within a few years of their

---

[60] Commissioner William Brooke, dissenting note to the final report of the Powis Commission on Primary Education, 1870, cited in Coldrey, *Faith and Fatherland*, 129.

[61] Coldrey, *Faith and Fatherland*, 56–7, 240; T. Garvin, *Nationalist Revolutionaries in Ireland, 1858–1928* (Oxford, 1987), 51.

[62] Annual Return of Schools and Database of Members of the Order (ACBGR).

[63] Coldrey, *Faith and Fatherland*, 39–41, 88.   [64] Lyons, *Ireland since the Famine*, 80 n.

[65] J. Hutchinson, 'Cultural Nationalism, Elite Mobility and Nation-Building: Communitarian Politics in Modern Ireland', *British Journal of Sociology*, 38/4 (1987), 492.

arrival, and that was still unresolved when he died in 1885. Both the Vatican Archives and those of the Christian Brothers' Generalate in Rome became stuffed over the years with complaints from both parties. Dorrian maintained that the Brothers' intended role had been to provide primary-level education for the many poor Catholics attending Protestant-managed national schools. In fact, he alleged, in a view shared by the Board inspector, their operation in Belfast had quickly become 'a sort of lower-middle-class school corporation', seeking to attract the best pupils away from Catholic-managed national schools.[66] Indeed, the transfer of the young Devlin to the care of the Brothers in 1878 was an example of this. More heinous still in the bishop's eyes, the Brothers were seeking to build up an intermediate department, offering free or very cheap secondary education, and enticing away families that ought to have been paying for their children to attend St Malachy's College, the diocesan seminary. In 1881 St Malachy's had nearly twice as many day-boys as the intermediate department of the Christian Brothers, but by the end of that decade the Brothers had a majority of the still very small number of Catholics progressing to secondary education. Dorrian thought that most of these boys were 'of a class who are not to be educated by collections from persons much poorer than themselves'.[67]

This dispute was bitter and protracted, and did not remain hidden from the pupils. Petty disputes festered and in 1882 Dorrian secured from the Superior-General of the Order an instruction to the Belfast Brothers to discontinue the teaching of Latin, a move calculated to restore St Malachy's as the sole provider of full Catholic secondary education; in response, the local Brothers hired an outsider (and a Catholic graduate of the banned Queen's college, to boot) to provide instruction in the subject after hours. The leading stirrer in this and other teacup storms was Brother Michael Stanislaus [O']Farrell, singled out in the correspondence with Rome as being particularly uncooperative.[68] Farrell was senior teacher at St Mary's in Devlin's time, and was later remembered by Joe as 'the best English master in the Order of Christian Brothers'. He also held an Irish history competition in the class every week.[69] Devlin was no doubt one of sixty-five boys present in Brother Farrell's classroom one day in June 1882 when the bishop's administrator called to enrol boys for the cathedral choir. Farrell replied that no boy could be released until the Intermediate entry examinations were over.[70] The head of the Christian Brothers' School at Richmond Street, Dublin, declared that 'Stan Farrell was really cracked . . . [and] . . . that most of those who were really great teachers like him were mad'.[71] Farrell's local Superior,

[66] Dorrian to Caton, 20 Mar. 1872 (ACBGR, 1949/006); Macaulay, *Dorrian*, 285.

[67] Hirst, *Religion, Politics & Violence*, 89: Macaulay, *Dorrian*, 299; Dorrian to Bro. R. A. Maxwell, Superior-General, 11 Aug. 1882 (ACBGR, 1949/020).

[68] Macaulay, *Dorrian*, 293, 298.   [69] MacSweeney, Memoir, ch. 2, p. 4; ch. 3, p. 3.

[70] Convery to Maxwell, 11 July 1882 (ACBGR, 1949/016).

[71] Bro. P. A. O'Ferrall to 'My Dear Bro. Assistant', 19 Dec. 1879 (ACBGR, 1949/013).

Brother James Slattery, complained that 'where is the young man of spirit who will remain in Belfast when he is emphatically told to teach nothing except the 3 Rs . . . We are to be mere tools for accomplishing ends for Dr Dorrian's seminary.'[72] Dorrian wrote to the Vatican that the Brothers were seeking to establish 'an *imperium in imperio* . . . to resist episcopal authority'.[73] At the same time, twenty-five of his Belfast clergy issued a statement claiming that, in the midst of thousands of mill-workers, the Brothers were educating only twelve children from such families, although 'the poorest and most numerous part of our Catholic community are the mill-workers'. The statement dismissed the fact that 234 labourers' children were at the school, on the grounds that such workers were not the poorest of the poor, as they tended to be elsewhere in Ireland. One of the signatories to this statement was Revd Dr Henry Henry, President of St Malachy's Diocesan College. It is a reasonable assumption that those who attended the Christian Brothers in Belfast during these years, including Devlin and many others who became active local Nationalists during the 1890s, were not educated in an atmosphere of excessive respect for the authority of their local bishop, nor for St Malachy's College or Dr Henry, of whom we shall hear much more later.

Devlin passed the junior honours grade Intermediate examination in English and in Natural Philosophy (for which he was the class's only entrant) in 1883, an achievement that earned considerable family congratulation and a listing in the local newspapers.[74] He had received an education that was strongly nationalist in tone so far as history, geography, and literature were concerned. His lifelong love of the singing and recitation of patriotic Irish ballads was certainly learnt from the Brothers. But, although the Christian Brothers' Schools—encouraged, *inter alia*, by the Intermediate Education Act of 1878—developed a strong commitment to Irish language teaching from the 1880s onwards, Devlin went through the system just too early to share in the revival of this particular element of Irish identity: CBS Belfast began the teaching of Irish with ten pupils in 1881, rising to twenty-five in Joe's final year of schooling. Likewise, Gaelic games did not become part of the Brothers' curriculum in urban centres until the turn of the century, for it was not common for day-schools in Ireland to provide organized sports of any sort before that date.[75]

Devlin left school in the summer of 1883, aged 12, and began work as a clerk in a jam factory at 2s. 6d. per week.[76] How long he stayed there is not known, but he claimed in later life that he had been denied a job as an office boy in a linen firm because of his religion. At all events, he did not stay in office work very long, and after a period of idleness went to work and live at a pub on the Antrim Road,

[72] Bro. J. P. Slattery to Bro. J. A. Hoare, Superior General, n.d. [Oct. 1879] (ACBGR, 1949/014).
[73] Dorrian to Maxwell, 16 Oct. 1882; abstract of Dorrian to Simeoni, Oct. 1882 (ACB-GR, 1949/020).
[74] *NS*, 27 Jan. 1906.   [75] Coldrey, *Faith and Fatherland*, 196, 161, 190–1.
[76] Biographical note on Devlin's mass card, Jan. 1934 (PRONI, Keating Papers, D/1919/16).

where his employer encouraged education.[77] His great enthusiasm was reading and recitation, and sometime in 1884, still aged only 13, he and a group of friends formed a reading and social club. Whether there was any adult influence in this is not clear, but certainly Devlin was elected chairman. A participant later recalled a programme of study and entertainment supplemented by 'excellent pastry' from Joe's mother, at which he was 'major domo' and very much the exuberant life and soul of the party.[78] About this time Devlin and some of the others joined an elocution class conducted by Professor Coleman of St Malachy's College, held in the evenings at St Mary's Hall, the new Catholic community centre in the city. Devlin's Christian Brothers' education soon brought him into conflict with the diocesan college ethos, when he challenged Coleman's use of Tennyson's 'Charge of the Light Brigade' as a suitable elocutionary text, persuading teacher and class that the Irish feats of valour described in Thomas Davis's 'Battle of Fontenoy' were more suitable subjects of study. He had learned it, he told Coleman, from A. M. Sullivan's *Story of Ireland*, staple reading for nationalists in most parts of late-nineteenth-century Ireland, but still new to the small Catholic elite of Belfast.[79] His schoolfriend Richard Carney later recalled that Devlin acquired some of his early ability in public speaking by attending open-air meetings at the Custom House Steps and arguing with members of the crowd who had come to hear the local anti-Catholic orators at work—a hazardous business![80]

Devlin's introduction to politics came when he was still only 14, in the autumn of 1885. The Nationalists had begun to take a serious electoral interest in north-eastern Ireland in 1883, when the Monaghan by-election marked the so-called invasion of Ulster. Notwithstanding strong support for the home-rule movement in Belfast from as early as 1872, and the strength of Fenianism in the town before that, Northern Catholics had hitherto been willing to return Presbyterian Liberals to Westminster. The situation was transformed by the victory of the Nationalist candidate T. M. Healy in Monaghan, resulting in the collapse of the Liberals (who had won the seat in 1880) into third place. In the general election of November 1885 the extension of the franchise coupled with redistribution of seats meant that the former two-seater constituency of Belfast was replaced by four individual seats, of which one, West Belfast, was finely balanced between Catholics and Protestants. A leading Nationalist from the south, Thomas Sexton, was prevailed upon to contest the Belfast seat. Local nationalists had already learnt that democratic electoral politics in a divided society were first and foremost a sectarian head count and that consequently much of the real battle had to be fought in the revision courts over the electoral register. Throughout the north, recalled the barrister A. M. Sullivan, 'the National League trained an army of

---

[77] Whitford, 'Devlin', 6.
[78] MacSweeney, Memoir, ch. 4, p. 3.
[79] Ibid., ch. 4, p. 6; R. F. Foster, *Modern Ireland 1600–1972* (London, 1988), 455.
[80] Ibid., ch. 5, p. 6.

young men and boys, taught them the Franchise Act, instructed them in the mysteries of the "inhabitant householder" and the technicalities of a lodger's claim, and sent them forth to find electors to put on the register'.[81] Joe Devlin was one youth so employed. Early in the campaign he offered his services and was asked to organize a group of boys to deliver leaflets. Efficient organization on both sides contributed to a turnout of 93 per cent, remarkable even by Ulster standards. In a straight fight with a Unionist, Sexton lost by the tiny margin of thirty-seven votes. But across nine-county Ulster, Nationalists won sixteen of the province's thirty-three seats.

Excited by the vision of electoral democracy unfolding before their eyes, and finding in the advance of nationalism resonances of their Christian Brothers' education, Devlin and his friends established a small but remarkable little organization, the Sexton Debating Society, 'founded for the purpose of creating a national taste for Irish literature among the youth of the city of Belfast, and for the fostering of a healthy spirit of educated criticism amongst its members'. Its motto was 'educate that you may be free', a slogan of the Protestant nationalist Thomas Davis, and it operated on a regular weekly basis for six years. Sexton, who turned the tables in the next general election in 1886 to 'win the West' by a margin of 103 votes, became patron of the Society, and addressed the young audience in July 1886. He told them that he had

listened to many speeches in my time . . . but I have never listened to one which gave me more pleasure than the one in which your chairman addressed me . . . [I regret] the rule which obliges all members of the House of Commons to be at least twenty-one years of age. For otherwise I think the chairman of this meeting would be amongst us.[82]

That chairman was the 15-year-old Joe Devlin. He was already demonstrating his magnetic personality and powers of leadership and organization.

Over the next five years the society maintained a membership of about thirty, with attendances in the region of a dozen or so. Most of the members were probably schoolfriends of Joe's. Their fathers' occupations were all humble enough, though in the truncated social structure of west Belfast they mostly ranked somewhat above the poorest class: dealer, fish salesman, mill-worker, fireman, clothier, french polisher, and flax carder being among those traced.[83] Meetings were occasionally addressed by outside speakers, but apart from Sexton they were all local figures. Devlin, it was said, 'simply bubbled over with fun and gaiety on these occasions, dressing always with care in the latest ties and collars, neat and fastidious, deploying witty and comic arguments'.[84] His first

---

[81] A. M. Sullivan, *Old Ireland: Recollections of an Irish KC* (London, 1927), 31–2.
[82] MacSweeney, Memoir, ch. 5, p. 6.
[83] Names of members from the Sexton Debating Society minute book (abridged copy in MacSweeney, Memoir), traced by surname where possible using the *Belfast and Province of Ulster Directory*.
[84] Whitford, 'Devlin', 20.

recorded speech, at the age of 16, was on the advancement of learning. He declared that 'the chequered history of Ireland . . . has in reality advanced the literature of our country'.[85] The programme of the society had a clear Irish nationalist agenda, but it was not exclusive or narrow. There were debates on various current parliamentary concerns, such as Sunday closing, and recitation evenings, where Devlin performed 'Hamlet's Advice to the Players', 'Rienzi to the Romans', 'Fontenoy', and his favourite party piece in adult life, 'Sentenced to Death'.[86] The Sexton Debating Society reflected the drive for self-improvement that characterized these years and that, in Britain, was later to generate bodies such as the Workers' Education Association. It predated the better-known 'Bounders' College' of Daniel McDevitt and his friends in the Belfast labour movement and, in the era of liberal nationalism, was precursor of a movement that was more commonly associated with early socialism a few years later.[87]

Beyond these society records, we know little of Devlin's youth. His future would have been hard to predict. He had demonstrated talents of organization and leadership; he was already an accomplished orator; he had the beginnings of an education of a typical late-Victorian literary kind, overlaid by a *fin-de-siècle* romanticism with a specifically Irish nationalist flavour. This had a particular resonance in the physically cramped and aspirationally restricted world of Catholic West Belfast. The way of advancement in such a society was by no means clear for a young man with no family capital, no patron, and an incomplete formal education. On the other hand, politics in the new democratic era, for a young man with Devlin's particular talents, appeared to offer a chance to break down or at least break out of the barriers that constrained that narrow world. In December 1890 Irish politics entered a new and, for a short while, exciting phase, beginning with the toppling of Parnell from the Party leadership and a withering-away following the defeat of the Parnellites in the general election of 1892. It was during this bitter and divided period of Irish history that Joe Devlin attained his majority and entered onto the wider political stage.

---

[85] *Belfast Morning News*, 7 Apr. 1887.

[86] Minute book of the Society; *Belfast Morning News, passim.*

[87] The 'Bounders' College' was a group of young self-educated socialists who met above McDevitt's tailor's shop in Rosemary Street, Belfast, during the Edwardian era. W. McMullen, *With James Connolly in Belfast* (n.p., n.d. [Dublin, 1951]), 22.

3

A Minority Divided, 1890–1908

The city of Henry Joy McCracken would have redeemed itself when it had restored West Belfast once more to Ireland.

(Joe Devlin, 1903[1])

When the Parnell split came in December 1890, Devlin's Ulster nationalist background made it very unlikely that he would take any route other than the Anti-Parnellite. It was during this crisis that a lifelong political association began between himself and John Dillon. Twenty years his senior, Dillon differed from Devlin in almost every way: tall, lean, ascetic, aloof, pessimistic and prone to bitterness, university educated, of well-to-do family and independent means. Dillon married late and, though soon widowed, raised four children. Devlin was short, thick-set, charming and charismatic, vulnerable, of humble family background, with a formal education that ended at the age of 12. He remained in precarious financial circumstances until he reached his mid-thirties. He never married. He was already a figure of some local standing in Belfast nationalist politics by the time of the split. For some time secretary of the Belfast Young Ireland Society, which he described as a 'political literary society', he was by the age of 19 on the committee of the Belfast branch of the Irish National League.[2] He was present at the foundation of the Anti-Parnellite Irish National Federation (INFed.) in Dublin, where his address on behalf of the Belfast delegates was described as 'capital'.[3] He then became secretary of the Belfast branch, a position he held throughout the decade of the INFed.'s existence. Dillon's acceptance of an invitation to give the Young Ireland Society's annual address on 11 November 1891 marks the beginning of a relationship in which Dillon identified Devlin as an energetic, competent, and trustworthy representative of nationalism in Ulster.[4]

---

[1] *NS*, 24 Oct 1903.
[2] See *Belfast Morning News*, 18 Feb. and 18 Dec. 1890, cited in Whitford, 'Devlin', 3.
[3] McCartan to Devlin, 7 Mar. 1891 (McCartan Letterbook, P11/B 336).
[4] Devlin to Dillon, 5 and 16 Oct. 1891 (DP 6729/1, 2).

FIGHTING PARNELL: 'KITTY O'SHEA! KITTY O'SHEA!'

The Parnell split ranged the Catholic Church and the English Liberals on one side of the divide, with Parnell's rickety alliance of 'hillside men' and 'conciliationists' on the other. In Belfast the Parnell Leadership Committee was headed by the veteran Irish Republican Brotherhood (IRB) man Robert Johnston, and was mainly Fenian in membership. Patrick McAlister, who had succeeded Dorrian as Bishop of Down and Connor in 1885, instructed his priests to withhold the sacraments from the Catholic members of this committee. Because of its minority status and restricted social structure, Ulster nationalism was more heavily dependent on clerical encouragement and leadership than the rest of Ireland. While Dublin was the strongest centre of Parnellism in Ireland, Belfast was the weakest. There was *some* sympathy for Parnell among the priests, but 'none among the secular clergy of this diocese'.[5] In May 1891 Parnell spoke in Belfast's Ulster Hall. Historians differ over the significance of his apparent offer of a new conciliatory approach to northern Unionists. Would it have been, in reality, a new way forward, or was it, like his more famous appeal to the hillside men, 'superficially striking but in reality meaning very little'?[6] Whether Devlin really jumped on to Parnell's carriage during the procession, yelling 'Kitty O'Shea! Kitty O'Shea!', as alleged by local Republicans, must remain conjecture.[7] Soon after this Devlin and his friend John Rooney went to help out at the Carlow by-election, where the Anti-Parnellites won with over 70 per cent of the vote. Devlin and Rooney thus helped to deliver the goods, applying their Belfast-honed electioneering skills to this new conflict.

In 1891 McAlister and Michael McCartan, the Belfast solicitor and MP for South Down, established the *Irish News* as a rival to the *Belfast Morning News*, which was hamstrung by the lack of Parnellite support in Ulster, and disappeared during 1892 following a lawsuit instituted by the bishop.[8] In the general election of 1892 the Parnellites secured only 1 per cent of the Nationalist vote in Ulster as against 26 per cent in the rest of Ireland. The police reported that 'the Roman Catholic clergy completely control the nationalist electorate in Ulster'. The INFed. had over 31,000 members in Ulster (including 2,000 in Belfast), while the Parnellite National League had less than a thousand (350 in Belfast).[9] But in Belfast, of course, there were also more formidable opponents. Sexton had lost the West to a Unionist by 37 votes in 1885 and won it by 103 votes in 1886. But since then some houses had been demolished in Catholic districts,

---

[5] McAlister to Kirby, 22 Jan. and 5 Feb. 1891 (KIR/1891/69).

[6] J. Loughlin, *Gladstone, Home Rule and the Ulster Question 1882–93* (Dublin, 1986), 245.

[7] P. McCullough, Camden, NJ, to his brother Denis, 1 Mar. 1947 (McCP, P120/53 (3)).

[8] McCartan to D. Sheehy MP, 28 Nov. 1891, and other correspondence (McCartan Letterbook, P11/B 372–5, 377).

[9] Loughlin, *Gladstone, Home Rule and the Ulster Question*, 246.

and many more had been built in the Protestant Shankill. Devlin ran the local campaign, organized around a corps of street captains to get out the vote, and the experienced 'labour nationalist' Michael Davitt was called in to mobilize workers' support and attempt to draw in a few much-needed Protestant votes. But Sexton lost to the Unionist H. O. Arnold-Forster by 839 votes. Devlin was now a part-time journalist on the *Irish News,* and early in 1893 Dillon helped him to obtain a more substantial position, running the *Freeman's Journal* office in Belfast.[10] A few weeks later the leading Federationists in Belfast honoured Devlin's youthful achievements with a dinner at Belfast's Linen Hall Hotel, where the proprietor and branch vice-president, Patrick Dempsey, made a presentation. At 22, Devlin was, he said, 'the guiding spirit' of the movement in the city.[11] Devlin's career seemed on the point of take-off, but the wider Irish picture within the Anti-Parnellite movement was less encouraging, and soon this was to have both a political and a personal impact on him.

FIGHTING HEALY: 'YOUR NAME IS DEVLIN, I SEE YOU HAVE YOUR MEN WELL PLACED'

After the death of Parnell, divisions within the Anti-Parnellite party became more bitter than the original split. Dillon and his old comrade-in-arms William O'Brien, with whom he continued to be cordially associated until 1903, approached the Parnell debacle from the point of view of damage limitation: they wanted to reconstruct Parnell's achievement, a united and tightly disciplined Parliamentary Party and national movement, without Parnell. Tim Healy, on the other hand, approached the struggle with Parnell with apparent relish. He had a different vision of the future, in which the grass roots of nationalism would predominate, rather than the Parliamentary Party, in the selection and control of MPs. In practice this really meant an enhanced role for the clergy: Healy had the support of many priests and was close to Cardinal Michael Logue, Archbishop of Armagh. Both Dillon and O'Brien, on the other hand, though far from being anti-clericals in the continental sense, held to a narrower interpretation of the priestly role in political life. Dillon never felt strongly enough to follow O'Brien's urgings and try to get Healy expelled altogether, although Healy's supporter Vesey Knox was expelled for transgressing in 1897. The Dillon–Healy split was essentially a battle of personalities, but it embraced live issues in a way that the Parnell split no longer did after the death of the Chief. It was about what sort of person should predominate in local politics, about how the Nationalist movement should approach difficult issues such as education (where the priests were always wary of the Liberals' policy on control of schooling), and about temperance and the role of the publican interest in the movement.

---

[10] Devlin to Dillon, 10 Mar. 1893 (DP 6729/3).   [11] *IN*, 19 Apr. 1893.

This was the young Joe Devlin's introduction to Irish politics, as, in the years after 1891, he was drawn increasingly into both a leadership role in Belfast nationalism and an active role in the wider work of the INFed. He became the civic delegate for Belfast on the Federation's ruling council in December 1892, while continuing his work in Belfast as secretary of both the Belfast branch of the Federation and the Young Ireland Society. His appointment as Belfast correspondent of the *Freeman's Journal* lasted only a few months. By the autumn of 1893 he was back full-time in the drink trade, as assistant manager of an old pub in Bank Street (known in more recent times as Kelly's Cellars). The neighbourhood was a cluster of narrow lanes between Royal Avenue and Smithfield that constituted the Catholic quarter of the city centre. The place was 'not a regular public house in the ordinary sense, but a semi-wholesale place where all is sold in bottles'.[12] It was owned by the Belfast whiskey distiller Samuel Young, who, at the age of 70, was returned to Parliament for the first time in 1892 as Anti-Parnellite MP for East Cavan. Young was a Presbyterian, but his business links were with the Catholic community: both in the liquor trade and as chairman of Hughes's Bakery. He was, he told Dillon, 'one of the few men living whose father had carried his pike and fought for liberty in '98'.[13] Although Devlin always needed to ask Young's permission to 'get off' for political work, it was generously given and often encouraged.[14]

By the early months of 1894 Devlin was speaking and organizing for the Federation throughout eastern Ulster. At Sheepbridge, in McCartan's constituency, the leading local activist invited Healy to speak on a Federation platform alongside McCartan and other Dillonite loyalists.[15] Although Healy scarcely touched on anything controversial, reported Devlin, he was 'completely howled down'. McCartan was 'received with enthusiasm', and the meeting from the Dillonite point of view was 'a most unqualified success'.[16] It was at this meeting that Devlin and Healy, who became opponents for a quarter of a century, first encountered one another. 'Healy came over to me, and he said "Your name is Devlin, I see you have your men well placed". I replied that his friends had the organization of the meeting, and as they had no supporters from Down he had to bring them in from Dundalk.' But Devlin too had organized in advance, arranging with friends from Lurgan to bring in 'a party of about 200 to attend and to make immediate protest if the affairs of the Irish Party are publicly introduced', while his clerical ally and lifelong friend Revd Frank O'Hare of Hilltown, Co. Down, had arranged that 'the men of Hilltown will be

[12] P. Flanagan to Dillon, 9 Jan. 1901 (DP 6781/1011).
[13] S. Young to Dillon, 12 July 1895 (DP 6760/1770).
[14] Devlin to Dillon, 24 Sept. 1893 (DP 6729/4).
[15] McCartan to Peter Byrne, 15 and 21 Feb. 1894 (McCartan Letterbook, 11B/527, 529).
[16] Devlin to Dillon, 16 May 1894 (DP 6729/9); McCartan to O'Connor, 23 Apr. 1894 (McCartan Letterbook, 1B/551).

instructed how to act the moment any attempt is made to create division at the meeting'.[17]

Buoyed up by the success of Sheepbridge, Devlin expanded his activities in rural Ulster. He told Dillon that 'home rule meetings are being held in parts of Ulster where previously they never could be held'.[18] Devlin's correspondence during this period indicates clearly the importance of help from the priests—although not always easy to obtain—in his plans for organizing the east Ulster countryside, supported strongly by his crowd management skills.[19] But the *Irish News* was somewhat unpredictable, and its London Letter, under the authorship of Healy's ally Vesey Knox MP, was especially unsympathetic.[20] A speech of Dillon's referring to Belfast was ignored in August 1894 in favour of coverage of 'obscure politicians that nobody knows', wrote Devlin, 'and I shall as a shareholder and as a Nationalist have the attention of the directors called to this. And if that fails,' he hinted darkly, 'there are other methods which can be resorted to.'[21] A few months later the Healyite MP for South Armagh, Edward McHugh, was put off the board, and Devlin reported that the directors were now 'unanimously in favour of party unity'.[22]

The collapse of Rosebery's Liberal Government and the ensuing general election of July 1895 left Healy 'caught at a great disadvantage by the suddenness of the dissolution', though his best hope lay in Ulster, where the priests were especially important.[23] There were bitter contests at several nominating conventions. South Armagh, rural and remote, provided the young Devlin with his first parliamentary temptation. From 1892 until 1918 its representation was effectively controlled by one or another strand of Belfast nationalism. Edward McHugh was on his way to the Convention when he encountered Devlin at Dundalk station. Devlin was actually en route for Dublin, but McHugh became alarmed, reflecting no doubt on the fate of a Healyite colleague who had been deselected in South Monaghan the previous day. He thus telegraphed to his clerical supporters that he had good reason to believe that Devlin was to be a surprise candidate at the Convention. When the lay delegates heard this, they were, according to Devlin, 'determined to stand by me almost to a man', in which case McHugh 'would undoubtedly have been defeated'. Had Devlin known the state of feeling in Armagh, he would certainly 'have given

---

[17] Devlin to Dillon, 30 Apr. 1894, and M. J. Kelly to Dillon, 19 May 1894 (DP 6729/8, 6772/307).

[18] Devlin to Dillon, 16 May 1894 (DP 6729/9).

[19] See, e.g., McCartan to Fr Lynch, 23 Nov. 1894, and to Dr McCourt, 8 Jan. 1895 (McCartan Letterbook, 11B/5586, 610); Devlin to Dillon, 9 Jan., 23 and 26 May, and 11 Aug. 1894 (DP 6729/6, 10, 11, 14).

[20] Devlin to Dillon, 9 Jan. 1894 (DP 6729/6).

[21] Devlin to Dillon, 11 Aug. 1894 (DP 6729/14).

[22] Devlin to Dillon, 21 June 1895 (DP 6729/22).

[23] T. M. Healy to M. Healy, 4 June 1895, in T. M. Healy, *Letters and Leaders of my Day* (London, 1928), ii. 419.

McHugh a fight'.[24] There may have been an element of youthful bluster here, for only a few months previously Devlin had told Dillon that he had 'little or no influence in Co. Armagh . . . the fact is I don't know half-a-dozen people in the whole county'.[25] As it was, McHugh's unsuccessful opponent at the convention was the Belfast publican M. J. Kelly, who attributed his defeat to 'all the Healyite priests of Armagh city'.[26] Dillon took up the matter of possible advancement for Devlin with his employer. Young agreed to release Devlin for ten days' election work, but regarded his protégé as 'young enough [i.e. too young] for a seat. He is better for a time in Belfast, but I should not stand in his way.'[27] It had been decided that there was no chance of regaining West Belfast in 1895, so Devlin led a flying column of young Belfast men, mainly schoolteachers, who, he told Dillon, were free 'to go to any part of Ireland where fight and work is to be done'. Anxious to get into the conflict, Devlin argued that 'with about a dozen of them we could make things mighty hot for Willie Redmond and Maguire [sitting Parnellite MPs] in Clare'.[28] We do not know if the Federation agreed to sponsor the 'election holiday' of these young workers, but Maguire in West Clare indeed lost his seat, a majority of 1,007 becoming a losing margin of 403, while in East Clare the Parnellite leader's brother barely hung on.

The outcome of the 1895 election encouraged Dillon to move more strongly against Healy. Healy's sponsor, the businessman William Martin Murphy, was humiliated by a Dillonite at a by-election in South Kerry in September 1895. This took the Dillon–Healy conflict onto the public hustings. Healy was expelled from the Irish National League of Great Britain, the Irish National Federation and the Committee of the Irish Parliamentary Party. Devlin, William O'Brien, and others had called for his expulsion from the Parliamentary Party itself, but Dillon calculated that his majority in the party was insufficiently decisive to risk it.[29] Devlin thought that, if Healy did not change his attitude before Parliament reassembled, 'the hitting should be straight from the shoulder and the methods adopted in dealing with him should be Healyite methods'.[30] But, although Dillon became Chairman of the Anti-Parnellites in February 1896, Healy remained an internal critic until the reunion with the Parnellites in 1900. In 1896–7 he set up his own political fund, much of the money coming from priests. At the core of this division were personality clashes between Dillon and Healy, and a contrasting view of party organization: Dillon wanted to retain the system of

---

[24] Devlin to Dillon, 11 July 1895 (DP 6729/24).

[25] Devlin to Dillon, 14 Dec. 1894 (DP 6729/17).

[26] Kelly to Dillon, 11 July 1895 (DP 6777/390).

[27] Young to Dillon, 12 July 1895 (DP 6760/11768).

[28] Young to Dillon, 10 July 1895 (DP 6729/23).

[29] F. S. L. Lyons, *The Irish Parliamentary Party, 1890–1910* (London, 1951), 52; Devlin to J. McVeagh, 23 Aug. 1895 (DP 6757/1164).

[30] Devlin to Dillon, 17 Sept. 1895 (DP 6729/26).

central control developed by Parnell, while Healy wanted constituency power. No doubt Healy's main objections to central party authority stemmed from his own remoteness from this particular lever of power. But his position did reflect a real community issue, in so far as 'constituency power' meant power for local notables—priests and the lay elite—against the party machine. In a Healyite universe, local social status would have guaranteed political status, regardless of the central party.

FIGHTING THE UNIONISTS: THE BELFAST CORPORATION BILL

Under Dorrian, the leadership of Belfast Catholicism had moved from a strategy of great caution to one of advancing the power and esteem of Catholicism, and of supporting moderate nationalism. The election of Sexton did not conflict with episcopal interests. On the contrary, his linking of Belfast nationalism to the wider world of Irish nationalist politics at Westminster opened up new possibilities. His skilful 'tacking' of other issues onto measures such as the apparently obscure Belfast Main Drainage Bill in 1887 and the Asylum Bill in 1891 brought a number of advantages to the Catholics in their previously unequal struggle with the Belfast Corporation. But two developments specific to Belfast, against the wider background of the Dillon–Healy controversy, were about to drive a breach deep into the politics of Belfast's Catholic community that would continue for more than a decade and have a lasting impact on Joe Devlin. The first was the death of Bishop McAlister on 26 March 1895 and his replacement by Revd Dr Henry Henry, formerly President of St Malachy's College, Belfast. The second was the decision of the Belfast Corporation in the late summer of 1895 to put forward a local bill requesting Parliament to grant a major extension of the city boundary and an associated reorganization of ward boundaries.

McAlister was seriously ill for much of 1894, but, despite several requests to Rome for a coadjutor bishop to be appointed, no appointment was made. The reason for this was probably doubt about the suitability of the priest most likely to be appointed in such circumstances, Daniel McCashin, Administrator of St Malachy's Church and McAlister's right-hand man.[31] The Rector of the Irish College at Rome, Revd Michael Kelly, customarily acted as the link between the Irish hierarchy and the Vatican, and was therefore in a position to exert some influence. Kelly was a leading total-abstinence campaigner, who may have been influenced by a letter he received in February 1895 from Revd J. C. McErlain, a former 'Roman' student from Down and Connor, now based

---

[31] McAlister to Archbishop T. Kirby, Rome, 19 Nov. 1894; McCashin to Kirby, 13 Dec. 1894 (KIR/1894/325, 358).

in New Jersey.[32] McErlain was a militant temperance advocate, who advised Kelly that

it would be an evil day for the Church and above all for the temperance cause if . . . the Rev. Daniel McCashin Adm. would become bishop: because practically he has been bishop these eight or nine years and during that time drunkenness and scandals prevailed to an alarming extent, justice set aside and every little clique advanced . . . I beg you . . . to use your influence at Rome to check the progress of those who will favour the sale of whiskey and uphold those in the fight against it.[33]

In fact McCashin was well regarded in the diocese, while McAlister had on occasion spoken out in favour of temperance.

More important to Rome than the liquor question, however, was the long-running dispute, started in Dorrian's time but continued by McAlister, between the diocesan authority and the Order of Passionist Fathers. The Passionists had been encouraged by Dorrian in the 1860s to establish themselves in the outlying mill districts of Ardoyne and Ligoniel to provide pastoral care at a time when the diocese's resources were severely overstretched. But after a while, as with the Christian Brothers, Dorrian found them to be too much of a good thing. There were disputes about their right to conduct fund-raising among Belfast Catholics, and the Passionists had to struggle on in temporary accommodation. In 1887 the Vatican tentatively intervened on the side of the Passionists, but McAlister, with strong support from McCashin, continued to put barriers in their way. When it appeared likely that McCashin would become coadjutor, a senior Passionist wrote to Rome that 'his hostility to them was notorious'.[34] On the death of McAlister in March 1895 a *terna* (a vote by parish priests of the diocese) was held, in which McCashin and Dr Henry tied.[35] The bishops of the Armagh archdiocese then advised Rome that, while both Henry and McCashin were able men, there was some basis for allegations that Henry held Parnellite views, and they recommended McCashin. But a prominent local priest, Revd Convery, had meanwhile written to all his colleagues in Down and Connor that he had it 'on high Roman authority that Fr McCashin had no chance for the mitre, and unless you want that young fellow O'Loan from Maynooth . . . you must vote for Dr Henry'.[36] Convery's information proved correct, and the Armagh bishops' advice was ignored. Pope Leo XIII made what proved to be the fateful choice of Henry Henry, who was consecrated Bishop of Down and Connor on

[32] Michael Kelly (1850–1940), Rector, Irish College, Rome, 1891–1901, Archbishop of Sydney, 1901–40.

[33] Revd J. C. McErlain, Jersey City, USA, to Revd M. Kelly, 1 Feb. 1895 (Kelly Papers, 1895/45).

[34] A. Macaulay, *Patrick McAlister: Bishop of Down & Connor, 1865–1885* (Dublin, 1987), 128–44.

[35] J. O'Laverty, *An Historical Account of the Diocese of Down & Connor*, v (Dublin, 1895), 634.

[36] Recalled after Henry's death by Revd J. F. Shiels to M. O'Riordan, 12 May 1908 (MOR 1908/37).

22 September 1895. Restrictions on the Passionists were removed, and their new church in Ardoyne opened in 1902.

McAlister and McCashin had regularly been referred to in fond terms by Devlin and his colleagues in Belfast. Henry, on the other hand, had remained outside the Federation circle. A native of North Antrim, he had been appointed a professor at St Malachy's College, Belfast, directly following his ordination in 1870, becoming President in 1876. His working experience had been in the world of the Catholic elite and their children, and he came to the bishopric with little experience of parochial work. During Dorrian's time he had worked in an atmosphere of conflict with the Christian Brothers' schools in the town. He was, therefore, remote from their alumni, and from the smaller publicans and the parvenu elements seeking to emerge from or lead the ghetto. Henry was a temperance advocate and an autocratic personality, determined to use his newly acquired authority to make a mark on Belfast. He was 'deeply impressed by the gravity of the *onus* imposed on me in this heretical see'.[37] Against this background, the need of the Belfast Corporation to petition Parliament for a new Act to extend its boundary offered a remarkable challenge and opportunity, both for the new bishop and for the political activists of the Catholic community. Since 1844, Belfast had been governed by a town council (a city council from 1888) elected on the customary Victorian franchise, restricted by wealth and sex. It was divided into five wards, the boundaries of which cut across the ethnic neighbourhoods, so that the Catholic population was in a minority in all wards.[38] Only three Catholics had ever served on the council, two as Liberals and one as a Conservative.[39]

Shortly after Henry's consecration, it became known that the proposed Corporation Bill to be submitted to Parliament was unlikely to be favourable to the Catholic position. He called a public meeting in St Mary's Hall to discuss the matter, refusing a request to involve the INFed. formally in the meeting. It would be a better strategy, he said, to contest the whole issue as a matter of Catholic civil rights, and not as a 'political' (that is, nationalist) issue. The Federation reluctantly agreed, believing that it had obtained from Henry a clear pledge that, if Catholic representation was obtained, 'the National Organization would be accorded the right to nominate the candidates and conduct the elections'. The Catholic Representation Association appointed a Catholic Committee of forty members, including thirteen Belfast priests. Fewer than half were associated with the local Federation.[40] The Committee's preferred plan for achieving Catholic representation was for 'cumulative voting' based on the four constituencies. It would have worked in practice rather like single-transferable-vote PR. Patrick Dempsey's brother James, the man with most experience of defeat under the old system, played a leading role in developing the plan. Others believed that it

---

[37] Henry to M. Kelly, 1 Sept. 1895 (Kelly Papers, 1895/212).

[38] In 1891, Catholic population percentages in the five wards were: Cromac 18.5, Dock 29.3, St Anne's 17.3, St George's 40.2, and Smithfield 33.2.

[39] Wright, *Two Lands*, 295.   [40] *IN*, 2 and 12 Oct. 1897.

was impracticable, or that it would not actually achieve the desired aim of an approximately 25 per cent level of representation for the Catholic community. Its advantage was that, if it did work, it would allow Catholics *wherever they lived* in the city to have some hope that the candidates for whom they voted might be elected. An alternative proposal was to divide the city into twenty-five small wards, drawn in such a way that Catholics would have the controlling influence in up to five of them. Some thought this safer than cumulative voting, but others were concerned that it placed too great a dependence on where people lived at the time, and would institutionalize religious residential segregation. Although Orange opinion later denounced this second alternative as a scheme of the priests 'to pen their followers into one special quarter of the city', the available evidence is rather to the contrary.[41] Henry had backed James Dempsey's cumulative voting scheme.[42] Finally the Catholic Committee put to the City Council a request to amend the Bill so as to attain minority representation *either* by ward *or* by cumulative voting. In November 1895 the Council rejected these proposals, and so it became necessary to challenge the Bill in Parliament.[43]

A petition to the House of Commons was drawn up by the Catholic Committee and presented to a meeting of 3,000 people in St Mary's Hall on 13 January 1896. Henry chaired the meeting, and Devlin read out the petition. It declared that, in a city 'where strong religious and political prejudices . . . have prevailed for a lengthened period, there ought to be a means adopted whereby practically disfranchised minorities of ratepayers would have their proper share in the management of corporate affairs'. A cumulative voting system was called for, as 'no system of division into wards without cumulative voting can assure any permanent representation to the Catholic minority'.[44] The Belfast Corporation Bill received a second reading in the House of Commons on 6 March 1896. Vesey Knox, the Protestant Healyite, moved its rejection. He argued for cumulative voting, as it was 'most undesirable that the House should do anything to perpetuate a condition of things by which the people of one religion should be huddled together in any one part of the town'. T. P. O'Connor pointed out that Catholic Irish Nationalists were returned as city councillors in Liverpool, Manchester, Bradford, and elsewhere, but not in Belfast. The second reading passed, but a delegation from the Catholic Committee persuaded Chief Secretary Gerald Balfour that the Bill should be sent to a Select Committee for revision. Dillon designated himself and Knox as the Irish Parliamentary Party's nominees, notwithstanding Healy's attempts to suggest that Knox's partner should be a second lawyer (just possibly himself!), so as to save the Catholics of Belfast the cost of hiring counsel to present their case to the Committee. Thus the only Ulster Nationalist expertise on the Committee was the Protestant Knox, who, ironically, was firmly in the camp of Healy and the bishop's party.

[41] *IN*, 14 July 1896.　　[42] *NS*, 12 Oct. 1897.　　[43] *IN*, 15 Oct. 1897.
[44] Ibid., 14 Jan. 1896.

The Select Committee sat for three weeks, interviewing 28 witnesses and asking 8,000 questions. Devlin was not included in the list of witnesses, because 'the Bishop said they did not want politicians there, and I was too much of a politician', but he felt he could 'afford to submit to insult for the victory has been entirely on our side'.[45] Catholic counsel pressed for a twenty-ward scheme, which would probably have given four wards with Catholic majorities, but the Select Committee thought fifteen wards sufficient for a city of Belfast's size.[46] Wisely, the Catholics would not agree to any ward scheme until boundaries had been mapped out that would deliver the intended goods. Once it was agreed that the Select Committee would take the unusual step of including in the Bill itself final confirmation of the detailed boundaries of two of the fifteen wards, the way was at last clear. A fifteen-ward scheme was implemented, which remained in operation until 1973 (Table 3.1).[47] Predictably the elderly South Belfast MP William Johnston of Ballykilbeg, Orange hero of the 1860s, protested that 'these two wards were pencilled out by a Roman Catholic priest', but the Bill passed its third reading without a division.[48]

The Catholic Committee had effectively ensured that eight seats out of sixty in the new council would be chosen by the Catholics of West Belfast, in what became the Falls and Smithfield wards of the city. It was a considerably smaller proportion than their 25 per cent of the population, although smaller Catholic concentrations in what became Dock and Pottinger wards were able to assist in the return of six Labour councillors, giving an initial opposition group totalling fourteen out of sixty. In Dock ward there was a compact Catholic area, and Court ward also included some small Catholic neighbourhoods. The largely suburban and Protestant Cromac ward had at its northern apex the small Catholic Markets district. But in general the sectoral ward pattern, with eleven of the fifteen wards radiating out from the central area to the city boundary, tended towards both ethnic and class mixing within wards. The small Catholic Short Strand neighbourhood and the large Protestant working-class vote of inner east Belfast were split between three wards. The Unionists jeered that the Catholic Church in fact preferred the relative certainty of the Falls–Smithfield concentration, because they wanted to encourage the growth of 'one big ghetto' in west Belfast. But cumulative voting would have brought Catholic representation closer to proportionality. It failed, not because the clergy wanted it to, but because the government opposed it, and because the predominantly southern Irish Parliamentary Party kept silent on the issue.

But as the Corporation Bill crisis unfolded, the Federationists' isolated position in Catholic Belfast became apparent. 'You can hardly imagine the difficulty of our position here for sometime,' wrote Devlin in what, for this early stage of his career, was an uncharacteristically low moment. The members of the deputation that

[45] Devlin to Dillon, 20 Apr. 1896 (DP 6729/31).
[46] *Select Committee on the Belfast Corporation Bill*, P.P., H.C. (1896), viii. 287.
[47] Ibid. 296.   [48] Parl. Deb., H.C., 4th series, xli. 1662 (23 June 1896).

Table 3.1. Wards by religion, Belfast, 1901–1937 (% Catholic)

Ward	1901	1911	1926	1937
Clifton	22.5	22.3	25.4	30.0
Court	18.6	23.2	22.9	24.5
Cromac	22.0	21.7	20.5	21.5
Dock	36.3	38.8	41.8	44.9
Duncairn	17.5	17.3	9.9	10.3
Falls	77.2	81.9	89.2	91.5
Ormeau	13.8	14.4	7.0	8.4
Pottinger	17.7	16.8	14.5	13.8
St Anne's	34.7	33.5	38.4	37.3
St George's	9.8	9.4	4.7	4.3
Shankill	7.6	7.1	4.5	5.0
Smithfield	86.9	89.6	91.0	91.0
Victoria	9.5	8.8	5.6	4.7
Windsor	15.1	14.9	16.5	15.1
Woodvale	10.7	9.9	4.8	4.5
CITY	24.3	24.1	23.0	23.8
*Dissimilarity Index =	39.3	39.3	49.4	49.7

* The Dissimilarity Index calculates segregation on a scale of 0–100.
Source: Census of Ireland, 1901, 1911; Census of NI, 1926, 1937.

went to London to present the petition 'were all either Healyites or Parnellites', and on reporting to the Catholic Committee on their return they 'did nothing all the evening but praise Healy and Knox'. The first split came at this meeting. The proposed resolution of thanks to Knox was countered by Devlin's amendment to thank Dillon and the Irish Party, which was lost by three votes. Devlin felt that the wisest policy was to continue to cooperate until the Bill was through Parliament, but he found the whole thing 'absolutely sickening'.[49] The Federation, as 'the national organization' in Belfast, assumed the right to represent the nationalist community, but it became clear that Henry and his supporters, having taken the lead in securing municipal representation, did not intend to leave the field. Henry produced a 'scheme', which he said had been formulated on the lines of the Catholic Union of the Archdiocese of Glasgow, for future Catholic municipal representation in Belfast. It proposed a Belfast Catholic Association, run by a central committee.[50] The bishop was to be president *ex officio*, and senior priests of the diocese were to occupy all the key positions. Effectively all decisions and appointments would be subject to the approval of the bishop. The proposal was unveiled at a large public meeting in St Mary's Hall on 25 October 1896. Devlin proposed an amendment 'that this Association take no part in municipal or national politics', but, as he had not been present to put his views at the earlier

[49] Devlin to Dillon, 27 Mar. 1896 (DP 6729/30).   [50] *IN*, 20 Oct. 1897.

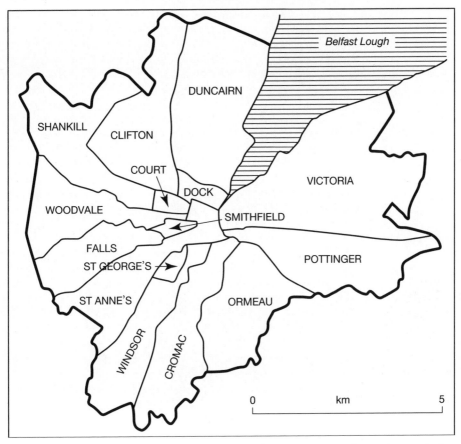

Fig. 3.1. Belfast municipal wards, 1896–1973. The city centre is at the northern end of St Anne's Ward, south of Dock Ward.

Committee meeting, the bishop ruled that 'Mr Devlin is out of order coming before us at all'. Uproar then ensued, and Devlin, accompanied by a number of Federationists, left the hall crying 'we will fight it at the November elections.'[51]

FIGHTING THE BISHOP: 'A VERITABLE BELFAST POOH-BAH'

Notwithstanding this humiliation, Devlin developed a renewed confidence and energy during the course of the winter. A major Federation rally was held at

[51] Ibid., 26 Oct. 1896.

Fig. 3.2. Belfast Nationalists, *c*.1897. John Rooney and Tim McCarthy (standing), J. T. Donovan and Joe Devlin (seated).

St Mary's Hall, with three of the six speakers being Protestants.[52] The *Irish News* continued to support the national work of the Federation, praising Dillon, denouncing Healy, and supporting moves for reunion with the Parnellites.[53] But, as the year advanced, the paper distinguished increasingly between local and national politics. By April 1897 Devlin thought that the *Irish News* 'has gone over body and soul to Bishop Henry, and we may shortly look for a dose of Healyism'.[54] In fact the *Irish News* went out of its way *not* to identify the Belfast Catholic Association (CA) with Healyism: its policy was now to support the Irish Parliamentary Party nationally, and to seek to identify the CA with it locally. But, beneath the veneer of harmony that the *Irish News* sought to create, battle lines were being drawn. On 9 July 1897 the local branch of the Federation met the remaining local members of the Parnellite Irish National League, formed a joint committee, and nominated candidates for all eight municipal seats in the Falls and Smithfield wards. The CA also nominated a full set of candidates for the two wards, after the Federationists had rejected the suggestion of a compromise ticket. Devlin was initially bullish. 'We are winning new friends every day . . . and the whole situation is most hopeful,' he told Dillon. The most serious problem was that the board of directors of the *Irish News* passed a resolution supporting the CA. The only policy in his view was to start a rival paper. 'The longer we delay the preparations for a paper the worse for ourselves . . . If we are beaten in this fight it practically means the extinction of nationality in Belfast if not in Ulster.'[55]

Devlin's new weekly was named the *Northern Star*, looking back to the Presbyterian-led republicanism of 1798, and forward in anticipation of the centenary celebrations in 1898. It had also been the name of the short-lived newspaper run in opposition to Bishop Dorrian by A. J. McKenna, and as such cocked an additional snook at Bishop Henry. The paper's banner read 'The Northern Star: A Nationalist Democratic Weekly', and its prospectus declared that

while placing the interests of the Irish national cause above and beyond all other considerations . . . [the paper] . . . will strenuously advocate the rights of the working classes to all that is claimed for them by their trade organizations, and while strongly maintaining the rights of the Catholics of Belfast and Ulster to their fair proportion of representation on all public boards and bodies, care will be taken to avoid encouraging any attempt to stir into activity the spirit of religious bigotry.

A young Corkman, Tim McCarthy, was appointed editor. He was to become a close associate of Devlin's when he returned to Belfast in 1906 as editor of the *Irish News*, the paper he was initially brought to Belfast to oppose. McCarthy was at this time a confidant of fellow Corkman William O'Brien MP, and sent him detailed accounts of his experiences in Belfast during these months. His first reports to O'Brien were encouraging, although he noted that 'the fight will be tough enough, and if we make headway against the influences at work, there will be ample reason for congratulation'.[56]

The campaign commenced in earnest during the first week of September 1897. Devlin was at the heart of the campaign, but did not stand himself. His

54 Recounted by McGhee to Dillon, 30 Apr. 1897 (DP 6757/1017).
55 Devlin to Dillon, 26 and 29 July 1897 (DP 6729/39, 40).
56 McCarthy to O'Brien, 8 Sept. 1897 (BLUCC, OBP, AH.69).

colleagues ran as the 'Joint Committee of the Irish National Federation and the Irish National League', thus achieving by local action that reunion of the Irish Party that was not realized at the national level until 1900. Two of their eight candidates came from the Parnellite side. The CA ran eleven candidates, three of them in neighbouring Dock ward. Their candidates were demonstrably a better-off group than their Joint Committee rivals. Only one CA candidate lived in Catholic West Belfast, the remainder all living in predominantly Protestant middle-class areas in the north or south of the city. Six of the eight Joint Committee candidates, by contrast, lived in Falls–Smithfield. In occupational terms the CA team included two hospital surgeons (both of whom were later knighted), a city-centre estate agent, a leading architect (many of whose commissions were from the local Catholic diocese), a large brewer, three solicitors, a city-centre draper, another house agent, and a publican. Devlin's team, on the other hand, included a Falls Road dispensary doctor and a Parnellite solicitor who lived at his parents' pub. These were 'the only men on the other side worthy of notice', said a CA candidate.[57] The other six included a licensed oyster-room proprietor, a publican, a commission agent, a cabinet-maker/shopkeeper, and a back-street butcher 'who carries a basket up the Falls Road'.[58] The second Parnellite was a manual worker and member of the Trades Council. He was described as a Labour-Nationalist, although the Trades Council denied that he had their formal support.[59] There is no doubt that the Joint Committee sought to add a 'labour/working-class' flavour to its campaign, although the overall impression is of a lower-middle-class leadership. This tension is illustrated by a Nationalist handbill from the election that claimed, on the one hand, that 'the needs of working people and the over-rated and over-taxed shopkeepers, and the interests of the rate-paying community will be their sole concern in the Corporation', and, on the other, that 'they will advocate and secure better houses, cheaper gas, better-lit streets and cheaper tram fares for the toilers of neglected west Belfast'.[60] Comparable to the classic rule-of-thumb division between the respectable and the unrespectable working class, the difference between the CA and the Devlinites in Belfast was very much that between a professional and commercial elite and a more marginal business group. 'The betting men . . . are almost every one Nationalists and strong supporters of ours,' Rooney told Dillon. 'The shopkeepers (publicans and grocers) are almost to a man in our favour,' added Devlin.[61]

The *Northern Star* made much play with the fact that a number of the CA candidates were rent agents with a vested interest in resisting stricter sanitary control of housing; they were denounced as 'hacks and self-seekers', men who

---

[57] *IN*, 26 Oct. 1897.   [58] *NS*, 23 Oct. 1897.

[59] J. W. Boyle, *The Irish Labour Movement in the Nineteenth Century* (Washington, 1988), 168.

[60] Election handbill (DP 6729/48a).

[61] Rooney to Dillon, 10 June 1896, and Devlin to Dillon, 29 July 1897 (DP 6773/703, 6729/40).

'in their inmost hearts spurn nationality and despise the labouring classes'; as 'gentlemen who came from other wards . . . to represent the working men of Falls and Smithfield'; as 'respectable folks—the elite of Catholic Belfast as they dub themselves . . . when will they be seen in the slums again?'[62] They were, said Devlin, 'men who knew nothing about the wants of the working classes'. The election was 'not a question of religion. It was a social question, of the happiness of the people, of open spaces for the children of the working classes, where they could enjoy themselves in the summer evenings, of district libraries, of decent houses, where the people could live after their hard day's work in the factories.'[63] The Nationalist candidates claimed 'to live and toil amongst you, and are no fair-weather friends striving to climb to place on your shoulders'.[64] Bishop Henry's right-hand man and successor as President of St Malachy's College, Revd Henry Laverty, who was the most irascible of the CA leaders, appeared to confirm this when, at a subsequent election, he declared that 'we do not want on the public boards of Belfast men without education, men without manners, men who would be a disgrace to the Catholic body'.[65]

Henry himself intervened heavily at key points. Early in the campaign he declared that his opponents, in attempting to secularize the selection of municipal candidates, were 'opposing the bishop'. It was necessary to keep 'party politics' out of 'the struggle for municipal rights in Belfast'.[66] The estate agent William McCormick, now chairman of the *Irish News* and aldermanic candidate for the Falls, maintained that they were all good nationalists 'but they knew that in Belfast where the shoe pinched was on account of religion'. P. J. Magee, another CA candidate, argued ingeniously if unconvincingly that the Association's city-wide parish structure was necessary because 'the Catholic wards' had been won from Parliament not just for the people of Falls and Smithfield, but had been 'conceded to the entire Catholic population of Belfast'.[67] Another candidate, James Corr, rebutted the charge that the CA candidates were not nationalists, but 'we do not flaunt Nationality in your faces, we come to be sent to the City Council to work for you'. His colleague, the irrepressible James Dempsey, on the other hand, declared that he was 'a Nationalist of Nationalists'; he could have stood for the other side, 'but local politics is local'.[68] The *Northern Star* and the Devlinite politicians, in public and private, characterized the CA as 'Healyite'. Dublin Castle's analysts of nationalist politics took the same view.[69] But neither Healy nor any of his supporters was invited to Belfast, by the CA or anyone else, and *Irish News* editorials went to some trouble to present the Association as a movement with entirely local concerns that at national level disapproved of Healyite 'faction'. P. J. Magee said that the CA would accept

---

[62] *NS*, 2, 9, 23 Oct., 24 Nov., and 4 Dec. 1897.   [63] Ibid., 23 Oct. 1897.
[64] Election handbill (DP 6729/48a).   [65] *IN*, 14 Jan. 1902.
[66] Ibid., 21 Sept. 1897.   [67] Ibid., 14 Oct. 1897.   [68] Ibid., 7 Sept. 1897.
[69] Return of Local Government Election Results, 1899 (TNA: PRO CO 904/184/1).

assistance from either Dillon or Healy.[70] Only James Dempsey allowed the veil to drop, reminding audiences of their previous relationship with 'our good friend Vesey Knox'. Curiously, in view of his endorsement of Knox, Dempsey then went on to present a frankly sectarian line: 'let them scratch a north of Ireland Protestant home ruler, and they would find an Orangeman.' 'The Orange vote will be cast for Mr Devlin's eight,' echoed the *Irish News* a few days later.[71]

Although he was not a candidate, *Irish News* editorials targeted Devlin for attack. He was predictably 'a young man in a hurry', but also 'a veritable Belfast Pooh-bah', speaking of pledging the honour of his organization, when in fact his audiences consisted of 'a dozen dupes and a score of whistling boys'. Matthew McCusker, owner of six city-centre pubs, took up the attack upon 'this youthful potentate Devlin . . . the manager of Sam Young's punch and judy show', for whom subscriptions for 'long service' had been solicited when he was 'about nineteen' (actually 22), since when 'Joseph has risen to political eminence in his own estimation'. McCusker continued what was essentially a snobbish attack on the Joint Committee candidates, referring deprecatingly to 'this man's oyster rooms' (Rooney), and saying that it would be a great service to Dillon and the Irish Party if the Belfast branch of the Federation were taken away from 'these miserable creatures'. McCusker said that, in contrast, William McCormick had 'conducted a large commercial business on his own account successfully', and that 'this was the class of man we want on the Corporation'.[72] The Joint Committee's campaign was not noticeably more salubrious. The Devlinites' regular characterization of Bishop Henry as a closet Parnellite had to be down-pedalled in a campaign fought jointly with the local Parnellites. It was persistently reported in the *Star* that James Dempsey had privately maligned the bishop to John Dillon while in London, and that he had urged Joe Devlin to 'join the CA and we shall burst it up from the inside'.[73] But, though very abusive, the Joint Committee's campaign did seek to focus on substantive issues. A Catholic organization was not an appropriate body to control political representation, the *Star* asserted. Did the Catholics of Belfast 'wish to inaugurate in this city a purely religious battle over matters entirely unconnected with the principles of their faith? Do they mean to . . . cast aside the teaching of every Irish patriot leader from Wolfe Tone . . . to Charles Stewart Parnell?' The rules of the CA, said Devlin, 'were an insult to public liberty'.[74] The bishop refused to allow the Nationalists to use St Mary's Hall for their meetings, and so many gatherings had to be held in the open air. At one large meeting 'of the working men of Falls ward' the chairman declared that 'this was the old fight of capital against labour'.[75] Only once did the Nationalists manage to get access to St Mary's Hall,

---

[70] *IN*, 26 Oct. 1897.   [71] Ibid., 14 and 26 Oct. 1897.
[72] Ibid., 20 and 26 Oct. 1897.   [73] *NS*, 27 Nov. 1897.
[74] Ibid., 2 and 9 Oct. 1897.   [75] Ibid., 2 Oct. 1897.

by inviting the leaders of the national movement, Dillon and O'Brien, to Belfast. This was intended as their trump card, the young parvenus parading through the streets of central Belfast with the 'leaders of the Irish people' while the bishop's supporters were excluded. It was also the first attempt to link the local election campaign with Devlin's emerging project of using the 1798 centenary as a means of achieving nationalist reunion. The Presbyterian republican William Orr had met his death in 1797, and the Nationalists proudly led Dillon and Co. through the centre of Belfast amidst banners proclaiming 'Remember Orr', 'Ulster wants Home Rule', and 'Who fears to speak of '98'. Dillon stressed the need for the unity of Irishmen 'of all creeds and classes', but made no reference to the local elections.[76] Devlin commented that 'the Catholic Association have one bishop out of twenty-three on their side'.[77]

But as the campaign continued its bitter course through November, the Nationalists became increasingly anxious, and Devlin made a desperate call for assistance to William O'Brien and to the labour Nationalist and Land League founder Michael Davitt. Tim McCarthy told O'Brien that 'on the other side the priests have been working more than devils and far more unscrupulously', while sympathetic priests could do no more than provide anonymous letters for publication in the *Star*:

Now the crisis has arrived . . . I am thoroughly in earnest when I say that a crushing defeat here would mean the extinction of Nationalism for all practical purposes in Belfast for years, the triumph of the worst and rottenest elements of public life under the dictatorship of a bishop who should never have been allowed outside an Infants' school . . . Now, I appreciate to the full . . . the inadvisability of identifying the *Irish Party* with the local fight. But something must be done . . . Davitt's presence would be decisive with hundreds of workingmen Catholics; yours would strengthen us and rally to our side the majority of the doubting Nationalists. Joe Devlin's name is on the memorial to Davitt as well as the candidates . . . If we fail for want of help from the Party there will be bitter feelings here. If this was placed before Dillon I am sure he would not object.[78]

Devlin wrote to Dillon along similar lines. In response to these entreaties, Davitt came to Belfast three days before the poll. St Mary's Hall was closed to him, but he led a torchlight procession of 20,000 people through the city centre from the Linen Hall Hotel and up the Falls Road. He made very clear, however, that he came 'without any consultation with his parliamentary colleagues', for the Nationalist movement 'did not seek to identify Irish parliamentarians with a municipal contest in Belfast'.[79] But he attacked the *Irish News* vigorously, and, although he had

not one word of disrespect to utter with reference to the Bishop of Belfast . . . we as Irish Nationalists and democrats have to make it plain to our Protestant fellow-countrymen

---

[76] *IN*, 15 Oct. 1897.   [77] *NS*, 23 Oct. 1897.
[78] McCarthy to O'Brien, 18 Nov. 1897 (BLUCC, OBP, AH.87, 88).
[79] *NS*, 4 Dec. 1897.

in Belfast and elsewhere . . . that we will not be dictated to in political matters by any man or any body of men who do not derive their authority directly from the people.[80]

The columns of the *Northern Star* in these early months of its existence identified strongly with labour and trade-union issues, both in reporting and in editorials, denouncing, for instance, 'capitalist efforts to smash the [almost exclusively Protestant] engineering unions' in recent strikes.[81] The *Star* warned that 'trade Unionism is a hard and solid FACT which employers of labour must recognize'.[82] But the outcome of the election, though not entirely unexpected by the Nationalists, contrasted sharply with the confident rhetoric displayed earlier. The CA won all eight seats, with 62 per cent of the vote in the Falls and 60 per cent in Smithfield. Elsewhere the Unionist Party won forty-six seats and Labour candidates won six.

The *Northern Star*'s response was predictably vigorous. 'Rent Agents in the Town Council—But the People Stand Firm—A Triumph for Gross Intimidation', cried its main headline.[83] Devlin and McCarthy sent private assessments of the result to their respective patrons, John Dillon and William O'Brien. Both placed their emphasis firmly on the role of Henry's priests. Devlin thought that an election petition to overturn the result on the grounds of clerical intimidation would have been successful, but was 'out of the question' in divided Ulster.[84] At the beginning of the campaign he had known that 'the shopkeepers (publicans and grocers) are almost to a man in our favour', but that 'an evening paper is wanted to combat the effects of the pulpit orations on the minds of the working people'.[85] McCarthy too stressed 'the real power wielded by the priests over the unfortunate poorer people—especially the women who . . . are nearly all old and illiterate—or pretend to be so'. In Smithfield the *Star* claimed that only 10 out of 220 illiterate voters cast their votes for the Nationalists.[86] McCarthy lamented that, although Davitt's visit

seemed to be a huge popular success . . . the appearance at the booths of the men and women who had votes completely dispelled from my mind the notion that the crowds in the streets [supporting Davitt] represented the poor creatures that were marched into the booth like sheep by the bishop's domineering force of curates. In my experience of elections I never saw anything so pitiable.[87]

But the Nationalist mood was not entirely defeatist. Devlin, ever the organizer, noted that all the local Parnellites who had supported the Nationalist candidates had now joined the local branch of the Federation, effectively ending the Parnellite split in Belfast. He claimed an increase in Federation membership

[80] *NS*, 27 Nov. 1897.   [81] Ibid., 11 Dec. 1897.   [82] Ibid., 6 Dec. 1897.
[83] Ibid., 4 Dec. 1897.   [84] Devlin to Dillon, 10 Dec. 1897 (DP 6729/44).
[85] Devlin to Dillon, 29 July 1897 (DP 6729/40).   [86] *NS*, 11 Dec. 1897.
[87] McCarthy to O'Brien, 29 Nov. 1897 (BLUCC, OBP, AH.94); *NS*, 11 Dec. 1897.

from 600 to 800, making the Belfast branch 'the largest and most important in Ireland'.[88] McCarthy wanted to continue as editor of the *Star*, but soon lost confidence in the paper's ability to pay his salary. 'I make no complaint,' he told O'Brien, 'but I have come to the conclusion that Belfast nationality, outside a few hundred good men, consists of religious bigotry and an ability to play the Boys of Wexford.'[89]

At the centre of the whole local conflict was the role of religion in politics. The young Co. Armagh Protestant and Oxford graduate W. D. Harbinson, McCarthy's assistant at the *Star*, though an active party worker and a well-regarded speaker, did not appear on a platform during the campaign.[90] Neither did the Ulster Protestant Nationalist Richard McGhee, President of the National Union of Dock Labourers (NUDL). Even after the election he was still 'of the opinion that being a Protestant it will be a mistake to address any meetings of the Federation at present'.[91] Dillon must have advised a less cautious approach, for McGhee duly delivered a major speech (on the benefits of the Liberal alliance) to the Federation in Belfast a few days later. There had been support from a small number of local priests for the Nationalist candidates, but in fact, so far as most priests were concerned, episcopal intimidation worked. Part of the problem was that, in Belfast, the bishop and priests had always had a very 'hands-on' role in leading a poor community with a truncated social structure. In Dorrian's time this had been very visible. McAlister's more consultative style had begun to acknowledge the existence of an educated laity, so that Henry's episcopal career was in fact an attempt to restore lay–clergy relations to an earlier epoch. In this he had the support, at least for several years, of Cardinal Logue of Armagh, who thought that 'things are coming to a pretty pass in Ireland when a bishop cannot change his curates without leave of the newspapers'.[92] Henry thought that 'a large number of our Catholics have substituted Nationality for Religion'.[93] But he was not opposed to nationalism as such. In 1898 he established in his diocese a confraternity magazine, *Sancta Maria*, which reflected a combination of temperance and cultural nationalist attitudes very similar to those that the *Leader* and its predecessor paper were disseminating nationally. But priests who adhered in public to the local Nationalist movement were likely to be transferred by Henry to remote corners of his diocese, and very few were prepared to speak out. On the other side, even the cautious Michael McCartan wrote to Dillon that 'the bishop, in his municipal mission of mischief . . . [is] . . . calculated to confirm the foolish notion that home rule means Rome rule'.[94]

[88] *NS*, 25 Dec. 1897.
[89] McCarthy to O'Brien, 6 Jan. 1897 [*recte* 1898] (BLUCC, OBP, AIA.8).
[90] *NS*, 11 Dec. 1897.   [91] McGhee to Dillon, 16 Dec. 1897 (DP 6757/1022).
[92] Logue to Walsh, 11 Aug. 1898 (Walsh Papers, 38).
[93] Henry to Kelly, 16 Nov. 1897 (Kelly Papers, 1897/504).
[94] McCartan to Dillon, 24 Mar. 1897 (DP 6756/978).

THE STRUGGLE CONTINUED, 1898–1903

Although Devlin and most of his friends were determined on a 'no surrender' policy in the aftermath of their defeat, Devlin himself wanted to get out of Belfast. He was almost 27 and rubbing shoulders with senior parliamentarians and professional men, yet he himself was the manager of a back-street bar, so it is scarcely surprising that he felt a sense of underachievement and dissatisfaction. Politically, also, he may have felt both that he might be more successful operating from a different base and that his continued presence in Belfast might act as a barrier to settlement of the local struggle. At a rally in Strabane in May 1898 he suffered the humiliation of being denounced from the platform by a local curate as 'more of a priest hunter than a nationalist', a fife and drum band then making it impossible for him to deliver his speech.[95] For the next three-and-a-half years Devlin plied John Dillon and others with requests for help in his personal career. In fact he was to remain in Belfast, living in the modest family home at 41 Alexander Street West, in the Lower Falls, until after his thirty-first birthday. His greatest achievement during this period was to organize a network of 1798 Centenary Clubs in Belfast, and then to transform them into branches of the newly created United Irish League (UIL).

The Protestant W. D. Harbinson succeeded McCarthy as editor of the *Northern Star* in the spring of 1898. The paper moved from a weekly loss in August 1898, with a circulation of 2,000, to a trading profit by April 1899, with circulation up to 2,500 in Belfast and 1,000 in the country, although it still fell some way short of repaying its capital costs.[96] These figures suggest that the *Star* was purchased by about one in six Catholic households in the city. Early in 1899 the paper's banner subtitle changed from 'A Nationalist Democratic Weekly' to 'Ulster's Nationalist Weekly', possibly in the hope of increasing rural sales. But the *Star's* future as an independent company was not secure, and in February 1900 Devlin and Rooney, aided by Michael Davitt, arranged with the newspaper baron and former Nationalist MP Charles Diamond to print the paper at his works in Glasgow. Diamond later stressed that his role in the *Northern Star* was simply that of printer.[97] But as he took over and merged various Glasgow papers, the *Northern Star*, for the rest of its brief life, effectively became the Belfast edition, its local coverage increasingly diluted by Scottish and Catholic news.[98] Devlin and his colleagues regarded the *Star* as very important, not just for countering the *Irish News*—which 'seems to have gone over body

---

[95] *IN*, 24 May 1898; seventy years later an 88-year-old member of this band recalled this event as the humiliation of 'one of Ireland's most traitorous sons' (*Donegal Democrat*, 8 Nov. 1968).
[96] Devlin to Dillon, 4 Apr. 1899 (DP 6729/63).
[97] *NS*, 21 Mar. 1903 and 9 Sept. 1905.
[98] McCarthy to O'Brien, 14 Feb. 1900 (BLUCC, OBP, AKA.99).

and bones and is now a Catholic paper pure and simple'—but because the voice of Dillon's Irish Party, the Dublin-based *Freeman's Journal*, gave poor coverage of the activities of Northern Nationalists, a fact not unconnected with the fact that *Irish News* editor T. J. Campbell was its northern correspondent.[99]

Much of Devlin's energy during 1899 went into establishing the National Club. This was necessitated by the need to compete socially with the CA.[100] Declaring that 'this is an age of clubs', Bishop Henry had begun the movement with the establishment of the Central Catholic Club, housed in ornate former hotel premises at 123 Royal Avenue.[101] The main target audience were 'young men engaged in business'. It sought to be both 'a means of innocent amusement' and 'a source of enlightenment'. Evening classes were offered, to provide a path 'to advancement and power for the working Catholic youth of the city who aspire to rise in the world'. While 'the humblest working man . . . will be as welcome in its halls as his wealthiest brother Catholic', the *Irish News* cautiously continued that 'all classes may not reap from it equal benefits, for all will not feel the same keen want of such a club'. Inevitably the bishop was *ex officio* Club President, and the Committee was dominated by his senior clergy and by laymen prominent in the CA. After six months of operation, it claimed 537 members. The National Club followed three years later. It was nearby, but in the narrow back lane that was Berry Street, rather than on the imposing façade of Royal Avenue. The sigh of relief is almost audible in Devlin's report to Davitt that now 'the Nationalists will have a club and hall second to none in Belfast and *it will be their own*'. By the end of 1900 it had a membership of 500.[102]

As the divided Irish parties at last achieved reunion in January 1900, the split in Belfast continued. In March Devlin and Rooney sought a settlement, but Henry presented them with a document for signature in which he called upon the Nationalists to express 'humble contrition for our past conduct' and 'profound regret', together with 'an appeal by us to his Lordship to allow us to conduct the national affairs of Belfast with the co-operation of the Catholic Association and subject to, and under his Lordship's guidance'. Devlin thought this would make it 'impossible for self-respecting men to take any part in the public affairs of their own city', and the negotiations ended.[103] He was concerned lest this move might be part of a ploy by the CA in the context of the party reunion. John Dillon had stepped down in favour of the Parnellite John Redmond as leader of the reunited party, and Devlin feared an attempt by the CA to bring Healy and Redmond to a public meeting chaired by the bishop, which he thought would lead to the destruction of the Nationalists in Belfast. Devlin addressed this long report to William O'Brien, with whom he was in close contact at this time, and

99 John Rooney to Dillon, 18 Feb. 1899 (DP 6773/704).
100 Devlin to Davitt, 28 Nov. 1899 (Davitt Papers, 9396/1451).   101 *IN*, 30 Apr. 1897.
102 Devlin to Davitt, 18 Nov. 1899 (Davitt Papers, 9396/1451); *NS*, 9 Feb. 1901.
103 Devlin to Dillon, 28 Mar. 1900 (DP 6729/69).

copied it to Dillon. He wanted O'Brien and Redmond to address a Nationalist meeting in the Ulster Hall, 'which we could easily fill'. Devlin thought that, although 'Redmond is not a favourite here', his presence would both 'dish the other party' and allow him to witness at close quarters the local popularity of O'Brien and reflect on the doubtful wisdom of playing 'the Healyite game in Belfast'.[104] These suspicions about a national Redmond–Healy axis proved to be unfounded, and on 14 September 1900 Devlin's dream of a great Belfast UIL demonstration took place. Both Redmond and Dillon went out of their way to praise Devlin's work for the national movement, noting in particular a talent 'rare in men of marked ability . . . his capacity to follow—his consistent and whole-hearted loyalty to constituted national authority'.[105]

The decline of Healy was beginning to rattle the local CA, and the confidence of the Belfast UIL began to grow. It was alleged by local Nationalists that the rank and file of the CA were anxious to join the UIL. There was a rumour that James Dempsey would resign from the City Council 'in disgust'. Dempsey, who had been mocked mercilessly by Devlin and the *Northern Star* in the 1897 council elections, contributed five guineas to a private testimonial for Devlin.[106] John Rooney told Dillon that 'Father McCashin, who ran a dead heat with Dr Henry for the bishopric, has been to Rome to seek for an investigation into Dr Henry's conduct, and a number of parish priests have sent a petition to Rome against Dr Henry'.[107] The CA, which was said to have collected £900 to contest the West Belfast seat against the sitting Liberal Unionist in the general election of October 1900, did not do so.[108] During 1901, Devlin's position, and that of the Belfast UIL, in the new Nationalist movement strengthened. The CA made a vain effort to persuade Redmond to recognize it, rather than the city's UIL executive, as the legitimate representative of the national organization in Belfast, but was instructed to route any communication with the Irish Parliamentary Party through the Belfast UIL Executive.[109] All the while the Devlin–Redmond alliance was being built on the basis of parliamentary work, designed to demonstrate to Belfast Catholics that national action at Westminster, not local action through the accommodationist policies of the local minority elite, was the way to secure advances.[110]

By the end of the year Devlin thought, somewhat prematurely as it turned out, that 'the Catholic Association here is practically broken up and absolutely discredited owing to internal dissensions . . . Last night there was a further row in the Catholic Club, fifty members of which joined us.'[111] Matt McCusker,

[104] Devlin to O'Brien, 28 Mar. 1900, copy (DP 6729/69).   [105] *NS*, 22 Sept. 1900.
[106] Testimonial to Devlin, 1st list of subscribers, *c*. Mar. 1901 (BLUCC, OBP, AL.6).
[107] Rooney to Dillon, 31 Aug. 1900 (DP 6773/705).   [108] *NS*, 6 Oct. 1900.
[109] P. J. Magee to Redmond, 14 Aug., 23 Sept., and 2 Oct. 1901; Redmond to Magee, 16 Aug., 26 Sept., and 7 Oct. 1901 (RP 15240/9–11).
[110] Redmond to Devlin, 4 July 1901, copy; Devlin to Redmond, 16 Aug. 1901 (RP 15181/1).
[111] Devlin to Dillon, 23 Dec. 1901 (DP 6730/81).

President of the Belfast and Ulster Licensed Vintners' Association (LVA), had been angered by the CA's decision not to select him for a municipal vacancy in the Falls ward, and stood as an independent. His supporters included Councillor James Dempsey. The local UIL, which had been struggling to deter its supporters from embarking on further municipal contests that they knew they could not win, did not formally adopt McCusker as a candidate, but gave him strong informal backing. A few weeks later his name topped the list of Belfast contributors to the Irish Party's Parliamentary Fund.[112] The campaign revolved around McCusker's abilities and motivation. One CA curate commented sarcastically that at least the publican McCusker knew 'the wants and the requirements' of the working classes in one sense.[113] McCusker lost, with a slightly lower share of the vote than the Devlinites had obtained in 1897, but this little tussle brought the split in Belfast's Catholic elite closer to a direct division between publicans and the rest.

In January 1902 Devlin left Belfast, and the local movement was left in the hands of John Rooney and the solicitor Thomas Maguire.[114] But the Belfast CA continued to be a force to be reckoned with, and the Nationalists did not attempt a second challenge in the municipal elections until 1904, and even then without success. In the spring of 1903 Belfast Nationalists were alarmed by the appearance of a wider threat, in the form of an All-Ireland Catholic Association that had been established in Dublin. The body was to be strictly non-political, and its stated objects were to forward the temporal interests of Irish Catholics. Fifteen bishops wrote letters of support, but the body did not obtain the endorsement of the Catholic hierarchy, and was opposed by Archbishop Walsh. The body disbanded itself in June 1904. One reason for its failure was its decision to accept the affiliation of the Belfast CA. This was done on condition that the latter would separate its political registration from its general work, but the damage was done. Many bishops were already nervously aware of the problems that their colleague Bishop Henry had brought down on his head. But in the early days it was the Belfast Nationalists who were more alarmed. Thomas Maguire wrote anxiously to William O'Brien in April 1903—on the eve of the latter's final separation from the mainstream of the Nationalist movement—calling on the UIL to denounce the All-Ireland Catholic Association. It was, he said,

being pushed to the front with the avowed object of securing future jobs and places for Catholic Whigs and Flunkeys . . . We in Belfast who have fought against the local shoneen forces during the past six years, view with anything but equanimity the way the All-Ireland Catholic Association are being allowed to further their schemes unchecked.[115]

Renewed pressure for Catholic unity in Belfast came in October 1903, when Arnold-Forster, Liberal Unionist MP for West Belfast since 1892, was appointed

---

[112] *IN*, 27 Jan. 1902.   [113] Ibid., 13 and 14 Jan. 1902.
[114] Devlin to Redmond, 23 Jan. 1902 (RP 15181/1).
[115] T. Maguire to O'Brien, 2 Apr. 1903 (BLUCC, OBP, AN.22).

to Balfour's cabinet as Secretary of State for War. In accordance with the parliamentary convention that prevailed before 1914, he resigned his seat and stood for re-election. Since 1892 the Nationalists had not forced a contest. Registration had for some years been in the hands of the CA. Should the Nationalists contest the by-election? Devlin, now based in Britain, feared that, if the Nationalists did not contest the seat, a 'Russellite' candidate might do so.[116] The local men believed that on the present register they were 280 short of a majority, and that the prospects for winning the seat at the general election were much better.[117] But Devlin was 'strongly in favour of a fight', and a candidate was sought.[118] The crucial issue was less who the candidate should be than how he should be chosen. Could the contest be used to achieve a measure of reunion with the CA, or alternatively to gain advantage over it? Devlin invited Henry to chair the nominating convention, concluding with what he must have hoped was his trump card: 'I may mention that the National Directory will be represented at the convention in the person of Mr John Redmond MP, chairman of the Irish Party.' Henry, uncompromising as ever, replied: 'If I had an assurance from Mr Redmond and from you that you would put an end at once to this foolish opposition to the Catholic Association and to me, I would then feel justified in entertaining the request contained in your letter.'[119] But by the time Henry sent this reply the nominating convention had already met. Redmond's attendance, at only two days' notice, indicates the seriousness attached by the Irish Party to the Belfast situation. No Belfast priests or CA elected representatives attended. The candidate chosen, Patrick Dempsey, was the least unpalatable of the local UIL activists so far as the CA was concerned. He was a member of the Catholic business elite of the city, on a par with the CA leaders in terms of age and social standing; his brothers Alexander (a senior hospital consultant in the city) and Alderman James were both active in the CA, while another brother, William, was a parish priest in the diocese. Patrick Dempsey was the nearest the UIL could get to a 'unity' candidate, in a situation where the opposite of unity prevailed.

Dempsey's campaign was one of the shortest in UK electoral history, his candidacy being announced only three days before polling.[120] Arnold-Forster did not appear in Belfast at all. It was announced that he was ill in London, although there were press claims that he was attending his office daily.[121] It was a difficult campaign for the Nationalists: on the one hand, they needed to bring out the full CA vote, which required them to be unequivocally 'Catholic', while,

---

[116] Devlin to Dillon, 27 Sept. 1903 (DP 6729/97). Liberal Unionist T. W. Russell left the government in 1900 because of his support for compulsory land purchase, becoming an Independent Unionist, and later a Liberal. In 1902–3 his supporters won two Ulster seats from the Unionists.

[117] *NS*, 10 Oct. 1903.   [118] Devlin to Dillon, 8 Oct. 1903 (DP 6729/98).

[119] *NS*, 24 Oct. 1903.   [120] Ibid., 24 Oct. 1903.   [121] Ibid., 31 Oct. 1903.

on the other hand, they knew that they could not win without attracting more than 200 Protestant votes. The Dublin-based *Irish Independent*, now owned by Healy's friend W. M. Murphy and rapidly emerging as Ireland's best-selling daily newspaper, declared that 'the only possible result of the insane policy of the local leaders of the UIL, approved as it is by Mr John Redmond, will be the infliction of a damaging defeat on the home rule cause'.[122] Arnold-Forster was returned by 3,912 votes to 3,671. The *Northern Star* blamed the CA for the defeat, first for publishing Henry's acrimonious correspondence with the UIL, secondly for refusing to make available to the UIL its updated version of the register. This action on the part of the CA is probably explained by its fears that the UIL would have subsequently been able to use the register should it decide (as it did) to contest the next municipal elections. It was claimed that Henry and three of his administrators abstained from voting, although the other fifteen priests did cast their votes. Three Belfast priests made donations, all anonymous, to the election fund.[123] Devlin returned immediately to London, telling the *Northern Star* that to have brought the Tory majority from 800 down to 241 was a great achievement, and he was confident that the division 'could be won handsomely at the general election'. There is no evidence that the labour movement identified with the Nationalists in the campaign, and hints of disenchantment with the prospects of converting Protestant working men were beginning to appear. Writing in the *Northern Star* shortly after the election, 'Stargazer' noted that the local trade-union party actually assisted in the re-election of Arnold-Forster, 'the sweater and friend of blacklegs'. The local trade-union body 'is nothing more or less than an ante-chamber of Orangeism', which in future 'need not look for any help from the Catholic and Nationalist working men of this city'.[124] In the general election of 1906 the line of argument was to be rather different.

'THE REBELS OF LUCIFER'

The high level of support for the UIL candidate, and the opportunity to pin the blame for his defeat on the CA, gave the UIL the confidence to mount its first municipal challenge to the CA since 1897. In January 1904 the UIL candidates secured an overall 44 per cent of the vote in the two wards, a modest improvement

[122] *Irish Independent*, 20 Oct. 1903.

[123] *NS*, 14 Nov. 1903. At this time the whole of Belfast was classified as one Catholic parish, of which the bishop was the parish priest, with each local church being headed by an administrator, who was in effect the parish priest for most purposes.

[124] Ibid., 14 Nov. 1903. 'Stargazer' was the editor of the *Star*, John T. Donovan, a close friend of Devlin's, and later a solicitor, barrister, and MP for West Wicklow, 1914–18.

on the 39 per cent achieved in 1897, when the all-Ireland Nationalist movement had itself been divided and weak, and Joe Devlin had been an 'upstart youth'. The result was, therefore, no more than mildly encouraging, but the response of the UIL to its defeat was confident and aggressive. Archbishop Walsh's pastoral letter denouncing the All-Ireland Catholic Association was circulated during the campaign, with Henry rather desperately rebuking those who circulated it without his permission (though it had already been published in *The Times*!).[125] He stressed that Walsh's strictures had no relevance to the Belfast CA, which was technically true, but the Belfast body had earlier successfully sought affiliation to the organization that was now denounced. The damage was done, and it seems likely that a highly political bishop like Walsh would have been well aware of the impact that his action would have on Henry's position in Belfast. The *Northern Star*, while reporting a clear election defeat for its own side at the hands of the CA, could in the same editorial call boldly on Henry to dissolve his organization.[126]

The UIL believed that time, as well as Henry's fellow bishops, were on its side. The *Star*, without giving any evidence, claimed that 95 per cent of Catholic men under the age of 35 voted for the UIL. It alleged that older voters, mainly women and especially those who were (or who, at the instance of the priest, claimed to be) illiterate voters, were the CA's main source of strength. The CA, declared the *Star*, had deliberately 'stuffed the register with women', who, it claimed, numbered 1,800 on the municipal register for West Belfast as a whole, which had the serious side effect of reducing the number of Catholic householders on the all-male parliamentary register. To counter this the UIL established its own West Belfast National Registration Committee, and three inspectors were appointed with a brief 'wherever possible to get the husbands, sons and brothers of the women tenants in west Belfast made the tenants of their places'. Although 'certain Catholic rent agents' (a reference to William McCormick and James Corr of the CA) had 'shown a reluctance to acquiesce in the good work', the *Star* alleged that most of the women concerned had, 'in a spirit of true patriotism', consented to the changes. It was also believed that the expansion of Harland and Wolff had encouraged a shift in the focus of Protestant population growth towards East Belfast, while building in the Clonard area had increased Catholic numbers in the West division. These developments, it was thought, would 'within a couple of years . . . [see] . . . the Green Flag . . . float off the citadel of West Belfast'.[127] All this emboldened the increasingly restive diocesan priesthood. In March 1904 the *Catholic Herald* reported that 'strong representations have been made to Rome by a large body of the clergy, as well as by the laity . . . for an inquiry into certain actions of Dr Henry . . . bearing on questions of policy'. The Bishop of Down and Connor may be 'a very saintly and holy man', the paper continued,

[125] E. Bolster, *The Knights of St Columbanus* (Dublin, 1979), 9.
[126] *NS*, 23 Jan. and 6 Feb. 1904.   [127] Ibid., 23 Jan., 6 Feb., and 28 May 1904.

'but as a bishop he has brought disorder, chaos and the most violent animosities into existence'.[128]

In January 1905 the local elections were again contested. One of the CA nominations, Councillor James MacEntee's cousin and fellow publican Joseph Smyth, was regarded by the CA as something a coup, for, although William McCormick 'detests the publicans', he wanted Smyth on the ticket on account of his board memberships and his Chairmanship of the LVA. But Smyth made the mistake in his election literature of appearing to use the latter position to advance his candidacy, and he was in consequence deposed from the chairmanship of the LVA. MacEntee and another politically active publican, Archie Savage, stayed with the CA, but its ethos was becoming increasingly anti-publican.[129] 'It has been openly stated in some circles', claimed 'Stargazer', 'that no publican is wanted among "the leaders of local Catholic society".'[130] Not only the predominantly small licensees' Spirit Grocers' Association but also the majority of the LVA now came to align themselves with the UIL against the 'respectable' professions predominating in the leadership of the CA. There was a new confidence, perhaps induced by the fact that Joe Devlin was by this time General Secretary at UIL headquarters in Dublin. The UIL and the *Northern Star* warned that any evidence of clerical intimidation would be taken before the courts, a course of action that back in 1897 Devlin had dismissed as quite out of the question, however strong the evidence. But the UIL lost the elections, with 42 per cent of the votes cast in the two wards, a slight decline on its previous performance. Henry denounced his opponents as 'Rebels of Lucifer'.[131]

Notwithstanding electoral failures, a further sign of confidence in the anti-Henry camp came when Down and Connor priests raised the flag of rebellion against their bishop's role in temporal affairs. Ironically this crisis was precipitated by a decision of the Irish hierarchy. Prompted by the failure of the Conservative Government's scheme for a Catholic university, their lordships resolved in January 1905 to give their full support to the Irish Party in the House of Commons to an extent that had not been the case for many years. Henry was now faced with the problem of reconciling the need to participate in the show of episcopal support for the Party with continued resistance to the local representatives of that Party. He sought a way out by having the CA take up its own collection in Belfast for the Parliamentary Fund, an activity previously left to the UIL. Two priests, Revd John Nolan and Revd Bernard Faloona, defied the bishop by sending their subscriptions to the Belfast UIL. Three more priests then wrote urging Redmond not to accept the CA's contribution, while a further twenty-four priests of the diocese, in forwarding their Parliamentary Fund subscriptions to UIL Headquarters in Dublin (to Mr Secretary Devlin, in fact!), made clear 'that our sole reason for not sending our contributions through

---

[128] *Catholic Herald*, 25 Mar. 1904.
[129] *NS*, 7 Jan. 1905. [130] Ibid., 19 Jan. 1903. [131] Ibid., 14 Jan. 1905.

the Belfast branch of the UIL as we were wont to do, is because we are prohibited, under pain of censure, from availing ourselves of this medium'.[132]

The presence of Devlin as General Secretary of the UIL was central to the way in which the Belfast Nationalists' all-Ireland strategy had outflanked the bishop's superior local strength and, at the practical level, hints at how the whole 'revolt of the priests' was carefully planned and orchestrated. After visiting Belfast to confer with local UIL officials, Devlin had, with Dillon, drafted a letter for Redmond to send to Bishop Henry. Following full discussion by the Party, wrote Redmond–Devlin, 'it was unanimously decided that in view of the relations which have existed for some time between the Catholic Association and the National organization in Belfast it would not be possible for the Irish Party to accept any contribution to the Fund collected through the agency of the Catholic Association of Belfast'.[133] The CA's cheque for £100 was returned to the bishop, and suddenly Henry's position was weakened dramatically. The *Star* published an anonymous call for his resignation as bishop.[134] Cardinal Logue thought Henry should be defended: 'it is only politics on the surface, but at the bottom a faction of rebellious priests.'[135] But Logue thought it was 'useless' to raise the matter with the Holy See, for 'when matters get into Propaganda they are buried'.[136] It was not in fact the cardinal but the intensely political Archbishop Walsh of Dublin and the strong Irish Party supporter Bishop Patrick O'Donnell of Raphoe who both, independently, visited Rome on ecclesiastical business at Easter 1905.[137] The advice they gave may have been rather different from Logue's. Bishop Henry, on the other hand, was not anxious to go to Rome in the wake of the revolt of his clergy. He postponed his five-yearly *ad limina* visit, due in April 1905, until the autumn.

The 'revolt of the priests' against Henry, together with Redmond's rebuttal, was a tremendous boost for the Belfast UIL: 'our friends are simply in ecstasies at the slap in the face Henry has got', J. T. Donovan wrote to Michael Davitt.[138] The contribution of £400 that the UIL was able to forward to the Parliamentary Fund underlined the CA's failure. Early in March the Belfast UIL offered to submit the whole issue to arbitration.[139] When Henry made no response, the confident local politicians threatened nothing less than the direct intervention of 'our high church authorities in Rome', warning that Henry's 'withdrawal from the diocese will be the heavy price the clergy and laity will demand for peace' if he did not dissolve the CA.[140] The local Nationalists were threatening

---

[132] Revd G. Crolly to Redmond, 12 Feb. 1905 (RP 15245/1); *NS*, 11 Mar. 1905.
[133] *NS*, 18 Feb. 1905; Devlin to Redmond, 25 Feb. 1905 (RP 15181/1).
[134] *NS*, 11 Mar. 1905.
[135] Logue to Archbishop Walsh, 3 Mar. 1905 (Walsh Papers).
[136] Logue to Mgr W. H. Murphy, 24 Feb. and 24 Mar. 1905 (Murphy Papers, 1905/27, 44).
[137] Walsh to Murphy, 25 Mar. 1905 (Murphy Papers, 1905/46); *NS*, 8 Apr. 1905.
[138] J. T. Donovan to Davitt, 3 Mar. 1905 (Davitt Papers, 9457/3724).
[139] *NS*, 4 Mar. 1905.   [140] Ibid., 11 Mar. 1905.

to get their bishop fired! But although the local men—Maguire, Rooney, and Donovan—appeared to be conducting the campaign, there is every sign that the strategy was being carefully considered and harmonized by the national leadership via Devlin, and also probably Bishop Patrick O'Donnell of Raphoe, the Party's closest friend in the hierarchy. In March 1905 Devlin held a private conference with the Belfast leaders, and on 17 April the CA agreed to participate in a peace conference, which met over three evenings in May at Patrick Dempsey's Linen Hall Hotel. The delegates agreed to keep their discussions confidential for a year.[141] The Nationalist press adhered to this, but someone leaked the details to the Unionist *Belfast Evening Telegraph*, which published what appears to be a well-informed account. Each side nominated six representatives, led by Devlin and the Very Revd Henry Laverty respectively. The main UIL arguments were that the undemocratic structure of the CA, and the episcopal veto, were 'a weapon . . . [in] . . . the hands of Orange and Protestant fanatics which they can use against us most effectively'.[142] The CA, on the other hand, could claim that it had been responsible for all registration work until 1904; that it had been established at a time when the national movement was divided and before the UIL came into being; that it had secured a strong majority of popular support in local elections in the two wards over a period of eight years; and that surrender now would be a great humiliation for the bishop and political suicide for his leading supporters.

The conference agreed to establish a joint committee to handle all electoral work. This was a victory for the UIL, for, though technically a neutral face-saver, the joint body would in effect become 'an auxiliary of the League'.[143] The *Irish News*, though still a CA mouthpiece, paid 'special thanks' to Devlin for the 'conspicuous trouble' he had taken to achieve an honourable settlement.[144] But, as Devlin and Dillon celebrated in the city, Henry threw another curve. In a letter to the *Irish News* he declared that, as a gesture towards peace, he would not renew the existence of the CA at its annual meeting the following March, in effect therefore unilaterally abolishing the Association.[145] What may have triggered his reaction was the news that a plan was in hand to add Devlin and Maguire to the board of directors of the *Irish News*. At the annual shareholders' meeting on 30 June 1905 the most notable absentee, apart from the bishop himself, was the chairman, William McCormick, whose health seemed to crack under the strain. After a long argument in private the remaining five directors emerged to announce that Patrick Dempsey would chair the meeting. Revd Henry Laverty had been sidelined, and he argued angrily against the whole trend of the meeting that followed. Dempsey reported that the paper was now in loss, and it was suggested that the divisions in the Catholic community and the

---

141 Ibid., 25 Mar. 1905 and 14 Apr. 1906.   142 Ibid., 20 May 1905.
143 *Belfast Evening Telegraph*, 23 May 1905.   144 *IN*, 18 May 1905.
145 Ibid., 1 July 1905.

paper's weak line on nationalism had adversely affected sales and advertising. The directors, with Laverty dissenting vigorously, proposed the addition of Devlin and Thomas Maguire to the board as a remedy and as an indication of a change of direction. This was agreed by the narrow margin of 2,005 votes to 1,901 (including proxies). Shortly afterwards McCormick resigned and Patrick Dempsey became chairman. During 1906 T. J. Campbell was replaced as editor by the Corkman Tim McCarthy, who had been the first editor of the *Northern Star* back in 1897—a particular snub to Henry and his followers.[146]

Henry continued his hostility to the local Nationalists. He maintained his ecclesiastical censures, forbidding priests to acknowledge the Belfast UIL, and he continued with punitive transfers. Parish priests, normally only moved by consent in Down and Connor, found themselves 'promoted' to other parishes. Laverty was promoted from the Presidency of St Malachy's College to be parish priest of St Matthew's in east Belfast, said to be the richest Catholic parish in the city, while the most senior of the bishop's administrators, Revd Daniel McCashin, continued to serve in the small and very poor Markets district, at St Malachy's Church.[147] The *Star* presented it as simply a question of Henry pursuing a vendetta against 'nationally-minded priests'. Certainly Henry handled the situation insensitively and, ultimately, disastrously. As Henry gradually disclosed his personal opposition to the peace settlement of May 1905, the *Northern Star's* attack on him revived, and switched its focus more towards his administration of the diocese. Cardinal Logue thought that 'the worst Billingsgate published in the Parnellite press was but a trifle compared with the scurrilous abuse of the Bishop which this paper publishes'.[148] But there was method in the *Star's* vituperation. Although Henry had postponed his five-yearly *ad limina* visit to Rome, he could not escape it altogether. By the time he did go, in the autumn of 1905, the troubles he had provoked were gathering about his head. He had instigated disciplinary proceedings against Revd John Nolan, and towards the end of 1905 Nolan travelled to Rome to present his appeal. 'The Cardinal [Gotti] was very kind to me,' he reported to Mgr Michael O'Riordan, the newly appointed Rector of the Irish College, and 'while matters are still in the Cardinal's hands, I have every reason to feel satisfied with the result'. In addition seventeen or eighteen parish priests sent a petition to Rome 'protesting against our bishop's action and his unfair treatment of his priests', and there was a similar petition from the laity.[149] Shortly after his return from Rome Nolan spoke at a major

---

[146] *IN*, 8 July 1905.

[147] Ibid., 11 Aug. 1906; Revd J. F. Sheils to O'Riordan, 12 May 1908 (MOR 1908/37).

[148] Logue to W. H. Murphy, 25 Mar. 1905 (Murphy Papers, 1905/24); Logue to Walsh, 3 Mar. 1905 (Walsh Papers).

[149] Revd J. Nolan to Mgr M. O'Riordan, 5 Dec. 1905 (MOR 1905/311).

UIL election rally in the Ulster Hall alongside Devlin and John Redmond. The Irish Party could not have signalled more strongly to the Vatican its support for him.[150]

THE END OF THE BELFAST CATHOLIC ASSOCIATION

During the last months of 1905 the conflict within the Belfast Catholic community died down. One reason for this was that the matter of Henry's temporal authority had been raised with the Vatican, and the time had now come for a period of calm until the outcome of his *ad limina* visit became apparent. More important, however, was that, as the Conservative Government disintegrated over the question of tariff reform, a general election came over the horizon. In West Belfast this was to bring about a triumph for the Nationalists and the return of Joe Devlin to represent his native city. Although Bishop Henry made no public statement regarding the election, it was reported that, unlike in 1903, he—along with his senior priests—did cast his vote.[151] Several leading CA members worked hard for Devlin's campaign. James MacEntee and James McDonnell, both publicans, were singled out for special praise in this respect.[152] Shortly after the general election the 'working towards equality' clause in the 1905 peace agreement was set aside so that Councillors MacEntee and McDonnell could be re-elected unopposed to the City Council without UIL opposition—a fact that cannot have been unconnected with their campaigning enthusiasm.[153] As Devlin celebrated his victory, his Belfast colleagues returned to the remnants of their conflict. Henry's decision to abolish the CA with effect from 31 March 1906 had been a petulant attempt to sidestep the implementation of the peace agreement of May 1905. Decisions were needed regarding future municipal representation and registration work. The Belfast UIL called a meeting in the National Club to which it invited all the city's Catholic priests and the members of the late CA. The meeting agreed to establish a 'National Registration Union of Belfast', to control local representation and registration, and to cooperate with the UIL with regard to parliamentary registration. Thomas Maguire, who became president of the new body, observed that 'nine years internecine fight in this city' had been closed not by the conference of May 1905 but 'with the recent parliamentary victory in West Belfast'.[154] This successful meeting was a major step towards the political reunification of Catholic and Nationalist Belfast. Part of the price was that the election rhetoric of 'Orange and Green will carry the day' switched in the editorial columns of the *Star* to a claim that Devlin's 'was a victory won by all the Catholic people'.[155]

150 *NS*, 23 Dec. 1905.   151 *IN*, 19 Jan. 1906   152 *NS*, 14 Apr. 1906.
153 Ibid., 5 Jan. 1907.   154 Ibid., 5 May 1906.   155 Ibid., 14 Apr. 1906.

A certain amount of urgency was injected into these reunion plans by the announcement that a branch of a new all-Ireland body, the Catholic Defence Society (CDS), had been established in Belfast. Quite correctly Maguire perceived the CDS, both locally and nationally, as a phoenix rising from the ashes of the CA. It was founded in Dublin in August 1905 with the 'cordial approval' of the Catholic hierarchy. A number of prominent Catholic intellectuals identified themselves with it, including Professor Joseph MacRory, later to become Bishop of Down and Connor and Cardinal Archbishop of Armagh. D. P. Moran of the *Leader* thought the movement 'a necessity in today's imperfect world', which could be disbanded whenever the Orange Order and the Freemasons ceased to exist. The CDS made little impact, continuing a shadowy existence until 1914. Its importance is really as a precursor of the more successful Knights of St Columbanus.[156] The *Northern Star* dismissed the Dublin CDS as 'a handful of Healyite clerics and a coterie of place-hunting shoneen adventurers . . . for Dublin jackeens of the Catholic snobocracy type'. The election of Belfast solicitor and diocesan attorney Councillor P. J. Magee, former secretary of the Belfast CA, to the national committee of the CDS was a clear indication of the new body's outlook.[157] On 25 March 1906 the indefatigable Magee unveiled a branch of the CDS in Belfast, just in time to replace the expiring CA. The Society would defend Catholic rights, 'not alone against their common enemy, but also against those Catholics who, considering solely their temporal advancement, give to their religion and the obedience and discipline it demands only a secondary place'. Henry, no doubt chastened by his visit to Rome, did not publicly endorse the CDS, but he did nothing to discourage it. The chips were now firmly down so far as Magee's CDS and the UIL/NRU were concerned, but, as the *Star* accurately predicted, 'the chips will never catch fire'.[158] It shortly became clear that the Belfast CDS intended to contest the municipal elections in January 1907, and to that end launched a new (and short-lived) journal, the *Vindicator*, its title harking back to Belfast's first nationalist newspaper of the 1840s. It had cautious support from the *Leader* in Dublin, which regretted the divisions in nationalist Belfast, wondering how far 'Mr Bung [the liquor trade] may be at the bottom of local difficulties'.[159] P. J. Magee and Dr Peter O'Connell, the aldermanic candidates, were leading CDS activists, as was the grocer and publican Archie Savage. Savage was something of a local character, who had been the leading figure in the weak attempt to float a branch of Tim Healy's People's Rights Association in the city during the late 1890s.

The year 1907 saw the first-ever victory for the Belfast Nationalists in a municipal contest. Whereas the Nationalists had lost with only 39 per cent of the vote in the Falls and Smithfield in 1897, 44 per cent in 1904, and 42 per cent in

---

[156] Bolster, *Knights of St Columbanus*, 11–13; D. W. Miller, *Church, State and Nation in Ireland, 1898–1921* (Dublin, 1973), 163.
[157] *NS*, 9 May 1905.   [158] Ibid., 2 June 1906.   [159] *Leader*, 5 Jan. 1907.

THE ONLY ISSUE !

Catholics
OF
Belfast!

RALLY ROUND YOUR REVERED BISHOP.

The Most Rev. H. HENRY, D.D.,
Bishop of Down and Connor,
Consecrated 22nd Sept., 1895,
Emancipated Belfast Catholics
1896.

Persecuted by irreconcilable
Factionists and
denied the right to direct and guide
Catholic Organization

Catholics   Smithfield Wards,

ANSWER :—

Do you approve of organised rebellion
against Ecclesiastical authority?

Do you approve of the alleged true
"democracy" — politics divorced . .
from religion?

Do you approve of yielding to the forces
of secularism?

Do you approve of the Berry Street War
Cry—"Less of the Bishop"?

IF YOU DO NOT,
AND WE KNOW YOU DO NOT,

VOTE FOR

O'Connell & Savage
IN SMITHFIELD WARD;

And VOTE FOR

Magee & M'Donnell
IN FALLS WARD.

God Save Ireland ❧

FROM ANTI-CLERICALISM.

Printed by H. Carswell & Son, Queen Street, Belfast, and Published at 1 and 3 Bank Street, Belfast

Fig. 3.3. Municipal election poster, Belfast, 1907, in support of the Catholic Defence Association, successor to the Catholic Association.

1905, now the UIL/NRU candidates reversed the position, defeating the CDS with 59 per cent of the vote.[160] The difference was partly a spin-off from Devlin's parliamentary victory in January 1906, and his general national prestige in the party. The key additional factor was the fact that the bishop and his Belfast priests kept out of it. The *Vindicator* claimed no clerical attendance at its meetings; the *Northern Star* did not repeat its previous diatribes against clerical interference. Most important of all was the changed posture of the *Irish News*, which had backed the bishop for so long, but which now had Devlin and Maguire on the board of directors, Patrick Dempsey as chairman, and Tim McCarthy as editor. In all these circumstances, and with a Liberal government that (in January 1907) was still expected to implement a measure of limited home rule in the immediate future, what is perhaps surprising is that such a lost cause as Magee's vampiric CDS should have retained as much as 41 per cent of the municipal vote in the two wards.

Bishop Henry now had the appearance of a broken man: 'Poor Dr Henry . . . is harassed almost beyond endurance', wrote Logue to Walsh, 'a number of his priests have got completely out of his hands and he can do nothing with them.'[161] He died very suddenly of a heart attack, aged 60, in March 1908.[162] Very shortly before his death Henry had set out to reward his loyal follower William McCormick with a papal countship. He was prepared to pay on McCormick's behalf the fee of £100. But McCormick went unrewarded because, by an unfortunate chance, the executors of Bishop Henry's will were none other than Revd Daniel McCashin, his opponent for the mitre in 1895, and Revd William Dempsey, brother of Patrick, James, and Alexander. As Logue noted, 'these gentlemen are supposed—whether rightly or wrongly I don't know—to belong to the party opposed to the bishop'.[163] Dr Peter O'Connell fared somewhat better in post-Henrician Belfast, becoming the first Catholic to serve as High Sheriff of the city, and in June 1908 being knighted for services to medicine. P. J. Magee remained a bitter political controversialist to the end, completing his political career with a pitifully unsuccessful attempt to prevent Devlin's re-election to the West Belfast parliamentary seat in January 1910. Yet in one sense the Associationists or their descendants triumphed over Devlin in the end, by becoming Sinn Féiners. Archie Savage moved directly from being a CA and CDS candidate in local elections to contesting in the Sinn Féin interest. James MacEntee's son Seán was a Republican from his teenage years. The family of the Belfast hide merchant Simon O'Leary, who signed CA nomination papers,

---

[160] *Leader*, 19 Jan. 1907.
[161] Logue to Walsh, 30 and 17 Nov. 1906 (Walsh Papers).
[162] Bishop C. McHugh to M. O'Riordan, 17 Mar. 1908 (MOR 1908/100).
[163] Henry to O'Riordan, 21 Dec. 1907; Logue to O'Riordan, 18 Mar. 1908 (MOR 1907/77, 1908/107).

later became Sinn Féiners, his son John ending his career as Master of the High Court in Dublin.[164]

Henry's death effectively brought the political schism in Catholic Belfast to an end. The conflict might have continued had Revd Henry Laverty succeeded to the diocese. He was elected Vicar-Capitular by his fellow priests during the interregnum, again in opposition to the unfortunate McCashin, but Henry's lamentable failure in the diocese was a powerful argument in favour of a new broom. Laverty was 'the public standard-bearer of the policy which had such lamentable results'. McCashin withdrew his candidacy 'when he saw such a partisan spirit on the Laverty side', and unsuccessful efforts were made to attract the Limerick-born writer and Rector of the Irish College in Rome, Mgr Michael O'Riordan, to Belfast.[165] In the end the mitre went to Revd John Tohill, PP, Cushendall, and previously Administrator of St Peter's Pro-Cathedral. He was a very different type of personality from Henry, and had demonstrated his capacity for clear-headed and useful work in his presentation of a brief to the House of Commons committee on the 1896 Belfast Corporation Bill. He could write with some justice in 1912 that 'I have succeeded in restoring peace to this diocese, which, as Propaganda can testify, was in a state of ecclesiastical turmoil and dissension under my predecessor'.[166] What he had not done of course was to set the clock back to an era when bishops could take final decisions in matters of temporal politics.

Did this protracted and bitter struggle between two sections of a minority in a hostile city have any long-term impact? One paradox was that the Federationist/UIL/Nationalist side, having been maligned throughout as anti-clericals and—at least once in Devlin's case—as a 'priest-hunter', had ultimately to become *more* 'Catholic' in order to come out on top, which effectively made them less attractive to non-Catholics and had the effect of discouraging the very tentative Protestant and labour links that the movement was attempting to build during the 1890s, and again during the 1906 general election. Devlin, in particular, had to demonstrate that he could be an effective spokesman for Catholic issues, and that a 'Nationalist' approach to the problem of Belfast could actually achieve more for the minority than Henry's 'Catholic' approach. After Devlin had taken on the secretaryship of the United Irish League of Great Britain (UILGB) in 1903, the *Northern Star* reported that 'Mr Devlin is continually presiding and speaking at purely Catholic functions, and of course the clergy gladly reciprocate'. When announcing Devlin's fundraising tour to Australia in the spring of 1906, the paper was quick to emphasize that he would be 'the honoured guest of the great Irish Cardinal and the Irish . . . bishops and

164 *IN*, 7 Jan. 1902; John O'Leary interview.
165 Revd J. F. Sheils to O'Riordan, 12 May 1908 (MOR 1908/37).
166 Tohill to O'Riordan, 26 Mar. 1912 (MOR 1912/64).

priests beneath the southern cross'.[167] Devlin would have been well aware that only the intervention of the wider Nationalist movement and the Party leadership had permitted the local Nationalists to win control of Catholic Belfast. This is what made the Ancient Order of Hibernians—previously of little importance in Ireland—attractive to Devlin. Effectively it was religion without the bishops.

[167] *NS*, 2 Jan. 1904 and 21 Apr. 1906.

4

The Organizer of Spontaneity

> The most difficult thing to organize is spontaneity.
>
> (attributed to Devlin by T. M. Kettle[1])

Two talents propelled Devlin from a back-street bar in Belfast to the forefront of Irish politics. One was his ability as an orator, a highly visible skill that facilitated his early advance to the forefront of Belfast and Ulster politics. This strength was supported, perhaps unusually in such an obvious 'front man', by an equally strong 'back-room' talent. Devlin was a formidable organizer of people and events. His oratorical skills will be considered more closely in the next chapter. Here we will focus on his skills as an organizer, skills developed first in Belfast, not just in the long struggle with the Catholic Association (CA) but also in the conflict with opponents of the parliamentary nationalist tradition over the organization of the '98 Centenary, and in the efforts to revitalize the constitutional movement in Ireland. This was a struggle that first of all put the urban Nationalists of Belfast in the forefront of a militant agrarian organization, the United Irish League (UIL), and that then led steadily to the export of Devlin's rhetorical and organizational skills to Glasgow, to the Irish communities in England, and to North America and Australasia. This in turn encouraged Devlin to develop the Ancient Order of Hibernians from what had been a predominantly American benefit society with a slightly anti-constitutional bias into an important support for the UIL and a powerful personal machine. His organizational skill also led Devlin to the General Secretaryship of the United Irish League of Great Britain (UILGB) in 1903 and the headship of the UIL headquarters in Dublin in 1904. These two talents—organization and oratory—made Devlin the only Nationalist of his generation who was able to join the leadership group of John Redmond, John Dillon, and T. P. O'Connor that, after the 1900 reunion, ran the Irish Parliamentary Party.

---

[1] Thomas Dillon interview.

FIGHTING THE REPUBLICANS: BELFAST, THE '98 CENTENARY, AND THE UNITED IRISH LEAGUE

Devlin was active at national level in Irish politics for most of the 1890s. But he remained a young man of very modest means, dependent on his employer for time to devote to politics. The Irish National Federation (INFed.) was always a struggling organization, both nationally and locally. In some of the rural areas of east Ulster, Devlin complained 'there is so much inactivity and apathy on our side'.[2] In Belfast, the position was so insecure that Devlin was 'entirely opposed' to starting additional branches. He thought that 'our branch has done as much good as fifty could do', and that, if ward branches were started, 'what guarantee have we that some of them might not be worked in the Healyite interest?'[3] The problems of the national movement, in Devlin's opinion, were to do with the fact that 'men who should have been faithful' to the Party's principles had instead refused 'to obey any leadership or display party discipline'.[4] This was to be a central motif for Devlin throughout his career, and was both his strength and his weakness. The main attempt by the INFed. to restore unity under its leadership was an international event, the 'Irish Race Convention' of September 1896. In itself it was a successful occasion, but it did little to strengthen the Federation or bring about nationalist unity.[5] One beneficiary of the event was Joe Devlin, his short speech being described as 'one of the very best delivered at the Convention'. This was his first appearance—and probably one of the first appearances of a Belfast accent—at an event of this nature. 'A warm buzz of general enquiry' went around the Dublin Rotunda, followed by cries of 'well done, Belfast!'[6] But the executive committee of the INFed. often struggled to achieve a quorum, and, despite the effort of fifteen paid organizers, the situation did not improve during the following three years.[7] There were 1,200 Catholic parishes in Ireland, but only 490 branches of the INFed.

A more promising influence for unity emerged in the form of widespread interest in the centenary of the rebellion of the United Irishmen in 1798. Somewhat problematic for all the constitutional parties was the fact that 1798 had, of course, been unequivocally a physical-force movement, but Dillon and Co. were able to get around this without too much discomfort by rhetoric of the 'that was then, this is now' type. A more serious complication was that the republican movement, which was at an even lower ebb than the constitutional movement, also saw in the centenary a potential lifeline. Early in 1897 a group in

---

[2] Devlin to Dillon, 14 Dec. 1894 (DP 6773/699, 6729/17).
[3] Devlin to Jeremiah McVeagh, 23 Aug. 1895 (DP 6754/1164).
[4] *IN*, 27 July 1896.   [5] Ibid., 29 Sept. 1896 and 13 Jan. 1897.
[6] Ibid., 4 Sept. 1896.   [7] Lyons, *The Irish Parliamentary Party*, 190–1.

Fig. 4.1. The Irish Race Convention, visit to Belfast, 1896. Front row, 3rd–7th from left: John Rooney, Joe Devlin, Sam Young MP, J. T. Donovan, W. D. Harbinson.

Dublin established a 1798 Centenary Committee under the chairmanship of the old Fenian John O'Leary. Both the constitutional parties then attempted to jump on the bandwagon, but the Provisional Committee would not accept MPs as members of the planning group, and the Anti-Parnellites then turned their backs on the Centenary Committee. In the summer of 1897, fearful that Redmond's party might end up benefiting from the activities of O'Leary's committee, the Dillonites decided to set up their own centenary organization. The drive and organizational skills of Devlin meant that Belfast came quickly to the fore. The '98 movement had particular attractions for him. As well as aiding the drive towards reunion at the national level, it constituted locally a non-sectarian activity in which his organization could take the lead. He established a series of '98 clubs around the city, and on 1 September 1897 called a meeting in St Mary's Hall—which the bishop had already closed to him for local INFed. activities. He invited representatives of all points of view, including the relatively small number of voices in Belfast sympathetic to advanced nationalism. Devlin sought to reflect the range of opinions by appointing as secretaries of the meeting his friend John T. Donovan, the local Parnellite leader Francis Connolly, and John Clarke, secretary of the Henry Joy McCracken Literary Society, a body founded by Belfast builder Harry Dobbyn, a veteran Fenian. Though small, the McCracken Society provided a platform for two talented women, the Protestant Alice Milligan whose Unionist father, Seaton F. Milligan, was a respected writer on Irish antiquities, and the Catholic Anna Johnston (whose pseudonym was 'Ethna Carbery'), daughter of another old Fenian leader, Robert Johnston. In January 1896 they founded a new Belfast-based journal, the *Shan Van Vocht* (1896–9). This was a powerful, if short-lived, voice for separatism, providing, *inter alia*, an early platform for the republican socialist views of James Connolly.[8]

Although Devlin's incorporation of the Belfast Parnellites into his plans for the '98 centenary proved successful, the open public meeting with Republicans failed. Alice Milligan urged Belfast nationalists to support the Dublin-based 1798 Centenary Committee and warned that, if the movement was seen to be in the hands of 'the existing political organizations in Ireland', the centenary would fail because of lack of American support. Milligan's motion was defeated by eighty-six votes to six, whereupon she and her colleagues protested against the '98 movement 'being made a tool for electioneering purposes', and withdrew from the meeting. Devlin's proposal to establish 'The Belfast United '98 Centenary Association' was then carried. Belfast's nationalist minority, already deeply engaged in a struggle between Federationists and the Catholic Association (CA), was now split three ways.[9] In January 1898 Dillon moved to draw Devlin's body and similar

[8] O. McGee, *The IRB: From the Land League to Sinn Féin* (Dublin, 2005), 243–4.
[9] T. J. O'Keefe, 'The 1898 Efforts to Celebrate the United Irishmen: The '98 Centennial', *Eire-Ireland*, 23/2 (1988), 64.

groupings elsewhere in Ireland into a newly created coordinating body, the United Irish Centennial Association.[10] The year of commemoration thus opened with two distinct national organizations competing for the honour of organizing it.[11] In private, however, both leaderships were aware of the impossibility of staging two successful rival centenaries. In May a new amalgamated body emerged in the nick of time. A public meeting in Dublin on 20 June confirmed by the presence of both sides on the platform that unity for the purpose of the centenary had at last been obtained: John O'Leary took the chair, flanked by John Dillon, the Dublin Parnellite MP William Field, Maud Gonne, and other advanced nationalists, together with Devlin and *Northern Star* editor W. D. Harbinson.[12] When the central event of the centenary year finally arrived on 15 August—the laying of the foundation stone for the Wolfe Tone statue in Dublin—John O'Leary as president of the Committee laid the stone, but Dillon and Redmond both spoke from the platform beside him.[13] Devlin was also present on the platform, and an estimated 2,000 supporters from Belfast attended the meeting. This unity did not survive for long. Maud Gonne later claimed that she was so disgusted to see parliamentary politicians presuming to involve themselves in an event celebrating separatists that she refused to participate in the ceremony, although it did not prevent her taking dinner in the same company later that evening.[14]

In Belfast on 6 June the Ulster '98 clubs held a procession to Hannahstown for which an attendance of 30,000 was claimed. Organizing the meeting had not been easy. As Devlin angrily reported to Dillon, 'out of sixty invitations sent to members of the Irish Party we only received some half-dozen replies (all refusals)'.[15] Many speakers, he believed, were kept away by 'alarmist rumours of riots, etc. raised for the purpose of damaging the meeting'.[16] The procession—peaceful as it was in itself—provoked two days of rioting, mainly on the Protestant Shankill Road, between the Protestants and the Royal Irish Constabulary (RIC). The West Belfast MP, Arnold-Forster, believing attack to be the best form of defence, went on the offensive in the House of Commons, describing Devlin's Hannahstown speech as 'an incendiary statement and an incitement to future rebellion', but Michael Davitt doubted whether 'the inhabitants of the Shankill Road bought the evening papers and coolly read the speeches before they went out and stoned the police'.[17] As had happened in 1886 and was to happen on a larger scale in 1912 and 1920, several hundred Catholics were excluded from their workplaces.[18] Devlin afterwards played down the incidents, telling Dillon that 'the police and the Shankill Road men can be safely allowed to deal with one another', and that 'our people are behaving splendidly', with no arrests and

[10] Ibid. [11] Ibid. 66. [12] *NS*, 25 June 1898. [13] Ibid., 20 Aug. 1898.
[14] O'Keefe, 'The 1898 Efforts', 68–73 [15] Devlin to Dillon, 28 May 1898 (DP 6729/47).
[16] Devlin to Dillon, 1 and 4 June 1898 (DP 6729/48). [17] *NS*, 18 June 1898.
[18] A. Boyd, *Holy War in Belfast* (Belfast, 1969, 1987), 181; Budge and O'Leary *Belfast*, 89.

'no interference of any sort with Protestant shopkeepers in Catholic quarters of the city'.[19] The more anxious Michael McCartan reported to Dillon that, on the Shankill Road, 'King Mob had full sway and exercised it with a vengeance', so that 'the public houses and property of Catholics have been smashed up and gutted'.[20]

As the centenary year progressed, Devlin and his colleagues worked hard at using the centenary to build unity with the Parnellites and to strengthen the struggling INFed. In November, speaking in the heart of industrial Belfast, Devlin called for a 'perpetuation of the work'. If the efforts of William O'Brien and the UIL 'to keep the land of Connaught for the people' were successful, he declared, then 'there would not be such an exodus to the towns, and as a result less competition amongst unskilled labourers and higher wages for working men'. O'Brien's rural movement was therefore of 'far-reaching importance to them in the cities and towns of Ireland'.[21] O'Brien's intention in launching the UIL had not only been to revive the dynamism of the Land League to support the struggle over the western grasslands, but also to link it to the '98 centenary and advance the recovery of the constitutional movement.[22] He had more success with this in the west than elsewhere, but Belfast was something of an exception. Devlin told Dillon enthusiastically in January 1899 that 'some of the members here are very favourable to establishing the ['98] clubs as branches of the United Irish League'. Dillon was initially sceptical, but Devlin and his Belfast friends pressed ahead. Not until August was Dillon persuaded that the UIL should be taken up as a national grass-roots political movement with a degree of control over the Parliamentary Party.[23] By this time the Belfast '98 clubs had already been converted into branches of the UIL, and Devlin was working hard to spread branches of the new organization throughout eastern Ulster. 'Nothing can now stay the progress of the League', he told O'Brien, except 'apathy, for opposition as far as I can see there is none'.[24] Devlin's correspondence with O'Brien during these months reflects an eagerness on the part of the younger man that normally only came across in his more sustained correspondence with Dillon. The advantages of O'Brien's new movement became apparent far sooner to the struggling Belfast Nationalists than to Dillon, whose priority remained a strong and reunited Parliamentary Party.

In January 1900 the Parnellites and Anti-Parnellites at Westminster at last achieved this. Parnellite leader John Redmond succeeded Dillon as Party chairman, a post he was to hold until his death eighteen years later. Dillon had some initial anxieties about Redmond's attitude to Healy and to the UIL, but as 1900

---

[19] Devlin to Dillon, 7 and 11 June 1898 (DP 6729/49, 50).

[20] McCartan to Dillon, 8 June 1898 (DP 6756/980). [21] McCartan to Dillon, 10 Dec. 1898.

[22] P. Bull, 'William O'Brien: Problems Reappraising his Political Career', in O. MacDonagh and W. F. Mandle (eds.), *Ireland and Irish-Australia: Studies in Cultural and Political History* (London, 1986), 54–5.

[23] F. S. L. Lyons, *John Dillon* (London, 1968), 202.

[24] Devlin to O'Brien, 9 Aug. 1899 (BLUCC, OBP, AJC/26).

progressed he was gradually persuaded by O'Brien and the Irish Nationalist leader in Britain, T. P. O'Connor, that it was his own lukewarmness about the UIL and aloofness from Redmond that was forcing Redmond towards Healy.[25] At the invitation of O'Brien, Devlin became a member of the joint committee of the UIL and the Irish Parliamentary Party to plan a major convention to ratify the reunion. John Redmond was in due course elected unopposed as President of the National Directory of the UIL. On 19 June 1900 the UIL was formally designated as the national organization, with a requirement that all parliamentary candidates must be selected by a duly constituted UIL-nominating convention in the constituency, overseen by a member of the National Directory. Despite the great stress laid on this, not least by Devlin, the immediate impact on the quality of Party personnel was limited. Forty-nine former Party MPs were returned once more in the general election of 1900, while of the thirty-one new members only about half a dozen had been involved actively with the UIL prior to Party reunion.[26] Parliamentary attendance in 1901 continued to cause Devlin concern: on two occasions, he alleged, only the absence of Irish Party members had saved the Government from defeat.[27]

But effective work by the reunited party at Westminster helped Devlin to forge links with Redmond, writing in August 1901 to express the thanks of the Belfast UIL 'to yourself and the Party for the splendid manner in which you have fought for the ratepayers of Belfast and for the victory you have won for them' over the City Rates Bill.[28] By October 1901 Devlin was able to persuade Redmond and Dillon—though not O'Brien—to appear alongside him at the Ulster Hall.[29] The *Northern Star* was ecstatic, losing no opportunity to contrast Belfast's new status in the national movement with the isolation of the CA. The UIL, Devlin told the annual end-of-year conference of Belfast branches, 'was not in any sense of the word a purely agricultural organization. The strongest and most virile branches existed in cities like Dublin, Cork and Belfast.' The UIL was taking up the town tenants' question, while the Party was following up a number of matters in Parliament that were of particular benefit to the Catholics of Belfast: a police barracks to protect Catholic workers in the shipyard, resistance to the Corporation's attempt to get a say in the control of the RIC in Belfast, and a parliamentary assurance that before the Corporation could purchase the Ulster Hall it would have to guarantee to accept bookings from all sides of the community.[30] Whereas the Federation in Belfast had always remained, at Devlin's insistence, a single branch, the UIL soon had ten branches in the various Catholic neighbourhoods of the city. But they were all controlled by a single 'watchful and efficient Divisional Executive', which Devlin chaired.[31]

25 Lyons, *Dillon*, 210–12. 26 Bull, 'William O'Brien', 54.
27 *NS*, 1 June 1901. 28 Devlin to Redmond (RP 15181/1).
29 Devlin to O'Brien, 30 Aug. 1901 (BLUCC, OBP, AL/77). 30 *IN*, 2 Dec. 1901.
31 Devlin to Dillon, 19 Dec. 1901 (DP 6729/80); *NS*, 5 July 1902.

FIGHTING FOR 'THE GREAT CHANCE OF HIS LIFE'

By 1901 Devlin had at least one eye on the post-Devlin era in Belfast Nationalist politics. A man of 30, still living in the modest parental home with several brothers and sisters, and managing a small bar for a living, he must have been increasingly aware of the gap between his personal and working life, on the one hand, and his public activities on the other—a world of mass meetings, growing national and international recognition of his abilities, and banquets, sometimes in his own honour. His political standing outside Belfast was considerably greater than it was at home, where he could still be characterized as a troublesome young man attempting to lead a minority political movement against his bishop. He had wanted to leave Belfast immediately after the municipal defeats of December 1897. A friend in the city had offered to provide some financial backing if he could find 'some distiller or brewer' who would secure a pub for him. Dillon had once promised to help Devlin get settled in a career—salaries for members of parliament still being ten years in the future—and Devlin now asked Dillon to help him to secure 'a house' in some city other than Belfast. Devlin himself had no capital or assets: 'for over six years, owing to my part in public affairs, I have been spending all I could earn, and of course this cannot go on.'[32]

A few weeks later he broached the subject again, asking Dillon if he had any influence with the Dublin branch of the Belfast Bank, which, he claimed, funded twenty or thirty Belfast pubs. Would they perhaps fund one in Dublin?[33] In July 1898 he pressed Dillon again. He had, he said, an opportunity to start a business in Belfast, but he thought that conflicting pressures on his time would prevent him from making it sufficiently successful to be able to repay his backers. He was beginning to feel a strong need to obtain 'some position of comparative independence', so that 'in a few years I would be in a position to be of far greater service than I am now'.[34] Dillon agreed to see what he could do, and Devlin replied that, while he would very much prefer London, if this were not possible he would be 'glad to get to Dublin or Glasgow'.[35] Dillon's suggestion, in the event, was not an introduction to a financial sponsor in any of these centres, but the offer of employment in the offices of the Irish National League of Great Britain. Devlin courteously but firmly declined this offer, as he did another suggestion from Dillon regarding some non-retail opportunity in business, for which Devlin thought he had no experience.[36] It is clear from Devlin's side of the correspondence, which is all we have, that Dillon did

---

[32] Devlin to Dillon, 10 Dec. 1897 and 21 Jan. 1898 (DP 6729/44–45).
[33] Devlin to Dillon, 10 Mar. 1898 (DP 6729/46).
[34] Devlin to Dillon, 12 July 1898 (DP 6729/51).
[35] Devlin to Dillon, 26 July 1898 (DP 6729/52).
[36] Devlin to Dillon, 16 and 24 Aug. 1898 (DP 6729/55, 56).

indeed trouble himself quite considerably on his protégé's behalf, but to no avail. Towards the end of 1898 Dillon was enquiring as to Devlin's intentions, but prospects of getting set up in London were fading.[37] As he had done six months earlier, he again stated his intention to resign his political positions in Belfast, and at the end of March 1899 he did indeed resign the presidency of the Belfast and Ulster Centenary Association, though retaining the title of honorary president.[38]

In August 1899, however, Devlin's personal circumstances remained unchanged. He offered to help William O'Brien with UIL work in the west during his vacation, but took the opportunity to hint more discreetly in the same direction as his more direct importuning of Dillon. 'Having charge of an important business which requires careful nursing and close attention,' he told O'Brien, 'it is difficult to get away, especially when the business belongs to another.'[39] Nothing came of Devlin's aspirations regarding London or Dublin, and during the next year he turned to his contacts in Glasgow, where the wealthy brewer Arthur Murphy was a leading figure in the national movement, as was the licensed restaurateur William McKillop, who had become a particular friend, and who was, with Devlin's help, returned as MP for North Sligo at the general election of 1900. Devlin's Glasgow friends were prepared to put up the £7,000 necessary for him to buy suitable premises in that city. The leading Belfast publican and loyal Devlinite Patrick Flanigan, proprietor of the Crown Liquor Saloon and the Adelphi Hotel, warned Dillon about this, pointing out that 'I need not say to you what a blow the national cause would receive if he accepts this, the great chance of his life. . . He is the life and the soul. . . Without him I cannot for the life of me see how the National Party or organization [in Belfast] could possible hold together or be of any service to the cause.' Flanigan and his friends contemplated asking Sam Young MP if he would 'sell the old tumble-down store' to Devlin. It was, said Flanigan, 'largely associated with Mr Devlin' and would otherwise be worth nothing. 'This Glasgow business will be settled before the end of the month,' so, Flanigan entreated, it would be most helpful if Dillon would put pressure on Young to agree to the sale.[40] We do not know whether Young offered his business to Devlin, or even whether Dillon approached him about it. In view of Devlin's previous declarations, it seems unlikely that he would have taken it. The Glasgow offer was much more attractive to Devlin, and he did agree to accept it. But at the last minute he was persuaded by John Rooney and other friends not to leave Belfast. They organized a major private testimonial for him, with a view to raising sufficient capital to enable him 'to secure a business house in Belfast'. Eighty-six subscribers

---

[37] Devlin to Dillon, 21 Nov. 1898 (DP 6729/60).
[38] Devlin to Dillon, 25 Jan. 1899 (DP 6729/62); *NS*, 1 Apr. 1899.
[39] Devlin to O'Brien, 9 Aug. 1899 (BLUCC, OBP, AJC/26).
[40] P. Flanigan to Dillon, 9 Jan. 1901 (DP 6781/1011).

contributed almost £300, which was the equivalent of a year's salary for a clerical worker.[41]

Whether Devlin did in fact purchase premises we cannot be sure, but it seems unlikely that he did, for a few months later the Dublin solicitor and political aspirant John Muldoon told Dillon that 'the latest is that Joe Devlin contemplates going to the bar', by which we may assume he meant the legal rather than the licensed bar! Muldoon thought this a very good idea, and one compatible with a parliamentary career, and he had strongly advised Devlin to do it.[42] How serious Devlin was about this kind of bar we do not know, but it soon became clear that the Party had other plans for him. Towards the end of 1901 Redmond asked him to undertake a fund-raising tour of the USA in the company of his brother William. Thus, after a series of dinners in his honour—in Belfast, Dublin, and London—Devlin at last left Belfast to became a full-time politician. He was paid expenses and an honorarium for the period of the tour. As we have seen, the local political situation in Catholic Belfast continued in disturbed vein for some years yet, but that now became a relatively small part of Devlin's life, as he left Belfast for the wider world of Irish nationalism.

DEVLIN AND THE DIASPORA

Between 1841 and 1911 the population of Ireland fell from eight and half million to four and half million, as a result of short-term famine and long-term emigration. Ever since the Fenian era, efforts have been made by various Irish nationalist organizations to mobilize these emigrant communities politically. In Parnell's time this had met with considerable success, partly because of the attractive nature of Parnell's non-violent but apparently effective strategy, and partly because by the 1880s Irish migrant communities were becoming more settled, stable, and organized, with a more broadly based class structure. The tramping labourer was no longer the typical Irish migrant; an educated and prosperous elite, capable of providing political leadership, had emerged. During the 1890s, as Irish nationalism struggled, emigrant enthusiasm for nationalist politics waned, but the social, economic, and associational development of migrant communities continued apace. When Irish constitutional politics revived after 1900, the situation was ripe for exploitation. Irish Catholic communities outside Ireland, stronger than they had ever been, offered to Irish nationalist politicians (and, of course, to revolutionaries as well) the prospect both of financial support on a scale unimaginable in Ireland itself, and also of significant political support.

Thus, after the reunion, John Redmond and his colleagues moved quickly to develop the emigrant dimension. Joe Devlin was the right man in the right place

[41] Rooney to O'Brien, 26 Mar. 1901 (BLUCC, OBP, AL/51).
[42] J. Muldoon to Dillon, 25 Oct. 1901 (DP 6734/61).

at the right time to play a leading part in this. In the autumn of 1901, as Redmond and two colleagues returned from an initial visit to America, they decided that Devlin, with support from Redmond's younger brother Willie, was the ideal person to undertake a more extended tour of the United States.[43] He was a fresh young face, a committed worker, and an experienced organizer without family ties, and was emerging as the most accomplished public orator of his generation. Unlike the other Irish political leaders, his whole experience in politics was in working with an Irish Catholic minority community in a city where the wider context was culturally alien if not directly hostile. It also involved electoral competition on a regular basis, rather than the virtually uncontested nature of southern Irish electoral politics after 1885. In several ways Irish Catholics in Belfast had more in common with their counterparts in Glasgow or Boston than with their fellow countrymen in Mayo or Kerry. Furthermore, Devlin's Belfast background, and especially his Belfast accent, were an added bonus. In the optimistic era of the reunion, an indication that Belfast—or at least part of it—was 'for Ireland' offered the promise of a solution to the emergence of *Ulster* Unionism as the main stumbling block to Irish legislative independence. So, although Devlin left Belfast early in 1902, and for the next eighteen years it became merely his base rather than his place of work or regular residence, in one sense he took Belfast with him into the wider world of international Irish nationalism.

Devlin and Willie Redmond disembarked at New York on 10 February 1902. It was the first time Devlin had 'trod on land where the British flag does not fly'.[44] Between then and June 1903 he was to spend more than eleven months on two gruelling American tours, followed in March 1906 by a twelve-month tour of Australia and New Zealand. John Redmond sent him his ticket and an expenses cheque for £100, and remuneration was arranged, which Devlin said could be allowed to 'accumulate until his return'. Devlin was also commissioned to send regular letters for publication to William O'Brien's Dublin weekly paper the *Irish People*, edited by his old comrade Tim McCarthy.[45] The main purpose of the trip was to develop a structure of UIL branches across the USA, as a basis for future fund-raising. A programme of forty meetings in twenty-eight days was organized by the United Irish League of America, the new organization founded in 1900. Press interest in the visit was intense, but, Devlin told Dillon, the reports were 'inaccurate in some respects and absolutely untrue in others . . . especially about winning Irish freedom by the sword, but we thought it better not to contradict any of the statements attributed to us'.[46] In New York, especially, they found a lack of leadership and 'a sheer lack of capacity and energy that is simply appalling', but they managed to start six or seven new UIL

---

[43] *Irish People*, 25 Jan. 1902.   [44] Ibid., 4 Mar. 1902.
[45] Devlin to Redmond, 23 Jan. 1902 (RP 15181/1).
[46] Devlin to Dillon, 16 Feb. 1902 (DP 6729/83).

branches before moving on. In Washington DC they found the work to be hard and 'at times discouraging' and the IRB-linked Clan na Gael to be 'extremely malignant and active'.[47]

As the weeks went by Devlin became more optimistic. In Baltimore he and Willie were received by Cardinal Gibbons, and in Washington DC by President Theodore Roosevelt.[48] From Chicago at the end of March he reported that the work was continuing 'most successfully, predicting that New York, Boston and Chicago would each have about 30 UIL branches'.[49] By the time Devlin sailed for home on 20 June, he and Willie Redmond had between them addressed 160 meetings in 4 months and started 186 branches. He was unusually frank in addressing the challenge from the physical force advocates. At the end of the tour he told New York's 'Northern Star' branch of the UIL, which was made up predominantly of Belfast men, that 'you Irish-Americans have not . . . sprung into the foremost position in this great free republic by insane methods or lack of logical appreciation of events . . . and we ask you to apply the same common sense to the Irish question'.[50] On his return, Devlin—still less than a year away from his previous career as a bar manager—was invited to join the Irish Party leaders at a dinner with the Canadian prime minister Sir Wilfrid Laurier. A *Freeman's Journal* report declared that, 'of the many ambassadors Ireland has sent to America, few roused Irish feeling there more noticeably than Mr Devlin'.[51] Although he asked for a quiet reception in Belfast when he returned home for the first time since the death of his mother four months previously, inevitably his success was used by the Belfast UIL in its struggle against Bishop Henry. 'No handful of factionists, cleric or lay,' declared the *Northern Star*, 'can now wreck the career of Joseph Devlin. He has been the great and honoured associate of Cardinals, Archbishops, and eminent ecclesiastics, not to mention Senators, Judges and lay celebrities in the vast American States.'[52]

Devlin was greatly impressed by the dynamism and brisk efficiency of America. Notwithstanding that Belfast was a busy, bustling place, he wrote in his column: 'the worker in New York would think he had a holiday if he got a job in my native city.' 'It is the air of freedom,' he continued, 'the thrilling feeling that one is living and toiling in a country when men are equal and where the rewards of zeal and industry are all his own.'[53] There is something similar in this thinking to the style of radicalism articulated by the young Lloyd George, who was appalled by 'the peacockism of royalty' but who once wrote to his wife that 'I am going to stay with a much richer man than the King, and a man who has made all that money himself'.[54] Such

---

[47] Devlin to Redmond, 17 Feb. and 6 Mar. 1902 (RP 15181/1); Devlin to Dillon, 6 Mar. 1902 (DP 6729/84).

[48] *Irish People*, 22 Mar. 1902.　　　[49] Devlin to Redmond, 28 Mar. 1902 (RP 15181/1).

[50] *Irish People*, 21 June 1902.　　　[51] *NS*, 5 July 1902.

[52] Ibid., 12 July 1902.　　　[53] *Irish People*, 4 Mar. and 19 Apr. 1902.

[54] K. O. Morgan (ed.), *Lloyd George Family Letters, 1885–1936* (London, 1973), 159.

enthusiasm for what he perceived as an open, meritocratic society left Devlin with something of a difficulty to reconcile, given that emigration was the *bête noire* of both Irish priests and Irish politicians. Towards the end of the same article—perhaps as an afterthought, perhaps at the suggestion of his travelling companion Willie Redmond or his editor in Dublin—he added a paragraph stating that, while 'very many of our people do well' in America, those who were unable to display the same level of 'intelligence, enterprise and ceaseless industry' were likely to 'go to the wall without delay...An alarming proportion of the emigrants from Ireland fall in the slums of the big and heartless cities.'[55]

Little more than three months later, transatlantic travel again loomed into Devlin's life. John Redmond, Dillon, and Davitt travelled to the United States in October 1902 to participate in the first national convention of the UIL of America. Within a few days of their arrival Devlin received a cable summoning him to join them. This arose from an invitation uttered at the Boston Convention. Devlin 'had no anxiety whatever to go there', but was 'strongly of opinion that I could do useful work'.[56] He promptly set off, knowing from the start that he would be expected to stay for six months or more and that he would travel the breadth of the country from Boston to San Francisco.[57] He was paid a salary of £20 per month from party funds, the same rate of pay as the grant for those Members of Parliament who needed support.[58] After the great Convention, he worked in New England for several weeks, then proceeded across the border to Toronto, Montreal, and Ottawa. The American UIL treasurer confirmed that by February 1903 $30,000 had been raised.[59] As the winter drew to a close, Devlin left the north-eastern seaboard to undertake a tour of the rest of the country. Where large public meetings were not possible, private meetings of thirty or forty people were organized, which, Devlin said, often raised more funds than large meetings.[60] In western New York State and in Ohio the meetings were 'not large', but contributions were generous.[61] During March he held fifteen meetings working out of Chicago. He then spent April proceeding via Minneapolis westwards as far as Salt Lake City, and then north to the copper-mining town of Butte, Montana, and on to Spokane in Washington State. He then returned via Kansas City. He had, he reported exhaustedly to Redmond when he reached Minneapolis, been 'practically living in trains for the last three weeks', the final leg being a non-stop train journey from Butte of 1,182 miles.[62] In the west Devlin found 'a terrible apathy and lack of interest in Irish affairs...For organizing purposes the East was a paradise compared with West.' But a private meeting in Omaha raised $1,000 and the visit to Butte and its neighbours produced $4,000. Butte, with a population of

55 *Irish People*, 19 Apr. 1902.
56 Devlin to Dillon, 10 Oct. 1902 (DP 6729/89); *NS*, 24 Jan. 1903.
57 *NS*, 15 and 22 Nov. 1902.   58 Devlin to Redmond, 18 July 1903 (RP 15181/1).
59 *NS*, 24 Jan. and 28 Feb. 1903.   60 Devlin to Redmond, 28 Mar. 1903 (RP 15181/1).
61 Devlin to Redmond, 6 Mar. 1903 (RP 15181/1); *NS*, 21 Mar. 1903.   62 *NS*, 25 Apr. 1903.

little over 30,000, was for its size the most Irish town in the United States—over 8,000 first- and second-generation Irish at the time of Devlin's visit, the majority of them hailing from the old copper-mining villages of west Cork, but with many also from Ulster.[63] He then went south to New Orleans, followed by visits to Birmingham, Montgomery, and Savannah. Some of his Irish-American advisers had argued against the trip, but in fact Devlin was pleasantly surprised by the quality of organization in the south, and $4,000 was raised. He returned for a final intensive tour of New England, with eighteen meetings in twenty days, together with a mass meeting in Quebec City attended by former Conservative premier E. J. Flynn.[64] Overall he estimated that $70,000 was gathered during his second tour. Everywhere he went, said American UIL Secretary John O'Callaghan, he had 'charmed the people' and, 'to use an American phrase, "he wears the same size hat returning to Ireland that he brought with him when he came" '.[65] After more than seven months in the United States, Devlin landed at Queenstown (Cobh) on 18 June.

Two-and-a-half-years later Devlin was on the seas again, travelling to Australia and New Zealand on a year-long tour with his Belfast friend John T. Donovan. They travelled overland across Europe, having an audience with the Pope in Rome before sailing from Naples and arriving at Perth in mid-April 1906. Western Australia detained them for a month, but yielded relatively little. 'There are a great many social functions at which we are kept busy,' he told Redmond, 'but they are not of any immediate or practical advantage.'[66] They then proceeded by ship to Adelaide and on to Melbourne. Contributions were 'not large' compared to what had been collected from individuals in the USA, but 'everyone at our meetings contributes something'. Devlin's mother had died while he was away in America in 1902, and early in the Australian trip he was to hear of the death of his father, and also of that of Michael Davitt, about which he expressed to Redmond great regret.[67] Most of the local committees would not agree to Devlin and Donovan having separate schedules, as was the practice in America. 'I am expected to go to every meeting,' Devlin told Redmond. 'It is pretty hard on the throat, but on the whole I am getting through the work alright.'[68] By late September Devlin's throat was giving him 'a great deal of trouble' and causing a painful earache. He therefore begged Redmond to cancel the planned additional speaking tour in America.[69] By December Devlin was en route for Tasmania, and on 1 January 1907 was in Rotorua, New Zealand. By

---

[63] Devlin to Redmond, 24 Apr. 1903 (RP 15181/1); *NS*, 25 May 1903; D. M. Emmons, 'Faction Fights: The Irish Worlds of Butte, Montana, 1875–1917', in Patrick O'Sullivan (ed.), *The Irish in the New Communities* (London, 1992), 82–98.

[64] *NS*, 6 June 1903.

[65] Ibid., 13 June 1903; Devlin to Redmond, 24 May 1903 (RP 15181/1)

[66] Devlin to Redmond, 23 Apr. 1906 (RP 15181/1).

[67] Devlin to Redmond, 2 June 1906 (RP 15181/1).

[68] Devlin to Redmond, 17 Aug. 1906 (RP 15181/1).

[69] Devlin to Redmond, 29 Sept. 1906 (RP 15181/1).

Fig. 4.2. Devlin in Australia, 1906.

the time Devlin and Donovan left Auckland for San Francisco on 7 February, a total of £22,000 had been raised. They crossed America as quickly as they could, before sailing from New York to Queenstown, where they arrived late in March.[70]

'A CATHOLIC ORANGEISM IN GREEN PAINT'?
THE ANCIENT ORDER OF HIBERNIANS

A central feature of Devlin's argument against Bishop Henry was that amelioration of the condition of Belfast Catholics would be won, not by purely local measures, but by binding the local movement firmly to the national movement, seeking advantages in the short term through action by the Irish Party at Westminster, and in the long term through home rule. After 1905 the growing role of the Ancient Order of Hibernians (AOH) turned this relationship around, so that it was the political ethos of the ethnically divided north that influenced the development of grass-roots politics throughout Ireland. This phase of Irish national politics has not had a good press. William O'Brien, whose fall from influence coincided with the AOH's rise, wrote in his voluminous memoirs that 'The Board of Erin Hibernians . . . debased the National Ideal . . . to the level of a Catholic Orangeism in green paint'.[71] The AOH has been presented as the voice of sectarian Catholic nationalism, although Cardinal Logue and several of his bishops opposed it; as an anti-labour organization, although its primary function was working-class welfare; and as a sinister secret society, although it was registered under the Friendly Societies Act and later recognized under the 1911 National Insurance Act. There is less dispute over the fact that, whatever else it was, the AOH became a personal political vehicle for Joe Devlin, and at the same time projected Belfast Nationalists into the heart of Irish Party activities.

The 'Ancient Order' traced its origins back to various episodes in the sixteenth and seventeenth centuries. It also acknowledged the Defenders and the Ribbonmen as part of its ancestry. But the Order's modern name dates from 1836, when St Patrick's Fraternal Society in New York sought authorization from the homeland to establish a benevolent society in America, which shortly became known as the 'Ancient Order of Hibernians'. As a sort of Irish Catholic freemasonry, combining nostalgia with benevolence, it satisfied a great need in immigrant America, and by the end of the century was the largest of all Irish-American societies, with over 100,000 members.[72] Although it normally strove to avoid any more specific political commitment than a broad espousal

---

[70] Devlin to Redmond, 18 Feb. 1907 (RP 15181/1).   [71] O'Brien, *Irish Revolution*, 31–2.
[72] J. O'Dea, *History of the Ancient Order of Hibernians and Ladies Auxiliary* (Philadelphia, 1923), ii. 1368.

of Irish nationalism, its wealth and sophisticated organization acted as a magnet for any group of Irish-Americans who sought access to the minds or pockets of their fellow exiles. Thus both the Molly Maguires (an intimidatory secret society operating in the Pennsylvania coalfield during the 1870s, which later gave the AOH in Ireland its derogatory nickname of 'the Mollies') and the Clan na Gael at one time or another succeeded in diverting the movement to their own ends. In Ireland itself, the organization was far smaller, offering similar provision to what were then more important bodies such as the Irish National Foresters. Joe Devlin later claimed to have joined the AOH sometime in the early 1890s, although there is no reference to it in his surviving correspondence until a decade later. The AOH first began to appear in reports of Nationalist activities in Belfast in 1899, when one division was affiliated to the Belfast and Ulster Centenary Association alongside the city's '98 clubs.[73] In the following year, 'an influential delegation from the AOH' took part in the local convention organized by the newly established Belfast divisional executive of the UIL, chaired by Devlin.[74] At this stage the AOH was simply regarded as another local body that it was helpful to have on side.[75]

What transformed the AOH in Devlin's eyes into something of major potential was his American experience during 1902–3. The AOH in America was essentially an Irish-American benevolent association, open to all Catholics of Irish birth or descent and embracing in a general way the cause of 'Ireland a nation'. The American Order had split in 1884 over a number of issues, and the split soon spread to Ireland. But by 1898 the American Order had reunited, and was a very large, rich, and powerful organization. It was agreed that the Order would not formally affiliate with its counterpart in Ireland until the latter was reunited and had received the approval of the Catholic Church.[76] During Devlin's first trip to the USA there was no mention of the AOH in his reports home, but contacts were made. At his farewell banquet in New York on 19 June E. J. Slattery, former state president of the AOH in Massachusetts, said that the time had come when 'the men of the AOH should make up their minds as to whether or not they are any longer to be inactive spectators of what is taking place in Ireland and in America with regard to the United Irish League'. He promised to raise the matter at the forthcoming AOH National Convention in Denver, when James E. Dolan, a man sympathetic to the constitutional movement, was elected president.[77] When Devlin returned to America in November 1902, he gave more priority to the matter: AOH divisions were more in evidence at his meetings, and he again met Slattery.[78] In one of his regular reports to Redmond he wrote that 'I am arranging to have meetings called of the State Boards of the Hibernians, and several have already promised to listen to a statement from me

[73] *NS*, 6, 13 20, and 27 May 1899.   [74] Ibid., 27 Oct 1900.   [75] Ibid., 4 Apr. 1903.
[76] M. Funchion, (ed.), *Irish-American Voluntary Organizations* (Westport, CT, 1983), 51–6.
[77] *Irish People*, 28 June 1902.   [78] *NS*, 29 Nov. 1902, 14 Feb. and 13 June 1903.

on the Irish question. Good will I think come out of this.'[79] A few months later he was able to report that 'after careful consideration the Directory of the AOH have given official sanction to the UIL by a vote of six to two'.[80] So large and disparate body as the American AOH was, however, hard to hold together in a united political policy. Thus a few days later Devlin wrote to Redmond again to report that 'the Directory of the Hibernians have issued a flabby approval of our movement and that makes a considerable advance, because we have practically had to cope with the opposition of the AOH as well as that of the Clan'.[81] It was a weak alliance, but it lasted throughout the presidency of James E. Dolan, 1902–6.[82]

From April 1903 the AOH began to feature prominently in the columns of the *Northern Star*. Devlin was by this time well aware of its potential as an organizational tool, especially since its Irish presence was greatest in Belfast and Ulster. It was not, however, the easiest of beasts to handle. It had a complex history of splits and rivalries, question marks over its financial arrangements, and differences of opinion—especially between urban and rural divisions—as to its primary purpose. An especially hot topic in Ireland and Britain was the question of whether or not the Order as a whole, or individual divisions within the Order, should register as a benefit society under the Friendly Societies Act. This would entail regular fixed contributions from members, in return for specifically stated welfare benefits. Urban divisions consisting mainly of workers tended to favour this, while many rural divisions were less enthusiastic, being more interested in the Order as a base for social activities. The registration issue began as a genuine difference of opinion and interests, but it became a very bitter dispute that, it gradually emerged, concealed other issues. Because this was unresolved, Devlin declined an invitation to chair the biennial national convention of the AOH, organized in Belfast in September 1904 by the Order's central body in Ireland, the Board of Erin. He did, however, attend as a keynote speaker. He called for an amicable discussion and settlement of the registration issue along the lines of no coercion of individual divisions. Many of the Belfast divisions favoured registration, but most of the Tyrone divisions, for instance, were against it. Ultimately the Convention accepted Devlin's suggestion to postpone any decision for a year. The meeting ended with a resolution calling on all members to support the UIL.[83]

Over the next year major efforts were made to modernize the administration and finances of the AOH Board of Erin. A Dublin insurance agent, John D. Nugent—soon to become a controversial figure in Dublin politics, but in later life a close friend and holiday companion of Devlin—became National

---

[79] Devlin to Redmond, 22 Jan. 1903 (RP 15181/1).
[80] Devlin to Redmond, 13 May 1903 (RP 15181/1).
[81] Devlin to Redmond, 24 May 1903 (RP 15181/1).
[82] Ibid.; Funchion, *Irish-American Voluntary Organizations*, 59.		[83] *NS*, 1 and 8 Oct 1904.

Secretary. When the next national convention of the organization was held, in Dublin on 21 July 1905, Devlin accepted the national presidency, a post he was to hold for the rest of his life. The Convention approved Nugent's new constitution, which required members to support the UIL and the Irish Parliamentary Party. After lengthy discussion it was decided that the Board of Erin would not itself register as a friendly society, but that individual divisions and county boards could do so. In his acceptance speech Devlin said that though in Ireland they were the parent body of the organization, they should not feel ashamed to follow the American AOH and 'emulate its progressive spirit'. He added that the AOH was not a narrow or sectarian association, but extended the hand of friendship to Protestants, and sought simply to obtain full equality for Catholics in all aspects of Irish life.[84] The following four years witnessed a tremendous expansion of the Order in Ireland. A membership of 10,000 in the autumn of 1905 had by 1909 expanded to 60,000.[85] Belfast and Tyrone led the way, but the Order became strong throughout Ulster, and in North Connacht.[86] By 1909 there were 19 AOH divisions in Belfast, totalling about 3,000 members, and 2,000 members in Dublin.[87] In Scotland also, it was claimed that, 'were it not for the AOH society', the leaders of the UIL 'might close their books'.[88] Generally speaking, the Order and the League worked well together. One factor in this was Devlin's double role. Another was the fact that there was most demand for AOH divisions in areas where the UIL had atrophied: by 1909, the RIC reported, it had to a great extent replaced the League in districts where land purchase had been extensive.[89]

Why was Devlin attracted to the AOH? He was a calculating and humane politician, well aware of the dangers of a sectarian appeal. His rhetoric shows that he knew from early days that for home rule to succeed at least some Protestants—and what he called 'the Orange democracy'—had to be won over. When Protestant Nationalists, like W. D. Harbinson, appeared in Belfast or elsewhere, he was quick to involve them in his operations. He had been keen to stress the non-sectarian character of the 1798 rebellion in Ulster, and to assign the names of its Protestant heroes to the branches of the '98 clubs. But he had noticed the power of history and pageantry to revive political movements, and the AOH could assist in this. As a rising young politician with a penchant for unity and tight organization, in an era when that was sadly lacking in the Nationalist movement, he was clearly impressed by the remarkable success of William O'Brien's United Irish League. The chance of building an organization in which he would be the central figure must have had attractions for him,

---

[84] Ibid., 29 July 1905.
[85] Monthly RIC Reports, Inspector-General, Oct. 1905 (INA), and July 1909 (TNA: PRO CO 904/78).
[86] Monthly RIC Reports, Inspector-General, 1905–8 *passim* (INA).
[87] *IN*, 12 Mar. 1909; *Hibernian Journal*, Nov. 1909.   [88] *WFJ*, 30 Jan. 1909.
[89] Monthly RIC Reports, Inspector-General, Jan. 1909 (TNA: PRO CO 904/77).

especially when it could be done in parallel with the League rather than in opposition to it. After O'Brien had fallen out with the mainstream of the Party in 1903, and as the UIL began to struggle to attract support outside areas where the land tenure crisis was acute, there was further reason to promote a new and additional organization. Among young men especially, the police noted, the Order was more popular than the League because 'it is more manifestly antagonistic to the Orange society'.[90] The Catholic North was the obvious place to find the energy to mobilize a new force, where the sense of grievance was acute, pervasive, and more or less classless.

There were further features in the AOH's favour. It was primarily an organization for mutuality—for providing a communal social life in the countryside and for providing economic help to the working man in times of personal hardship. This was the era in which such voluntary provision was at its height, state provision still being some years in the future. Another feature, especially attractive to Devlin in view of his long battle with Bishop Henry, was that the AOH offered the possibility of a lay-led and lay-controlled Catholic nationalism. The AOH was in fact less about sectarianism than about secular leadership. In the sense that many of the bishops in Ireland and Scotland were hostile or at least suspicious of it, it appeared to some as an anti-episcopal movement, but it could scarcely be dismissed as an anti-clerical movement. Senior clergy differed in their attitudes towards it. In the very different circumstances of the American immigrant community, many regarded the Order as an important support for Catholicity. In Ireland itself, Bishop Patrick O'Donnell of Raphoe, later to become Cardinal Archbishop of Armagh, was a strong supporter. He thought that 'it is greatly to the credit of the Board of Erin that it pulled so many men out of secret societies and formed them into an organization with Irish Catholic principles . . . The poor fellows are anxious to have their priests with them . . . I have been on their side from the start.'[91] Independence from the bishops and clergy also had a practical attraction. One of the AOH's main activities was to raise funds to provide halls and other meeting places. Once the AOH had established itself, Nationalist organizations could no longer be denied a meeting place by a hostile bishop or priest, or a Unionist-controlled municipal council. There was in fact a practical similarity between Hibernianism and Orangeism, for, just as the Orange Order, with its Orange Halls, provided an neutral base where Presbyterians, Episcopalians, Methodists, and Baptists could come together as 'Protestants', so Hibernian Halls provided the same kind of lay independence of the clergy without losing the dynamic force of religiosity. Finally, of course, a central attraction of the AOH, of which Devlin was especially aware, was that it provided the possibility of bringing the American Irish in numbers into political and financial support for constitutional nationalism.

[90] Monthly RIC Reports, Inspector-General, Feb. 1909 (TNA: PRO CO 904/77).
[91] O'Donnell to O'Riordan, 13 Dec. 1909 (MOR 1909/101).

Devlin declared in January 1908 that 'he would like to see a public hall in every parish in Ireland... It should be a centre from which would radiate life, and light and warmth... the light of education revealing to them the past and preparing them for the future... There they would become acquainted with the language and music of Ireland; there they could hold their dances and merry meetings.'[92] The *Leader* agreed that 'these are effective instruments in preventing emigration as they provided amusement and attraction which relieve the monotony of rural life'.[93] It was indeed the case that the AOH was in principle committed to the encouragement of Irish games, the work of the Gaelic League, and the fostering of Irish industries.[94] The Belfast Hibernian Club ran a successful cycling club and swimming club. It also formed the Ulster Hibernian Literary Society, though there were soon reports of poor attendances.[95] Some years later the *Leader*, no uncritical friend of the Irish Party, still took the optimistic view that 'a goodly number of AOH men are strong Irish-Irelanders and we hope that Irish-Ireland points of view will be pushed on as far as possible in the clubs and halls'.[96] But Sinn Féiner Eoin MacNeill, reflecting in later years, wrote:

When Mr Devlin came to the front with his organization of the revived AOH, the Irish language appeared as an article in their programme. But I had no difficulty in recognizing a very thorough hostility towards the whole Irish language movement within the Hibernian organization. I can remember at a public meeting... hearing the Irish language described as 'that gibberish'.[97]

Likewise the *Sinn Féin* newspaper observed, with more relish than regret, that 'the classes occasionally started in Hibernian circles die an easy and natural death'.[98]

How did the Catholic Church respond to the sudden expansion of this lay-led Catholic organization? In America there was no problem with it after the reunion of 1898: the AOH helped to keep Irish-American Catholics inside a religion-based community. In Britain and Ireland the situation was different, given the Order's historic links with violent secret societies. The Scottish bishops had imposed a ban in 1882. In 1907 they reconfirmed this, but in December 1909 were notified by the Vatican that the ban was rescinded.[99] In Ireland the ban had been lifted earlier, but the hierarchy had a range of views about it. Bishop O'Donnell and several of his Raphoe clergy were members and strong supporters. Other bishops were mainly circumspect or neutral. Henry Henry, obviously, was opposed. The long-standing national chaplain of the Order,

[92] *NS*, 11 Jan. 1908.　　[93] *Leader*, 16 Jan. 1915.　　[94] *NS*, 29 July 1905.
[95] Ibid., 13 Oct, 3 Nov., and 1 Dec. 1906.　　[96] *Leader*, 16 Jan. 1915.
[97] MacNeill, memoir, in M. Tierney, *Eoin MacNeill: Scholar and Man of Action* (Oxford, 1980), 80–1.
[98] *Sinn Féin*, 12 Oct. 1912.
[99] *NS*, 7 Sept. 1907; J. Handley, *The Irish in Modern Scotland* (Cork, 1947), 293.

Revd J. J. McKinley, was a Down and Connor priest, and Henry denied him promotion, transferred him from one end of Co. Antrim to the other against his will, and restricted his participation in AOH ceremonials.[100] But the only senior member of the hierarchy to oppose the Order strongly and steadily was Cardinal Logue. He was not against benefit societies as such. The Irish National Foresters, for instance, he declared to be 'good sterling Catholics . . . blessed by religion'.[101] One of his senior priests, Canon McCartan of Donoughmore, thought that 'our Hibernians [in Ireland] are simply Ribbonmen with oaths, signs and passwords and the poor dupes pay 1/- a quarter to men who render no account of the money nor do any of them if sick get any help from them'.[102] In 1903 Logue denounced the Order and said that it had no foothold in Ireland. On another occasion he denounced the Tyrone AOH as 'a cruel tyranny, an organized system of blackguardism'.[103] Perhaps provoked by this, in September 1907 Devlin held a rally of 15,000 Hibernians close to Logue's palace in Armagh City.[104] The Irish Parliamentary Party also had a range of attitudes to the AOH. A recent historian of the Party has estimated that around seventeen of the Party's eighty-odd MPs were members of the Order. Most of the others were happy to accept the constituency benefits that it delivered, including Devlin's mentor John Dillon. The Dublin MP Tim Harrington voiced concerns to Redmond about the sectarianism of the AOH, while Stephen Gwynn, a cultivated and nominally Protestant MP, wrote to Dillon that, 'while the Mollies are excellent people with Devlin at their head . . . their existence has always disquieted me a little about the future and you may take it that it is disquieting more than [a few] . . . good people'.[105]

By 1909 an observer might have been pardoned for thinking that the AOH in Ireland had reached the limits of its expansion. Such predictions could scarcely have been more wrong. Between 1910 and 1916 the Board of Erin spread its organization substantially through the whole of Ireland, to such an extent that the police of many southern and midland counties regarded it as the leading nationalist society.[106] By 1915 it claimed 1,800 branches in Ireland with 100,000 members, in addition to 200,000 insurance members.[107] This was a tribute to the assiduous organization of Devlin, Nugent, and others, and a reflection of the Irish Party's apparently dominant position at Westminster, together with the tremendous boost gained by the Order from Lloyd George's National Insurance Act of 1911.

[100] *NS*, 8 Apr. 1905.   [101] *IN*, 5 Oct. 1896.
[102] Canon McCartan to Bishop O'Donnell, 8 Nov. 1900 (DP 6764/55).
[103] *NS*, 23 May 1903; *Catholic Herald*, 25 Mar. 1904; Maume, *Long Gestation*, 95.
[104] *NS*, 28 Sept. 1907.
[105] J. R. R. McConnel, 'The View from the Backbench: Irish Nationalist MPs and their Work, 1910–1914', Ph.D. thesis (Durham University, 2002), 60–1.
[106] B. MacGiolla (ed.), *Intelligence Notes, 1913–16* (Dublin, 1966), *passim*.
[107] *Leader*, 16 Jan. 1915.

While the Board of Erin AOH was expanding, those who had seceded in 1905, the 'Scottish Registered Section', had taken a very different direction. The *Northern Star* continued to take a neutral line on the registration issue until well into 1905, but there were growing signs that a political difference was concealed within the debate. The old Belfast Fenian Harry Dobbyn was associated with the registered section from 1903, and by 1905 was Vice-President. 'To mention his name', declared the *Star*, 'is enough for every man who knows anything about Belfast affairs.' But the paper seemed to consider him more a figure of fun than a serious threat. 'Did anything ever prosper, or even partly succeed, that Mr Dobbyn had a hand in?' it asked.[108] Early in 1905 the Registered Section met in Glasgow and voted by a small majority to register themselves as a separate body, 'The AOH Benefit Society', which would seek to affiliate with the American AOH. This probably marks the point when the IRB elements made their move. In an attempt to resist this takeover, the Devlinites themselves registered a code of rules under the name 'The Board of Erin Ancient Order of Hibernians', following which the Registered Section applied unsuccessfully for an injunction to prevent the Devlinites from using the title AOH.[109] By this time the *Star* was getting a clearer picture. In August 1905 it denounced the Registered Section as under the control of 'extreme nationalists'. The Registered Section hit back at the Board of Erin in its short-lived journal, the *Hibernian Banner*, as being 'not sufficiently advanced nationalists', and dubbed Devlin 'a sworn loyalist of England'. But it was struggling. In October 1905 the police estimated that the Registered Section had 4,000 members in Scotland and around 1,000 in Ireland, but thought that even these figures exaggerated the extent of its support.[110] Many of the divisions affiliated to the Registered Section had taken such action for non-political reasons. It took some time for the real situation to become apparent, but by the end of 1907 the section was reported to be 'decreasing in strength'. The Registered Section's court case over the use of the name was quietly dropped.[111]

The Registered Section did ultimately wither away, but it would have done so earlier had it not been for the fact that the Board of Erin lost the foothold that Devlin had established in America in 1903. At the AOH Convention in Saratoga Springs in August 1906 the four-year presidency of James E. Dolan came to an end, and it soon became clear that the new president, Matthew Cummings, had very different views. The Secretary of the UIL of America described him as 'the Clan tool'.[112] In 1907 the American Order's house journal, the *National Hibernian*, declared its support for the new Sinn Féin Party in Ireland.[113] Cummings's election encouraged the extremists in Ireland to preserve their

108 *NS*, 19 Sept. and 7 Nov. 1903, and 22 July and 12 Aug. 1905.   109 Ibid., 4 Aug. 1906.
110 Monthly RIC Reports, Inspector-General, Oct. 1905 (INA).
111 RIC Special Branch Monthly Précis, Reports on Secret Societies, Dec. 1907 (TNA: PRO CO 904/117); *NS*, 11 Aug. 1906.
112 John O'Callaghan to Redmond, 18 Sept. 1906 (RP 15524).   113 *NS*, 26 Oct. 1907.

AOH structure, and it became their turn to press the American Order for recognition.[114] The Saratoga Convention resolved that no steps should be taken until there was proof that harmony prevailed among the Hibernians of Britain and Ireland. In the spring of 1909 Cummings made an official visit to Ireland to 'investigate' the matter, but he spent most of his time with the remnants of the Registered Section. The latter had rented large offices in Dublin on a short-term let, to make a favourable impression. Cummings had just one meeting with Devlin and Nugent. His demands were that the Board of Erin would have to dissociate itself from the constitutional movement and subject itself to the American Order if it wanted recognition. Clearly he did not intend this meeting to have any practical result. Although the physical-force wing of the Order in Ireland had become pitifully small, all it needed to achieve its objective was to demonstrate its existence, thus enabling Cummings to report back that the AOH in Ireland was not united.[115] But the deed proved to be his undoing, and in 1910 he narrowly lost the AOH presidency to James Regan, who agreed in future to recognize transfer cards from the Board of Erin.[116] Reflecting the general climate of Nationalist confidence during the years of the Third Home Rule Bill, the American Order gave its support to the Irish Party until the outbreak of war in 1914.[117]

The rise of the AOH in the Nationalist movement after 1905 was the product of underlying social forces, as well as a tribute to the organizing abilities of Joe Devlin and a consequence of the 1911 Insurance Act.[118] The Order was more urban than previous nationalist organizations—two-thirds of its insurance membership was so classified in 1913—while in rural districts its recruits were drawn 'chiefly from the labourers and landless men'.[119] The social aspirations of both urban and rural labourers might have dislocated national unity at this time had not the AOH offered a way of retaining these forces in support of a political programme that otherwise would have lacked meaningful social content. Its prominence was also an indication of the increasing importance of Ulster Nationalism relative to the movement as a whole. Nationalist Ulster provided much of the real vigour of the parliamentary movement between 1905 and 1914—hence the widespread allegations made by all the Party's critics during these years of 'cartloads of Hibernians' and 'hooligans from Belfast' breaking up election meetings in North Leitrim; of 'Mr Devlin's friends' arriving in West Mayo to assist the Party candidate against William O'Brien in December 1910; of 'paid roughs, imported from Belfast' guarding the Dublin Mansion House

---

[114] R. Johnston to John Devoy, 5 Feb. 1907; P. McCartan to Devoy, 20 Feb. 1909, in W. O'Brien and D. Ryan (eds.), _Devoy's Postbag_, ii (Dublin, 1953), 357–8, 376–7.

[115] _IN_, 31 Aug. 1909; DMP Monthly Précis, Reports on Secret Societies, Apr. 1909 (TNA: PRO CO 904/12); _Hibernian Journal_, Nov. 1909.

[116] O'Dea, _History of the AOH_, ii. 1420.

[117] Ibid., 1499; Funchion, _Irish-American Voluntary Organizations_, 59.

[118] See Ch. 5, pp. 132, 134.   [119] _The Times_, 26 Dec. 1911.

during a great home-rule rally in 1907; and of 'a special train full of armed men from Belfast' brought in to dominate the so-called Baton Convention in 1909.[120] These were gross exaggerations by hostile critics. But there is no doubt that Devlin did make special efforts to find men he could trust for security duties, and such developments were indicative not only of the ruthless centralism with which he sought to infuse the organization, but also of the increasing extent to which the movement relied for its vigour on Ulster Nationalism.[121]

'A PAID POSITION': RUNNING THE UNITED IRISH LEAGUE

While still on his second American tour in May 1903, Devlin was appointed General Secretary of the United Irish League of Great Britain (UILGB). Five years earlier, at the time of his first efforts to leave Belfast, he had been offered a position within what was then the Irish National League of Great Britain, but felt 'compelled to decline'. He could not, he told Dillon, 'under any circumstances accept a paid position in connection with the National movement'.[122] But once he had accepted a seat in Parliament in 1902 (still, of course, unpaid) and spent more than a year of his life working for the movement in America, his circumstances were very different. The opportunity for building up an independent income as a publican prior to re-entering politics had gone. Working for the Party in a senior paid position at least offered a reasonable income, and more dignity than existing on handouts from the Parliamentary Fund. Devlin had already amply demonstrated his organizational skills. He was sounded out by UILGB President T. P. O'Connor about his new post in March 1903, but, with typical modesty and diffidence, had replied that he would be willing to be considered only if two others, 'both of whom were more experienced and better qualified than I could claim to be', were no longer in the race.[123] T. P., however, speaking in July at the London dinner to honour Devlin's appointment, declared that 'almost by a miracle of simultaneity his name came to the lips of every member of the executive'. 'The more I see of Devlin', he added privately, 'the more confidence I have in his intelligence.'[124]

A perennial problem facing the Irish Party in Britain was conflicting interests among expatriate Irish voters. The Party's strategy was to keep 'the Irish vote' together as a bargaining weapon, to be cast for the party most likely to bring forward a Home Rule Bill. But other interests could pull Irish voters in different

---

[120] *Sinn Fein*, 22 Feb. 1908; *The Times*, 13 Dec. 1910; *Sinn Fein*, 14 Sept. 1907; W. O'Brien, *An Olive Branch in Ireland* (London, 1910), 443.
[121] Hepburn, *Past Apart*, 170.   [122] Devlin to Dillon, 16 Aug. 1898 (DP 6729/55).
[123] Devlin to Redmond, 28 Mar. 1903 (RP 15181/1).
[124] *NS*, 18 July 1903; O'Connor to Dillon, 4 Oct. and 19 Dec. 1903 (DP 6740/127, 129).

directions. An early test for Devlin in his new role was the Gateshead by-election of January 1904. Many Irish workers were gravitating towards the emerging political Labour movement, but many Catholics also supported the education policies of the Conservatives, as being more sympathetic towards funding for Church schools. The Irish vote in Gateshead, estimated at some 1,800, was one of the largest in the country. The local priests called on Catholics to vote for the Conservative candidate rather than the Lib–Lab, who was a strong home ruler. The local UIL was in chaos. O'Connor sent Devlin to the constituency, where he issued a manifesto calling on Irish voters to vote Liberal, asking 'are you for Ireland or against Ireland?' Sixty voluntary canvassers were assembled and Devlin held 'three or four meetings every night in the Irish quarter'. The Lib–Lab won the seat with a majority of 1,205. In an interview with John Redmond, Cardinal Bourne of Westminster 'went as near condemning as he could the action of the Irish priests with regard to Gateshead', although Cardinal Logue of Armagh wrote to his fellow prelate Archbishop Walsh that Redmond and Dillon had signed a manifesto 'urging Irish Catholics to vote contrary to the religious interests of themselves and their children'. But by November of the same year some of the very priests who had led the support for the Conservative back in January organized a home-rule meeting at which Devlin was the main speaker. The *Northern Star* could not resist contrasting the action of these Gateshead priests in 'publicly declaring their mistake' with the attitude of Bishop Henry in Belfast.[125]

By the summer of 1904 Devlin's success at the London office had earmarked him for greater things. The UIL HQ in Dublin was running less smoothly, partly because of a clash of personalities, and partly because of the fact that the General Secretary, John O'Donnell, had allied with William O'Brien in the conflict over the 1903 Land Act. O'Donnell's immediate colleague in the Dublin office was Laurence Ginnell, a 'briefless barrister' in his late forties, a highly strung man of militant and eccentric views, who became an Irish Party MP in 1906, an independent Nationalist in 1916, a Sinn Féiner following the Rising, and an Anti-Treaty TD in 1922. Ginnell reported to Dillon in August 1903 that the conflict over the Land Act was leading to disruption in the office, poor attendance at the UIL standing committee, and a general decay of the movement.[126] Dillon relied to some extent on Ginnell, as the only senior figure in the office sympathetic to his critical line on the Land Act, but found him to be in 'a terrible condition of excitement' and believed that O'Brienite influence would 'certainly drive the poor creature out of the office and possibly into a lunatic asylum'.[127] By January 1904 Ginnell was virtually a spy for Dillon at UIL HQ. At last O'Donnell

[125] *NS*, 26 Nov. 1904; L. W. Brady, *T. P. O'Connor and the Liverpool Irish* (London, 1983), 163; Devlin to Dillon, 14 and 17 Jan. 1904 (DP 6729/102, 103); O'Connor to Dillon, 3 Mar. 1904 (DP 6740/133); Logue to Walsh, 20 Jan. 1904 (Walsh Papers, 76).

[126] Ginnell to Dillon, 20 Aug. 1903 (DP 6732/209).

[127] Handwritten note by Dillon on letter from Ginnell, 9 Sept. 1903 (DP 6732/212).

vacated his post, and it must have been a tremendous relief both to Dillon and to Redmond when they were able to move Devlin into the vacant position. Devlin accepted the post at the same level of pay as O'Donnell, £7 per week, though it represented a reduction from his London salary.[128] Under the new regime Ginnell soon began to complain of overwork, whereas a year previously he had believed the office to be overstaffed.[129]

In January 1901 Devlin had written to William O'Brien that 'you can count on my loyalty to yourself personally', complimenting O'Brien on his 'single-minded devotion, undaunted courage and above all magnificent political foresight and judgement'.[130] The split over the 1903 Land Act and O'Brien's resignation from the UIL brought all this to an end. In Belfast the UIL was unruffled by O'Brien's resignation, for disagreements over the Land Act had little relevance, while O'Brien's mild anti-clericalism ensured that his activities would not attract Bishop Henry. But in July 1904 Devlin was concerned that O'Brien 'now intends to open a campaign against the Party and if possible to start a new movement'.[131] By October 1905, however, he thought that O'Brien, 'who finds now that he cannot smash up the movement and destroy the unity of the country from without thinks that the best thing to do is to try and patch things up and have a change of tactics'.[132] Devlin also thought that 'a better spirit . . . now prevailed between the [O'Brienite] Land & Labour Association and the United Irish League', and rejoiced 'that labourers as well as farmers recognized the obvious need for the union of all classes of Irish Nationalists'. He acknowledged that a mistake had been made when the Land Bill was going through Parliament that sufficient pressure had not been brought to bear on the government 'to do something for the agricultural labourers of the country', but he believed that 'the labourers' case was being made merely a pretext . . . to create division amongst the people'.[133]

Devlin was not always able to get his own way. On his return from New Zealand in 1907 the Party leaders were keen to obtain a seat in Parliament for John T. Donovan, Devlin's fellow envoy. Donovan had also served the National movement well, if controversially, through his editorship and 'Stargazer' column in the *Northern Star*, and was active in the AOH. In May 1907 he was put forward for a vacancy in North Monaghan. A young local lawyer, James Lardner, was already in the field, with the support of UIL branches and several priests. But AOH divisions outnumbered UIL branches in the constituency, and Dillon advised Redmond that Donovan might be carried at a Convention.[134] The Protestant Dillonite Richard McGhee attended as representative of the UIL

[128] Ginnell to Dillon, 17 Sept. 1904 (DP 6732/264).
[129] Ginnell to Dillon, 21 and 31 Dec. 1904 (DP 6732/267, 268).
[130] Devlin to O'Brien, 2 Jan. 1901 (BLUCC, OBP, AL.1).
[131] Devlin to Dillon, 16 July 1904 (DP 6729/107).
[132] Devlin to Dillon, 16 Oct. 1905 (DP 6729/112).   [133] *NS*, 30 Sept. 1905.
[134] Dillon to Redmond, 11 May 1907 (RP 15182/12).

National Directory. When the Convention opened, it was alleged that many of the AOH divisions were 'overnight' creations, and the Revd Chairman thereupon closed the meeting and walked out with 140 delegates. There remained 160 delegates, almost all AOH, along with McGhee, and Donovan was nominated. Those who had left reconvened elsewhere and nominated Lardner.[135] For a week it seemed that there would be an electoral contest, but then Redmond summoned Donovan to Dublin. He 'behaved admirably', in Redmond's opinion, and agreed to withdraw.[136] Devlin was angry, and pressed Redmond not to admit Lardner to the Party.[137] But in fact Lardner proved to be a loyal and useful member for the rest of the Party's existence. The incident was in essence a triumph of localism over the central Party, in a case where both candidates were of higher than usual calibre. But it damaged the AOH and also damaged Donovan, who was not able to obtain a parliamentary seat until 1914.

A very different kind of body with which Devlin came into regular contact was the Young Ireland Branch (YIB) of the UIL. The YIB was founded in Dublin in November 1904 with the support and encouragement of Devlin, who made meeting rooms at UIL HQ available to it.[138] T. M. Kettle, the first branch president, shared the *Leader*'s view that 'nationalism is more than politics', and that the UIL should acknowledge that the language and industrial revival movements are not incompatible with the national movement. The old firm of 'Honest Johns' and 'People's Williams' were by themselves not enough, in the opinion of the *Leader*, which was glad to see that Kettle 'and other distinguished young university men' were getting involved in politics.[139] 'What we all want to do is drive out the moneychangers and to purify and harden the constitutional movement by bringing into it young, capable and enthusiastic men,' said Kettle.[140] These Young Irelanders, well-educated Dublin students and professional men, were a few years younger than Joe Devlin, the under-educated and distinctly Belfast figure who had come amongst them as the paid boss of the UIL. They were fascinated by his power, charisma, and charm, but slightly appalled by the pragmatism of the full-time politician. Other leading members of the YIB, alongside Kettle, included two more future Nationalist MPs, Richard Hazleton and Stephen Gwynn, the parliamentary candidate and future barrister W. G. Fallon, Frank Sheehy-Skeffington, Francis Cruise O'Brien, and the future republicans and Sinn Féiners Thomas MacDonagh, Joseph Plunkett, Thomas Dillon, and Rory O'Connor. By 1908 membership of the branch had reached

---

[135] *WFJ*, 22 June 1907.   [136] *IN*, 11 Mar. 1909.

[137] Devlin to Redmond, 22 June 1907 (RP 15181/1).

[138] Two sources date the foundation of the YIB a year later than this (Jesuit Fathers (ed.), *A Page of Irish History* (Dublin, 1930), 491, and J. B. Lyons, *The Enigma of Tom Kettle* (Dublin, 1983), 61–2). But two contemporary sources, the *NS* of 10 Dec. 1904 and the *Leader* of the same date, confirm that 1904 is correct.

[139] *Leader*, 10 Dec. 1904.   [140] Lyons, *Tom Kettle*, 62.

a hundred. 'The welding-together of these hitherto comparatively dormant forces [students and young business/professional men] is a telling tribute to the organizing ability and the magnetic influence of Mr Devlin,' declared the *Northern Star*.[141]

But the Party leadership and the YIB soon found one another mutually exasperating. A few days after the introduction of the government's Irish Council Bill—a halfway-house measure of home rule—in May 1907, the YIB met and decided to oppose the measure at the forthcoming convention in Dublin. On the eve of the convention Devlin was sent by Redmond to meet the branch but, according to some members who were present, Devlin was more or less won over to their point of view.[142] Although the Party leaders ultimately decided to oppose the Bill, causing it to be withdrawn, the failed measure created problems for the Party with regard to Irish public opinion. Its immediate response to the crisis was to make things difficult for the government by kindling a campaign of militant opposition, in the form of organized 'cattle drives', to the eleven months' system of cattle ranching in some of the midland and western counties. Agrarianism had little appeal to the YIB, however. It became increasingly critical of the Party leadership, and in 1908 was denied further use of meeting rooms at UIL HQ.

At the beginning of 1909 the YIB sponsored a motion by Thomas Dillon that the Party should cease to trouble itself with 'minor measures' such as land reform, but should bring an end to the Liberal alliance and focus policy entirely on home rule. The branch secretary, Frank Sheehy-Skeffington, declared, 'in a spirit of absolute loyalty to the Parliamentary movement . . . [that] we cannot conscientiously bring ourselves to believe that the present tactics of the Irish Party are the best that could be adopted'. Over four years, he claimed, the YIB had kept 'the educated and thinking nationalists of the younger generation' involved in the movement, and 'we can hardly believe that the leaders of the Parliamentary movement would act wisely in estranging the one body of nationalists of the younger generation which supports them in Dublin'.[143] Kettle then arranged a meeting in Dublin between Devlin and about ten leading YIB members. Rather than discuss the matter in detail, Devlin, according to Thomas Dillon's recollection more than half a century later, delivered a public oration to the group, 'as if addressing 10,000 people'.[144] The outcome was that the YIB stuck to its guns and raised the motion a few weeks later at the UIL National Convention. Devlin—prompted, according to Thomas Dillon's recollection, by a signal from

---

[141] W. G. Fallon interview; E. MacNeill to Redmond, 29 May 1914 (NLI, MacNeill Papers, 15204): F. Sheehy-Skeffington to UIL Standing Committee, 11 Jan. 1909 (NLI, Sheehy-Skeffington Papers, 33612/6); *NS*, 10 Dec. 1904.

[142] Jesuit Fathers (ed.), *Page of Irish History*, 492.

[143] F. Sheehy-Skeffington to UIL Standing Committee, 11 Jan. 1909 (Sheehy-Skeffington Papers, 33612/6).

[144] Thomas Dillon interview.

Redmond—then rose and demolished their arguments, while belittling them personally.

Relations between Devlin and the YIB therefore deteriorated, as youthful idealism and political pragmatism came into conflict. Francis Cruise O'Brien articulated the YIB view most fully in a profile of Devlin in the *Leader* in 1910. He described the General Secretary as 'the most powerful man in Ireland...a crowd-pleaser, a man who never stops to have "a good think"', a speaker who 'confuses adjectives with arguments...Ideas to Mr Devlin spell faction...He is the most dangerous, because the most unthinking force in Irish politics... Mr Devlin set out to get there, and he has got. It does not matter to him where. He has never thought of it.'[145] Following this article, the Dublin UIL Executive called upon the YIB to expel Cruise O'Brien. When it refused to do so, the branch itself was expelled from the City Executive. The YIB remained loyal to the Party until it faded out around 1914, although many individual members drifted into the Sinn Féin or Republican ranks. When Cruise O'Brien died, still a relatively young man, in 1928, Devlin donated five guineas to his memorial fund.[146]

The attitude of the Party leaders, including Devlin, did little to keep the YIB on board, especially when the home-rule policy began to go sour in 1913–14. A letter from the Sinn Féin journalist William Sears of the *Enniscorthy Echo* to Sheehy-Skeffington a few days after the 1909 UIL Convention indicated the opening that this treatment of the YIB gave to opponents of the Party:

The same crowds that cheered Mr Devlin and Mr Dillon at the Convention last week would do the same next week and every other week for the rest of their lives...I know the country delegate well...He wants to be bossed and bulldozed. He wants a Devlin and he has the right man in Joe. The young men in the country are different. They are thinking for themselves, they read the *Irish Nation* every week and *Sinn Féin*. They look down with contempt on the UIL, the Party and the *Freeman*. Are you not on the wrong side? Come over to us.[147]

Francis Cruise O'Brien, W. G. Fallon, and other YIB members remained with the Party until the end, but many others sooner or later followed Sears's advice. Sheehy-Skeffington became an independent socialist-feminist, and his nephew Conor Cruise O'Brien regarded him as being in effect an 'extreme nationalist' by 1916.[148] Thomas Dillon left politics to become a professor of chemistry in 1919, but not before he had participated in the Easter Rising, married a sister of Joseph Mary Plunkett, and helped to draft the Sinn Féin constitution of 1917. Rory O'Connor trained as an engineer, and emigrated to Canada. He returned to Ireland in 1914, intending to join the British Army, but was dissuaded from

---

[145] *Leader*, 19 Feb. 1910.   [146] Receipt dated 30 May 1928 (Fallon Papers, 22582).
[147] William Sears to F. Sheehy-Skeffington, 15 Feb. 1909 (Sheehy-Skeffington Papers, 33611/1).
[148] C. C. O'Brien, *Memoir: My Life and Times* (London, 1998), 9–10.

doing so by Thomas Dillon.[149] He subsequently became a leading figure in the IRA, opposed the 1921 Treaty, led the Four Courts insurgency in 1922, and was executed without trial by decision of the Free State cabinet as a reprisal later the same year.

Like most successful orators and organizers, Devlin made enemies as well as friends. But a great part of the opposition to him derived from his success. His abilities and energy provided a vital prop to the Irish Party at a difficult time. Redmond, Dillon, T. P. O'Connor, and most of the rank and file of their parliamentary colleagues were well into their middle years by the time that Devlin joined their ranks. Of the younger men who came into the movement in the years either side of 1900, few had Devlin's ability and commitment. Some sided with O'Brien and were effectively lost after 1903; the young Mayo solicitor and MP Conor O'Kelly did a fund-raising tour, but the American UIL asked Redmond not to send anyone like him again; Kettle had the ability, but not the mental stability, and left Parliament to take up a chair in the National University; Jerry McVeagh stayed the parliamentary course, but the Party leadership became increasingly disenchanted with him; Richard Hazleton appeared to be more promising, but was ground down for years by bankruptcy arising out of an electoral dispute with Tim Healy; John T. Donovan was a good supporting figure, but was unable to get into Parliament until 1914. Added to his personal abilities, Devlin also brought the urgency and electoral experience of Catholic Belfast into the leadership of the national movement. In areas of the south of Ireland where the land-tenure question was not acute or was resolved, Nationalism seemed to run out of steam in the Edwardian era. A 'classless' movement found it increasingly hard to attract landless people and city labourers: as Augustine Birrell told Asquith in September 1913, the great Dublin strike and lockout 'lifted the curtain upon depths below Nationalism and the Home Rule movement'.[150] Students, intellectuals, and young professionals might be drawn to nationalist ideals, but, to a purchased farmer or a country shopkeeper, 'alien rule' was something over the horizon. It was more visible to those with experience of migration to Britain, to those seeking career mobility into the upper echelons of business and the professions, and, most of all, to the Catholic minority of Belfast and Ulster.

---

149 Thomas Dillon interview.
150 Leon Ó Broin, *The Chief Secretary: Augustine Birrell in Ireland, 1907–16* (London, 1969), 75.

5

'A Theatre where we may Expose the Wrongs of Ireland': Parliamentarian

We want to make the House of Commons a theatre where we may expose the wrongs of Ireland.

(Joe Devlin, 1903[1])

Devlin was a member of the Westminster Parliament for twenty-five years, including seventeen representing Belfast. He was initially reluctant to accept a seat, though several were pressed on him, but in later years he found re-entry difficult, taking seven years to get back after he had left West Belfast in 1922. His personal charm and oratorical skills equipped him well for success at Westminster, and he became a very popular figure in the Commons. Central to his efforts was the urge to demonstrate—especially to the working people of West Belfast—the value of parliamentary work. The most prominent part of his activities at Westminster was in the area of labour questions, where he was one of the Commons' leading social radicals at a time when Labour was still a small group. When Devlin left Parliament in 1922, Labour had 63 MPs; when he returned in 1929 they had 288 and formed the government. He was also frequently called upon to defend aspects of Catholicism from criticism, including the Anderson case in 1904, the McCann case in 1911, and several attacks on the Ancient Order of Hibernians (AOH).

FROM NORTH KILKENNY TO WEST BELFAST

The leaders of the Parliamentary Party, both before and after the reunion of 1900, frequently expressed concern about the quality and the commitment of many of their MPs.[2] It was, therefore, scarcely surprising that they were keen from an early stage to draw Joe Devlin into their ranks. But he showed no great

---

[1] Speech at Providence, Rhode Island, *NS*, 10 Jan. 1903.
[2] e.g. O'Connor to Dillon, 19 Dec. 1903 (DP 6740/129); O'Connor to Redmond, 3 Mar. 1904 (DP 6740/133); E. Blake to Elizabeth Dillon, 22 Jan. 1906 (Blake Papers, mic. 4683, fo. 582).

anxiety to get into Parliament. On half a dozen occasions he refused to allow his name to go forward. Redmond and Dillon urged him to stand at the general election of 1900, but he declined, and asked Redmond to remove his name from the list of available candidates. He urged him to consider instead the Co. Armagh Protestant W. D. Harbinson, 'a very brilliant young fellow who would be of immense service in the new Party'.[3] 'All over the Midlands', where he was hard at work electioneering for others in 1900, people were saying 'what a pity it is that Mr Devlin declines to enter the Irish Party'.[4] William O'Brien also pressed Devlin to enter Parliament. Though Devlin still had

the same objections . . . as I had from the beginning . . . it is very hard for me to refuse anything you ask of me and I make this promise that if you should still think it desirable when a vacancy (other than South Down) arises that I should become a member of the Party I will endeavour to accede to your request . . . I am bound to support McVeagh for South Down.[5]

A few months later Devlin asked Redmond not to suggest his name for the by-election vacancy in Galway.[6] By this time he was reportedly 'sought after by constituencies all over the country', though he was not acceptable everywhere.[7] In the South Monaghan by-election at the end of 1901 the retiring MP James Daly told Dillon that the priests would run a rival candidate if Jerry McVeagh were nominated, and that 'Mr Devlin was another man that would not be acceptable'.[8] As he departed for the USA in January 1902, Devlin again told Dillon that he did not want to be nominated for Parliament while he was away.[9] But less than a month later he was selected as the Party's candidate at the North Kilkenny by-election, and was returned to Parliament unopposed.[10] He made his first appearance in the constituency on 13 July, declaring that

no one more keenly realises than I do the necessity for close attention to those local interests which require to be promoted and safeguarded from time to time, and I regard it as a most patriotic act on your part to overlook this drawback in the case of myself by returning a man who, at least so far as Kilkenny County is concerned, was an absolute stranger.[11]

Ten days later he made 'a maiden speech of great force and eloquence' in the House of Commons.[12]

In October 1902, just a few days after the election of the Independent Orangeman Tom Sloan as MP for South Belfast, Devlin led a debate on the adjournment, drawing attention to the clash at Belfast's Custom House Steps

[3] Devlin to Redmond, 25 Sept. 1900 (RP 15181/1). Harbinson in fact left politics and became a Dublin barrister.
[4] *NS*, 20 Oct.1900.　　[5] Devlin to O'Brien, 2 Jan. 1901 (BLUCC, OBP, AL.1).
[6] Devlin to Redmond, 18 Oct. 1901 (RP 15181/1).　　[7] *NS*, 18 May 1901.
[8] Daly to Dillon, 19 Dec. 1901 (RP 15240/12).
[9] Devlin to Dillon, 18 Jan. 1902 (DP 6729/82).　　[10] *Kilkenny People*, 15 Feb. 1902.
[11] Ibid., 19 July 1902.　　[12] *The Times*, 24 July 1902.

Fig. 5.1. Joseph Devlin MP,
1902 and 1915

the previous Sunday between the Sloanite and Trewite wings of the Belfast Protestant Association. His aims were, first, to emphasize splits within the Unionist camp, and, secondly, to highlight the differences between the treatment of Nationalists in the west of Ireland and Unionists in Belfast: 'if a Nationalist looked sourly at land grabbers, he was hauled before two resident magistrates and condemned to a plank bed, while an Orangeman might say with impunity that he would make mincemeat of one of the highest judicial functionaries of Ireland (laughter and cheers).'[13] It was a sharp and witty speech, though it passed over the fact that Sloan's more outspoken rival, Arthur Trew, had in fact just served a year in prison for his activities in Belfast. Devlin and McVeagh called for the railing-in of the Custom House Steps to put an end to meetings there, but Sloan countered that he had seen more disorder in his first week in the Commons, and proposed railing in the Nationalist benches. Chief Secretary Wyndham said there has been far too much 'railing' already, and the debate came to an end.[14] One of the London daily papers reported that 'Mr Devlin has power and character, and held the fairly crowded House as he worked up his picture of Belfast rowdyism'.[15] But for much of his first eighteen months as an MP Devlin was on Party business in America. Shortly after his return, in July 1903, he continued his attacks on the Chief Secretary's law-and-order policy. He seized on the case of Constable Anderson, a Protestant policeman who had been dismissed from his position in December 1903 following a police disciplinary inquiry, on the grounds of personal misbehaviour of various kinds, including, it had been alleged, 'improper conduct' with a local Catholic girl to whom he was said to be engaged. Ulster Unionist MPs claimed that the whole affair was a Catholic conspiracy against Anderson, led by the local priest. Devlin raised the case nine times between June 1904 and May 1905, in order to 'protest with all his strength against this conspiracy to hold up the Irish people as bigots who would not allow Protestants to live in Ireland'.[16] At a time when he and his Belfast colleagues were still deeply embroiled in their local struggle with Bishop Henry's Catholic Association, the issue provided a good opportunity for Devlin to present himself as a defender of the good name of Catholicism.

The most important issue during Devlin's first term in Parliament was the impact of the Land Act of 1903 on relationships within the Irish Party, sparked by William O'Brien's newfound enthusiasm for the policy of 'conference, conciliation and consent'. Dillon and Devlin, followed somewhat more cautiously by Redmond, believed that the Act was far too generous to the landlords and, in Devlin's view, did nothing for rural labourers and very small farmers. Ultimately

---

13 *The Times*, 24 Oct. 1902.
14 Parl. Deb., H.C., 4th series, cxiii. 687–702 (23 Oct. 1902).
15 Cited in *NS*, 1 Nov. 1902.
16 Parl. Deb., H.C., 4th series, cxxxvii. 1038–9 (7 July 1904).

the Party leadership rode the storm and O'Brien was marginalized, but the United Irish League (UIL) was for a while under considerable pressure. The other major Irish issue during Devlin's first term was the devolution controversy. The Under Secretary, Sir Antony MacDonnell, in collaboration with a reforming Irish landlord, the Earl of Dunraven, developed a plan for administrative reform and devolution in Ireland. When the plan became public early in 1905, opposition from the government backbenches forced the resignation of the Chief Secretary, George Wyndham. T. P. O'Connor described devolution as 'the Latin for home rule', but the other Irish leaders were less convinced. Devlin's own position was spelled out in a letter to his constituents. The men of North Kilkenny, he wrote, 'will never consent to a whittling down of the National demand for a free and unfettered Irish parliament, nor seek the co-operation of a few aristocratic nobodies who make the preposterous demand that our national aspirations should be weakened in order that we may enjoy the luxury of their aristocratic company in the struggle that lies before us'.[17] In the event the crisis subsided, but MacDonnell remained in post, and the issue returned to challenge the Irish Party again in the next Parliament.

'TRIUMPH OF THE LITTLE CORPORAL': WEST BELFAST, 1906

The Conservative Government was destroyed by the tariff-reform controversy, and resigned prior to a general election. Campbell-Bannerman's Liberals took power in December 1905, and the election followed in January. In Britain the new government won a very large overall majority. In West Belfast the decision of the sitting Unionist H. O. Arnold-Foster, 'with the characteristic courage of a War Minister', as Devlin put it, to move to a safe English seat was an encouraging sign for the Nationalists, while other electoral developments in Belfast can only have increased Nationalist confidence further.[18] In South Belfast the Independent Orangeman T. H. Sloan had won the seat from the Unionists in 1902, while in North Belfast the British Labour supporter William Walker came close to winning a by-election in 1905. The land agitation had also permitted followers of T. W. Russell MP to win two by-elections against the Unionists in rural Ulster. We now know that these splits were no more than minor shocks to the Unionist political monolith, which presaged absorption into the mainstream movement rather than a fundamental restructuring or a bridging of the ethnic divide. But in 1905–6 change seemed to be in the air. In particular it was not unreasonable for Nationalists in West Belfast to think that a sufficient number of working-class Protestants might vote across the divide to help them regain the seat.

[17] *The Times*, 19 Sept. 1904.   [18] *IN*, 8 Jan. 1906.

By September 1905 the Nationalists had decided to contest West Belfast.[19] On 13 December Redmond and T. P. O'Connor spoke at a rally in the Ulster Hall with Devlin in the chair. No candidate was named, but Devlin's statement that 'although I have been, perhaps, a considerable time absent from Belfast I think I could nearly know the face of every man and woman in this hall' may have been a sufficient hint.[20] Though prudently retaining his uncontested candidacy in North Kilkenny, he was nominated unanimously for West Belfast at a convention on 7 January. His campaign rhetoric was skilful, but not disingenuous. Notwithstanding the ten-year battle with Bishop Henry and the consequent need to avoid the slightest hint of anti-clericalism in order to secure a full turnout of Catholics—the majority of whom had, of course, opposed his local colleagues in the municipal elections between 1897 and 1905—he was able to square the circle of securing a full Catholic vote while making a coherent appeal for working-class Protestant support. Unlike the other candidates, he was, he said, 'a Belfast man . . . sprung from the people', and 'as devotedly attached to the cause of labour as . . . to the cause of Irish nationality'. He claimed Arthur Henderson, Keir Hardie, and John Burns among his 'close personal friends'.[21] He had been 'in close and active association with the Labour Party' in the previous parliament and was in favour of the taxation of land values, improved housing and the protection of town tenants, old age pensions, and state ownership of Irish railways. His address did not include the term 'home rule', stating simply that the prosperity of the country and its people could be properly advanced only 'by the Irish people having the right to manage their own affairs'.[22] The *Irish News* cautiously admitted that Devlin lacked 'the official endorsement of the Labour Representation Committee, not being the nominee of any trades council', but he was shortly afterwards able to secure the official support of the Belfast Trades Council as 'the candidate most in harmony with the demands of the workers'.[23] Devlin also brought William Walker, the Labour candidate for North Belfast, to address UIL meetings. Walker was an opponent of home rule, and the City Police Commissioner thought that his UIL appearance was 'a sign of the times'.[24] Devlin declared that, while he would continue to differ from Walker and Sloan on fundamental questions, if they were elected he would 'co-operate with them in everything that can appeal to the cause of labour'.[25] Sloan was re-elected, but Walker once again lost narrowly.[26]

Devlin's various appeals for Protestant support have been regarded with some scepticism, both by political opponents and by historians. Certainly it is true that, while the UIL's campaign song was 'Orange and Green will carry the day', Devlin's campaigning had in practice to be restricted to Catholic

[19] *NS*, 30 Sept. 1905.   [20] Ibid., 23 Dec. 1905.   [21] Ibid.
[22] Ibid., 13 Jan. 1906.
[23] *IN*, 12 Jan. 1906; letter from J. Murphy, Secretary, Belfast Trades Council, *IN*, 16 Jan. 1906.
[24] RIC County Inspectors' Reports, Belfast, Jan. 1906 (INA).
[25] *NS*, 20 Jan. 1906.   [26] John Gray, *City in Revolt* (Belfast, 1985), 36–41.

neighbourhoods. But he did have offprints made from the *Irish News* report of his speech calling for Protestant support, which suggests the intent to circulate them in neighbourhoods where the *Irish News* would not be read.[27] The *Star* claimed that 100 Protestants had attended the meeting in West Belfast UIL Hall, and 'twice that number were present in the National Club'.[28] Two prominent Protestant labour leaders later testified that the UIL had given them 200 tickets for Devlin's Ulster Hall meeting to distribute on the Shankill, and that they had used their influence to encourage Protestant workers to vote for Devlin.[29] Devlin's non-sectarian labour appeal may have been over-optimistic—hopelessly so in the light of what was to happen a few years later—but the appeal was coherent and, in the context of 1906, not entirely unrealistic. The Russellite and Sloanite movements had made him more optimistic about the conversion of the 'Protestant democracy'. There was a strong class base to the Conservative and Unionist Party, especially visible in its selection of candidates. Likewise there was a growing Labour movement in Belfast, and even in the changed atmosphere of 1912–22 there was a group of rising trade-union activists who were converted by the ideas of James Connolly, with a significant following of 'rotten Prods' who were driven from their work alongside the Catholics in 1912 and 1920.

But skilful rhetoric was not the only, and probably not the most important, factor in Devlin's campaign. Even where genuine appeals were made to the other side, a key part of voting was still the ethnic roll-call. The *Northern Star* could write that 'the Protestant and Catholic working-man fought shoulder to shoulder on behalf of the great principle of democratic progress', while warning in the same paragraph that 'it is in the registration courts . . . that the fight is really won'.[30] Catholic and Protestant newspapers agreed that there was still a Protestant majority on the West Belfast electoral register: 4,704 to 4,168, or a Protestant advantage of 536.[31] In fact Devlin won the 1906 election by a majority of sixteen over his Liberal Unionist opponent, Captain J. R. Smiley, and was hailed by the *Northern Star* as 'the "little corporal" who has gallantly carried the flag of Liberty and Democracy to success'.[32] It was claimed that, in an overall turnout of 95 per cent, the 'Nationalists' (that is, the Catholics) had polled 96 per cent of 'their' vote and the Protestants/Unionists 94 per cent of theirs. In these circumstances the *Northern Star*'s estimate that somewhere in the region of 380 Protestants—or at least Devlin's own claim of 200—must have voted for Devlin does not seem unlikely.[33] But the crucial factor in this outcome was the intervention of a third candidate, Alexander M. Carlisle, who stood as an independent Liberal Unionist, 'opposed to home rule . . . and a staunch supporter of Free Trade', winning 153 votes.[34] He was the brother-in-law and

[27] James Wood Archive (LHL).   [28] *NS*, 20 Jan. 1906.
[29] Boyle, *Irish Labour Movement*, 316.   [30] *NS*, 28 July 1906.
[31] A. Morgan, *Labour and Partition* (London, 1991), 32.   [32] *NS*, 27 Jan. 1906.
[33] Ibid. For Devlin's claim, see *Leader*, 17 Feb. 1906.   [34] *NS*, 13 Jan. 1906.

senior colleague of W. J. Pirrie, Chairman of Harland and Wolff. Pirrie had been greatly angered when passed over for the Unionist nomination in South Belfast in 1902, and was again ignored for the West Belfast nomination in 1906. He then immediately joined the Liberal Party and funded it to such a level that he was raised to the peerage as Baron Pirrie of Belfast in June 1906. Less publicly, but no less certainly, he helped to bring about Devlin's victory by encouraging his brother-in-law to split the Unionist vote.[35] Home rule was clearly regarded by this ultimate symbol of Ulster Protestant capitalism as less objectionable than allowing a personal slight to go unanswered.

It seems unlikely that Devlin or his friends were actively involved in instigating Carlisle's candidature, but once it was announced it quickly became clear from Devlin's rhetoric that he had grasped the situation and knew how to milk it for all it was worth. He suggested that the 'deadhead' Smiley, son of a landed baronet, was less of an electoral challenge than the 'capitalist' Carlisle, who was 'the formidable opponent in this contest'. His colleague Denis Kilbride MP said that 'if Mr Carlisle by any misfortune ever got into the House of Commons he would be the greatest foe they ever had to fight . . . If Captain Smiley got in . . . no one would care two pence what he said.'[36] In effect these two Catholic Nationalists were discreetly campaigning by remote control in Protestant West Belfast so as to maximize Carlisle's vote. This was just as well, for Carlisle held no meetings at all. After the election the Nationalists changed their tune, dismissing his campaign as 'merely a protest' that 'no one ever took . . . seriously', but discreetly thanking him by expressing admiration for his character 'as a self-respecting citizen who refused to be intimidated'.[37] After the election was over, and Devlin had paraded as 'the man who won the West', the Nationalist election rhetoric of 'Orange and Green will carry the day' switched, at least in the editorial columns of the *Star*, to claims that Devlin's 'was a victory won by all the Catholic people'.[38]

'IN THE CLOSEST SYMPATHY WITH ADVANCED OPINIONS': DEVLIN AND LABOUR

Devlin was once described to King Edward VII by Winston Churchill as belonging 'to a new type of Irish politician—progressive, democratic and radical; and he is of course in the closest sympathy with advanced opinions in Great Britain'.[39] Jim Larkin and James Connolly, on the other hand, denounced Devlin as an enemy of labour, Connolly equating him with Carson as a sectarian leader. The revived grouping of Nationalist Party MPs that Devlin led in Northern

---

[35] Emmet Larkin, *James Larkin: Irish Labour Leader, 1876–1947* (London, 1965), 285–86; Herbert Jefferson, *Viscount Pirrie of Belfast* (Belfast, 1948), 100, 135–6.
[36] *IN*, 13 Jan. 1906.   [37] Ibid., 20 Jan. 1906.   [38] Ibid., 14 Apr. 1906.
[39] Churchill to King Edward VII, 27 Apr. 1910 (CP 12/15/65).

Fig. 5.2. Two hostile impressions of Catholic West Belfast by a Unionist cartoonist, *c.*1912

Ireland after 1925 later came to be characterized as 'green Tories'. On several occasions, as an Irish Nationalist, Devlin worked against Labour candidates at elections—in British elections prior to 1918, where his party almost always supported the Liberals; in Dublin College Green, in the by-election of 1915, where his AOH colleague John D. Nugent was opposed by a candidate of the recently formed Irish Labour Party; and in Northern Ireland in 1929. When standing as an Independent candidate for Liverpool Exchange in the general election of 1922 he chose to accept the backing of the Liberals rather than take the *Catholic Herald*'s advice and seek the support of Labour.[40] His friends, especially in his later years, tended to be small businessmen, professional people, and priests, rather than labour activists. Yet the *Northern Star*—his journalistic mouthpiece during his early career—was a voice of trade-union as well as national issues. In 1906 the *Star* declared that 'the democracy of Belfast . . . should put every ounce of energy they possess into the fight against the grasping greed of capitalism and the overweening vanity of deadhead politicians'.[41] Throughout his parliamentary career Devlin was strongly associated with radical industrial reform; he was, and remained, the idol of the Belfast mill girls; in 1918 William O'Brien thought dismissively that he would become 'a mere English Labourite with a Belfast accent'.[42] The brief answer to all this is that he was a party organizer and a political pragmatist who was an established, socially radical member of a Nationalist party before Labour seriously entered the national political scene in either Ireland or Britain. But, in a survey of his activities in relation to both labour and Labour, it is possible to discern an implicit ideology.

During the 1890s there was growing interest in the Catholic community in social questions—manifested especially in Pope Leo XIII's *De rerum novarum* of 1891, which proscribed socialism but embraced social reform. The early Scottish Labour MP, and later cabinet minister, John Wheatley, an Irishman by origin who had begun his career in the Lanarkshire UIL, said that this made British socialism acceptable to Catholics.[43] Speaking in Hyde Park in July 1903, Devlin described both Cardinal Manning and Pope Leo XIII as having been 'champions of the working people'.[44] Opposition to capitalism was associated with opposition to emigration. The *Northern Star* thought that the values of 'Henry George's triumphant democracy' in America were being replaced by 'grasping, grinding, soulless monopolists'.[45] The pre-socialist radicalism of Henry George, with its emphasis on land values, was Devlin's implicit guiding ideology. A long-serving colleague of Devlin's was Michael McKeown, who was a leading Belfast trade unionist, a Trades Council member, and a branch chairman of the UIL. In 1907 McKeown was elected to the Belfast City Council as a Nationalist. The Trades

---

[40] *Catholic Herald*, 11 Nov. 1922.   [41] *NS*, 10 Nov. 1906.

[42] O'Brien to T. M. Healy, 18 Sept. 1918 (NLI, OBP 8556/20).

[43] J. J. Smyth, *Labour in Glasgow, 1896–1936: Socialism, Suffrage, Sectarianism* (East Lothian, 2000), 134.

[44] *IN*, 27 July 1903.   [45] Ibid., 25 Dec. 1897.

Council withdrew its candidate, while the advanced nationalist and socialist Daniel McDevitt—later an ally of Connolly and of Sinn Féin—declared that McKeown was 'a very good labour man'.[46] But, from 1908, Labour ceased to give nationalism a free ride in the Falls and Smithfield council wards. The reasons for this are several: the collapse of the Belfast Catholic Association meant that Labour could intervene without creating any undesired side effects; the development of political Labour in Britain, together with the beginnings of Larkinite militancy in Ireland, meant that Labour was no longer inclined to wait; the fact that Labour had lost all its seats on the Belfast City Council in 1907 meant that the Party could no longer afford to regard the Catholic quarter of the city as off limits; while the developing connection between militant socialism and militant republicanism gave another string to the bow of those opposed to the UIL.

In the long run British Labour became a home-rule party, but in the early years it sought to be more flexible. On the one hand, Keir Hardie declared that 'the truest representatives of democratic feeling in the House of Commons were the Irish Parliamentary Party, a fact which the workers of Britain would do well to recognize', while the LRC and the ILP did not regard membership of the UILGB as incompatible with Labour membership. But, when the ILP came to Belfast's Ulster Hall for its annual conference in January 1907, Hardie said that, while he personally favoured home rule, each Labour member was free to vote as he pleased. George N. Barnes 'went so far as to say that the people of England and Scotland had made up their minds that home rule was unattainable', while Arthur Henderson spoke more equivocally in favour of preserving 'one imperial family, and restricting home rule to local matters'.[47] Despite Devlin's alliance with William Walker during the 1906 election, debate at the annual congress of the Irish Trades Union Congress (ITUC) a few weeks later indicated that the sectarian banner was still not entirely broken. A Belfast representative exempted both Tom Sloan and Joe Devlin from the charge that Belfast MPs never voted in the cause of labour, but the predominantly Protestant Belfast Trades Council leadership made its customary proposal that the ITUC should affiliate to the British-based Labour Representation Committee.[48] This was countered by the usual amendment that 'the Irish Party is everything that labour requires'. The former motion was defeated by a combination of UIL and advanced nationalists, while the latter amendment was defeated by a combination of Belfast Protestants and advanced nationalists.[49]

Early in 1907 the Belfast labour picture was transformed dramatically by the intervention of Jim Larkin, a Liverpool Irishman by background and newly appointed organizer for the Liverpool-based National Union of Dock Labourers (NUDL). At this stage Larkin, while opposing the Irish Party's claim to represent Irish labour, still identified with the British-based Labour

[46] Boyle, *Irish Labour Movement*, 288.   [47] Ibid. 324, 240, 243.
[48] Ibid. 235.   [49] Ibid. 234–5.

Representation Committee. William McMullen, then a young shipyard worker at Harland and Wolff, who met Larkin during the 1907 strike, thought him 'vain and petty'.[50] A labour organizer in the docks, reflecting for a BBC programme many years later, thought Larkin 'the best organizer that ever set foot in Ireland—but he wasn't the best negotiator. His attitude—"hit the table and make it bounce"—didn't settle the question.'[51] A fellow veteran thought Larkin 'a brilliant man . . . he had the magnetism for drawing a crowd. He actually made you listen to him . . . But I wouldn't say he was as clever as Connolly . . . whenever he got you organized you see—he just couldn't handle you the same as Connolly.'[52] In February 1907 Larkin was recruiting dockers and carters to his new branch of the NUDL. Then, between April and June, strike activity built up. At the peak, 370 dockers and 200 carters had come out on strike, the combined total rising to 2,340 only when those locked out were included.[53] In June Larkin supported the Labour candidate in the Jarrow by-election against an Irish Nationalist, but in Belfast he declared during the same month that 'Mr Devlin was a working-class member' and had his support. At the same time he appointed Devlin's ally Michael McKeown as secretary of the Belfast branch of the NUDL.[54] Having returned from New Zealand at the end of March 1907, Devlin spent the next three months working in London and Dublin, making arrangements for the Party's nationwide response to the Irish Council Bill debacle. When Redmond suggested Belfast for a major meeting as part of the post-Council Bill campaign, Devlin—without mentioning the strike, or the Orange marching season—suggested that it might be 'better to wind up the series of Home Rule demonstrations, say at the end of December, in Belfast'.[55] Normally never one to miss an opportunity of raising the flag in his native city, Devlin clearly thought that a major Nationalist event in the midst of the strike could only damage the cross-communal (and anti-Unionist) spirit that the strike seemed to be producing.

At the beginning of July troops were sent into Belfast, as the Royal Irish Constabulary (RIC) national reserve force was engaged elsewhere. On 8 July Devlin raised the matter of the strike in the House of Commons for the first time. He drew attention to the fact that, 'owing to the trade dispute in Belfast and the occupation of the streets by armed troops, the trade of the town was almost at a standstill', and called upon the Chief Secretary to press for a settlement by means of government arbitration. Augustine Birrell replied that he could do nothing unless invited to do so by both sides.[56] At this stage a series of

[50] William McMullen interview.

[51] Statement by Mr Hunter. Transcript of BBC NI Radio programme on Larkin and the 1907 Strike, 1957 (Sam Hanna Bell Papers, D3358/1).

[52] Statement by James Clarke, ibid.

[53] Larkin, *James Larkin*, 22; Morgan, *Labour and Partition*, 97.

[54] Gray, *City in Revolt*, 57.   [55] Devlin to Redmond, 29 June 1907 (RP 15181/2).

[56] Parl. Deb., H.C., 4th series, clxxvii. 1174 (8 July 1907).

unsigned letters appeared in the Belfast press complaining about police working conditions. Several policemen were involved in this, and their protest almost culminated in a police strike. Devlin raised the matter in the Commons on 25 July, saying that there was a risk of police mutiny. He suggested that part of the cause was that the police had been instructed 'to put every obstacle in the way of those engaged in the entirely legal occupation of picketing', and called upon the government 'to see that the forces of the Crown were not used entirely in favour of one of the parties to the dispute, but that they were called upon to act impartially'. Moving on to the strike itself, Devlin again urged Birrell to bring about a settlement by arbitration. 'He did not propose to discuss the merits or demerits of the strike. He simply wanted to say that . . . widespread misery was being caused to the masses of the people, and great injury was being done to the industrial progress of the city itself.'[57]

The character and intensity of the conflict changed dramatically in mid-August. This was the classic time of the year for militant demonstrations in the Catholic community, around the Feast of the Assumption on 15 August—known to Belfast Protestants as 'the Micks' Twelfth'—which habitually followed on from Orange domination of the streets during July. Larkin arranged a mass rally at the Custom House Steps for 10 August, inviting the city's four MPs to attend.[58] It was expected that Devlin and Tom Sloan would accept the invitation, but at the last minute Sloan—perhaps sensing the ethnic turn that the police 'mutiny' and the introduction of troops into the city was likely to provoke—declined, leaving Devlin as the sole parliamentarian on the platform. Over 10,000 were present. Devlin's speech was covered more thoroughly in the Unionist papers than in the *Irish News*, though the latter paper was broadly sympathetic to the strike, unlike the Unionist dailies.[59] He declared first that he had 'practically held aloof from any expression of opinion on the issue' lest what he called 'the capitalistic press' might try to characterize the strike as Catholic and Nationalist. He then complained that the employers had refused to submit the matters in dispute to arbitration, and 'there was no necessity for the soldiers at all'.[60] There is no reason to doubt Devlin's reasons for having previously kept public silence on the strike. Had he attempted in any way to take a lead, it would indeed have enabled the Unionists to dismiss the strike as essentially a nationalist activity, as they were to do after the events of 11–12 August. His parliamentary interventions indicated his sympathies, while the *Irish News*, the paper of which he was a director, had been sympathetic to the strike from the beginning, as was his own weekly *Northern Star*.[61] Since it was expected until the last minute that Sloan would also appear on the platform alongside him, it was reasonable for him to expect that

[57] Parl. Deb., H.C., 4th series, clxxix, 207–8 (25 July 1907).
[58] Morgan, *Labour and Partition*, 110.
[59] Larkin, *James Larkin*, 289.   [60] *The Times*, 12 Aug. 1907.
[61] Larkin, *James Larkin*, 30; *NS*, 20 July and 10 Aug. 1907.

the event might help to build on the tentative alliance of the 'orange and green democracies' that had flourished at the time of the 1906 general election.

But on the evenings of 11 and 12 August there were large-scale riots in the Falls area, during which forty-five policemen were injured and soldiers fired on the rioters, leaving two innocent bystanders dead and five injured.[62] It has been suggested that Devlin's criticism of the presence of the military was responsible for provoking the trouble, which was confined exclusively to the Catholic quarter, one historian describing it as 'shameless Nationalist opportunism'.[63] Certainly the Unionist papers thought it was evidence that the whole thing was a nationalist conspiracy.[64] In fact Larkin was probably not far wrong when, on his return to the city the next day, he said that 'drink was at the bottom of all that had occurred', while Devlin had no record of inciting violence in his speeches.[65] In any event the second week in August, leading up to the 15th, was the peak of the Belfast Catholic rioting year. Furthermore, Larkin had recently extended his strike-organizing activities directly into the Falls, where the mainly Catholic deep-sea dockers, at first not directly involved in what had been a predominantly Protestant strike, had now been laid off. On 8 August Larkin, with some degree of success, urged mill-workers in the Falls to join the strike. On the 9th, the day before Devlin's speech, trouble began on the Falls when strikers and mill-workers attacked some strike-breaking carters, which brought the military into the district.[66] Devlin's intervention was thus far from central to the events that followed.

The day after the riots, though five weeks after Devlin had first urged the idea in the House of Commons, the government sent a Board of Trade industrial negotiator, George Askwith, to Belfast. About 1,000 carters, many of whom had originally been locked out, got a favourable deal, with wage increases and shorter hours.[67] In the case of the 500 dockers who were still on strike, the outcome was less satisfactory, with 'considerable discontent on the waterfront after Larkin quit the city'.[68] Larkin was to admit before a later government inquiry in 1912 that 'the Belfast strike eventually ended in disaster for the men'.[69] Askwith's contribution, however, backed by a certain amount of government pressure on particular firms, was a positive one. Despite the Prime Minister's rejection of Devlin's subsequent call for 'a permanent board of arbitration', the Belfast case turned out to be the first of many such missions that George Askwith undertook between then and 1919.

The 1907 strike was for the most part a cross-communal class movement, involving unskilled and previously non-unionized workers. A relatively small proportion of the city's workforce came close to bringing trade to a standstill, while

[62] Ibid., 30; Gray, *City in Revolt*, 156–9.   [63] Gray, *City in Revolt*, 152–3, 209.
[64] Ibid. 163.   [65] Ibid. 164.   [66] Ibid. 154
[67] Larkin, *James Larkin*, 32.   [68] Morgan, *Labour and Partition*, 114.
[69] John McHugh, 'The Belfast Labour Disputes and Riots of 1907', *International Review of Social History*, 22/1 (1977), 17.

Fig. 5.3. The orator,
1915 and 1922

MR. JOSEPH DEVLIN,
Independent candidate for Exchange, 1922

the street-based nature of most carting work made it possible for sympathizers not directly involved in the strike to intervene effectively in bring work to a halt. The majority of the strikers and their local leaders were Protestants, though Catholics were also involved in significant numbers. This reflected the ethnic industrial balance, for almost three-quarters of the city's carters and three-fifths of the city's dockers were Protestants (see Table 2.5). The strike clearly had support on both sides of the ethnic divide. To this extent it was a continuation of the alliance of 'orange and green democracies' that Devlin had been seeking to build. The restriction of the serious riots of 11–12 August to the Catholic quarter drove a fissure into this alliance. As the future Ulster Volunteer Force (UVF) gun-runner Fred Crawford wrote to a friend: 'what a blessing all the rioting took place in the Catholic quarter of the city. This branded the whole thing as a nationalist movement.'[70] The Unionist press also reported allegations that, whereas Protestants had borne the brunt of the strike hardships, Catholics had been favoured in payouts from the Dockers' and Carters' Strike Fund. On 5 September the Trades Council proposed an investigation into charges of 'sectarian favouritism', but nothing further came of it.[71] Fifty years later a carter and survivor of the strike named John Orr—a name more often Protestant than Catholic—stated on a BBC Northern Ireland radio feature that 'it was just all the same to him [Larkin] no matter what you were—Roman Catholic or Protestant you got—you just got the same as the rest—you got ten shillings a week of strike money'.[72]

A few weeks later Devlin came under attack from the other flank. On 29 September Cardinal Logue declared that 'it is a very ominous thing when we find the politicians of this country entering into an alliance with secularism and socialism under the pretence of securing home rule for Ireland'.[73] Thus by the autumn there was pressure on Devlin to distance himself from Larkin and the strike. 'I knew nothing about the strike in its inception', he said in the Ulster Hall, and 'nothing whatever about the strike in its progress...I have never spoken to Mr Larkin in my life but once.'[74] But this mild backtracking was all that Devlin needed to do to keep the Catholic inter-class alliance together. Unlike in the Protestant community, where the events of 1907 began to drive a wedge between trade-unionist activism and the wider Protestant community, within the Catholic community 'there was little scope for friction between the working class and those who constituted the nucleus of a future Catholic bourgeoisie'.[75]

It has often been said that the social radicalism of the Irish Party was restricted to agrarian matters. But Devlin, representing an industrial constituency, spoke frequently and consistently at Westminster on urban labour issues. His main

---

[70] Hepburn (ed.), *Conflict of Nationality*, 67.   [71] Morgan, *Labour and Partition*, 115.
[72] Statement by John Orr. Transcript of BBC NI Radio programme on Larkin and the 1907 Strike, 1957 (Sam Hanna Bell Papers, D3358/1).
[73] Gray, *City in Revolt*, 166.   [74] Larkin, *James Larkin*, 34.
[75] Gray, *City in Revolt*, 214.

concerns were with conditions and wages in the linen and related industries (the main employer of his own constituents), with unemployment and distress, and with the fair resolution of strikes. He was an admirer of the radical Liberal Sir Charles Dilke (1843–1911), who, he told Dilke's biographer shortly after his death, was 'an example and inspiration to younger men . . . I myself can never forget all his kindness in the House of Commons and the generous assistance he always gave me in the social work in which I was interested.'[76] In 1907 Devlin pressed the government to implement more effective inspection of the sanitation and ventilation of mills and factories, drawing attention to the high death rate from consumption.[77] He was especially concerned about the conditions of female workers, of whom there were between 30,000 and 40,000 in Belfast. The wages of women and girls, he alleged, ranged for 7*s.* to 10*s.* per week and they were 'worse paid in Belfast than in any other city in the United Kingdom', and he called for an extension of the activities of the Commission on Sweating.[78] He frequently raised the matter of the violation of the Truck Acts, alleging that employers of outworkers deducted wages from employees in ways that were illegal or that should be made so.[79] He drew public attention to the situation of 'half-timers'—that is, children between the ages of 12 and 14, who were permitted to work for half the week in factories. Around 2,000 were so employed in Belfast, working from 6.30 a.m. to 6 p.m. on three alternate days per week for a wage of 3*s.* to 4*s.* per week (see Table 5.1).[80] During the linen-trade depression of 1907–8, Devlin called for local-authority relief works to be organized, and for an allocation to Belfast of funds from the Unemployed Workmen Act of 1905.[81] In 1910 he declared that

in Belfast there were sweated women and children and unemployed men, who felt the curse of the whole social system as deeply as it was felt in England, and was he to sit here and listen to fiscal fables in the supposed interest of distillers and landlords while his constituents were to be robbed of all the beneficent advantages they hoped to secure through the agency of the budget?[82]

In June 1910 he persuaded Churchill to instigate an inquiry by the factory inspectorate into the system of fines for 'late attendance and other trivial offences' that was being enforced by employers.[83]

The most important issue in which Devlin took a prominent role was the pressure for the extension of the new Trade Boards Act to include the Irish linen industry.[84] This arose from the 1909 report of Dr Bailie, Belfast's Medical Officer of Health, which drew attention to the poor 'conditions of

---

[76] Devlin to G. Tuckwell, 20 May 1911 (Dilke Papers, Add. MS 43967, fo. 211).
[77] Parl. Deb., H.C., 4th series, clxxv. 854–5 (6 June 1907); ibid. cvxxiii. 287 (25 Apr. 1907).
[78] Ibid. 1566 (13 June 1907).   [79] Ibid. 658 (5 June 1907).
[80] Ibid. clxxiii. 869 (1 May 1907); clxxxiv. 811–12 (19 Jan. 1908); clxxxvii. 187 (6 Apr. 1908); ibid., 5th series, i. 1005 (25 Feb. 1909).
[81] Ibid., 4th series, clxxxix. 187, 740 (21 and 25 May 1908).   [82] *The Times*, 28 Apr. 1910.
[83] Parl. Deb., H.C., 5th series, xviii. 671 (27 June 1910).   [84] Ibid. xix. 342 (13 July 1910).

Table 5.1. Number of persons employed in the Belfast linen industry, 1901 and 1904

Employees	1901		1904	
	Number	% female	Number	% female
Persons above 18 years of age	20,916	76.9	21,437	77.8
Full-timers aged 13–17 years	5,170	68.1	5,172	69.1
Children employed as half-timers	2,591	66.3	1,951	65.0

Source: Parl. Deb., H.C., 4th series, clxxxiv. 1569–70b (25 Feb. 1908).

work and the rates of payment to outworkers and in-workers in connection with the linen trade'. Bailie's work was taken up by other activists, including the Presbyterian clergyman David Purves, who thought it remarkable that Dr Bailie, 'this underling of the Corporation, whose appointment was one of their pet jobs, has been a Daniel come to judgment on the city'.[85] Bailie's report revealed grossly low wages and harsh 'fines', together with appalling conditions in the homes of outworkers, and Devlin made the additional allegation in Parliament that employers were evading their legal responsibilities by deliberately discontinuing the employment of outworkers during the two short periods each year in which returns of information were required.[86] In 1911 his continued pressure on this matter began to produce action from the government. He pointed out in March that there were more than 8,000 home-workers in the Belfast linen trade, that in 174 cases it had been necessary to issue cleansing orders regarding such homes, that the rates of pay were often less than 1*d.* per hour, that time spent delivering material to the factory, maintenance of sewing machines, and the cost of thread were none of them paid for by employers, and that 'it cannot be too frequently or strenuously insisted that such underpaid labour must inevitably cripple, and in great part nullify, the good effects of any scheme of health reform'.[87] Shortly afterwards Devlin told Dilke's biographer that 'you will be glad to hear that we are getting the Inquiry into sweating in Belfast'.[88] When the Committee reported in 1912, Devlin called upon the government to 'take steps forthwith' to have the provisions of the Trade Boards Act applied to the trades concerned.

Another major issue for the Liberal Government during these years was the question of women's suffrage and the related matter of suffragette militancy. Devlin was a supporter of women's suffrage, and, writing in his diary in 1913, the

[85] Revd D. Purves to Sir C. Brett, 18 and 29 Aug. 1910 (Lestrange & Brett Papers, D1905/3/15).
[86] *The Times*, 16 Sept. 1910.   [87] Parl. Deb., H.C., 5th series, xxii. 703 (2 Mar. 1911).
[88] Ibid. xxiv. 434 (11 Apr. 1911); Devlin to G. Tuckwell, 20 May 1911 (Dilke Papers, Add. MS 43967, fo. 211).

Manchester Guardian editor C. P. Scott described him as 'a suffragist'.[89] Devlin was, however, opposed to the more extreme suffragette methods, as he was to the physical-force movement in Irish nationalism. In reply to an inquiry in 1912 he wrote that

I can assure you that no organization that I have any connection with will follow the tactics of the English suffragettes. Being myself a strong supporter of the movement for the enfranchisement of women, I resent as deeply any attacks on suffrage meetings as I do the conduct of suffragettes who have damaged, if they have not destroyed, a great cause.[90]

He was, however, criticized by the suffragette newspaper, the *Irish Citizen*, for 'leaving the wives out of the Home Rule Bill'.[91] One factor that caused some confusion over his views was a practical one. So long as women did not have the vote in parliamentary elections, it was in the interests of the political parties for the designated ratepayer in each household to be, so far as possible, an adult male. Devlin on one occasion in 1913 told a female audience in St Mary's Hall that it was

in the revision Courts that elections were fought and won, and nothing could be finer or more unselfish than the manner in which the working women of West Belfast came to the court to secure votes for their husbands and fathers and brothers. The position which they occupied on the Register was due in a large degree to the self-sacrifice of the women of the division.[92]

This complex and, at times, controversial procedure was in fact a pragmatic reason for Devlin to support the enfranchisement of women!

Devlin continued to be active in Parliament on social and industrial matters, taking up, especially, such matters as the reinstatement of activists following the railway strike of 1911 and the payment of relief to Belfast labourers put out of work by the British coal strike in the same winter.[93] In the case of the railway strike he declared that 'the whole cause of the strike was the conduct of the railway directors and the scandalous wages they paid to their workers'.[94] All in all there is no reason to doubt the sincerity of Devlin's social radicalism or to suggest that it was a mere front for nationalism, any more than Connolly's socialism should be dismissed as a front for republicanism. Devlin's views on social questions and his parliamentary methods were very similar to those of the Lib–Labs and early Labour Party members in Britain, who achieved so much in the first era of radical social reform. Connolly and Larkin, whose standing in Irish popular memory is so much higher, were in fact marginal figures in terms of achievement, comparable with Tom Mann or Ben Tillett in Britain.

---

[89] T. Wilson (ed.), *The Political Diaries of C. P. Scott, 1911–1928* (London, 1970), 65.
[90] Devlin to Mrs F. Cox, 1 Aug. 1912 (Sheehy-Skeffington Papers, 33603/17).
[91] *Irish Citizen*, 24 Jan. 1914.   [92] *IN*, 1 Sept. 1913.
[93] Parl. Deb., H.C., 5th series, xxxi. 1203; xxxii. 32 (22 and 29 Nov. 1911); xxxiv. 1553 (29 Feb. 1912).
[94] Ibid. xxxiv. 1397 (28 Feb. 1912).

SCREECHING WILLIAM AND THE LITTLE BAG
OF VENOM: THE BREAK WITH O'BRIEN

By 1908 it was fairly clear that attempts to patch up William O'Brien's relationship with the mainstream of the Irish Party had failed. Once the Party leadership had persuaded the Liberal Government to introduce a new land bill, applying radical changes to the 1903 Act, the ground was prepared for a major battle. O'Brien believed that the changes would wreck land purchase by removing the financial oil that had enabled it to progress to the extent it had, and he advanced these views strongly at a meeting of the Irish Parliamentary Party in April 1908. Majority opinion, however, took the view that the 1903 Act was grinding to a halt, that its finances needed restructuring, that prices needed bringing under control if it was to work more effectively, that something had to be done about the eleven-month grazing system, and that an element of compulsory sale needed to be introduced. Thus, when the party's national convention was called for 9–10 February 1909 to seek approval for its policies, O'Brien proposed an amendment to the effect that 'such a bill must lead to the stoppage of land purchase for an indefinite number of years' and postpone for at least fifty years the solution of the problem of congestion in the west and of the untenanted grasslands.[95]

The Convention met in Dublin, with around 3,000 delegates. John Redmond took the chair, with Devlin at his side, on a small dais. Most of the party's MPs, together with a few other prominent figures, sat on the platform.[96] The first morning was occupied with a routine resolution in support of home rule, followed by a resolution in support of the Irish Party, which was the subject of several amendments, including one from the Young Ireland Branch (YIB), which supported the Land Bill but otherwise called for 'strenuous opposition' to the Liberal Government. In a speech in Belfast a fortnight before the Convention Devlin had stated that during the past year the Liberal Party's position on home rule had become 'clearly ascertained and fully defined'. His response at the Convention was marred only by a touch of arrogance towards those young men of the YIB, whom he sarcastically referred to as 'these eminent statesmen'. 'I tell Mr Cruise O'Brien and Mr Sheehy-Skeffington here today that the Irish Party do not require to receive advice or dictation from them,' he said. He 'demolished their case', reported the *Irish News* unsurprisingly, but 'it was perhaps too merciless a performance'. On the second day, when the attendance was considerably smaller, it was the YIB's turn to achieve some success, on the question of whether matriculation in Irish language should be a requirement for

---

[95] *IN*, 10 Feb. 1909.
[96] Details of the Convention are taken from the *IN* reports of 10 and 11 Feb. 1909.

entry into the new National University. Despite a strong speech opposing this along classic liberal individualist lines from John Dillon, the proposal was passed by a vote of three to one.

But the main business came in the first afternoon, in the form of a vote of confidence on the Party's support for the Land Bill. Redmond opened the debate, then William O'Brien introduced his amendment. He was on his feet for more than an hour but was shouted down for most of the time. At one point his ally Eugene Crean MP moved from his seat on the platform towards the dais, apparently with the intention of urging O'Brien to give up the impossible challenge. Intercepted by stewards, he then approached Redmond from behind, with a view to gaining his attention. Redmond later testified in court that a scuffle broke out behind him on the platform and that the first he knew of it was when his chair was 'violently seized, and he turned round and saw Mr Crean in a state of the greatest possible excitement—perfectly white with excitement—clutching the back of the chair'.[97] The O'Brienites alleged that Crean was handled roughly and that Devlin, in the midst of the two-minute furore, had called 'throw the fellow out'. O'Brien and his seconders then continued amidst great opposition. The resolution in support of the Land Bill was then passed on a show of hands, in which it was stated by Redmond from the platform that only ten delegates had voted for O'Brien's amendment. This figure perhaps strains credibility—giving evidence in the subsequent court case the O'Brienite Revd James Clancy claimed that 400 or 500 people out of 2,200 present in the hall did not raise their hands in support of the Party's Land Bill motion.[98] But there is no doubt that O'Brien and his colleagues suffered a resounding defeat. A month before the Convention the *Leader*—which had long since nicknamed O'Brien 'Screeching William'—commented that the whole object of the enormous gathering was 'to trump O'Brien', and that anyone who set out to move an adverse resolution would want 'the lungs of Stentor'.[99]

Although the O'Brienites had been humiliated at the Convention, they did not let the matter rest. Eugene Crean brought criminal charges against Devlin and Assistant Secretary Denis Johnston on the grounds that they had acted in a disorderly manner with the intention of preventing the meeting from transacting its intended business, that they had incited others to do likewise, and that Devlin had 'procured the commission of an assault upon the complainant'. The action was brought under legislation passed in 1908, known popularly as the 'Suffragette Act'. Tim Healy was retained as senior counsel for the plaintiff, Serjeant Moriarty defended Devlin, while the former *Northern Star* editor W. D. Harbinson, now a Dublin barrister—though denounced by the plaintiff's solicitor during the trial as 'an insulting pup'—was Devlin's junior counsel.[100] The case was heard over no less than seven days in the Dublin Police Court. During the proceedings it was

---

[97] *IN*, 10 Mar. 1909.   [98] Ibid., 9 Mar. 1909.
[99] *Leader*, 9 Jan. 1909.   [100] *IN*, 9 and 6 Mar. 1909.

confirmed by the defence that 100 stewards had been appointed to keep order during the Convention, some of whom were volunteers and others of whom were paid 10*s.* for the two days, and that 50 of them were issued with wooden batons, which all pertinent witnesses stated they were instructed to keep in their pockets except in extreme circumstances. Only two of the stewards, it was claimed, were Hibernians.[101] Redmond testified that batons had never previously been issued at Party conventions, but reference was made by the defence to the fact that at a previous convention of 1907, when no stewards were employed, a serious attempt had been made by 250 Sinn Féiners to storm the doors.[102]

In a long opening address, and an even longer five-hour closing address, Healy made repeated references to 'Belfast' and 'Belfastmen' as being the core of the problem. 'Everything in this case had a Belfast flavour . . . The [admission] tickets were printed in Belfast, the agenda was printed in Belfast, the bludgeon-men came from Belfast and Mr Joseph Devlin represented Belfast.' At one point Moriarty asked: 'What was the object of introducing the question of Cork accents or Belfast accents?'[103] In fact 'Belfast' was throughout used by Healy as a term of abuse, implying sinister, behind-the-scenes influence. In his cross-examination of Redmond, he 'asked why the whole of the arrangements for this convention were given into the hands of the Belfast clique', to which Redmond replied 'they were not. They were given into the hands of the General Secretary of the organization and his staff.' Redmond acknowledged, however, that Belfast was 'ahead of any place in Ireland' in terms of its contributions to Party funds.[104] Belfast in turn was linked by Healy to the AOH — or rather to 'the ancient remains of the Molly Maguire faction', which Devlin had 'galvanized' and 'dubbed' the Ancient Order of Hibernians in an attempt to 'usurp the copyright' of the AOH in America, 'a noble and honourable institution . . . [that] . . . had no connection with Ireland'. It was these Molly Maguires, claimed Healy, who supplied the 'poor dupes who were imported at ten shillings a head to create this disorder . . .' Why should these 'sturdy agriculturalists of the Falls Road, who probably would not know how to tell a plough from a poleaxe', be so interested in the price Irish farmers were giving for their land. 'Instructions were given', he continued, 'that any man with a Cork accent was not to be allowed near the platform.' Another Cork witness claimed that during the disruption of O'Brien's speech 'men with Northern accents were around, and were using filthy expressions'.[105] The disruption of O'Brien's speech, claimed Healy, 'came from a small section — Mr Devlin's importations from Belfast'. Redmond, who had been sitting beside Devlin, denied that his colleague had shouted any such words as 'throw the fellow out' at any point.[106]

The whole case was something of a shambles, with the prosecution witnesses providing very little evidence to support the charges. Healy's first three witnesses

---

[101] Ibid., 6 Mar. 1909.   [102] Ibid., 8 and 10 Mar. 1909.
[103] Ibid., 10 Mar. 1909.   [104] Ibid., 11 Mar. 1909.
[105] Ibid., 8 Mar. 1909.   [106] Ibid., 10 Mar. 1909.

were all stewards hired in Dublin. They each received 10*s.* for their efforts, and denied having been provided with alcohol during the day. They saw no batons being used. The first two witnesses both took the view that the uproar during O'Brien's speech seemed to arise from 'a general wish not to hear Mr O'Brien' rather than from any organized disruption by a particular group. Healy's third witness betrayed him altogether, stating that he had not been issued with a baton, had seen no batons in the hall, and had heard 'no talk about men with Cork accents'. Finally Healy had to request the magistrate's permission to treat him as a hostile witness.

The main defence argument was that O'Brien was shouted down because of the Convention's general dislike of what he was saying. It was the planned intention of the O'Brienites, they alleged, to attempt to talk out the first day so as to postpone the vote on the Land Bill until the second day, by when the Belfast special train would have returned home and the attendance would have been considerably smaller. Crean, in particular, was questioned about what had taken place at an informal gathering called by O'Brien at the Imperial Hotel on the previous evening.[107] Moriarty asked him if he had heard O'Brien say that 'Joe Devlin was a little bag of venom'. Crean would neither confirm nor deny this.[108] Moriarty claimed that only 24 of the 100 stewards came from Belfast. The Belfast stewards were selected by Hugh Martin, a Falls Road tobacconist and long-standing member of the Belfast UIL Executive. Only seven of the twenty-four, he claimed, were paid a fee for their two days' work, and only two of them were on duty inside the hall. Dan McCann JP, treasurer of the Belfast UIL, testified that 193 men and women had travelled on the special train, of which only 55 were from Belfast, 27 representing the UIL and 18 the AOH. Healy declared that he would show that there were a great many more, but the list of Belfast delegates printed in the *Irish News* on the day of the Convention included 25 UIL delegates, 24 AOH delegates, and 6 Nationalist members of the Belfast Corporation, confirming a total of 55 with only slight internal discrepancies. This total included several professional men and a number of prosperous publicans, further eroding Healy's 'Belfast roughs' characterization. The *Irish News* list indicated clearly that the overwhelming majority of Ulster delegates represented rural areas.[109]

Healy concluded sarcastically that Redmond was entitled to say the discussion should have concluded on the first day, 'because the sturdy agriculturalists of the Falls Road were anxious to get home to their bullocks and turnips'.[110] He called for Devlin to be convicted.[111] But the magistrate's decision, announced some weeks later, was that the charges were not upheld, and that Crean would have to pay the defendants' costs of £150 or face two months' imprisonment. The

---

[107] *IN*, 11 Mar. 1909.   [108] Ibid., 9 Mar. 1909.
[109] Ibid., 10 Feb. and 12 Mar. 1909.
[110] Ibid., 12 Mar. 1909.   [111] Ibid., 13 Mar. 1909.

Irish Independent, not a newspaper normally friendly towards the Irish Party, commented that 'anyone who has followed the evidence' could have anticipated no other verdict. 'Irregularities there were at the Convention which could not be justified . . . but the police court was not the way to deal with it.' Likewise the *Independent* did 'not see our way to joining the attacks which were made on the AOH'.[112] The *Leader*, a very independent and critical supporter of the Irish Party, dismissed the court case as 'simply a device by which William might again appear before a public that is heartily sick of him'. The 'real villain', it thought, was Healy—'What did he ever do for Catholic Ireland except take briefs from it?'[113] O'Brien subsequently suffered a health breakdown and spent several months recuperating in Italy. Before he left he closed his Dublin-based weekly paper, the *Irish People*, and began a Cork-based weekly, the *Cork Accent*. At the same time he established a new organization, the All-for-Ireland League or, as the *Leader* called it, the 'All-for-William League'.[114]

The whole thrust of the O'Brien–Healy case had been that the AOH Board of Erin had penetrated to the heart of the UIL and injected it with Belfast sectarianism. O'Brien continued to believe that Devlin was 'the real author of his downfall', one of the chapters in his volume of memoirs dealing with this period being entitled 'Molly Maguire Imperatrix'. He continued to maintain that he was shouted down by a 'victorious minority', who were 'mostly young tradesmen or labourers, who assuredly knew little more of the land bill under debate than of the latest Assyrian inscriptions'.[115] But the Protestant Nationalist Richard McGhee thought that O'Brien's 'rascally attacks on the AOH are about his greatest disgrace . . . I well remember how warm he was in their praise when we were organizing for the 1900 Convention . . . beside being a fanatic he is also a most infernal hypocrite.'[116] But, despite his humiliation on this occasion, O'Brien was to raise the whole matter of the AOH again in Parliament two years later.

'ROME RULE': THE McCANN CASE, THE NATIONAL INSURANCE ACT, AND THE AOH AGAIN

As home rule moved towards the top of the government's agenda, the Ulster Unionists, aided to some extent by the All-for-Ireland League (AfIL), sought to draw the attention of Ulster Protestant and British audiences to some of the dangers inherent in a home-rule regime in Ireland. One example was the McCann case. Alexander McCann, a Catholic, had married a young Presbyterian

---

[112] *Irish Independent*, 16 Apr. 1909; O'Brien, *Olive Branch*, 454.
[113] *Leader*, 20 Mar. 1909.   [114] Ibid., 13 Mar. 1909.
[115] O'Brien, *Olive Branch*, 451–2.
[116] McGhee to Dillon, 26 Mar. 1909 (DP 6757/1048).

at a Presbyterian church in Ballymena, Co. Antrim, in May 1908. Their first child was subsequently baptized by the same minister. The family then moved to the Falls Road area of Belfast, the customary location for mixed marriages in the city. The marriage got into difficulties, and the police were called several times to deal with domestic conflict. McCann left the family home in October 1910, taking the children with him, shortly after which he attempted to have the second child baptized in St Paul's RC Church in West Belfast. Mrs McCann attempted to disrupt the ceremony, and, following a scuffle, the couple had to be ejected by the sacristan. McCann and the children then went missing, it later being rumoured that McCann had left Ireland for New York and that the children had been brought to New York to join him by a young woman in February 1911.[117]

The case came to public attention in the context of the *Ne Temere* decree issued by the Vatican on 19 April 1908. It ruled that only marriages made by a Catholic priest were valid in the eyes of the Church, whether or not both parties to the marriage were Catholics. Patrick McKenna, the Bishop of Clogher, took the view that, rather than 'allow parties to combine in concubinage', a priest ought to assist at a mixed marriage even if the Protestant partner refused to give the guarantees. But, when McKenna sought to put these views to his fellow Irish bishops, 'he was looked at as a dangerous sort of fellow, smelling of heresy'.[118] It was alleged that the McCann marriage had broken up after a Belfast priest told them that their marriage was null and void, and they would need to remarry in a Catholic ceremony, which Mrs McCann refused to do. McCann then departed with the children—or, in another version of the story, the priest took the children.[119] A statement along these lines was then issued on behalf of Mrs McCann, and was widely used as propaganda against Devlin in West Belfast during the general election of December 1910.

The matter came before the House of Commons on 7 February 1911, in a motion raised by the Unionists. The new leader of the Ulster Unionist Party, Sir Edward Carson, described Mrs McCann's treatment at the hands of the Catholic Church as 'a grave public scandal'.[120] The case had occurred in Devlin's constituency, and appeared to suggest to Northern Protestants the kind of treatment they would get under home rule. Devlin therefore had a heavy responsibility in his role as main respondent for the Irish Party. His speech, Winston Churchill reported in the Home Secretary's daily report to the King, was a highly successful rebuttal: 'Mr Devlin, who is the one new figure of distinction in the Irish Party, made a powerful reply and showed that the whole case, which was an ordinary tale of a private quarrel, had been used deliberately on the eve of the Belfast election as a means of exciting partisanship. This speech

---

[117] *Northern Whig*, 2 Mar. 1911.
[118] Bishop McKenna to O'Riordan, 27 May 1914 (MOR 1914/79).
[119] *Northern Whig*, 19 Jan. 1911.
[120] Parl. Deb., H.C., 5th series, xxi. 166 (7 Feb. 1911).

practically settled the incident.'[121] Devlin had obtained through Bishop Tohill statements from the three priests of St Paul's parish, who were the only ones who could have been involved. These statements Devlin read out in the House, and made the basis of his counter-attack.[122] Mrs McCann's statement, he said, appeared five days before the West Belfast election and had been circulated widely in English and Scottish constituencies as well as around the north of Ireland. 'Mrs McCann', declared Devlin, 'has been the greatest asset of the Ulster Tory Party since the days of King William III.' The statements from the three priests all denied that they had told her she was not properly married. 'Irreligion, and not religion, was responsible for all these troubles,' declared Devlin, and the whole business is 'one of the most scandalous political dodges ever known'.[123] Speaking in London three weeks later, he pointed out another weakness in the charge of Catholic exclusivism: 'while the Nationalists had eight Protestants in the [Parliamentary] Party, they in England only returned five Catholics out of six hundred members of Parliament' and there were no Catholics in the Ulster Unionist Parliamentary Party.[124]

But, as the prospect of home rule drew nearer, the Irish Party had a difficult tightrope to walk. On the one hand, it had to deny that home rule would mean Rome rule, while, on the other, it had to avoid offending those senior members of the Catholic clergy who were less than 100 per cent enthusiastic about the Party. Shortly after the debate on the McCann case, Redmond published an article on nationalism and religion in his colleague T. P. O'Connor's *Reynolds' Newspaper*. Cardinal Logue wrote to the Rector of the Irish College at Rome that 'it does not sound very complimentary to the Holy See; and I doubt very much whether it is quite orthodox. I fear very much, from the present tendency of things, that if home rule be granted, it will mean freedom for Irish Protestants and forge shackles for Irish Catholics.' At the same time the Archbishop of Dublin's secretary forwarded to the Rector a copy of the newspaper, referring sarcastically to 'the edifying contribution of the Leader of the Irish Race at Home and Abroad'.[125]

A more long-running issue than the McCann case was the role of the AOH in the national movement. This was important for two reasons. First, although it had originally been just another Unionist anti-home-rule argument, it was taken up vigorously in Parliament by O'Brien and Healy. Secondly, the Order was now associated with a major piece of UK-wide social legislation, the National Insurance Bill of 1911. Essentially a non-party measure in England,

[121] Churchill to George V, 8 Feb. 1911 (Randolph S. Churchill, *Winston S. Churchill*, ii. 1034–5).

[122] Tohill to Devlin, 2 Feb. 1911 (RP 15181/3).

[123] Parl. Deb., H.C., 5th series, xxi. 166–72 (7 Feb. 1911).

[124] *Northern Whig*, 2 Mar. 1911. Denis Henry became the first (and only) Catholic Unionist MP in 1916.

[125] Logue to O'Riordan, 24 Feb. 1911; M. J. Curran to O'Riordan, 25 Feb. 1911 (MOR 1911/43, 45).

it aroused considerable controversy in Ireland. To provide compulsory state health insurance for wage-earners without antagonizing insurance companies and friendly societies, Lloyd George had devised a scheme for administering benefits through existing private organizations. Almost any corporate body could become an 'approved society' under the act, so long as it operated the state-insurance section of its affairs on a non-profit basis. Participating societies were to receive an administration allowance of 3*s*. 8*d*. per member per year from public funds.[126] Such an arrangement was of special interest to the Hibernians, because Ireland, unlike England, had no tradition of private insurance and was not covered by a network of friendly societies. Under the Bill as first introduced, only the Hibernians and the Irish National Foresters would have had enough members to qualify for the allowance.[127] The Foresters' Society was very much the larger of the two, but, apart from a broad espousal of the national cause, it played no part in politics. The AOH was thus in a position to extract a unique advantage from the Act. One prominent Hibernian publicly expressed the hope that the government's Bill would 'enable them to plant the organisation in every town and village in Ireland'.[128] It was true, of course, that societies would have to set up a separate section for handling state insurance, and that ordinary membership of a society was not required for state insurance purposes, but the AOH was nonetheless given a whole new dimension, at the state's expense.

There was considerable opposition to the National Insurance Bill in Catholic Ireland. In June 1911 the Hierarchy called on the Irish Party to press for Ireland to be excluded from the measure, on the grounds that most Irish workers were not wage-earners, that adult sons and daughters working for their parents, and live-in workers of various kinds, would have to be paid for by their employers but would not be eligible for most of the benefits.[129] Devlin, however, was a 'powerful advocate' for the Bill, referring to its 'noble aims and magnificent scope', and making a strong speech in which he 'joined issue with the Roman Catholic bishops, the Irish doctors, the farmers and the traders' and with the *Freeman's Journal*, which had warned him that he was 'going too far and too fast'.[130] But an Irish Party committee then studied the Bill in depth, and recommended unanimously that the Party should support the Bill, subject to some amendments.[131] At this point the bishops dropped their opposition, but the AfIL MPs seized on the issue as an opportunity to differentiate their policy from that of the Irish Party and, furthermore, to draw attention to the advantage

---

[126] H. Eckstein, *The English Health Service: Its Origin, Structure, and Achievements* (Cambridge, MA, 1958), 17–29.

[127] *The Times*, 29 May 1911.

[128] J. J. Bergin, editor of *Hibernian Journal* (*Sinn Féin*, 17 June 1911).

[129] Miller, *Church, State and Nation*, 274–5.

[130] Lyons, *Tom Kettle*, 200; Stephen Gwynn, *John Redmond's Last Years* (London, 1919), 55; *The Times*, 3 July 1911.

[131] Devlin to Dillon, 4 July 1911 (DP 6729/153); Minutes of Irish Parliamentary Party, 1 June and 12 July 1911 (NLI 12082).

that the AOH would gain from the legislation. *The Times*, a strong opponent of the Irish Party, continued into the autumn of 1911 to claim that 'the whole Irish people' want Ireland to be excluded, but 'Mr Devlin wants the Insurance Bill, because his society . . . will obtain a handsome grant under it'.[132]

The fact is [continued the paper] the Bill is being imposed on Ireland in the interests of the industrial population of Belfast . . . Due to the increasing apathy of the agricultural population in the matter of home rule . . . the professional politicians have been obliged to look for a new following, and Mr Devlin has found it for them in the democracy of the cities and larger towns under his *de facto* leadership. The policy of the Nationalist party is ceasing to be agricultural and is rapidly becoming industrial.[133]

Opponents of the Irish Party, both O'Brienite and Unionist, were up in arms over what they saw as the government's subsidy of a political organization—although the 'Orange and Protestant Friendly Society' was in fact to be another beneficiary of the Act. An effort to expose in Parliament the AOH's secret and sinister influence in Irish politics resulted only in an abysmally bad evening of debate, for which William O'Brien was primarily responsible. O'Brien moved an amendment to exclude from the list of approved societies in Ireland 'any society whose rites of initiation or rules confine membership thereof to persons of a particular religion, and whose meetings, signs and passwords are of a secret character'. Redmond replied that signs and passwords were common features of a number of friendly and other benevolent societies, including the American Knights of St Columbus, of which he was himself a member. Only four members, he said, of the twenty-man Standing Committee of the UIL were AOH members, and none of the four UIL treasurers. The AOH, he concluded, was 'an honourable and a useful and patriotic organization'.[134] Dillon then weighed in, attributing the recent spread of the AOH in the south of Ireland to a backlash against O'Brien's 'crusade of vilification . . . The truth is that the most efficient organizer and spreader and promoter of the Ancient Order of Hibernians in Ireland is not the hon. member for West Belfast but the hon. Member for Cork himself.' There were now, claimed Dillon, in the region of 15,000 AOH members in Co. Cork. At an election for town surveyor in Cavan the previous week, he claimed, the Protestant candidate who defeated his Catholic rival was in fact nominated by the county head of the Hibernians.[135] Healy then joined the attack, denouncing 'a society for grabbing the loaves and fishes . . . having the mask and pretence of religion'. Devlin had intended to keep silent, allowing Redmond and Dillon to counter the charges, but Healy's speech goaded him to take the floor. He recounted how 'many years ago' the AOH 'was an organization largely composed of an undisciplined and chaotic body of men'. He and Dillon, he pointed out, had a decade previously

---

[132] *The Times*, 17 Oct. 1911.   [133] Ibid., 16 Nov. 1911.
[134] Parl. Deb., H.C., 5th series, xxxi. 298–303 (14 Nov. 1911).   [135] Ibid. 311–16.

opposed O'Brien's decision to admit AOH representatives to UIL nominating conventions.[136] Lloyd George concluded that if O'Brien's amendment was carried it would rule out 'societies which have got hundreds of thousands of members in this country and which are doing good work'.[137] The amendment was overwhelmingly defeated, the AfIL MPs voting with the Ulster Unionists and the Conservatives.

O'Brien claimed, perhaps more mischievously than seriously, that the Order's secret password for the quarter was 'Will the times be good?—Yes, when we are insured.'[138] In particular, it was rumoured that John D. Nugent would be appointed Ireland's chief insurance commissioner.[139] This post in fact went to the chairman of Galway County Council, a Presbyterian insurance manager with a Gaelic League background, and, of the twenty-three provincial organizers, even *The Times* could not associate more than half a dozen with the AOH in any way.[140] But large numbers of temporary canvassers and instructors were also appointed under the Act, and here local AOH officials probably made something of a killing, for they were in many places the only ones qualified for the work. By 1914 the Order had almost 170,000 members in its insurance section, nearly one-fifth of the total number insured and about one-quarter of the insurable Catholic population.[141] It had, as its critics claimed, received a tremendous fillip from the Act, and Lloyd George was surely disingenuous in expressing surprise at the 'explosive material' that his 'innocent non-party measure' had uncovered.[142] Parliamentary sniping at the AOH continued, with Devlin feeling obliged to make a personal explanation in the Commons in January 1913, following a public speech by the Conservative MP Brigadier Thomas Hickman claiming that the old Ribbon Society oath, which spoke of wading 'knee-deep in Orange blood', was the oath of the modern AOH. The AOH remained the bogeyman for Unionists, O'Brienites, and Republicans, but no direct hits were scored by its opponents.

[136] Parl. Deb., H.C., 5th series, xxxi. 326–7 (14 Nov. 1911).
[137] Ibid. 318.   [138] Ibid. 290–329.   [139] Ibid.
[140] *The Times*, 20 Feb. 1912; *Sinn Fein*, 21 Dec. 1911.
[141] Parl. Deb., H.C., 5th series, lix. 606. The total number of insured in Ireland in 1912 was 825,000 (*The Times*, 14 Oct. 1912).
[142] Parl. Deb., H.C., 5th series, xxxi. 318 (14 Nov. 1911).

6

'The Real Chief Secretary': Centre Stage, 1910–1914

The Government of Ireland is carried on at 39 Upper O'Connell Street, Dublin, and Mr Joseph Devlin is the real Chief Secretary.

(John Redmond, 1910[1])

Lloyd George's Budget of 1909 set the Commons and Lords on a collision course. The general election of January 1910 gave the Irish Party the balance of power in the House of Commons for the first time since 1895. Then the sudden death of King Edward VII brought about a further general election in December 1910. This replicated the results of the first one, and so did not ultimately divert the Government–Irish Party alliance from its chosen path. But it caused further delay, thereby providing more time for stoking the fires of opposition to home rule in Protestant Ulster. The length of the delay was then doubled by the provisions of the Parliament Act, which required any bill that the Lords rejected to be carried through the Commons again, unchanged unless by agreement, in two successive years before it could become law without the Lords' approval. Thus home rule, which was firmly on the agenda from February 1910 onwards, could not finally pass until 1914. Short of the government reneging on its home-rule pledge altogether, nothing could have been more helpful to opponents of home rule. A third unforeseen factor was, of course, the outbreak of the First World War in August 1914. While the progress of the attempted settlement was undermined by all sorts of failings—most notably, little Nationalist thinking until very late in the day about how to deal with the Ulster difficulty—seldom can the proponents of such a major piece of legislation have been so severely hit by the impact of extraneous 'events'.

---

[1] Speech at Utica, New York (*The Times*, 25 Nov. 1910).

ON THE UP: FROM BUDGET AND VETO
TO HOME RULE

An initial irony was that the so-called People's Budget of 1909, which began the sequence of events leading towards the Irish Party's ultimate goal, was in fact a controversial and unpopular measure in Ireland. The main Irish Party concern was the proposed increase in the taxation of liquor. The Belfast and Ulster Licensed Vintners' Association (LVA) asked the government not to increase the scale of licence fees, which would 'ruin publicans'. During the summer Devlin and his colleagues met Lloyd George twice, but he offered only a modest reduction in licence fees.[2] This setback threw Devlin into one of the periodic bouts of depression that tended to afflict him in later life, and he withdrew for one of his regular short breaks at Harrogate.[3] T. P. O'Connor, who was closer to Lloyd George than were his colleagues, warned the Chancellor that 'you will understand how far feeling has gone when Joe Devlin—one of the most sanguine, ablest and truest men in our Party—said to me on Friday night that Healy was right; and that we ought to have fought the budget from first to last'.[4] T.P. told Dillon that a 50 per cent reduction in the proposed licence fee was certain, but 'Joe Devlin does not think even the 66 per cent will save Belfast. Indeed Devlin is in a strangely pessimistic mood about everything.'[5] The rejection of the Budget by the Lords then offered some respite, and the election that inevitably followed enabled them to put home rule in the forefront more convincingly than for many years. Redmond called for an official declaration that the government would deal with home rule 'on the lines of national self-government, subject to imperial control, in the next parliament'. If this did not happen, 'not only will it be impossible for us to support Liberal candidates in England, but we would most unquestionably have to ask our friends to vote against them'.[6] Asquith duly declared at the Albert Hall for a policy that, 'while explicitly safeguarding the supremacy and indefectible authority of the Imperial Parliament, will set up in Ireland a system of full self-government in regard to purely Irish affairs'.[7]

Given the careful preparation of the People's Budget, and the strongest appeal to Irish voters in Britain for almost twenty years, the election result was disappointing for the Liberals. With 275 seats to the Conservatives' 273, they were totally dependent on Nationalist support for a Commons majority. Although Labour reached a new high with forty seats, it was not enough to counterbalance the Nationalists. The Irish Party was now in a position to

---

[2] Lyons, *Dillon*, 309; D. Gwynn, *The Life of John Redmond* (London, 1932), 162–4.
[3] Devlin to Dillon, *c*.20 Sept. 1909 (DP 6729/144).
[4] O'Connor to Lloyd George, 25 Sept. 1909 (LGP, C/6/10/1).
[5] O'Connor to Dillon, 'Thursday' [i.e. 23 Sept. 1909] (DP 6740/161).
[6] Redmond to Churchill, 27 Nov. 1909 (CP 2/39/113).   [7] D. Gwynn, *Redmond*, 169.

determine the government's priorities. This notwithstanding the fact that its own parliamentary numbers were the lowest they had been since the days of the Parnellite split. O'Brien's All-for-Ireland League (AfIL) won six of the nine seats in Co. Cork, and four elsewhere, leaving the Irish Party with sixty-nine seats. In West Belfast, Devlin—rather than the Unionist candidate, as had been the case in 1906—was challenged by the third candidate. But the dogged P. J. Magee, still seeking to fly the flag for the late bishop as an Independent Nationalist, flopped with only seventy-five votes. The Catholic position on the register had improved since 1906, and Devlin secured 53 per cent of the vote and a margin of 587 over his Unionist opponent. The latter, said Devlin, 'had a lot to say about tariff reform, which meant robbery of the poor by the rich . . . But he had not a word to say as to what the Tory Party proposed to do for the workers of the Falls and Shankill Roads, who were forever haunted by the twin spectres of unemployment and starvation.'[8] In other parts of the city, however, the threat of home rule was enough to reverse the Unionist decline of 1906. The Independent Unionist radical Sloan, who had won the previous two elections in South Belfast easily, gained only 38 per cent of the vote in a straight fight, while in North Belfast the Labour candidate's vote fell from 48 per cent in 1906 to 39 per cent. This pattern suggests that it is unlikely that Devlin's non-sectarian labour rhetoric had much impact on his own result.

As the parties returned to Westminster, Asquith sounded out Churchill about replacing Birrell as Chief Secretary. Churchill replied that 'three or four years ago I would have gone' (a sly reminder that he had offered to go in January 1907), but 'the office does not attract me now'.[9] Churchill went to the Home Office, while Birrell remained at the Irish Office, despite many attempts to resign, until the humiliation of Easter 1916. Birrell was to become increasingly less pivotal to Irish policy, and one wonders what might have happened if an ambitious and rising cabinet heavyweight like Churchill had in fact been at the helm. He continued to take an active interest in Ireland, but it remained a spasmodic interest for a man running, first, the Home Office during a period of acute industrial tension, and then the Admiralty as Britain prepared for war with Germany.

The policy of the Irish Party, now dominant in the Commons, was 'no veto, no budget'.[10] Speaking at Dumbarton on 14 March, Devlin said that, unlike most of the Irish Party, he was positively in favour of the Budget, but priority had to be given to removal of the veto.[11] On 13 April Asquith informed the King that, if the Lords rejected the veto resolutions, he would ask him to dissolve Parliament and promise to create enough peers to overcome Lords resistance should the Liberals be returned to power again. The Irish Party then voted for the Budget, to which Devlin gave his 'unqualified support'.[12] The fact that the

[8] *IN*, 15 Jan. 1910.   [9] Churchill to Asquith, 5 Feb. 1910 (CP 2/45/10–12).
[10] D. Gwynn, *Redmond*, 173.   [11] *IN*, 15 Mar. 1910.
[12] Ibid., 16 Apr. 1910.

burden of increased liquor taxes had now shifted from the retail publicans to the mainly Protestant whiskey distillers made it easier for Devlin to take this line. But Churchill, in his daily report to the King, reported that Devlin 'made a really fine speech—full of courage and of a high order of eloquence . . . Most Irish members have attempted a sort of apology for supporting it. Mr Devlin made a bold and able defence of it as a good budget for Ireland.'[13] Speaking in Donegal, a few weeks later, Devlin declared that the budget was one of the best measures for the Irish people ever passed, for he did not believe that 'the fate of Ireland was bound up with the brewers, distillers and landlords' who were funding the opposition to home rule. The budget 'taxed the luxuries of the rich, not the necessities of the poor'. Half a million pounds in extra taxation for Ireland would be more than compensated for by two and quarter million invested in old age pensions.[14] By the end of April 1910 the route to home rule appeared to be opening up. Then the whole situation was disrupted by the sudden death of Edward VII. During May and June Redmond lay low in Ireland, while Devlin busied himself at the United Irish League (UIL) office in Dublin, preparing for another general election where it would be a matter of priority to prevent further O'Brienite inroads. Meanwhile the British parties went into conference, seeking an agreed settlement on the Lords issue, which threatened to remove the Irish Party from its new-found position of power. This uncertain situation continued through the summer, but the conference ultimately ended in failure—to the great relief of the Irish Party leaders. On 18 September Redmond and Devlin set off on a fund-raising tour of America, where they raised $100,000 and were received by President Taft.[15] The mission greatly strengthened the election war chest, although their opponents in Ireland and Britain did their best to pillory Redmond as 'the dollar dictator'.[16]

The December election produced little change. The Liberals lost 3 seats and the Conservatives 1, leaving them on 272 each. Labour gained two. In Ireland the AfIL fell to eight seats, while the Irish Party number rose to seventy-five. In West Belfast Devlin's vote fell only fractionally, to 52.7 per cent in a straight fight. But elsewhere in the city the Unionist Party resurgence continued. In North Belfast Labour conceded a walkover, while in South Belfast Sloan's share of the vote fell further, to 32 per cent. In Ulster home rulers now held sixteen of the thirty-three seats, including one Liberal, thus coming very close to justifying Devlin's ironic repetition during the election of Lord Randolph Churchill's 1886 rallying cry to Unionists, 'Ulster will fight and Ulster will be right!'[17] Nationalists and Liberals thus returned to Parliament with increased confidence and a sense of common goals. The Parliament Bill was introduced into the Commons immediately, the King having pledged, if necessary, to create

---

[13] Churchill to King Edward VII, 27 Apr. 1910 (CP 12/15/65).   [14] *IN*, 30 May 1910.
[15] *The Times*, 4 and 11 Oct. 1910.   [16] D. Gwynn, *Redmond*, 184.
[17] Ibid., 30 Nov. 1910.

additional Liberal peers. The Lords finally gave way and passed the measure on 10 August 1911, and the Parliament Act became law, restricting the Lords' veto to one year on financial bills and two years for all other legislation. This meant that a Home Rule Bill would have to pass the Commons in the same form during three consecutive sessions of Parliament before it became law. Any changes made during the Bill's second or third passages would have to be in the form of suggestions and consent. This technicality was in due course to become a matter of some significance. But in 1911 such problems were still in the future. In February Asquith made the long-awaited statement that a Home Rule Bill would follow the Parliament Bill. Churchill spoke very supportively in the Commons, but in March submitted a paper to the cabinet in which he proposed a form of home rule all round. This idea did not get very far, but it suggests the beginnings of concern that home rule for Ireland should not appear to be about the dismemberment of the United Kingdom.

The Irish Party had never addressed the question of Ulster Protestant opposition to home rule, except to see it as a simple matter of persuasion. Indeed, since a distinct *Ulster* Unionist movement did not appear in Ireland until 1905, and since even in 1911 all wings of Unionism were opposed to home rule altogether, it is not difficult to understand why this should have been the case. Devlin, for instance, speaking in Donegal on 15 August 1911, acknowledged that the conflict in Ulster over home rule would be short and sharp, but was in no doubt that it would be successful.[18] By the end of 1911 the Irish leaders had the substance of the home-rule proposals before them. 'In some respects they are better than I had hoped for', wrote Redmond, and 'in other respects objectionable. But I am very hopeful'.[19] Meanwhile the Government's programme of home rule activity by ministers began to expand. Churchill accepted an invitation from the Ulster Liberal Association to speak in Belfast early in 1912.[20] At an early stage it was recognized that the Ulster Liberals did not have sufficient support to arrange a large meeting, so that the involvement of Devlin and the Nationalists would be required. Birrell, who was not consulted until after the commitment had been made, did not like the idea very much, telling Churchill that 'I don't think it is *possible just now* to appease Protestant sentiment in Ulster . . . If that can be done it can only be done after the Bill has been . . . passed through the *House of Commons.*'[21] The planned visit attracted major press interest. The *Northern Whig* declared that the idea of Churchill 'joined with Molly Maguires and England-haters' was 'an insult to the imperial idea in the mind of every loyal Belfast man'. William O'Brien's *Cork Free Press* asked: 'What on earth is the use of delivering speeches in Belfast? We never met a Belfast man whose political

---

[18] *IN*, 16 Aug. 1911.
[19] Redmond to O'Donnell, 26 Dec. 1911 (P. O'Donnell Papers, IV, 5).
[20] Elibank to Churchill, 18 Dec. 1911 (CP 2/53/81).
[21] Birrell to Churchill, 4 Jan. 1912 (CP 2/56/10).

views were so pliable as to be moved by the oratory of Cicero, Joseph Devlin or [Ulster Unionist] William Moore.'[22] By this stage Churchill himself was picking up some of Birrell's anxiety, expressing to Redmond his doubts as to 'whether our joint appearance in Belfast will really conduce to the public advantage'. But his problem was that the Nationalist Party had to play the principal part in organizing and sustaining the meeting. The Ulster Liberal Association, though of value as a figurehead, could not fill a hall.[23]

At this stage the Ulster Unionist Council booked the Ulster Hall for the evening before Churchill's speech, intending to remain in occupation afterwards and so prevent his meeting. Churchill then held a meeting with Devlin, Pirrie, and others. Pirrie initially advised abandoning the meeting, and Birrell reported that St Mary's Hall was 'repugnant to the fine susceptibilities of the Ulster Liberals'.[24] The venue finally agreed on, Churchill told his wife, was 'deep in the heart of the Falls neighbourhood . . . a whole block of old houses will be pulled down and a beautiful tent erected with sounding boards, etc. to hold 10,000 . . . We shall make a great torchlight procession down the Falls Road three miles long, surrounded by the Nationalist army . . . The police will draw a cordon between the two parts of the city.'[25] He did not mention the 5,000 soldiers who were to be on duty, most of whom Birrell thought could be hidden from view.[26] Attendance was calculated by the Liberal *Ulster Guardian* at 8,000, but its estimate that 5,000 of these were Protestants seems unlikely.[27] The meeting ended with the singing of the national anthem. Churchill concluded by saying that 'we have done a good day's work and I do not think any of us will ever have cause to regret it'.[28] The Belfast Police Commissioner, on the other hand, reported that it was 'difficult to describe adequately the bitter feeling caused' by the visit.[29]

On 31 March 1912 a major home-rule rally was organized in Dublin. Speakers included Redmond, Devlin, Eoin MacNeill, and Patrick Pearse. Devlin was responsible for the organization. Pearse, in his pseudonymous series of open letters to public figures in his short-lived Irish-language newspaper *An Barr Buadh*, congratulated Devlin on this achievement:

The sign of your hand was apparent on the occasion—the hand of a young person. I like young people. The Irish like young people. The Irish like you. You were the idol of the crowd on Sunday and not John Redmond. You have a young heart, O young man! Be careful that it does not petrify, with so many venerable colleagues around you . . . You

[22] *Cork Free Press*, 5 Jan. 1912.

[23] Churchill to Redmond, 13 Jan. 1912 (Randolph S. Churchill, *Winston S. Churchill*, ii. 1380–1).

[24] Birrell to Churchill, 28 Jan. 1912 (ibid. 1388–9).

[25] Churchill to Clementine Churchill, 23 and 24 Jan. 1912 (ibid. 1383–4).

[26] Birrell to Churchill, 28 and 30 Jan. 1912 (ibid. 1388–9).

[27] *Ulster Guardian*, 10 Feb. 1912.   [28] *The Times*, 9 Feb. 1912.

[29] RIC County Inspectors' Reports, Belfast, Feb. 1912 (TNA: PRO CO 904/86).

spoke in a lively fashion on Sunday. Some of your words I found distasteful. Will you be loyal to the British crown when Dublin has a home rule parliament? I do not think that you will. Reflect on this question.[30]

Then on 23 April about 3,000 delegates gathered at Dublin's Mansion House for the UIL Convention on the Bill. Devlin, whom *The Times* described as 'the real author of the day's triumphs', sought to cut through diversions regarding home-rule finance by taking

the high idealistic line that freedom should come first and finance afterwards, and that the Celtic genius for government would conquer any difficulties inherent in the Bill. In other words . . . it would be all right on the night. This easy optimism enthralled the Convention, but when Mr Devlin went on to say that home rule would release new liberal and democratic forces in Ulster there was a certain silence in the audience.[31]

The long-awaited Home Rule Bill was at last introduced into the Commons in April 1912. Devlin made a long speech on the second reading, focusing on religious discrimination in employment and related matters. The Unionist elite, he claimed, 'do not so much dislike the Pope and Papists as they do the Pope's Encyclical on Labour'. Conversely, he also drew attention to the lack of concern that Lord Pirrie and some other tycoons had about the economic dangers of home rule. A month later the suggestion of partition was raised for the first time by a Liberal back-bencher, who called for the exclusion from the Bill of the four counties of Antrim, Armagh, Down, and Londonderry. In a two-day debate Devlin was one of the last speakers, though pointing out that he was the first of the four Belfast MPs to speak. 'If Ulster, or any portion of Ulster,' asked Devlin, 'wants to be cut off from Ireland, why does that proposition not come from an Ulster member?' Protestants on public boards in the South tended to be over-represented in relation to their numbers, he argued, whereas the Catholic position in Ulster was the opposite. It was in Belfast where the discrimination lay, he said, such as the recently appointed insurance committee of the Belfast Corporation, which had not one Catholic among its fifteen members. He then pointed out that Belfast would have 16 MPs in an Irish Parliament of 160 members and that, overall, Protestants would be able to elect 60 MPs of their choice. 'When we get an Irish Parliament, security for a minority will be found . . . in the union of the Protestant workers of the north with the Catholic labourer of the south, in the union of the privileged classes of the north with the farmers and the tillers of the soil of the south. There will be a complete transformation of parties and classes . . . You are not fomenting religious strife by this Bill, but obliterating it.'[32] It was conciliation of Protestant Ulster by promises and the rhetoric of moderation, rather than by political concession.

---

[30] S. Ó Buachalla (ed.), *The Letters of P. H. Pearse* (Gerrards Cross, 1980), 260.
[31] *The Times*, 24 Apr. 1912.
[32] Parl. Deb., H.C., 5th series, xxxix. 1154–67 (13 June 1912).

During the summer of 1912 the icing on the home-rule cake became somewhat flaky. Carson, James Craig, and their colleagues, fully supported by Conservative leader Andrew Bonar Law, organized anti-home-rule rallies in north-east Ulster and spoke of an Ulster provisional government. Unionist Clubs were drilling, and there were rumours of 'large importations of arms into the Orange counties'.[33] More seriously, a clash occurred on 29 June in the village of Castledawson, Co. Londonderry, between members of the Ancient Order of Hibernians (AOH) returning from a home-rule rally and a Sunday School excursion parading with Union Jacks, on a day out from the north Belfast industrial suburb of White-house. The AOH members, allegedly under the influence of drink, appear to have started the trouble, and the incident was reported in the Unionist press as a Hiber-nian attack on children. Redmond later confided privately that the result of the incident 'was to seriously prejudice our cause in Great Britain and in the House of Commons'.[34] By 2 July the more excitable elements in Protestant Belfast were up in arms about this. At Workman, Clark's north shipyard, which was only a couple of miles from Whitehouse, groups of apprentices and young labourers began to drive Catholic workers from the yard. The trouble quickly spread to the other shipyards, to engineering works, and to some linen mills. A second wave of expulsions occurred three weeks later, as the big firms reopened after the holidays. About 2,000 were expelled during the first week in July, and another 1,000 towards the end of the month.[35] At the end of July soldiers were brought in to assist the police, which helped return the situation to what passed for normal in the city, although troops remained at the main flash points until mid-September. Most expelled workers returned to work by early autumn. Unsurprisingly, bitter-ness about these events continued for much longer. About 20 per cent of those expelled were Protestants, mainly trade-union activists and others who had failed to identify themselves with the Unionist cause. On 7 July Bishop Tohill estab-lished a relief fund. Almost £5,000 was collected, and at the high point 1,366 weekly claims were being paid.[36] Anxious to put an end to these sectarian clashes, which were such a threat to the home-rule band-wagon, Devlin cancelled all the AOH meetings scheduled to take place across the north of Ireland on the Catholic holiday of 15 August.[37] Neither side could expect to derive political benefit from the expulsions. For the Nationalists, evidence of strong popular Protestant feeling against home rule—no matter how crudely and unattractively expressed—was not the message they wanted to go out to the British electorate. Likewise for the Unionist leadership, the suggestions that their followers could behave so unpleas-antly and uncontrollably was not the image of Unionist 'law and order' that they customarily sought to present as a contrast to the 'lawlessness' of the South.

[33] Churchill to his constituency chairman in Dundee, Sir G. Ritchie, 14 Aug. 1912 (Randolph S. Churchill, *Winston S. Churchill*, ii. 1394).
[34] Redmond to Bishop McHugh, 26 Feb. 1914 (P. O'Donnell Papers, IV, 5).
[35] *The Times*, 1 Aug. 1912.   [36] Morgan, *Labour and Partition*, 134.
[37] *The Times*, 6 Aug. 1912.

When, in July 1912, the strongly pro-Unionist Conservative F. E. Smith claimed that by-elections were showing a swing to the Conservatives, Devlin offered to resign his West Belfast seat at once and fight Smith in a by-election.[38] This confidence by the holder of a marginal seat may have been stimulated by a report that his friend Dan McCann sent to Redmond that 'we now have on the register a purely Catholic majority (exclusive of Protestant home rulers) of 525, so that West Belfast for the present at least is as safe as even Waterford'.[39] One factor that improved the situation for Nationalists was the appointment in 1911 of a Revising Barrister who took a more favourable view of cases based on 'double tenancies'—that is, small houses occupied by more than one household. 'The sole question', it was reported, was 'had the people living above, to whom the people living below had sub-let, the right to go through the kitchen for the purpose of getting water, and for the purpose of getting to the yard?' Once this has been established, protested the Unionist solicitors, every Nationalist downstairs claimant came into court and swore to his fellow tenant that 'with my permission you can go through the kitchen'.[40]

On 22 September 1912 Devlin was being driven through Donegal to a meeting in a hired car, along with John T. Donovan and two other friends. Because of an error by the chauffeur, the vehicle ran backwards out of control down a steep hill, causing Devlin and a friend to jump out, injuring themselves in the process. Devlin, his counsel claimed at the later court case, 'received a grave injury to the kidneys as a result of shock from his injury'. He was ordered to cancel all engagements for six weeks, and attended only to minimal duties at the House of Commons. By the time he had recovered, the Ulster situation was beginning to dominate the debate.

THE ULSTER CRISIS

Churchill and Lloyd George had, since the autumn of 1911 if not earlier, privately taken the view that some concessions would have to be made to address the Ulster difficulty. In August 1912 Churchill told Lloyd George that 'we ought to give any Irish county the option of remaining at Westminster for a period of five to ten years, or some variant of this'.[41] Once the Irish Parliament was up and running, he maintained, the economic pressure of the rest of Ireland on Belfast, plus the success of the Parliament, would resolve matters.[42] But it was to be another year before the government as a whole began to think seriously about resorting to concessions—rather than Devlin's moderation and optimism—as a means of resolving the Ulster difficulty. In April 1913, after

[38] Ibid., 15 July 1912.   [39] McCann to Redmond, 12 and 17 Oct. 1912 (RP 15254).
[40] *The Times*, 4 Feb. 1914.   [41] Churchill to Lloyd George, 21 Aug. 1912 (CP 13/5/30).
[42] Churchill to Ritchie, 8 Sept. 1912 (Randolph S. Churchill, *Winston S. Churchill*, ii. 1396–7).

the Belfast shipyard troubles and the formation of the Ulster Volunteer Force (UVF), the Under Secretary Sir J. B. Dougherty, himself an Ulster Presbyterian, advised Birrell that any trouble over the Home Rule Bill would be no more than the usual rioting: 'the constabulary, with some assistance from the military garrison, will be adequate to deal with any disturbance that is likely to occur in Ulster.'[43] Likewise Devlin declared in the Commons in June that 'all the talk about civil war in Ireland was humbug, sham and hypocrisy, organized by lawyers who, if they had not been so successful at the English bar, would have ranked among the foremost stage managers on the London stage'.[44] Privately too, Devlin told several parliamentary colleagues that he believed 'Ulster' was bluffing.[45] The capture by a Liberal home ruler of the marginal Derry seat in January was another encouraging development for the Irish Party, enabling it to say that the parliamentary representation of Ulster was 17 to 16 in favour of home rule. Redmond also put a brave face on things, telling Bishop O'Donnell that 'Carson's campaign has been a veritable Godsend to us'.[46] But by September 1913 it was in fact becoming clear that some sort of offer would have to be made to Ulster. Speaking in Kerry on 14 September, Devlin told his audience that 'we would be prepared to make any concessions short of sacrificing the nationhood of Ireland if by doing so we could get a solution acceptable to all Irishmen'. But he then added that 'I know Ulster and I know Belfast, and I know that the way to reach an agreement with them is not by crawling or cringing, but by standing up to them . . . This talk about solution by consent is not, to my mind, made in good faith as man to man, but is for the purpose of trying to defeat home rule.'[47]

This was provoked by a letter in *The Times* on 11 September from the former Lord Chancellor, Lord Loreburn, calling for a settlement of the problem by consent. It was, Lloyd George told T. P. O'Connor, written without any consultation with his colleagues, and many Liberals were bitter about it.[48] Asquith still thought that 'an ungovernable Ireland is a much more serious prospect than rioting in four counties', but he told Churchill that, 'in the end, we should probably have to make some sort of bargain about Ulster as the price of home rule'.[49] Devlin had until this stage kept an unusually low profile in debate, probably in the hope of avoiding further provocation of Orange opposition, just as he had suppressed the 15 August demonstrations for two years. But now that the question of special treatment for Ulster was coming to the fore, he became a major focus of interest for both his colleagues and the government. On 30 September Lloyd George told T. P. O'Connor that the Conservative and Ulster Unionist leaders were now on board for 'a settlement in which Ulster

[43] Memo. by J. B. Dougherty, 9 Apr. 1913 (BOD, Birrell Papers, MS Eng *c.*7034, fo. 36).
[44] Parl. Deb., H.C., 5th series, liii. 1540 (10 June 1913).　　　[45] Maume, *Long Gestation*, 132.
[46] Redmond to O'Donnell, 1 July 1913 (P. O'Donnell Papers, IV. 5).
[47] *The Times*, 15 Sept. 1913.　　　[48] O'Connor to Devlin, 1 Oct. 1913 (RP 15181/3).
[49] Asquith to Churchill, 12 and 19 Sept. 1913 (Randolph S. Churchill, *Winston S. Churchill*, ii. 1399–1401).

counties would have the right to exclude themselves'.[50] In a long letter to Devlin, T.P. then began the process of softening up his younger colleague. Although no concessions should be flagged up for the moment, he said: 'it would be well for us to consider some means by which the Orangemen could save their faces, such as complete control of education and religion by the four counties themselves . . . In the last resort I would suggest a modified form of self-government subject to the Parliament in Dublin.'[51] This was the approach that became known as 'home rule within home rule'. Perhaps relieved at the limited extent of this proposed concession, Devlin, in a speech at Dundalk the following Sunday, repeated Redmond's recent statement that, although the Irish Party would 'never' agree to the exclusion from home rule of the four Ulster counties, if the Carsonites would accept an Irish Parliament with a responsible executive, 'we will gladly go into a conference . . . to settle the details of a bill that would be acceptable to all sections of Irishmen'.[52]

Churchill, it was feared, was 'unsound' on Ulster. T. P. O'Connor wrote to him on 7 October that 'the only minority in Ireland that suffers from religious persecution is the Catholic minority in the north'.[53] But, speaking in his Dundee constituency the next day, Churchill declared that Ulster's claim for special treatment 'could not be ignored or brushed aside'.[54] Although the speech ended with a peroration in favour of home rule, it caused much concern in Catholic Ulster. Bishop O'Donnell, the Party's strongest episcopal supporter, wrote immediately to Redmond to declare that, while the conciliation of the Orangemen was desirable, nothing could justify cutting off the Northern Catholic minority from their claims under the Bill and 'deliberately leaving them under a harrow that might be worse than what they have endured. Autonomy in education, etc. for the N.E. corner would be queer autonomy for them.' There was, warned O'Donnell, 'a good deal of feeling' that Ulster Nationalists should have special representation at any conference.[55] 'The thing I have always dreaded', he later wrote to O'Riordan, 'is an administrative council for Ulster under the guise of home rule within home rule.'[56] Redmond sought to counter Churchill's Dundee speech in Limerick the following Sunday, declaring that 'the two-nation theory is to us an abomination and a blasphemy'.[57] Speaking at Portsmouth a few days later, the twelfth speech he had given in England in three weeks, Devlin said that 'while the door was still open for conciliation and for concession there must be no divorce either of Ulster or of any portion of Ulster from the rest of Ireland'.[58]

---

[50] Lyons, *Dillon*, 333.   [51] O'Connor to Devlin, 1 Oct. 1913 (RP 15181/3).
[52] *FJ*, 6 Oct. 1913.
[53] O'Connor to Churchill, 7 Oct. 1913 (Randolph S. Churchill, *Winston S. Churchill*, ii. 1401–2).
[54] Lyons, *Dillon*, 332.   [55] D. Gwynn, *Redmond*, 231.
[56] O'Donnell to O'Riordan, 6 July 1914 (MOR 1914/154).   [57] D. Gwynn, *Redmond*, 232.
[58] *The Times*, 23 Oct. 1913.

Home rule within home rule appeared to be a more palatable concession, but it alarmed the Northern bishops. The South Down MP Jerry McVeagh, who was close to Cardinal Logue and some of the other bishops—though not as close to Devlin and Dillon as he had been a decade previously—sided with the bishops. Any autonomy for Ulster 'would mean the placing of the neck of the Ulster minority under the heel of a majority that has never failed to make a tyrannical use of its power'. McVeagh thought it would be much better to offer a set of alternative concessions, including increased Ulster representation in the Irish parliament for a fixed period of ten years, elections by proportional representation, and recruitment to public-sector jobs via an Irish Civil Service Commission, so that political patronage would be brought to an end.[59] Devlin meanwhile was beginning to feel uneasy about all this. He was annoyed that, having 'rallied the Irish and labour vote despite the intervention of a Labour candidate' in the Keighley by-election, the Liberal whom he had helped to elect afterwards spoke in support of the exclusion of part of Ulster. On 7 November he wrote in these terms to the Liberal chief whip, Percy Illingworth. 'On his individual responsibility,' Devlin informed Illingworth that 'everyone concerned may rest assured that the exclusion of Ulster or any portion of Ulster is outside the realms of compromise'.[60] This was a new role for Devlin, dealing directly with the Liberals on central questions of policy. But he was careful to copy the letter to Redmond, saying that 'it commits no one', and to Dillon, adding almost apologetically that 'coming from me I don't think the letter can do any harm'.[61]

At this stage Lloyd George persuaded the cabinet to support an offer based on the temporary exclusion of the four Protestant majority counties—Antrim, Armagh, Derry, and Down—for a period of five or six years. Redmond attacked this as distinctly unfair to Northern Catholics, predicting that exclusion would erect 'sharp, permanent, eternal dividing lines between Catholics and Protestants'.[62] He persuaded Asquith that it would be better to hold back any offer to 'Ulster' until the last moment, which then might possibly be along home-rule-within-home-rule lines. In a parallel meeting, Dillon gave Lloyd George the impression that he would at some future stage be more favourable to temporary exclusion than to the home-rule-within-home-rule approach—which he disliked for the same reasons as Bishop O'Donnell—though he anticipated great difficulty with Devlin over any sort of exclusion proposal.[63] But, privately, Redmond and O'Connor had by this time agreed that the temporary exclusion of 'Ulster' would be better than the loss of the Bill. Redmond, reported T.P. to Dillon, thought what an 'immense drawback it would be to the working of the Irish Parliament if we had bloodshed and smouldering rebellion in Ulster'. 'I

---

[59] J. McVeagh to Redmond, 28 Oct. 1913 (RP 15205/4).
[60] Devlin to Illingworth, 7 Nov. 1913, copy (DP 6730/164).
[61] Devlin to Redmond, 12 Nov 1913 (RP 15181/3); Devlin to Dillon, 12 Nov 1913 (DP 6730/164).
[62] *The Times*, 15 Nov. 1913.   [63] Lyons, *Dillon*, 339.

cannot communicate your letter to Joe Devlin', replied Dillon, 'because of the sentences conveying the impression that I had agreed to the temporary exclusion of Ulster.'[64]

On 9 December Devlin spoke at a by-election on behalf of the newly appointed cabinet minister C. F. G. Masterman. He told Masterman 'that the Irish Party will not consent to anything in the nature of exclusion for Ulster and that the Irish leaders could not, if they would, carry such a proposal with their followers'.[65] When T.P. asked Devlin his view on four-county exclusion, 'his reply was prompt and peremptory: if we brought any such proposition *at any time*—as I understood him—before the Party it would be rejected'. He did not, however, 'raise anything like the same heated objections' to home rule within home rule. T.P. thought this 'a declaration so absolute' against exclusion that he immediately arranged to take Devlin to see Lloyd George.[66] When Devlin made clear to the Chancellor of the Exchequer his view that home rule within home rule was the more palatable option, Lloyd George expressed his own preference for temporary exclusion, but concluded that the decision was

essentially an Irish question; and that if we deliberately thought that home rule within home rule was better than exclusion, it was not for him to object. He was satisfied with it as a concession which would justify the position of the Government; and, if rejected, would also justify the Government in any steps which they might find necessary to put down violence.

O'Connor, the weathercock, now told Dillon that, 'with Devlin's view of Irish feeling, and added to that his own strong personal position . . . exclusion is a policy we should find it difficult *at any time* to acquiesce in', whereas, O'Connor believed, 'we can carry with us opinion in favour of home rule within home rule—temporarily, of course, and not as the last and final settlement of the Irish question—and that then we might have peace on terms rather better than exclusion'.[67]

Dillon told T.P. that he had favoured home rule within home rule as the best concession since the summer, but he may have been dissembling somewhat, as this was not the impression he had given to Lloyd George in November. He agreed that temporary exclusion might be impossible to sell to their followers, but he considered Lloyd George's idea of temporary exclusion 'may be right as a tactical move', and wanted to keep himself 'perfectly free in the improbable event of such a situation arising'.[68] O'Connor once again reiterated his preference for home rule within home rule, arguing that 'any form of exclusion of Ulster will

---

[64] O'Connor to Dillon, 26 Nov. 1913, and Dillon to O'Connor, 27 Nov. 1913 (DP 6740/212, 213).

[65] Lord Riddell, *More Pages from my Diary, 1908–14* (London, 1934), 189.

[66] O'Connor to Lloyd George, 10 Dec. 1913 (LGP, C/6/10/6).

[67] O'Connor to Dillon, 17 Dec. 1913 (DP 6740/617).

[68] Dillon to O'Connor, 20 Dec. 1913 (DP 6740/218).

place us in an almost impossible position. I fear that we should lose Devlin and all that he represents, and you know what a loss that would be to us.'[69] But the Conservative Austen Chamberlain heard from John Morley at a dinner party that Redmond and Dillon 'might sulk a bit but would not oppose' exclusion, while Dillon was reported to have told Morley that 'Devlin would stick by Redmond whatever happened', by which he no doubt meant 'stick by Dillon'.[70]

The issue surfaced once again at the beginning of February 1914. Devlin continued to maintain in public that the whole Unionist policy was 'a gigantic game of bluff', but there was growing concern at the possibility of armed UVF resistance, and Redmond was later to write to Asquith that 'the Nationalists of Ulster are seriously disturbed by the apprehension of isolated attacks on life and property'.[71] In taking the public line that they did, therefore, the Nationalists were postponing a hard decision on Ulster. Devlin denied that all the businessmen of Ireland were against home rule, and 'the only claim Sir Edward Carson had to speak for businessmen was that he himself was a manufacturer of calumny against his fellow-countrymen'.[72] At Swansea on 20 February he said that Asquith's offer of conciliation to the Unionists 'had been treated with contempt as soon as made', and, unless the Unionists were prepared to meet in a spirit of goodwill, the current home-rule policy would be carried through to completion.[73] Observing sardonically from the sidelines, as always, Tim Healy thought that 'either Devlin's colleagues were concealing the true situation from him, or he has not the parliamentary instinct to discern what is being arranged, if he has not also surrendered'. A couple of days later he concluded that 'Devlin cannot give in, but I see Dillon arguing with him constantly'.[74]

Soon after this, Devlin circulated a long memorandum to his immediate colleagues and to leading members of the government. He argued that the majority for the Bill in the House of Commons was undiminished, and that British public opinion, 'as evidenced at by-elections and at public meetings, is overwhelmingly in favour of the passage of the Bill'. He dismissed the civil-war threat: 'We have exceptional sources of information in regard to the Ulster Volunteer movement, and we are convinced that its danger is grossly exaggerated . . . In Belfast . . . where the Catholic and Protestant home rulers would be among the first victims of any outbreak among the Orangemen, the home rulers regard the whole thing with absolute contempt.' He thought the Bill as it stood contained ample safeguards, but if further concessions were proposed by the government they should preserve the unity of Ireland under the Bill. Devlin himself proposed three concessions: (1) the right of Ulster counties to opt

---

[69] O'Connor to Dillon, 30 Dec. 1913 (DP 6740/219).

[70] Austen Chamberlain to Lord Lansdowne, 9 Dec. 1913, in A. Chamberlain, *Politics from Inside: An Epistolary Chronicle, 1906–14* (London, 1936), 586.

[71] Redmond to Asquith, 15 May 1914 (RP 15169).

[72] *The Times*, 2 Feb. 1914.   [73] Ibid., 21 Feb. 1914.

[74] Healy to M. Healy, 11 and 13 Feb. 1914 (Healy, *Letters and Leaders*, ii. 533–4).

out of home rule after ten years; (2) extra representation for Ulster in the Irish Parliament; and (3) 'such an arrangement of the Senate as would afford them an additional safeguard against unfair treatment'.[75]

In a sense Devlin's proposal offered the Ulster Unionists less than home rule within home rule, for it retained in Dublin the control of administration; in another sense it offered more, in that it accepted the principle, albeit deferred, of exclusion. His document was not as compelling as it might have been, for it devoted too much space to generalized assurances of 'a fair deal' for Protestants, and to denials of the seriousness of the security situation in Ulster. In private negotiation, neither of these arguments was likely to carry weight. The memo elicited a long reply from Lloyd George setting out the case for four-county temporary exclusion. Neither home rule within home rule nor the delayed opt-out plan, he argued, would be accepted by the Unionists in Parliament, thus leaving the government no constitutional alternative but to force the original Bill through, using the provisions of the Parliament Act.[76] He thought that Devlin underestimated the danger of civil disturbance in Ulster, which the government would be prepared to face down only after it had been made clear 'to every reasonable mind in Great Britain that the rioters have refused all reasonable accommodation'. The alternative of home rule within home rule would, Lloyd George deftly maintained, amount to a government admission that the unqualified home-rule policy offered inadequate safeguards to Ulster Protestants. Lloyd George thus proposed offering temporary exclusion until after another general election to any county that requested it in a referendum. In practice this would exclude four counties. In the interim the Ulster Unionists would find it very difficult 'to get up another movement such as they have organized at such great expense during the last couple of years . . . [and] . . . the Irish Parliament will then have been established at College Green, and will have got over most of its preliminary difficulties'.[77] What this really implied was that London, rather than Dublin, would have responsibility for defusing the UVF, an approach that may in fact have had attractions for the southern-based Nationalist leaders. Like the boundary commission clause of the 1921 Treaty, it had the characteristic stamp of a Lloyd George negotiation, whereby those on the other side of the table had to meet their part of the bargain first.

Redmond, O'Connor, and Devlin met Asquith, Lloyd George, and Birrell on 3 March.[78] Afterward Lloyd George told his journalist friend Lord Riddell that 'the Irish are tough negotiators. They bluff so well you really cannot tell whether they are bluffing or not.' 'Has Devlin agreed?' asked Riddell. 'Yes,' replied Lloyd

[75] 'Mr Devlin's memo', 20 Feb. 1914 (RP 15181/3).
[76] 'Response to Mr Devlin's memo', 23 Feb. 1914 (LGP, C/20/2/7).
[77] Memo, 23 Feb 1914 (LGP, C/20/2/7).
[78] D. Gwynn, *Redmond*, 267.

George, 'he has acted well. He is the man who will have the troublesome task.'[79] Devlin was increasingly in the spotlight. 'The adhesion of Mr Devlin is of the first importance to the Ministry,' declared *The Times*. 'He is their guarantee for the goodwill of the Ulster Nationalists.'[80] At this stage Devlin had in fact reverted to his more customary role of organization man, accepting the policy of temporary four-county exclusion that he had previously resisted so firmly and, on Redmond's instructions, taking up the challenge of selling it to Catholic Ulster. He had satisfactory meetings with Charles McHugh, Bishop of Derry, with Bishop O'Donnell, and with the dying Bishop Tohill.[81] On 6 March he held a private conference in Patrick Dempsey's Linen Hall Hotel, 'of all those people whom I thought it advisable to see' from across the province—a total of thirteen priests and ten laymen. This group gave the temporary exclusion proposals 'their fullest and most unqualified support'.[82] Devlin was not the best person to call on Cardinal Logue, whose disapproval of the AOH had not relented, so that part of the mission was undertaken by Jerry McVeagh and James Lardner. McVeagh reported that Logue 'doesn't *love* the concessions, but will not object'.[83] He was putting the best gloss on the meeting that he could, for Logue told Archbishop Walsh a few days later that he thought the home-rule concessions 'would be a bad business for us in the north', leaving them more than ever under the heel of the Orangemen, who would be 'free to tamper with our education'.[84]

Thus Devlin was brought for the first time to swallow the principle of exclusion. The primary reason for his doing so was clearly the pressure that had been put on him by his southern colleagues within the Party leadership. Observers outside the movement, conscious of Devlin's force in debate and ruthless efficiency in organization, constantly predicted that he would revolt. In 1913 some Tories had thought that he was laying the groundwork for a seizure of the Irish Party leadership on an anti-exclusion ticket. During his mission to Ulster in March 1914 the *Times* correspondent reported a rumour 'that Mr Devlin and some of the younger members of the Party are not in agreement with Mr Redmond on vital questions of policy'. Devlin, it was said, was strongly in favour of putting the government's proposals to a national Convention in Dublin—a position that he had indeed maintained earlier.[85] But following Devlin's progress round the Ulster dioceses, the *Times* correspondent completely misread what was happening. Devlin, he thought, was holding these hastily arranged meetings 'to seek encouragement for his side as against Mr Redmond's... Few in the inner circles of northern Nationalism will be surprised if it should be found that Mr Devlin believes his nominal chief has gone too far, and is going to say so emphatically.'[86] As we

---

[79] Riddell, *More Pages*, 202.   [80] *The Times*, 7 Mar. 1914.
[81] Ibid., 7 Mar. 1914 (RP 15181/3).   [82] Ibid., 6 Mar. 1914 (RP 15181/3).
[83] McVeagh to Redmond, 'Friday night' [6 Mar. 1914] (RP 15205/4).
[84] Logue to Walsh, 13 Mar. 1914 (Walsh Papers, 120).   [85] *The Times*, 5 Mar. 1914.
[86] Ibid., 6 and 7 Mar. 1914.

have seen, the opposite was in fact the case. Dillon had been right when he told Morley that 'Devlin would stick by Redmond [or Dillon] whatever happened'.

Bishop O'Donnell took a more positive view of developments following his meeting with Devlin. He told O'Riordan in Rome that he did not think 'that the day of their enjoying an Irish parliament is postponed very much, if at all'. His only fear was of 'any reversion to "home rule within home rule" at the last moment on the part of the Government'.[87] On the same day, Churchill, now fully behind the government's offer of temporary four-county exclusion, sent a squadron of battleships to stand to off Belfast Lough. Speaking at Bradford, he delivered a fiery attack on the Conservatives' Ulster policy and declared that 'if Ulstermen extend the hand of friendship it will be clasped by Liberals and by their Nationalist countrymen'. Redmond welcomed this 'superb speech', which he thought confirmed that the Nationalists' last word on the subject of concessions to Ulster was also the government's last word.[88] By coincidence, Devlin spoke in Bradford just twenty-four hours after Churchill. It was an angry speech. The government had given way to pressure, he said, 'not of the Protestants of Ulster, but of a little section of political conspirators against democratic liberty', as a result of which Asquith had given certain counties permission to vote themselves out of home rule for six years.[89] Four days later, Devlin made another angry speech in the Commons, 'a rude and bitter attack' on Carson, as Austen Chamberlain described it.[90] Carson then strode out of the House en route for Belfast, and the Conservative benches rose in a body to cheer him, disrupting Devlin's speech.[91] Then, putting the argument in favour of what he stressed was not the Nationalists' but the government's concession on Ulster, Devlin stated that a temporary six-year exclusion, with two British general elections intervening, would give every encouragement to the Irish Parliament to develop a conciliatory approach throughout the period, whereas with the Unionist demand of 'permanent' exclusion would come 'the old passions inflamed, old prejudices reinforced, old hatreds encouraged'.[92]

While the war of words continued at Westminster, seventy army officers based at the Curragh camp, in Co. Kildare, refused to participate in the 'coercion' of Ulster if instructed to do so. It was an alarming hint of mutiny, provoked by incompetent handling of the matter at a higher level, though it had no immediate impact on the wider political situation. Then, on the night of 24–5 April, 30,000 guns and ammunition were run into Larne by the UVF and rapidly distributed around the province, in an operation involving 12,000 men, news of which did not reach Dublin Castle until noon the next day. This, hard on the heels of the Curragh incident, was a grave setback for the government and

[87] O'Donnell to O'Riordan, 14 Mar. 1914 (MOR 1914/69).
[88] D. Gwynn, *Redmond*, 275.   [89] *The Times*, 16 Mar. 1914.
[90] A. Chamberlain, *Politics from Inside* (London, 1936), 641.   [91] *The Times*, 20 Mar. 1914.
[92] Parl. Deb., H.C., 5th series, lix. 2278–86 (19 Mar. 1914).

for the Irish Party. Churchill was deluding himself when he wrote to his wife that 'from a parliamentary point of view' this had altered the situation very much in the Government's favour . . . They have put themselves entirely in the wrong.'[93] But, speaking in the Commons on 28 April, he 'threw a sentence across the House to Carson which has revolutionized the situation, and we are all back again in full conciliation'.[94] The sentence was to the effect that, if Carson would accept the government's Ulster concessions, Churchill 'in return will use all my influence and goodwill to make Ireland an integral unit in the federal system'. A colleague told him afterwards that his remark had aroused great fury 'in the Irish Party . . . Devlin is beside himself with rage, and is openly telling everyone that you have betrayed the Irish cause'.[95] He seems to have quickly calmed down, however, for afterwards Austen Chamberlain heard that the members of the Irish Party held 'a stormy meeting' and were 'with difficulty restrained by Devlin, who persuaded them that it was impossible for Carson to accept Winston's proposal'.[96] Ulster Unionist opposition to anything short of permanent exclusion for the entire province brought this phase of the crisis to a halt.

Viewing things from a Westminster perspective, Redmond thought that 'there is nothing new of importance. The [Home Rule] Bill is certain to become law as it stands and will leave this House before Whitsuntide. If an amending bill is introduced *then* the danger will be on us.'[97] But opinion in Nationalist Ulster was uneasy about the whole exclusion business. The Bishop of Clogher, whose diocese straddled the south Tyrone borderland, thought that 'things are looking bad'. He feared that, 'if temporary exclusion is once granted and the system works fairly well, it is almost certain to become permanent'. He pinned his hopes on the expectation that 'the Unionists of Ireland will not accept exclusion and this will save us the necessity of making up our minds'.[98] On 23 June an amending bill was introduced into the Lords, providing for temporary six-year exclusion by county option, but the Lords amended it to indefinite exclusion of the entire province of Ulster. A meeting of party leaders then took place at Buckingham Palace on 21–4 July. Only two leaders from each of the four sides were invited. Augustine Birrell, cabinet minister responsible for Ireland, and Winston Churchill, who had taken such an active and provocative part in the crisis, were two notable omissions, and Joe Devlin, the voice of Ulster Nationalism, was another.[99] At the conference Carson said he would accept the so-called clean cut of nine-county

[93] Churchill to Clementine Churchill, 27 Apr. 1914 (Randolph S. Churchill, *Winston S. Churchill*, ii. 1502–3).
    [94] Churchill to Clementine Churchill, 29 Apr. 1914 (ibid. 1418).
    [95] R. Harcourt, MP, to Churchill, 28 Apr. 1914 (Randolph S. Churchill, *Winston S. Churchill*, ii. 1419).
    [96] Chamberlain, *Politics from Inside*, 642.
    [97] Redmond to O'Donnell, 11 May 1914 (P. O'Donnell Papers, IV. 5).
    [98] P. McKenna to O'Riordan, 27 May 1914 (MOR 1914/79).
    [99] Maume, *Long Gestation*, 145.

Ulster exclusion, which would offer a better prospect of reunification in the long run. Redmond and Dillon shared his assessment, but said there was no way they could sell it to their supporters. The conference discussed both area and time limit, but no decision was reached.

On 4 August the United Kingdom entered the European war, and Ireland was suddenly reduced to a question of minor concern. On the previous day, after Sir Edward Grey had made his epic speech, Redmond—in the absence of Dillon and after whispered advice from T. P. O'Connor not to speak—declared that Ireland would defend its own shores against the German enemy.[100] That day Redmond also had a private interview with Asquith, who was too overwhelmed by the wider situation to give Redmond confirmation that the Home Rule Bill would be put onto the statute book. Afterwards Devlin was 'raging' about this 'in his operatic way, and declares he himself will get up and denounce the Government'. He told T.P. that the Party's position in Ireland would be intolerable without the Bill, 'with the Sinn Féiners and that crew denouncing the Government for treachery and calling for German success'. Redmond, however, was convinced that the Party would see the passage of the Bill before the end of 1914.[101] Devlin sent a desperate telegram to Dillon urging him to come to London.[102] T. P. O'Connor's biographer suggests that it was Redmond's pledge in the Commons that had enraged Devlin.[103] The next day, presumably after he had received some 'feedback' from colleagues, Redmond wrote to Churchill to ask for his help in persuading Asquith to act. He was, he said, very aware that in his speech of the previous day he had taken 'very great risks . . . if the Home Rule Bill be postponed . . . [My people] will consider themselves sold and I will be simply unable to hold them.'[104]

LABOUR IN BELFAST AND DUBLIN

In Belfast in 1907 Jim Larkin had no political party and, in so far as he constituted a political challenge, it was to the Unionists. He did not seem to constitute a threat to the Nationalist movement, and, to the extent that he drew Catholic and Protestant workers together in common action, his contribution was from Devlin's point of view a helpful one. In the south of Ireland the situation was different. The Irish Party had no need of Larkin there, and he was later to complain that Devlin, who had professed friendship in Belfast, worked against him in Cork and Wexford.[105] When he arrived in Dublin, Larkin's first political

---

[100] D. Gwynn, *Redmond*, 355.   [101] O'Connor to Dillon, 4 Aug. 1914 (DP 6740/223).
[102] Devlin to Dillon, 4 Aug. 1914 (DP 6730/165).   [103] Brady, *T. P. O'Connor*, 218.
[104] Redmond to Churchill, 4 Aug. 1914 (Randolph S. Churchill, *Winston S. Churchill*, ii. 1422).
[105] J. M. Hone, 'James Larkin and the Nationalist Party', *Contemporary Review*, 104/786 (Dec. 1913).

move had been to seek to re-establish a branch of the British-based Independent Labour Party (ILP) in the city. Likewise in August 1908, speaking at the Dublin Trades Council, he opposed the expansion of Irish-based unions. But on 7 December 1908, following several clashes with his executive, he was suspended by the National Union of Dock Labourers (NUDL). His national views were rapidly reversed, and on 4 January 1909 the Irish membership of the NUDL became the basis for Larkin's new union, the Irish Transport and General Workers' Union (ITGWU).[106] Although it drew its initial energy from the reputation that Larkin had established in Belfast, the ITGWU was a Dublin-based union, which associated itself frankly with radical nationalism. It was disliked as much by the Catholic Church as it was by Unionists, but it found a significant base of support among the unskilled working class in the cities of southern Ireland. Meanwhile in Belfast the NUDL, now led locally by Alex Boyd, became a union supported mainly by Protestants, as the southern-based ITGWU began to organize among Belfast Catholics. Boyd made rather clumsy efforts to prevent this, which may have been counterproductive: 'The ITGWU was a Sinn Féin organization', he declared, that 'not even a decent Nationalist in Belfast would have anything to do with'.[107] But it was not until the arrival of James Connolly in Belfast in June 1911 that the ITGWU gained any strength in the northern capital, with a membership of between 600 and 800 men, almost all from the Catholic-dominated deep-sea docks.[108] Connolly developed an analysis that linked the national and the social struggles, but that also split the labour movement into pro- and anti-nationalist factions, as was happening at the same time in other ethnically divided regions of Europe.[109] In Belfast he had some industrial success, though little political success, in drawing Catholics into a cohesive labour organization. Perhaps his most distinctive achievement in the city was to lead a group of Protestant labour activists to a republican socialist position. Several such individuals made what proved to be a lifetime commitment.[110]

William McMullen was a young shipwright at Harland and Wolff when he met Connolly on the latter's first visit to Belfast in 1910. Son of a Presbyterian RIC pensioner, he became a socialist at an early age, but not till he met Connolly did he become aware of a socialist school of thought in anything other than the British tradition. Connolly soon persuaded McMullen that the old ILP line, of socialism being compatible with views for or against home rule, was not acceptable and that henceforth it was to be stated unequivocally in all parts of the city that 'we favoured the granting of home rule to Ireland, and that it was entirely inconsistent with the principles of socialism to deny such a right'. In

---

[106] A. Mitchell, *Labour in Irish Politics* (Dublin, 1974), 25–6; Morgan, *Labour and Partition*, 116.

[107] *Northern Whig*, 23 Jan. 1909.

[108] Statement by James Clarke. Transcript of BBC NI Radio programme on Larkin and the 1907 Strike, 1957 (Sam Hanna Bell Papers, D3358/1); Larkin, *James Larkin*, 99.

[109] A. C. Hepburn, *Contested Cities in the Modern West* (London, 2004), 233.

[110] McMullen, *With James Connolly*.

1912 McMullen attended a meeting in Dublin, along with Connolly and others from Belfast, at which it was agreed to reorganize the Socialist Party of Ireland as the Independent Labour Party of Ireland. A Belfast branch, with McMullen as chairman, was formed, which sat alongside the four branches of the British ILP in the city. But after the pro-unionist William Walker had left the Labour movement for an appointment under the National Insurance Act, there was for a while in Belfast a joint committee of the local ILP and ILP (Ireland) 'to conduct propaganda'. Connolly stood as a Labour candidate for the Belfast City Council in Dock Ward in January 1913. He obtained only about 900 votes, mainly from the Catholic side of the local community, and was defeated by two to one in a straight fight with a Unionist.[111] Increasingly he was able to speak only in Catholic neighbourhoods, and even there he was several times attacked by Nationalist youths over his criticism of Redmond's and Devlin's apparent concessions on Ulster home rule.[112] As war in Europe drew near it became increasingly difficult for the ILP (Ireland)'s regular open-air meetings to get a hearing, and soon after the war had started the branch voted to discontinue them, to the annoyance of Connolly and McMullen.

The unskilled working class in Dublin at this time was one of the poorest in Europe. Dublin's death rate was the highest of any large city west of Moscow. During the great Dublin strike and lockout of Autumn 1913 the young lecturer Tom Dillon, who worked on a peace committee organized by T. M. Kettle, wrote later that it would be 'difficult for anyone who got any insight into the plight of the Dublin labourer in those days not to come down' on Larkin's side, but 'the labourer did not always receive the sympathy of the grades of worker above him'.[113] Larkin's agitation began with a strike by drivers of the Dublin Tramway Company, which was owned by William Martin Murphy. A meeting called by Larkin in O'Connell Street for Sunday 31 August was banned, but Larkin, in disguise, suddenly appeared on the balcony of the Imperial Hotel—also owned by W. M. Murphy—at the appointed hour, and began to address the large promenading crowd below. He was quickly seized by the police, but meanwhile a major police baton charge took place, in which it was alleged that 200 people, mainly bystanders, were injured. Devlin's paper, the *Irish News*, though it denounced the police baton charge as 'a thoroughly brutal and disgusting performance', dismissed Larkin's balcony appearance as 'a trivial, tawdry, undignified and stagey trick'. Larkin had called a strike of tramway men, only about one-tenth of whom had responded, it claimed. No strike pay was available for the 150 men who were out. Opponents of home rule, declared the paper, were making much play with events in Dublin as an indication of

[111] Ibid. 4–5, 7, 26–7, 28, 30.

[112] Peter Collins (ed.), *Nationalism and Unionism: Conflict In Ireland, 1885–1921* (Belfast, 1994), 138.

[113] Thomas Dillon, unpublished memoir, 'Events of 1916–17' (deVP, P150/576).

what might happen under an Irish Parliament.[114] Dillon's conclusion was that 'Murphy is a desperate character, Larkin as bad. It would be a blessing to Ireland if they exterminated each other.'[115] While Murphy's stubborn resistance finally broke Larkinism as an industrial force, the political impact of the movement was curtailed somewhat earlier. When Larkin thoughtlessly allowed some radical suffragettes to start a scheme for the evacuation of starving Catholic children to England for the duration of the strike, he provided both an opportunity for Archbishop Walsh to denounce him and a practical issue around which a rival force could organize on the streets. Hibernian mobs, with young priests at the head, were able to picket ships bound for England and trains destined for Belfast, in order to save young Catholic souls.[116] The *Irish News* denounced the evacuation plan as a 'vile and sinister campaign', although Michael McKeown, a Belfast UIL city councillor and Devlinite, who was employed as organizer for the ITGWU, was involved in organizing the exodus of the children.[117]

It is easy to understand how Larkin and Connolly came to regard the Hibernians as the storm troopers of capitalism. In Dublin, the AOH had led the resistance to the Sinn Féin challenge during the lean years after 1906, and it responded to Larkinism in very much the same way. If its action gave assistance to William Martin Murphy—whose newspaper and whose political associates had been hostile to the Irish Party for many years—it was not because the AOH was anti-labour but because Murphy's challenge to the Party had at that stage been ineffectual and Larkin's had not. The Hibernians opposed Larkin, not because they were a 'bourgeois organization', but because they saw Larkinism primarily as a dangerous challenge to Party authority and a divisive force in the Nationalist ranks. The conflict was more about party politics than social revolution. The conservative Nationalist Tim Healy told his friend Murphy that 'I should prefer Larkin to Devlin'.[118] Likewise, Carson's fellow Unionist MP for Dublin University, James Campbell, declared in a speech during the strike that 'I would rather suffer under the whips of Larkin than under the scorpions of Joe Devlin. I honestly believe I would have a greater chance of liberty, of personal judgement and of conscience under Jim Larkin and the Irish Transport Union, than I would have under Joe Devlin and the Molly Maguires.'[119] Larkin, too, thought that 'John Redmond only dances when Joe whistles'.[120] But James Connolly thought that Devlin might be in ignorance of the 'yellow unionism' with which the AOH had been associated. Once home rule came in, he wrote, 'should "Wee Joe" elect to follow the democratic path, I should not be surprised to see the AOH break with him and brush him

[114] *IN*, 1 and 8 Sept. 1913
[115] Padraig Yeates, *Lockout: Dublin, 1913* (Dublin, 2000), 240.
[116] Arnold Wright, *Disturbed Dublin* (London, 1914), 223–5; Desmond Greaves, *The Life & Times of James Connolly* (London, 1961), 258.
[117] *IN*, 22 and 23 Oct. 1913   [118] Yeates, *Lockout*, 238.
[119] Ibid. 445.   [120] Ibid. 421.

contemptuously aside'.[121] The writer J. M. Hone took a different view again, commenting that the AOH 'is attacked also by conservative Nationalists of the type of the farmer, who fears that his newly-won prosperity will be endangered by radical legislation, and looks on Mr Devlin as the boon companion of Mr [Lloyd] George'.[122]

'THE EDGE OF THE VOLCANO': POLITICIANS AND VOLUNTEERS, 1914

Shortly after the Home Rule Bill had passed the Commons for the first time in January 1913, the 'Ulster Clubs' were formally redesignated by the Ulster Unionist Council as the Ulster Volunteer Force, a private army that by the end of that year had grown in membership to more than 90,000 men. There was much mockery of this force from the Nationalist side, and the word 'bluff' was never far from the lips of Liberal and Nationalist politicians. The Belfast Police Commissioner agreed that the leaders might be bluffing, but thought it 'impossible to doubt the fanaticism and determination of the rank and file'.[123] Although Ulster Nationalists, in particular, were said to be unimpressed by the threat, as the UVF grew it inevitably encouraged the emergence of similar instincts on the other side. In November 1913 Eoin MacNeill published an article entitled 'The North Began', calling for the creation of an Irish Volunteer Force and suggesting—somewhat bizarrely—that Carson's UVF had set a good example to the Irish people by standing firm against the British, and followed it up with a mass meeting in Dublin. The Irish Volunteers came into existence almost immediately in Dublin, and soon appeared in provincial towns, mainly with non-Irish Party figures to the fore. A meeting in Cork a few days later went badly wrong when MacNeill's fatuous call for 'three cheers for Carson' was misinterpreted as a call for some kind of O'Brienite conciliation. The day after MacNeill's meeting Devlin called on Dillon, who expressed anxiety about the new development. Devlin, on the other hand, thought that, if ignored, it would fizzle out.[124] Lord Dunraven was nearer the mark when he told O'Brien that 'We are sitting on the very edge of a volcano'.[125] The Irish Party leaders made no public comment for some time. John Muldoon MP wrote in mid-December that 'Redmond does not like this thing, neither does Devlin, but they are loath to move at present'.[126] In January 1914 Devlin advised the Newry AOH leader

---

[121] *Forward*, 30 Aug. 1913.   [122] Hone, 'James Larkin', 786–7.

[123] RIC County Inspectors' Reports, Belfast, July 1913 (TNA: PRO CO 904/90).

[124] Dillon to O'Connor, 26 Nov. 1913 (DP 6740/211a).

[125] Sally Warwick-Haller, 'Seeking Conciliation: William O'Brien and the Ulster Crisis, 1911–14', in D. George Boyce and Alan O'Day (eds.), *The Ulster Crisis, 1885–1921* (London, 2006), 162.

[126] J. J. Horgan, *Parnell to Pearse* (Dublin, 1948), 229.

to have nothing to do with it, just as in Belfast in 1912 he had 'swiftly quashed proposals to found a Catholic military corps'.[127] Nonetheless the movement began to spread steadily. The poet and teacher Thomas MacDonagh, later executed for his part in the Rising, wrote enthusiastically to a colleague in New York that, while 'a good part of the old generation' are against us, and 'think it is our business to fight not England but Ulster . . . we have with us our whole generation, including such men as Joe Devlin', a claim that was totally untrue.[128]

By April 1914 membership of the Irish Volunteers stood at 19,000.[129] On 23 March Colonel Maurice Moore, a retired British Army officer from a west of Ireland Catholic gentry family, who had been appointed Inspector-General of the Volunteers by MacNeill's provisional committee, met Redmond, Dillon, and Devlin at Westminster. Dillon reiterated his opposition to the movement, but Redmond said—according to Moore's memoirs—that he was beginning to swing in favour of the idea, as was Devlin.[130] This preliminary meeting set in chain a long series of negotiations, culminating in an effective takeover of the Volunteers by the Irish Party in June 1914. The central point of discussion was control of the force. It had a provisional committee of twenty-five members, few of whom had any public association with the Irish Party and a significant number of whom were Irish Republican Brotherhood (IRB) men and/or Sinn Féiners. Devlin told the Volunteer leaders on 15 April that Redmond must 'dominate' the Volunteers. The growing popularity of volunteering had thus forced the Irish Party to rethink. Redmond and Dillon drafted a statement saying that Carson's behaviour, the Curragh incident, the Larne gun-running, and the government's failure to deal with it 'convinced the leaders of the National Party that they could no longer withhold their sanction from the creation of a National Volunteer force', while John D. Nugent circulated all AOH divisions with advice to join their local Irish Volunteer unit or, where none existed, to start one.[131] Negotiations between the Party and the Volunteer leaders finally collapsed, whereupon Redmond issued an ultimatum demanding that a matching number of nominees should be added to the twenty-five members of the Provisional Committee, or he would start a rival organization. The Provisional Committee decided by majority vote to agree. By that stage the Irish Volunteers numbered about 100,000 men, of whom 35,000 were ex-army.[132]

The Irish Party was no longer perceived as being against the Volunteer movement, but a few days later Patrick Pearse told Joseph McGarrity of

[127] RIC Crime Special Branch, Précis of Information, Jan. 1914 (TNA: PRO CO 904/120/1); Bardon, *History of Ulster*, 442.

[128] F. X. Martin and R. J. Byrne (eds.), *The Scholar Revolutionary* (Shannon, 1973), 177.

[129] Cabinet paper, 30 Apr. 1914 (TNA: PRO CAB 37/119/60).

[130] Col. M. Moore, 'History of the Irish Volunteers', written 1918 (*Irish Press*, 8–10 Jan. 1938); Tierney, *Eoin MacNeill*, 129.

[131] Typed draft, and draft in Dillon's handwriting, n.d. (RP 15182/22); circular from Nugent, 9 May 1914 (NLI, Eamon Ceannt Papers, 13070).

[132] *The Times*, 11 June 1914.

Philadelphia that Redmond 'wants to arm them not against England, but against the Orangemen. The Volunteers are to be used to force home rule on Ulster, and possibly to enforce the dismemberment of Ireland.' A standing committee was formed, and Pearse lamented to McGarrity that of its thirteen members all but five 'will do exactly as Redmond tells them', but he thought that they should not break away until 'our men are at least armed'.[133] Meanwhile Redmond arranged to buy from Belgium 6,000 rifles of what Moore called 'a discarded type', which they imported via the Holyhead mailboat with government approval, although the Redmondites later tried to create an illusion of 'gun-running'.[134] Pearse told McGarrity that the committee had 'officially decided to send all arms to Ulster—which means to Devlin's followers. We are determined not to acquiesce in this.'[135] Then on 26 July 900 guns and ammunition were delivered into the small port of Howth, near Dublin, and marched into the city in broad daylight. A further 600 rifles were landed further down the coast in Wicklow. This was instigated by dissident members of the Irish Volunteers. Many of the Howth guns reappeared on the streets of Dublin at Easter 1916.[136] Only twenty-five were recorded as reaching Belfast.[137] As the weapons from Howth, accompanied by a very large crowd on a summer Sunday afternoon, reached the centre of Dublin, a unit of British soldiers retaliated to abuse and stoning by firing on the crowd at Bachelor's Walk, killing three people and wounding thirty. This incident was to have enormous repercussions. Pearse's instant reaction was that 'the whole country has been re-baptized by bloodshed for Ireland'.[138] Devlin asked Birrell in the Commons to explain 'the differential treatment by the authorities of the Ulster Volunteers in Belfast, as compared with their action in regard to the Irish Volunteers in Dublin yesterday'.[139] The senior police officials responsible for the handling of events on 26 July resigned, and subsequently the enactment against arms importations was repealed.

The outbreak of war in Europe, on the one hand, shifted Ireland from the centre to the periphery of British cabinet priorities, but at the same time brought military concerns, drilling, arms, and recruitment to the forefront of public interest. Military men like Moore were concerned that the mobilization of British Army reservists immediately left the Irish Volunteers in a fix—'it takes away in one swoop some 25,000 of our soldiers and most of our instructors, just when they were most wanted'.[140] For Eoin MacNeill, still trying to sit on the fence between the Irish Party and the serious revolutionaries on the Volunteer committee, the situation was of increasing concern, and on 9 August he wrote

---

[133] Ó Buachalla (ed.), *Letters of P. H. Pearse*, 316–21.
[134] Typescript, 'History of the Irish Volunteers', 291–3 (MMP 8489/5).
[135] Ó Buachalla (ed.), *Letters of P. H. Pearse*, 322.   [136] Ibid. 325.
[137] Berkeley, Memoir, 37 (NLI, Berkeley Papers, 7880).
[138] Ó Buachalla (ed.), *Letters of P. H. Pearse*, 322.
[139] Parl. Deb., H.C., 5th series, lxv. 936 (27 July 1914).
[140] Moore to Redmond, 8 Aug. 1914 (RP).

to Redmond that 'it would be well if you were represented in Dublin by some person in close and immediate relation with yourself and recognized to be in that position, such as your brother or Mr Devlin'.[141]

VOLUNTEERING IN BELFAST

Advanced nationalism was weak in the North in the first years of the twentieth century, as it was elsewhere in Ireland. When the young Ulster Protestant Ernest Blythe went to Belfast in 1909, having been converted to republicanism during his spell as a Dublin civil servant, he joined the Belfast Circle of the IRB, which then had about fifteen members.[142] Among the most prominent of the younger generation, however, were two Belfast men, Bulmer Hobson and Denis McCullough, both of whom faded into the background after 1916. The 'No. 1 Dungannon Club' was founded in Belfast in 1906. The club's membership numbered about two dozen, including several from the South of Ireland. In 1907 Hobson raised £100 in America, which enabled the branch to publish a few issues of a journal, the *Republic*. Seán McDermott was employed at the modest wage of 15*s.* per week to work as Ulster organizer. Hobson invited selected members of the Club to join the IRB. On several occasions Club members debated the politics of physical force versus constitutionalism at the National Club with some of Devlin's supporters, who were 'men of mature years'. The republicans made no headway, which convinced Hobson that converts to physical force could not be made among grown-up men, and that efforts should be concentrated on the youth. 'The members of the Dungannon Club earned very modest livelihoods,' recalled one member, 'but they were confirmed in the view that the question of freedom was more important than better social conditions.' Shortly afterwards the Dungannon Clubs, although their beliefs were republican, merged into Arthur Griffith's Sinn Féin movement.[143]

For some years prior to 1914 a 'Freedom Club' also operated in Belfast. It appears to have had a very similar membership to the earlier Dungannon Club, and it was associated with the *Irish Freedom* newspaper. Its immediate aim was 'educational', focusing on the young people of the Fianna, but essentially it was an IRB front organization.[144] Its membership included McCullough, Hobson, Ernest Blythe, Cathal O'Shannon, Seán Lester (later to become League of Nations High Commissioner in Danzig), and Joseph Connolly. Blythe and Hobson were Protestants, as was Rory Haskin, a Belfast man with six years' service in the British Army behind him. He joined the Orange Order in 1912,

---

[141] MacNeill to Redmond, 9 Aug. 1914, cited in Tierney, *Eoin MacNeill*, 144.
[142] E. Blythe, unpublished memoir, 4a (Blythe Papers, P24/173).
[143] Liam Gaynor witness statement, 21 Oct. 1948 (BMH, witness statement 183).
[144] Thomas Wilson witness statement, 19 Oct. 1948 (BMH, witness statement 176).

and then the UVF, before being converted to republicanism by a friend, who took him to the Freedom Club. Blythe and Lester later swore him into the IRB.[145] Casement and Eoin MacNeill were initially against starting the Irish Volunteers in the North, but Joseph Connolly called for it in an appeal, 'The Need of the North', which Arthur Griffith endorsed in *Sinn Féin*. In March 1914 the Freedom Club invited all nationalist organizations to a meeting to establish the Irish Volunteers in the city. McCullough was elected chairman, Joseph Connolly vice-chairman, and Michael Carolan secretary, all of whom were later prominent in the Republican movement. Another leading figure was Seamus Dobbyn, son of the old Belfast Fenian and AOH (American Alliance) activist Harry Dobbyn. When McCullough opened the meeting, a Board of Erin Hibernian read out a letter from Devlin 'expressing his approval of forming the Volunteers as a protection against Carson's Ulster Volunteers, but he did not approve of the time or place of forming them'. The republicans present took the view that this was intended as a blocking move by Devlin, 'to influence his supporters not to get mixed up with our formation'. But, according to Tom Wilson's account, another Hibernian spoke in favour of the proposal, which 'gave us the necessary support to get a start made'. A 'governing committee' was created, which soon divided into a 'civil committee' with overall control and a 'military committee'. Most of the men who joined the Volunteers at the start, recalled Wilson, were 'men of good national background, who looked upon the Volunteer organization as an essential safeguard for all nationalists against the attentions of the Carsonite Volunteers. The welding of all the men who joined . . . in the direction of extreme republicanism was the task undertaken by the small number of IRB men in Belfast.'[146]

The majority of the civil committee were republicans.[147] Among those on the military committee were Peter Burns (chairman), the Army reservist NCO Seán Cusack, and the ex-soldier Rory Haskin. George Berkeley, later appointed by Moore as inspecting officer for Belfast, described this committee as 'the most august assembly of which I have ever been a member', for it was made up mainly of NCOs who had served at Spion Kop, Ulundi, and other great imperial battles of the previous generation. These men, Berkeley continued, even though they in practice ran the companies and trained the officers, would not agree to become officers: 'they considered that it would be more to the credit of the movement if the officers came from the richer classes.'[148] Only six members of the two committees were IRB men—McCullough, O'Shannon, Tom Wilson, Frank Booth, Cusack, and Peter Burns.[149] Seán Cusack and Haskin led the training, until Cusack was recalled

---

[145] Rory Haskin, witness statement, 13 Oct. 1948 (BMH, witness statement 223).
[146] Wilson, witness statement 176.   [147] Ibid.
[148] Ibid.; Berkeley, Memoir, 49 (NLI, Berkeley Papers, 7880).
[149] Frank Booth, witness statement, 14 Oct. 1948 (BMH, witness statement 229).

to the British Army on the outbreak of the First World War, when Peter Burns took it over.[150]

In April 1914 the movement in Belfast had little more than 100 members, drawn from Sinn Féin, the Gaelic League, the IRB, and the Freedom Club. The City Police Commissioner reported that the clergy and the Nationalist leadership opposed the movement and that the local UIL and AOH had threatened their members with expulsion if they joined.[151] But once the Irish Party leaders put word around the country to its supporters to join, the position in Belfast changed, as it did elsewhere. From the end of May the Belfast Volunteers were 'practically swamped with recruits'.[152] Devlin, who according to *The Times* had been elected commanding officer in Belfast, held a major review of the city's Volunteers on 7 June. The *Times* reporter was impressed with the appearance of the troops who, 'for the most part . . . were of the same type as many of the men in the Unionist ranks—young fellows out of shops and offices with a sprinkling of older recruits . . . [but] . . . The skilled artisan element, which is so valuable to the UVF, seemed to be lacking altogether.'[153] Many more ex-British Army NCOs joined at this time, but their political outlook was different from that of the local founders. 'They were enthusiastic about the idea of fighting against Carson's Ulster Volunteers,' recalled Seán Cusack, 'but the idea of fighting for independence seemed hopeless in their eyes.'[154]

Following Redmond's national takeover, the local Belfast committee was asked to admit nominees proposed by Devlin, Tom Wilson advised McCullough not to do it, 'as the admission of Mr Devlin's followers would weaken instead of strengthen the morale of the organization'. If the matter had gone to a vote on the Belfast committee, in Wilson's view, the proposal would not have been carried. But McCullough had received instructions from Dublin and the proposal was accepted without a vote. One Devlinite nominee was Bernard Campbell, who later became a Sinn Féiner, following a transition through the Irish Nation League (INL). Other prominent members were Devlin's old colleague Thomas Maguire and Charles McLorinan, a former 'bishop's man'. According to Wilson, although 'the Devlin partisans were endeavouring to control or to smash up the organization', the Belfast executive committee 'remained soundly republican'. There was some friction with Devlin's nominees, 'which did much harm but did not effect any change in policy'.[155] The police, however, thought that the Devlinites were in effective charge, with 'the original leaders gradually being

[150] Cathal McDowell, witness statement, 14 Oct. 1948 (BMH, witness statement 173).

[151] RIC County Inspectors' Reports, Belfast, Mar. and Apr. 1914 (TNA: PRO CO 904/92, 93); Haskin, witness statement 223; Seán Cusack, witness statement, 23 Apr. 1948 (BMH, witness statement 9).

[152] Haskin, witness statement 223; Cusack, witness statement 9.

[153] *The Times*, 8 and 11 June 1914.   [154] Cusack, witness statement 9.

[155] Wilson, witness statement 176.

ousted'.[156] Devlin confidently advised Dillon that 'the rank-and-file will get rid of the local leaders'.[157] In Dublin Devlin told the Provisional Committee at the first meeting that the Redmondites attended, on 14 July, that he had just run enough guns into Belfast to arm his men, including two machine guns. 'All this would be excellent if the men were genuine nationalists,' lamented Pearse to McGarrity, 'but they are only home-rulers-at-any-price.'[158]

At the end of June 1914 an Englishman born in Dublin into an Anglo-Irish gentry family, George Fitzhardinge Berkeley, was appointed commanding officer of the Irish Volunteers in Belfast. Rory Haskin, by this time a committed republican, reflected in later years that 'this man's idea was probably the use that could be made of Volunteers on the British side in the war'.[159] But unlike many Southern ex-unionists who sought to join the Irish Volunteers in July and August 1914, Berkeley had long identified with the home-rule cause and had been incensed by the establishment of the UVF and the workplace expulsions of 1912. He was in his mid-forties, with some very limited and distant military experience.[160] He made a financial contribution to the Howth gun-running plan, but opted out of participating, as he was prone to seasickness. By way of compensation he said: 'I'll go to Belfast. That is the place where there is sure to be trouble.' He went to Dublin and sought out Colonel Moore, after which he spent a weekend touring Ulster. On a Volunteer platform at Dungannon on 6 June he met McCullough and Casement. Berkeley was slightly taken aback by the separatist tone of their speeches, but put it down to the enthusiasm of the moment. He noted that 'Mr Devlin and the Nationalist Party knew what they were about; in any case I regarded them as my governing body'.[161] Afterwards Casement asked Berkeley to go to Belfast as organizing officer.[162] Berkeley accepted on the basis that his authority to use force came from the parliamentary majority of the Irish people. His Unionist cousins in Co. Cork warned him that 'you and others are forging a weapon that will be turned against you'.[163]

On 6 July Berkeley took up his post in Belfast. The first people he met were McCullough and two of the most prominent British Army people in the movement—both, in fact, committed republicans—Joe Burns and Seán Cusack. Berkeley thought McCullough 'nice-looking and nice-spoken . . . But at first sight I saw no particular reason for the influence which undoubtedly he possessed.'[164] Berkeley was able to demonstrate his seriousness of purpose by

[156] RIC County Inspectors' Reports, Belfast, May, June, and Aug. 1914 (TNA: PRO CO 904/93, 94).

[157] Dillon to Redmond, 3 June 1914 (RP 15182/20).

[158] Ó Buachalla (ed.), *Letters of P. H. Pearse*, 319–20.   [159] Haskin, witness statement 223.

[160] Berkeley, Memoir, Introduction (NLI, Berkeley Papers, 7880).   [161] Ibid. 38.

[162] Berkeley, witness statement, 1 July 1954 (BMH, witness statement 971).

[163] R. E. Longfield to Berkeley, 8 and 10 Sept. 1914 (CCCA, Berkeley Papers, PR12/104, 106).

[164] Berkeley, witness statement 971.

buying a small number of guns for the Volunteers immediately. His duties were mainly administration in the mornings, searching round the city and nearby countryside for suitable drill and musketry sites in the afternoons, and attending several parades every evening, before returning to a life among the journalists at the Grand Central Hotel. The Catholics of Belfast, he thought, were 'iniquitously treated'. Several of the first Volunteers he met, including a sergeant-major with twelve years' experience in the British Army, had been victims of the expulsions. Many of his men he found to be uneasy about drilling in the open or where they could be observed, as some had already lost their jobs owing to their participation in the Volunteers. 'Our system', he wrote to his wife, 'is to work entirely in the Catholic quarter of the town.'[165] As the summer went by, Berkeley was increasingly concerned that when the Home Rule Bill passed into law there could be an attack by the UVF. His forces had very few rifles, and many of the men were untrained in rifle-shooting. One night a UVF unit marched through a Catholic neighbourhood at 2 a.m. The Bachelor's Walk incident made him even more anxious, for the UVF still outnumbered the Irish Volunteers in Belfast by about five to one. He was relieved shortly after that when Colonel Moore and his deputy Colonel Cotter visited Belfast. A meeting of 'about a hundred responsible and sober-minded residents' took place, 'to decide the momentous question of defence'.[166] They 'evolved a complete plan of action in case of any attack by the UVF', with detailed preparations covering the Falls area, and also Catholic areas in north, east, and south Belfast.[167]

For some months after Redmond's takeover of the Volunteers their status in the eyes of the authorities, even in Belfast, was almost semi-official. Berkeley recalled that policemen in the Falls area used to salute him. On 15 August he rode on 'my noble black steed' at the head of his battalions down a Falls Road absolutely brimming with crowds, thirty or forty thousand people he estimated, and felt 'as if he had done great things . . . It is rather touching how grateful these poor harassed people are for the very little that one can do for them.'[168] Belfast, he thought, was 'the noisiest [town] that I have ever been in; far worse than Milan'.[169] Recruits were joining the Volunteers at an ever-faster rate, and for a while Berkeley's team could scarcely cope. When he joined in July 1914, the Irish Volunteers in Belfast numbered about 3,000, in five battalions. During his time in charge he estimated that about 5,000 passed through the ranks, half of whom, he thought, 'got any real training'. A few Protestant home rulers joined

[165] Berkeley to his wife, 13 and 14 July 1914 (NLI, Berkeley Papers, 13266/1).

[166] E. Cotter to Berkeley, 27 July 1914 (CCCA, Berkeley Papers, PR12/58); Berkeley, Memoir, 51 (NLI, Berkeley Papers, 7880).

[167] Berkeley, witness statement 971; 'Confidential memorandum', 5 Aug. 1914 (CCCA, Berkeley Papers, PR12/10).

[168] Berkeley, Memoir, 53–4, 80 (NLI, Berkeley Papers, 7880); Berkeley to his wife, 16 Aug. 1914 (NLI, Berkeley Papers, 13266/1).

[169] Berkeley to his wife, 10 Aug. 1914 (NLI, Berkeley Papers, 13266/1).

the Irish Volunteers, 'but it was very difficult for them to do so'.[170] Once the Home Rule Act became law, on 18 September, Berkeley took the view that his work was done, and he left Belfast. For most of the war he was a musketry officer at Bisley, before serving in France and Italy from late 1917 onwards.[171]

Of the Volunteers whose army service Berkeley admired so much, the most prominent was Seán Cusack, a long-standing NCO in the British Army who, by 1912, was in his forties and living as an army reservist with his family in Belfast. For some years he had taken the view that constitutional nationalism was unlikely to achieve its objectives. He contacted the AOH (American Alliance), which led to a visit from two local IRB men, and he was sworn into that body early in 1912 in the house of Denis McCullough's parents in Grosvenor Road. Until the Irish Volunteers were formed in Belfast, his activities were limited to attending meetings of the IRB, Gaelic Athletic Association (GAA), and Gaelic League. He was present at the meeting that established the Volunteers in Belfast, and was appointed senior instructor. After the Devlinites had joined, the new military committee suggested to him that he, as a military man, should replace McCullough as O/C. He sensed, however, that there was a political motive behind this, and refused. At the outbreak of war he was recalled to the British Army as a machine-gun instructor based at Holywood, Co. Down, but his circumstances permitted him to continue his work with the Volunteers. He took the republican side in the October split, and believed that knowledge of this fact was the reason why the military authorities posted him to France on 23 November 1914.[172] He left behind him a very small group of Irish Volunteers and a very large group of Devlinite Volunteers. This situation was to change little during the following two years.

---

[170] Berkeley, Memoir, 53–4, 80 (NLI, Berkeley Papers, 7880).
[171] Berkeley, witness statement 971.   [172] Cusack, witness statement 9.

7

Belfast, Ireland, and the War, 1914–1918

Heaven knows what the future holds if England is drawn into this European war.

(Patrick Pearse, 1914[1])

Destroy this constitutional movement and we will see if you can settle this question by relegating it to the immensity of time.

(Joe Devlin, 1916[2])

The years 1913–14 were a time of some concern for Belfast nationalists. Although they were the most populous and concentrated Catholic community in the north-east of Ireland, there seemed to be no kind of compromise that would benefit them. The government's drive for an exclusion-based scheme, on the one hand, and the apparent determination of the Ulster Unionists and the Ulster Volunteer Force (UVF), on the other, together with the bishops' opposition to an alternative such as home rule within home rule, seemed to be boxing them in. It was a time of trial for Devlin, from the pressure to accept temporary exclusion in February 1914 to the unwelcome emergence of paramilitary forces on both sides and then his personal exclusion from the Buckingham Palace Conference. His reaction was relatively buoyant. The Unionists appeared resistant to all suggestions of compromise short of permanent six-county exclusion, which the government still seemed to regard as a demand too far. Thus Nationalists could still convince themselves that the original Home Rule Bill would win through. Devlin remained optimistic, supportive of the Liberal Government, and, for the first time in his career, closer to Redmond than to Dillon in terms of positive support for the war effort. But the next four years were to see a downward spiral. The Volunteer movement brought violent revolution and repression, which drove an ever-deeper wedge between the two communities in Belfast and destroyed the constitutional movement across the country, while the government at Westminster degenerated into coalitions that were more concerned with

---

[1] Ó Buachalla (ed.), *Letters of P. H. Pearse*, 324.
[2] Parl. Deb., H.C., lxxxiv. 2185 (31 July 1916).

maintaining their own stability (and winning the war) than with settling the Irish question. Meanwhile, the Catholic Church was more concerned to run with popular opinion than to take political risks in order to achieve a compromise settlement.

VOLUNTEERS, RECRUITS, AND REBELS

On 22 August 1914 it was reported from Enniskillen that companies of the UVF and Irish National Volunteers had joined together to form an escort of honour for the Inniskilling Fusiliers as they set off to war. Redmond thought: 'if the National Volunteers could succeed in inducing the Ulster Volunteers to combine with them . . . there might be such alleviation of the present bitter feeling as would induce the Ulster Volunteers to fall in with their countrymen.'[3] But, if the government failed the Irish Party, he warned Asquith, 'all the old suspicions would be revived; the forces, small but loud, which at present I am able to control, would break loose'.[4] Eoin MacNeill thought that England's difficulty might become Ireland's opportunity in a new way. He outlined to Devlin a scheme whereby the Irish Party leaders, in the crisis brought on by the war, should 'declare themselves to be by virtue of their election the proper authority for regulating the affairs of Ireland . . . they should claim the direction of administration and should set up a committee for that purpose'. In present circumstances, thought MacNeill, the British Government could not resist such a request. Devlin replied that this 'would be too great a responsibility'. MacNeill concluded that, if 'this was the view of the youngest and most active and enterprising of the Party leaders, the case of the Party appeared to me altogether hopeless'.[5]

Relations within the Provisional Volunteer Committee rapidly worsened. At one meeting Devlin got into an argument with the republican Eamonn Ceannt. 'There is only one name', he said, 'that I can call such a man.' Then, according to a republican witness, Ceannt stood up and

looking straight at Wee Joe said, as he placed his hand containing the pencil behind his back, 'Say that word!'. Wee Joe didn't say that word. His followers, and particularly Father [Frank] O'Hare of Newry, yelled out 'He's going to draw a revolver' and there was a little excitement. Devlin finished his speech very lamely, I thought, and sat down.

The discussion continued in heated vein, as John D. Nugent 'made himself very obnoxious' to the republicans present, charging Pearse with contradicting a statement he had made earlier on. Pearse denied this, and Nugent called him

[3] *WFJ*, 22 Aug. 1914.
[4] Redmond to Asquith, 22 Aug. 1914 (BOD, Asquith Papers, 36, fo. 77).
[5] MacNeill, Memoir (Tierney, *Eoin MacNeill*, 147).

'a lying, contemptible cur'. Pearse then struck Nugent and a few blows were exchanged. 'Peace was made, but not before Father O'Hare rushed down to Ceannt, and with a small automatic pistol in his hand, challenged Ceannt to draw his revolver now! Ceannt only smiled.'[6]

Once the Home Rule Act had been passed (and suspended) on 18 September, Redmond urged Volunteers to sign up for the war 'wherever the firing-line extends'. Devlin soon echoed these sentiments. 'He was delighted to hear the declaration by Mr Redmond that this was not England's war. This was a battle for the rights of small nations.'[7] In August 1914 a huge cartoon was drawn on the pavements of West Belfast, portraying the Kaiser sacking Catholic convents.[8] Devlin urged Irishmen to fight for Catholic Belgium, which, in Protestant republican Rory Haskin's recollection, was the direct cause of the Volunteer split in Belfast.[9] The Belfast committee called for an order to forbid Irish Volunteers from enlisting in the Army. Berkeley thought that McCullough was at the bottom of it, though 'it was proposed by a conceited young ass named [Joe] Connolly'. Devlin was very angry when Berkeley told him of this attempt at anti-recruiting, and stamped about the room saying 'some of these men are no better than pro-German'.[10] The Volunteer split in Belfast took place shortly ahead of the national split.[11] At a city-wide meeting of the Volunteers, Devlin claimed that the fate of home rule hung on acceptance of Redmond's line. He had the support of the majority of people in the hall, and Denis McCullough made only a very brief speech.[12] After a while someone called out 'Come out of that Denis. That man [Devlin] is only twisting.' There was uproar in the hall, and Devlin 'seemed nervous'.[13] According to Joe Connolly's recollection, McCullough

made a futile effort to state our point of view but it was quite evident that the vast majority had been organized to howl down any person who was opposed to the new departure and recruitment for the British Army. We were ejected from the meeting and later when we took stock of the position, we reckoned that only about 200 remained loyal to the original Volunteers.[14]

Across the rest of the country the Royal Irish Constabulary (RIC) estimated that after the split 10 per cent remained with the Irish Volunteers, whereas in six-county Ulster the figure was 4 per cent.[15] In Belfast the police estimated that there were 3,250 National Volunteers and 300 Irish Volunteers, but noted that

　　[6] Seamus O'Connor, statement to the Bureau of Military History, 14 June 1948, copy (MacNeill Papers, LA1/G/117).
　　[7] D. Gwynn, *Redmond*, 392; *The Times*, 26 Sept. 1914.
　　[8] Berkeley, Memoir, 84 (NLI, Berkeley Papers, 7880).　　　　[9] Haskin, witness statement 223.
　　[10] Berkeley to M. Moore, 2 Sept. 1914, copy (CCCA, Berkeley Papers, PR12/97).
　　[11] McDowell, witness statement 173.　　　　[12] Cusack, witness statement 9.
　　[13] James Smyth witness statement, 23 Mar. 1949 (BMH, witness statement 234).
　　[14] Connolly, witness statement 124.
　　[15] RIC and DMP Reports on the Volunteer Split, 31 Oct. 1914 (NLI, 15258).

the latter group 'contained men of considerable influence'.[16] They believed that the leaders of the 'Sinn Féin Volunteers' in the city were Denis McCullough, Joseph Connolly, Herbert Pim (a convert to Catholicism and republicanism who was later to revert to being a Unionist propagandist), Cathal O'Shannon, and Peter Burns.[17] The number remaining with them included several ex-British Army men and reservists, including Seán Cusack. On Easter Sunday 1915, 1,000 Belfast National Volunteers attended an all-Ireland review in Dublin, with 27,000 on parade.[18] The Belfast contingent were all armed with rifles and bayonets, and led the parade. The Cork leader J. J. Horgan wrote enviously that 'I think we were as well-drilled as any there, but the Belfast uniforms gave them a real advantage'.[19] Even the *Leader*, not slow to criticize the Nationalist political establishment, commented that 'in so far as the review was a demonstration against the partition of Ulster it was significant that Belfast should have made the best and most soldierly display, for the nationalist minority in Belfast must naturally be opposed to partition in a more intense degree'.[20] The Irish Volunteers in Belfast, meanwhile, remained essentially the same small group who had started the organization. Rebuilding after the split was, according to Rory Haskin, 'slow, disheartening and heartbreaking work'. The RIC became more antagonistic.[21] The butcher Tom Wilson felt that Devlin's 'deliberate action in splitting the Volunteers was unpardonable, as he well knew that the result of such a split in the city's nationalist population would put the unfortunate Catholic minority in most Orange districts at the mercy of Orange fanatics'.[22] Throughout the pre-Rising period the Irish Volunteers drilled weekly, with a regular attendance of about forty-five. Denis McCullough continued as civilian commander with Peter Burns as O/C. About fifty of them travelled to Dublin in 1915 for the funeral of O'Donovan Rossa.[23] Early in March 1916 Patrick Pearse gave a lecture at St Mary's Hall, inspected a small Volunteer parade, and marched up the Falls with them.[24]

On the eve of the First World War, the proportion of Irishmen in the British Army fractionally exceeded the Irish proportion of the UK population. But during the war recruitment across Ireland, though initially substantial, was lower than in Britain, and fell away sharply after 1916. Eric Mercer has calculated that 144,000 Irishmen were recruited during the war (in addition to regulars and reservists), of whom 46,000 came from Belfast. Catholics,

---

[16] B. Mac Giolla Choille (ed.), *Intelligence Notes, 1913–16* (Dublin, 1966), 73–4.

[17] RIC County Inspectors' Reports, Belfast, Nov. 1914 (CO 904/95)

[18] *National Volunteer*, 10 Apr. 1915.

[19] Horgan to Moore, 6 Apr. 1915 (MMP, 10561/18).   [20] *Leader*, 10 Apr. 1915.

[21] Haskin, witness statement 223; David McGuinness witness statement, 28 July 1950 (BMH, witness statement 417).

[22] Wilson, witness statement 176.

[23] RIC County Inspectors' Reports, Belfast, Apr. 1915 (CO 904/96); Booth, witness statement 229.

[24] Ó Buachalla (ed.), *Letters of P. H. Pearse*, 357.

who constituted 23.2 per cent of the male population of the city, contributed 23.1 per cent of the city's recruits in 1914 and 27.3 per cent in 1915. By December 1915 over 7,800 Belfast Catholics had enlisted since the start of the war, including 2,200 National Volunteers. Belfast men, Catholic or Protestant, were four times as likely to enlist as other Ulstermen. The early weeks of the war were bad for the Belfast labour market. When the economy picked up, recruiting slowed, and was increasingly drawn from the unskilled working class. Unskilled wages in Belfast were in the region of £1 a week. An Army recruit in 1914 earned 7*s.* per week, of which half went direct to his wife if he was married, but his wife also received 12*s.* 6*d.* per week separation allowance, rising to £1 per week for a woman with three children. Recruiting levels were also high from the upper middle class in the city, but skilled workers and lower-middle class categories such as clerks and shop assistants were under-represented.[25] Urbanization levels and socio-economic status were far better predictors of recruiting than was religious denomination. Several Nationalist MPs took commissions, including 53-year-old Willie Redmond, 50-year-old Stephen Gwynn, the former MP Professor Tom Kettle, and three others. Kettle and Redmond were both killed at the front, as were three sons of Nationalist MPs. Devlin was regarded as the most effective member of the Irish Party on recruiting platforms, and at 43 was younger than three of the Nationalist MPs who did serve. According to Stephen Gwynn, Devlin 'wished to join also, but Redmond held that he could not be spared from Ireland . . . Everyone . . . knew that his chief attribute was personal courage. But he was indispensable.'[26] Not everyone liked Devlin's recruiting rhetoric. In a speech in Enniskillen he denounced 'Prussian militarism' and declared that 'we are pursuing the policy of Parnell under the altered circumstances that the Home Rule Bill stands upon the statute book'. An anonymous correspondent from Tipperary sent the press cutting to Dillon, declaring that 'this ranting runt of a Devlin is doing more harm that good. He isn't fit to fight a cat.'[27]

Another matter of concern was how to deal with anti-recruiting literature. Devlin thought that these papers had no practical impact on recruiting and that suppression would only 'make martyrs of them'.[28] Sinn Féin opposition to recruiting was based on arguments regarding 'personal morality' as well as those of 'Irish freedom' and 'no quarrel with Germany'. The British Army, it was alleged, had 'created the market for prostitution which so befouled the O'Connell

[25] E. Mercer, 'For King, Country and a Shilling a Day: Belfast Recruiting Patterns in the Great War', *History Ireland*, 11 (Winter, 2003), 29–33.

[26] S. Gwynn, *Redmond's Last Years*, 183.

[27] Anon. to Dillon, 31 Jan. 1915, encl. *FJ* 29 Jan. 1915 (DP 6730/167).

[28] Nathan to Birrell, 10 Nov. 1914 (BOD, Birrell Papers, MS Eng. C.7033, fos. 22–4); Birrell to Nathan, 4 Nov. 1914 (BOD, Nathan Papers, MS 449, fo. 21); Nathan to E. O'Farrell, 10 Nov. 1914 (BOD, Nathan Papers, MS 462, fo. 107).

Street area' of Dublin. The 'separation women', whose husbands had enlisted, were said to spend their allowances on drink and were portrayed as a disgrace to Irish womanhood. It was alleged that Devlin had formed a secret alliance with the Grand Orient Lodge of the Freemasons, and that the Irish Party brought godlessness and freemasonry into Ireland.[29] Linked to this line of criticism was a visit that O'Connor, Devlin, and a group of Irish parliamentarians made to Paris in April 1915. 'Joe is delighted', T.P. told Dillon, 'at the prospect of seeing Paris from the inside.'[30] They met France's leading political and church figures, including President Poincaré and Premier Viviani. Their aim was to influence Irish and Catholic opinion around the world in support of the war. But in the advanced nationalist press much was made of Viviani's freemasonry and his prominent role in the secularization of public education in France.[31] The mounting carnage at the front during 1915 gave the advanced nationalists another propaganda weapon. James Connolly, although himself working determinedly towards revolutionary violence in Ireland, lost no opportunity to belabour Devlin with responsibility for death in the trenches.[32]

In May 1915 the last Liberal Government collapsed under pressure of the munitions crisis, and a Liberal–Conservative Coalition took over. Asquith remained Prime Minister, Birrell remained at the Irish Office, and the government was still predominantly Liberal. But it was no longer dependent on Irish Party support. Worst of all, Sir Edward Carson accepted a seat in the cabinet. John Redmond was also offered a seat, 'some unknown and unnamed English office', but declined it on the traditional grounds that the Irish Party was pledged not to accept office until home rule was attained.[33] In private T. P. O'Connor took a different view. If not Redmond, he thought, then some other member of the Party should have joined the government. 'If Joe could take the job and do it, I'd sooner see him than anybody, as counter-poise to Carson.'[34] Likewise the *Leader* thought that times had changed and that 'Redmond should go into it and take responsibility; if not Redmond, let Devlin go in; or why not both of them'.[35]

By the autumn of 1914 the infrastructure of the United Irish League (UIL) was beginning to crumble. In three of the eight by-elections that occurred in Catholic-majority constituencies between August 1914 and the Rising, nominating conventions could not be held because the local UIL was too frail. But local Party men were still elected. Only in Dublin College Green, where it defeated Irish Labour with 57 per cent of the poll, was the Party seriously challenged.

[29] B. Novick, *Conceiving Revolution* (Dublin, 2001), 116, 157, 168.
[30] O'Connor to Dillon, 25 Apr. 1915 (DP 6741/249).   [31] Maume, *Long Gestation*, 165.
[32] *Workers' Republic*, 28 Aug. 1915.
[33] Redmond to Asquith, 7 June 1915 (BOD, Asquith Papers, MS 36, fo. 89).
[34] Dillon to O'Connor, 24 May 1915, and O'Connor to Dillon, 25 May 1915 (DP 6741/251, 252).
[35] *Leader*, 26 May 1915.

There was no evidence from these by-elections of a rise in popular support for advanced nationalism. But, in more politically conscious circles, problems were beginning to arise. In July 1915 an order was issued under the Defence of the Realm Act, expelling four Sinn Féin organizers from Ireland. The Party's attempts to distance itself from the expulsions were ineffectual. The *Leader* declared that the Party was 'on the run . . . and the country is disgusted with them'.[36]

THE EASTER RISING

On 10 April 1916 Devlin, in a private outburst against the British administration, told Dillon that 'the amazing thing to me is that everybody in Ireland has not been driven into the Sinn Féin movement. It is perhaps dishonest and illogical but, at any rate, it gives the people a chance of saying what they think.' The government, he thought, had 'nothing but the most absolute contempt for us'.[37] Two weeks later 3,000 armed men of the Irish Volunteers poured onto the streets of Dublin, seizing control of a number of key buildings, which they held for almost a week; 450 people were killed, 2,614 were wounded, and 15 leaders and others were subsequently executed.[38] While the Rising was in progress in Dublin, the 16th (Irish) Division was in the forefront of the fighting on the western front, with 1,970 casualties including 570 killed.[39]

By contrast, the involvement of the Belfast contingent of the Irish Volunteers in the Rising was not tragedy but farce, from which Denis McCullough's reputation never recovered. The number of men available for duty was about the same as the number at the time of the 1914 split.[40] McCullough, one of the organizers imprisoned under the Defence of the Realm Act (DORA) for disobeying an expulsion order, was released in November 1915. Early in December he was elected President of the Irish Republican Brotherhood (IRB) Supreme Council. He had wanted to propose Patrick Pearse for the job, but Seán McDermott had said 'sure, we couldn't control the bloody fellow', and pressed McCullough to take it. Being based in Belfast, McCullough was ill placed to give strong direction to a Dublin-based movement, and in later years came to think that he had really been elected as a front for McDermott.[41] This is confirmed by the fact that he knew nothing of the intended Rising until a few days before it happened. He was then given instructions to lead the Belfast regiment, via Tyrone, to join up with the Connacht men around Galway. When he protested about evacuating Ulster,

---

36 *Leader*, 7 Aug. 1915.   37 Devlin to Dillon, 10 Apr. 1916 (DP 6730/169).
38 Lyons, *Ireland since the Famine*, 375.
39 Charles Townshend, *Easter 1916: The Irish Rebellion* (London, 2005), 270.
40 Wilson, witness statement 176.
41 McCullough, Memoir on 1915–16 (McCP, P120/31/3).

James Connolly replied: 'if we win through, we can think of Ulster and deal with it then.'[42] McCullough thereupon issued orders to the Belfast men to prepare to travel to Tyrone on Easter Saturday for week-end manœuvres.[43] The rifles were taken by taxi to Coalisland, and 130 Belfast Volunteers travelled by train to Dungannon. Frank Booth had heard from fellow-IRB man Peter Burns that the move to Tyrone would mark the beginning of the Rising, but most of the men did not know the trip's real purpose until it got under way. They stayed over the Saturday night in barns and outhouses, having marched from Dungannon station to the mainly Catholic Coalisland district.[44]

On the Friday evening McCullough stayed with the Tyrone Volunteer leader Dr Patrick McCartan at Carrickmore. The next day he accidentally shot himself in the hand while unpacking his pistol. McCartan treated the wound, and, later that evening, they received news of the MacNeill countermand.[45] Early on Easter Sunday McCullough therefore returned to Coalisland and ordered the three company commanders to prepare to return to Belfast. Cathal McDowell sought to argue, reminding McCullough of Pearse's instruction to ignore any countermand. A meeting of officers and the civil committee then took a majority decision to return to Belfast, which McDowell reluctantly accepted, though he believed that, if there had been no mix-up, 'the Belfast men would have gone into action without any misgivings'.[46] Having sent his men home, McCullough decided to make his own way to Dublin, but on the way to the main-line station at Portadown McCartan's car broke down, and McCullough instead procured a lift by motor cycle back to Cookstown, where he rejoined his men.[47] Roger McCorley, still a 14-year old boy at the time, concluded from the Belfast regiment's ineffectual performance that 'a few determined men could have taken action which would have compelled most, if not all, of the British garrison to remain in Belfast. It was from this that my detestation of faint-heartedness in war originated.'[48] Meanwhile, Joe Connolly had developed such a low opinion of McCullough as a military leader that he chose to join up with a Dublin company at Easter 1916 rather than go with the Belfast regiment. He travelled to Dublin on Easter Saturday, but on hearing of MacNeill's cancellation returned home again the next day, and worked at his furniture business during Easter week.[49]

The British Army NCO and IRB member Seán Cusack returned to Belfast on a week's leave in August 1915, but before he could return to France was taken seriously ill and regraded as fit for home service only. From November 1915

[42] McCullough, Memoir on 1915–16, and statement to Pensions Board, June 1942 (McCP, P120/31/5, 12 and P120/26/10–11).

[43] Ibid. (McCP, P120/31/12).

[44] McDowell, witness statement 173; Booth, witness statement 229.

[45] McCullough, statement to Pensions Board (McCP, P120/26/2).

[46] McDowell, witness statement 173.

[47] McCullough, statement to Pensions Board (McCP, P120/26/12–14).

[48] McCorley, witness statement 389.   [49] Connolly, witness statement 124.

until Easter 1916 he worked as a British Army recruiter in central Belfast by day and a training officer for the Irish Volunteers in the evenings. While changing trains at Portadown on Easter Saturday with Rory Haskin, he was told by a messenger from McCullough that everything was off, and that they should return to Belfast. McCullough believed that Cusack 'never forgave me, because he was not let fight'.[50] On Easter Monday Cusack went to the Belfast Gaelic League premises, where he heard that the Rising had commenced in Dublin. The general view was that it would be impossible to do anything in Belfast, as all their arms and ammunition had been left in Tyrone. The next day Cusack returned to his British Army recruiting duties. Soon afterwards he was arrested when a raid on the Volunteers' office turned up an incriminating note in his handwriting. He was put before a military court, which, taking into consideration his long Army record, decided that he was 'innocently drawn' into his part of the affair. Having agreed to give an undertaking that he would not in future consort with people he knew or suspected of being subversives, he was released and returned to duty.[51]

After the Coalisland fiasco, the Belfast Volunteers arrived back in the city on Easter Sunday night. 'All during Easter Week', recalled Tom Wilson, 'the Volunteers kept quietly in contact. Mr McCullough was not moving about at the time [he was in fact lying low at a house in the Protestant Sydenham neighbourhood of east Belfast], and his absence seemed to leave the Volunteers in a confused position.' Like Cusack, several other leading Volunteers met regularly during Easter Week at the Gaelic League rooms to discuss what was going on in Dublin, although 'there was no possibility of doing anything'.[52] The following week twenty-six were arrested in a police round-up, most of whom were then interned at Frongoch. In all 83 people were arrested in Ulster out of a total of 3,343 throughout Ireland.[53] The young David McGuinness escaped arrest, but afterwards he recalled that 'a feeling of despair existed . . . and the movement in Belfast became totally disorganized. We had no leader as all the prominent men were in prison or scattered.' But 'comradeship' was maintained throughout 1916. Three priests, Robert Fullerton of St Paul's, Charles O'Neill of St Peter's, and John Hassan of St Mary's, 'did a lot to keep the fires alive'.[54] Joseph MacRory, former President of St Malachy's College, who had been appointed Bishop of Down and Connor in August 1915, thought the Rising 'a shocking and idiotic tragedy . . . engineered by a few desperate socialists and a few sincere but silly patriots . . . Belfast remained quiet, thank God, throughout all the excitements.'[55]

[50] McCullough, Memoir of 1915–16 (McCP, P120/31/16).
[51] Cusack, witness statement 9; McCullough, (McCP, P120/31/13).
[52] Wilson, witness statement 176; McCullough, Memoir of 1915–16, and statement to Pensions Board (McCP P120/31/20, P120/26/2).
[53] Mac Giolla Choille (ed.), *Intelligence Notes*, 241, 267.
[54] McGuinness, witness statement 417.
[55] MacRory to O'Riordan, 4 May 1916 (MOR 1916/19).

Devlin was in Belfast for Easter, and as late as the evening of Tuesday 25 April appears to have been unaware of what was happening in Dublin. He spent the day fund-raising for soldiers' families, claiming in a speech that the Falls and Smithfield wards had now sent over 6,000 men to the front.[56] He returned to Dublin on 5 May. A worrying feature was that many National Volunteer and Ancient Order of Hibernians (AOH) members around the country who had no sympathy with Sinn Féin had been arrested, while by 7 May Dillon had noted that feeling in Dublin was becoming extremely bitter over the ongoing executions.[57] Even Asquith was surprised at the rapidity of the first three executions, on 3 May, but was persuaded, since three other Sinn Féiners had received much lighter sentences on the same day, that General Maxwell was adopting a balanced attitude and should be left to his own discretion. Revd Michael Curran, Archbishop Walsh's secretary and an enthusiastic Sinn Féiner, wrote to Rome that 'the national soul is roused; scoffers of Sinn Féin are now sympathizers'.[58] The Inspector-General of the RIC took a similar view, reporting that, 'throughout the country generally, popular sympathy is turning in favour of the rebels'.[59] T. M. Kettle, who was soon to die in the trenches, wrote, on the other hand, that 'the Sinn Féin nightmare upset me a little, but then if you tickle the ear of a short-tempered elephant with a pop gun and he walks on you that is a natural concatenation of events'.[60] In the mindset of British Army generals in the midst of the First World War, such ruthlessness is comprehensible. But politically it was a dreadful mistake. Redmond was on the right lines when he drew attention to the compassionate treatment by the South African Government of the leaders of the rebellion of 1913–14, while T. P. O'Connor pointed out that the United States had not executed a single leader of the Confederate rebellion after the Civil War and that Joseph Chamberlain had overturned the death sentences passed on the Jameson raiders.[61] General Maxwell's inadvertent contribution to the victory of Sinn Féin is incalculable.

'PARTITIONIST!': THE 1916 NEGOTIATIONS

Even as the Rising in Dublin petered out on 1 May, T. P. O'Connor reported that in London political circles there was 'a strong feeling that the Irish question should be settled now and at once'.[62] On 14 May he and Devlin dined at Walton Heath, Lloyd George's weekend retreat. Lloyd George then spoke to the leading

[56] *IN*, 26 Apr. 1916.   [57] Dillon to Redmond, 1, 2, and 7 May 1916 (RP 15182/22).
[58] M. J. Curran to O'Riordan, 29 May 1916 (MOR 1916/37).
[59] RIC Inspector-General's Report on the state of public opinion, May 1916 (BOD, Asquith Papers, MS 44, fo. 24).
[60] Kettle to H. McLaughlin, 7 Aug. 1916 (Kettle Papers, LA34/397).
[61] Tierney, *Eoin MacNeill*, 225; *Reynolds's Newspaper*, 18 June 1916.
[62] O'Connor to Dillon, 1 May 1916 (DP 6741/301).

newspaper proprietor Lord Northcliffe, who, himself an Irishman by birth, invited Devlin to his home the next day.[63] Northcliffe expressed his abhorrence at the executions, but thought that the Rising was 'of very little consequence' except that it 'afforded British politicians an opportunity of immediately settling the [Irish] question on lines which could be agreed upon'. He advised Devlin that the best policy for the Irish Party was to take what they could get now, and look for more in the future. Devlin agreed that 'the policy of marking time' had now been proved fatal and things could not go on as they were.[64] Northcliffe then arranged a secret meeting between Lloyd George, W. M. Murphy and Tim Healy in an attempt to get the *Irish Independent*—now selling 120,000 copies per day—onside for a settlement. But Murphy regarded the existing Home Rule Act as simply giving the Irish Parliament 'the privilege of distributing amongst place hunters the proceeds of taxes collected by the imperial Parliament', and the exclusion of Ulster as 'unthinkable'. Lloyd George urged Murphy 'not to make mischief in Ireland', but the *Irish Independent* continued its critical course without deviation.[65]

The Irish Party leaders knew nothing of this fruitless sideshow. Devlin remained in London, and on 22 May visited Rising prisoners in Wandsworth Jail. T. P. O'Connor, now highly enthusiastic about prospects for a settlement, was with him 'almost night and day'. Devlin had bouts of regretting that he had ever agreed to his colleagues' 1914 plan for concessions on Ulster, but he ultimately came round to the view that 'there must be some sacrifices about Ulster'. He, O'Connor, and Redmond all agreed to push for a settlement. Dillon, as so often, was more sceptical, telling C. P. Scott that he regarded Lloyd George as 'a slippery snake'.[66] Asquith then asked Lloyd George to seek a solution. The Chancellor proceeded through separate meetings with the Irish Party leaders and with Carson and Sir James Craig. He suggested that the Home Rule Act be brought into immediate operation accompanied by an Amending Act for the duration of the war, which provided for the Irish MPs to continue at Westminster in full numbers, and for six Ulster counties to remain under direct rule from Westminster until the war was over. After the war the future of Ireland would be considered by an Imperial Conference. Redmond and Carson agreed to consult their supporters.[67] Initial responses on the Nationalist side were not encouraging. Devlin visited several of the Ulster bishops. MacRory 'would not entertain the proposals', and, while he was, according to Devlin, 'not

[63] O'Connor to Dillon, 14 May 1916 (DP 6741/306); Lord Riddell, *Lord Riddell's War Diary* (London, 1933), 182.

[64] 'Memorandum by Mr Joseph Devlin MP', encl. with Devlin to Dillon, 15 May 1916 (DP 6730/170).

[65] R. Pound and G. A. Harmsworth, *Northcliffe* (London, 1959), 501; Cecil Harmsworth to Northcliffe, 26 May, W. M. Murphy to Northcliffe, 28 May, Lloyd George to Murphy, 8 June and 17 June, Murphy to Lloyd George, 20 June 1916 (LGP, D/14/1/22, 29, D/14/2/10, 18, 190).

[66] Wilson (ed.), *Diaries of C. P. Scott*, 207.

[67] D. Lloyd George, *War Memoirs* (London, 1938), i. 419–21.

a politician in the sense of Derry or Raphoe. . . his opposition would influence a section of his clergy'. McHugh of Derry dismissed the proposals as 'rot'. Even O'Donnell would go no further than county option. In Belfast Devlin found that his closest associates, Patrick Dempsey, Dan McCann, and others, would support the proposals, but recognized that it would be impossible to get the west Ulster Nationalists to agree. As in 1914, Jerry McVeagh again reported that Logue was 'not averse', but the *Irish Independent* reported the Cardinal as saying that it would be 'better to remain as we are for fifty years' rather than accept the proposals.[68] Devlin was initially apprehensive, and Dillon thought that 'we are heading for disaster', but the Irish Party leaders decided to hold a major conference of Ulster Nationalists. T.P. told Lloyd George that 'up to the present the signs are very bad outside Belfast. . . but if Joe only makes the same speech as he did at our meeting yesterday, he will carry everybody except the secret enemies of home rule—clerical and lay'.[69] Devlin was, by this stage, 'very strong in favour of accepting your proposals', wrote Dillon to Lloyd George, saying that he did not 'entirely despair of the Ulster conference, but I am far from sanguine. . . You have let Hell loose in Ireland, and I do not see how the country is to be governed.'[70] O'Connor reported that Devlin 'is in danger of becoming a popular hero in England. . . When I told L.G. that we talked of him as "the Lloyd George of Ireland" he said that of course they were alike in their perfect simplicity and freedom from guile.'[71]

On 16 June the five Northern bishops told Redmond that the Ulster conference would be lost by 'an overwhelming majority', while Devlin was 'in a *very fighting mood*, but not sanguine of carrying conference'.[72] On 18 June Devlin addressed 2,000 people in St Mary's Hall. It was, he told Redmond, 'a magnificent success'. Only 'about twenty' opposed the proposals, led—in the absence of the internees—by Dr Russell McNabb, 'a young fellow not heretofore known in local politics'. According to a hostile observer, Revd James Hendley of St Malachy's College, McNabb was 'hustled off the platform' by Dan McCashin. Sixteen or more Catholic clergymen, 'all the important priests in Belfast', were won over.[73] The *Daily Mail* correspondent R. Montague Smith, who was present, reported that the majority of northern priests, led by Bishop McHugh, were seeking to harden opinion against the proposals, but that Devlin probably had 50 of the

[68] McVeagh to Redmond, n.d. [early June 1916] (RP 15205/4); M. Laffan, *The Resurrection of Ireland: The Sinn Féin Party, 1916–23* (Cambridge, 1999), 59.

[69] Dillon to O'Connor, 7 June 1916 (DP 6741/313); O'Connor to Lloyd George, 9, 'Sunday' [11 June], and 13 June 1916 (LGP, D/14/2/23, 27, 35).

[70] Dillon to Lloyd George, 11 and 16 June 1916 (LGP, D/14/2/25, D/14/3/1).

[71] O'Connor to Dillon, 13 June 1916 (DP 6741/18).

[72] Dillon to Lloyd George, 16 June 1916 (LGP, D/14/3/2); Dillon to O'Connor, 17 June 1916 (DP 6741/320).

[73] Devlin to Redmond, telegram, 18 June 1916 (RP 15181/3); J. Hendley to O'Riordan, 7 July 1916 (MOR 1916/77); W. H. Owen, 'Convention of Ulster Nationalists', 23 June 1916 (LGP, D/15/1/15).

170 priests expected at the Convention on his side, mainly from Down and Connor. What Montague Smith called the 'unscrupulous opposition' of the *Irish Independent* was countered in eastern Ulster by the strong support of the *Irish News*.[74] After this meeting, Devlin's confidence grew rapidly. Redmond's secretary, T. J. Hanna, reported that McCashin was doing all he could to influence priests who would be attending the conference. On 21 June Devlin published a letter that summarized his argument: the proposals would inevitably lead to the unity of the country; Ulster Unionists should be conciliated and not coerced; partition was unthinkable, but these proposals offered the best way of preventing a resurgence of Carsonism; the settlement would permit an amnesty for Rising prisoners; and Ulster would remain under the administration of the Imperial Parliament during the interim period. The only alternative to all this would be a continuation of military despotism and the postponement of home rule for a generation.[75] On 21 June Lloyd George told Redmond that Asquith has personally approved his proposals, but they would not go to the cabinet until they had received the approval of the Irish leaders. Lloyd George believed that Carson and many Conservative ministers would stand by the proposals, but that Walter Long and Lords Selbourne and Lansdowne were set to resign. O'Connor passed this information from Redmond on to Dillon, but did not copy it to Devlin, who was preparing for his Convention challenge.[76]

The Ulster Convention met in Belfast on 23 June, with Redmond, Dillon, and Devlin all present (Table 7.1). Canon Keown of Enniskillen spoke against the scheme, doubting its temporary nature, alleging that there would be a devolved Unionist regime in Belfast and arguing that a courageous rejection of the proposals would produce a better offer. The forty-five-minute speech by Devlin, who followed, was 'wonderfully eloquent and delivered with great force'. He warned the Convention that if the proposals failed the whole struggle for home rule would be greatly set back, while if the proposals were adopted the benefits of home rule would soon become apparent to the excluded counties. He and Redmond would support the appointment of a committee of clergy who could join in the Irish Party's deliberations on the details of the scheme. When the moment arrived for voting, each delegate was called by name and required to pronounce 'yes' or 'no' to the proposal for the exclusion of the six counties as a 'temporary and provisional settlement of the Irish difficulty'. The voting was 475 in favour and 265 against. Lloyd George's observer, Captain W. H. Owen, estimated that over 100 of the 265 opponents were priests.[77]

---

[74] R. M. Smith to Lloyd George, 20 June 1916 (BOD, Asquith Papers, MS 37, fo. 64); Dillon to Redmond, 19 June 1916 (RP 15182/23).

[75] T. J. Hanna to Redmond, 19 and 20 June 1916 (RP 15193/5); *IN*, 21 June 1916.

[76] R. M. Smith to Lloyd George, 20 June 1916 (BOD, Asquith Papers, MS 37, fo. 64); Lloyd George to Asquith, 20 June 1916, copy (LGP, D/14/3/21); O'Connor to Dillon, encl. O'Connor to Redmond and Lloyd George to Redmond, all 21 June 1916 (DP 6741/325).

[77] W. H. Owen, 'Convention of Ulster Nationalists' (LGP, D/15/1/15).

Table 7.1. Attendance and voting at the Ulster Nationalist Convention, 23 June 1916

Attendance	Antrim	Armagh	Down	Derry (*city*)	Tyrone	F'nagh	Total present
MPs	1	1	1	0	1	1	5
Priests	47	29	11	26	13	4	130
UIL	29	10	20	16	16	6	97
AOH	13	4	5	9	3	1	35
INF	11	4	5	15	4	5	44
Public							
Boards	46	65	88	66	132	77	474
TOTAL	147	113	130	132	169	94	785
Voting							Total vote
Voted YES	129	62	117	67 (7)	64	36	475
Voted NO	7	32	13	60 (30)	95	58	265
Did not vote	11	19	0	5	10	0	45

Source: W. H. Owen, Report of Ulster Nationalist Convention (HLRO, LGP, D/15/1/15 (corrected)); Report of UIL National Directory, 3 July 1916 (NLI, MS 708).

An exultant Devlin sent a telegram to Lloyd George proclaiming 'magnificent convention. Proposals carried by nearly 200 majority' (in fact it was 210). The *Irish Independent* presented a different view, dismissing 'Mr Lloyd George's revolting scheme', and, while denying any desire to 'split the movement', denouncing the 'sheer weakness and backbonelessness' of the leadership.[78] There were allegations, but no evidence, that the Convention had somehow been rigged.

When the Irish Party met on 26 June, all but two of the fifty MPs present supported the proposals.[79] Meanwhile T.P. reported that Lloyd George was 'grappling with the Tory members of the cabinet who threatened to resign', and begged his colleagues to join him in London.[80] Redmond and Dillon declined for personal reasons, and Devlin was sent across to London alone. On 29 June he met Lloyd George and Bonar Law, who suggested that the Amending Bill should reserve some matters to the Westminster Parliament for the duration of the war. Devlin agreed that, provided the arrangement for the administration of the six excluded counties was acceptable, this would not be a problem. Devlin and T. P. O'Connor again dined at Lloyd George's weekend retreat, where the journalist Lord Riddell found Devlin 'a charming little man', but thought that both he and Lloyd George 'looked very weary'.[81] Dillon, the pessimist, correctly

[78] Devlin to Lloyd George, telegram, 23 June 1916 (LGP, D/14/3/36); *Irish Independent*, 24 June 1916.

[79] *Irish Independent*, 27 June 1916.

[80] O'Connor to Dillon, 28 June 1916, and Dillon to O'Connor, 28 June 1916 (DP 6741/328, 330, 331); O'Connor to Lloyd George, 28 June 1916 (LGP, D/14/3/44).

[81] Riddell, *War Diary*, 196.

suspected that something was about to undermine the scheme. On 22 June
Austen Chamberlain joined the cabinet rebels. On 28 June Lord Lansdowne
expressed to Asquith his doubts as to whether a Nationalist regime would be
able to quell disorder as effectively as would Westminster.[82] The UIL National
Directory on 3 July voted to accept the proposals, much to the anger of the
Irish Independent, which reported the meeting under the headline 'The Latest
Sham'.[83]

On 10 July Asquith set out the main features of the agreement. But, in
response to a question from Carson, he said that exclusion could never be
ended 'without the free will and assent of the excluded area'.[84] O'Connor
wrote to Lloyd George the following day that 'Joe is in a perfect fury over
Asquith's answer to Carson... See us if you can. Joe will have to be treated
with the utmost tenderness, and we must have regard to his great difficulties
with his own people.'[85] On the following evening Lansdowne, speaking in
the Lords, said that the new scheme would be 'permanent and enduring'.[86]
O'Connor warned Lloyd George that, unless Asquith distanced the government
from this, 'I think the whole thing is broken up'.[87] Lloyd George told Riddell
that 'I have pledged my word to the Irish, and if the pledge is not fulfilled
I shall have to resign', though adding that, in view of the military situation,
'a break-up of the cabinet just now would be a misfortune'.[88] On 22 July
he told Redmond that the cabinet had decided to add two new conditions
to the proposals, one providing for the exclusion of the six counties to be
permanent, and the other removing the provision to keep the full number of
Irish MPs at Westminster during the transitional period. Redmond bitterly
denounced the changes: 'I warn the Government that if they introduce a
bill on the lines communicated to me, my friends and I will oppose it at
every stage.'[89] Dillon later wrote privately that these negotiations 'struck a
deadly blow at the Irish Party', while Redmond's first biographer and party
colleague wrote that 'that day really finished the constitutional party and
overthrew Redmond's power'.[90] It was reported to Lloyd George that 'Devlin
is a bit sick and... it is doubtful if [he] will enter into further negotiations
for some days. He is upset.'[91] But on 31 July Devlin delivered an angry
speech in the Commons. 'If ever I march through the division lobbies again,'
he declared, 'it will be for the purpose of clearing the present Coalition
Government out of power... I would never agree to the permanent exclusion

[82] Lansdowne to Asquith, 28 June 1916 (Lloyd George, *War Memoirs*, i. 423–4).
[83] *Irish Independent*, 4 July 1916.   [84] D. Gwynn, *Redmond*, 519.
[85] O'Connor to Lloyd George, 11 July 1916 (LGP, E/2/22/1).   [86] Lyons, *Dillon*, 401.
[87] O'Connor to Lloyd George, 12 July 1916 (LGP, E/2/22/2).
[88] Riddell, *War Diary*, 201.
[89] Parl. Deb., H.C., 5th series, lxxxiv. 1429–34 (24 July 1916).
[90] Dillon to O'Connor, 20 Dec.1918, cited in Phoenix, *Northern Nationalism*, 35; S. Gwynn, *Redmond's Last Years*, 239.
[91] W. Sutherland, memo to Secretary of State for Munitions, 28 July [1916] (LGP, E/1/4/2).

of Ulster. I agreed to these proposals precisely because I thought it was a temporary war measure.'[92]

The affair was mishandled and demonstrates that Lloyd George was less than infallible as a political negotiator. But at this stage in his career his personal ambitions surely dictated that he would have wanted his proposals to succeed rather than to fail. K. O. Morgan has written, somewhat kindly, that 'the failure in July 1916 was not basically Lloyd George's fault at all'.[93] The Liberal minister Christopher Addison wrote in his diary that 'there is much disgust with the P.M. [Asquith] and the way he has messed up the Irish business. He has never displayed any firmness or decision in connection with getting the Bill forward.'[94] Balfour, Bonar Law, F. E. Smith, and Carson had all been prepared to accept the settlement—though with different expectations in the long term than the Nationalist leaders—but Lansdowne, Long, Selborne, and others had not. Lloyd George frequently used the resignation threat during these weeks, but when the threat did not work he always withdrew it, and it came to carry little weight.[95] The impact of the failure was serious in both Britain and Ireland. Addison thought that it 'contributed more substantially than has often been supposed' to the December collapse of Asquith's government.[96] In July a Unionist lawyer, Henry Duke, was appointed Chief Secretary. Shortly afterwards the Inspector-General of the RIC reported that 'the Sinn Féin movement is gaining strength in Belfast, and Mr Devlin's influence is waning'.[97] In fact the opposite was the case. Ironically it was in the south of Ireland, where, in reality, concern for Catholic Ulster was no more than skin deep, that the negative effect of the 1916 negotiations made most impact.

NATIONALISTS AND SINN FÉINERS, 1916–1917

In the country as a whole, popular reaction against the Irish Party followed swiftly upon the executions and the failed negotiations. The emergence of a coherent movement to lead this reaction emerged more slowly, the various advanced nationalist groupings coming together as a reconstituted Sinn Féin in the autumn of 1917. But a series of by-elections during the first eight months of the year provided clear evidence of the changing state of popular opinion in the country. Devlin was laid low with influenza for the first of them in North Roscommon when Count Plunkett, standing essentially as 'the father of a martyr', won with 56 per cent of the vote. A few weeks later Devlin was active

[92] Parl. Deb., H.C., 5th series, lxxxiv. 2182–90 (31 July 1916).

[93] K. O. Morgan, 'Lloyd George and the Irish', in British Academy and Royal Irish Academy, *Ireland after the Union* (Oxford, 1989), 91.

[94] Christopher Addison, *Politics from Within, 1911–18* (London, 1924), i. 258.

[95] Wilson (ed.), *Diaries of C. P. Scott*, 222–3.   [96] Addison, *Politics from Within*, i. 256.

[97] RIC Inspector-General, 'State of Public Feeling in Ireland' (TNA: PRO CAB 37/152/11, 23).

in what appeared to be a more hopeful contest in South Longford. But on the eve of the poll Archbishop Walsh wrote to the press that 'anyone who thinks that partition, whether in its naked deformity, or under the transparent mask of "county option" does not hold a leading place in the practical politics of today, is living in a fool's paradise'.[98] A republican prisoner won by thirty-seven votes. Then, when John Redmond's brother Willie, MP for East Clare, was killed at the front in June, Eamon de Valera walked away with the seat, with 71 per cent of the vote. His opponent was an unofficial pro-Irish Party candidate, and Devlin kept well out of the campaign. In Kilkenny City a few days later, it was rumoured locally that Devlin, previously a Kilkenny MP, intended to resign West Belfast in order to fight the seat, but in the event a local UIL councillor stood, and was defeated by W. T. Cosgrave with 66 per cent of the vote.[99] It seemed that the Sinn Féin advance was unstoppable. The *Leader* commented that 'what the Irish Party are up against today is not a policy but a protest . . . a national resurrection'.[100] In most of these by-elections the clergy were a help to Sinn Féin. Dillon thought that Sinn Féin would have got nowhere near winning in Roscommon, Longford, and Clare 'had it not been for the frantic activity of the young priests—who seem to be possessed by a poisonous hatred of the Party'.[101] The Irish Party's remaining strength was believed by both sides to be in the towns—Boyle, Longford, Ennis, Kilkenny—due mainly to the high level of Army recruitment, but this had not proved enough. Another issue, which was to come up more frequently in the 1918 by-elections, was the Sinn Féin allegation that the Irish Party was propped up by the 'unionist vote', a curiously sectarian argument.

In West Ulster during the summer of 1916 a breakaway group of constitutional nationalists formed the Irish Nation League to oppose exclusion. On 22 August the formation of a Belfast branch was announced in the press, but, as the local leader, the solicitor Bernard Campbell, was on holiday, nothing happened.[102] After a further failed meeting in September, the League finally took off in Belfast on 22 October, with about 400 present, 90 of whom signed up as members, and Campbell made some anti-recruiting statements. By December the INL had 150 members, led by Campbell and Archie Savage, but according to the police 'the movement does not appear to be a success'.[103] In October the annual meeting of the Belfast Gaelic League was held in St Mary's Hall with an attendance of 1,200, including 'all the local Sinn Féin and Irish Volunteer suspects'. Revd Robert Fullerton, who presided, said that they were bound to

[98] Thomas J. Morrissey, *William J. Walsh, Archbishop of Dublin, 1841–1921* (Dublin, 2000), 300–2; M.Coleman, *Co. Longford & the Irish Revolution* (Dublin, 2003), 62; Miller, *Church, State and Nation*, 356.

[99] *Kilkenny Journal*, 21 July 1917.   [100] *Leader*, 29 Sept. 1917.

[101] Dillon to O'Connor, 4 Sept. 1917 (DP 6741/416).

[102] RIC County Inspectors' Reports, Belfast, Aug. 1916 (TNA: PRO CO 904/100).

[103] Ibid., Sept.–Dec. 1916 (TNA: PRO CO 904/101).

continue the work begun by 'the heroes who went to Heaven last Easter'.[104] The Irish Volunteers in Belfast were led for a time by Liam Gaynor, a Belfast schoolteacher and section leader in the Tyrone fiasco, who had escaped arrest in May 1916, and became head of the IRB in Belfast and eastern Ulster. Once the Belfast prisoners had been released, there was a move to reorganize. An event in St Mary's Hall to welcome them home in January 1917 was attended by 650 people.[105] Meanwhile Gaynor worked with Seán Cusack to reorganize the Belfast companies, after a while persuading Cusack to accept appointment as commanding officer.[106] Remarkably, while doing this, Cusack remained a British soldier on active service at Carrickfergus during the day, until he was discharged on medical grounds in the autumn of 1916, after which he worked as an electrician at Harland and Wolff. Roger McCorley, later to emerge as one of the most active IRA men in Belfast, managed to enrol, though under age, in the newly formed 'C' Company. Each company had a 'civil' or 'political commissioner', to teach the men about history and politics after parades. Harry Dobbyn had this role in 'C' Company.[107] GHQ in Dublin was not enthusiastic about the addition of 'C' Company until Companies 'A' and 'B' had reached full strength, but its leader, Peter Burns, persuaded Cusack that a number of his men were civil servants and business people who needed to keep their activities secret, whereas he suggested that many members of 'A' and 'B' companies were already well known to, and watched by, the police.[108] The strength of these companies in 1917–18 ranged from twenty to forty. There was no battalion level of organization until after the Volunteer Convention of October 1917.

Some time after the return of the internees, Tom Wilson's butchery business was raided, and the RIC took away a very old and complicated machine gun. After examining it at the local barracks, officers 'said it was not a machine gun but a sausage machine', and it was returned.[109] Meanwhile Seán Cusack was instructed to interview Denis McCullough and find out what his intentions were regarding a future military role. McCullough replied that what had been asked of him at Easter 1916 was beyond reasonable expectation for such a small force, and for that reason he had accepted Eoin MacNeill's countermand. Cusack replied that many in the Belfast force felt that McCullough had 'to some extent let us down' and 'that the rank and file of the Volunteers would be relieved to know that he would not again attempt to assume leadership'. McCullough agreed that he would no longer seek an active role in the IRB or the Volunteers

[104] RIC Crime Special Branch, Belfast, 1916 (TNA: PRO CO 904/23/3).

[105] RIC County Inspectors' Reports, Belfast, Jan. 1917 (TNA: PRO CO 904/102).

[106] Gaynor, witness statement 183; Thomas Fox witness statement, 25 Mar. 1950 (BMH, witness statement 365).

[107] McCorley, witness statement 389.

[108] Seán Cusack witness statement, n.d. (BMH, witness statement 402).

[109] Booth, witness statement 229.

but would continue to undertake fund-raising and other national work.[110] Then in September 1917 delegates were selected to attend the Volunteer Convention in Dublin. The four Belfast delegates included a Dubliner and a Cork man, both then resident in Belfast. The convention was held in the upstairs hall of a 'ramshackle' building near Croke Park. Cusack was proposed as Ulster representative on the Executive, but backed off and proposed Seán MacEntee, who then replaced Gaynor.[111]

In June 1917 there were 2 Sinn Féin clubs in Belfast, with a total of 500 members. 'They seem to have got hold of the younger members of the nationalist community', observed the City Police Commissioner, and 'the movement will sooner or later become a force that must be reckoned with here'.[112] By November 1917 there were 9 clubs, with a total of 780 members.[113] This provoked new activity in the UIL, which opened two new branches during the month, giving it a total of seventeen in Belfast. The AOH was also reported to be 'fairly active'.[114] The National Volunteers made desultory attempts to re-form during 1917, but the *Leader* more or less wrote their epitaph on 24 November, asking 'when last did anyone see a National Volunteer in this land, and what is their policy?'[115]

THE IRISH CONVENTION: CONSTITUTIONALISM'S LAST THROW

In December 1916 Asquith was toppled in a cabinet coup, and Lloyd George became Prime Minister of a second coalition government with considerably greater Conservative representation. He told T. P. O'Connor that an Irish settlement was 'most necessary', but was more concerned about reports that Irish recruiting had fallen to eighty per week. T.P. privately urged the government to consider imposing an Irish settlement 'somewhat independently of both Irish parties'. Henry Duke, he thought, was hoping to get away from the dead-end of partition by 'his idea of a concordat between north and south'.[116] On 7 March the Irish Party introduced a Commons resolution calling for the conferment upon Ireland of 'free institutions' without further delay. The debate went very badly, Lloyd George winding up with proposals very similar to those that the Irish Party had rejected in July 1916. Anxious to secure his position as head of a now Conservative-dominated coalition, he declared that the Ulster

---

[110] Cusack, witness statement 402.   [111] Ibid.; Gaynor, witness statement 183.
[112] RIC County Inspectors' Reports, Belfast, June 1917 (TNA: PRO CO 904/103).
[113] Ibid., Oct.–Nov. 1917 (TNA: PRO CO 904/104).
[114] Ibid., Sept. 1917 (TNA: PRO CO 904/104).
[115] DMP report on National Volunteer Convention, 28 Sept. 1917 (TNA: PRO CO 904/23/5); *Leader*, 24 Nov. 1917.
[116] O'Connor to Devlin, 22 Jan. 1917 (DP 6730/176).

Protestant community was 'as alien in blood, in religious faith, in traditions, in outlook from the rest of Ireland as the inhabitants of Fife or Aberdeen'. It was another devastating blow, and Redmond led his Party out of the chamber in protest.[117]

But on 22 March the Conservative W. A. S. Hewins observed a 'sudden *volte-face* of the Government on the Irish question'.[118] Addison noted on 4 April that 'Irish matters are not going very well, but we have decided to bring in a bill to apply home rule with excluded areas and to offer great inducements to the parts that stand out to come in'. On 16 April Addison, Duke, and Lord Curzon were appointed to draft a bill.[119] Duke was 'convinced that preferably the right thing to do is not to encourage Ulster to vote itself out by counties. . . but to take the bold line and include Ulster; giving protection by conferring a veto on acts proposed to be applied to themselves, with a separate organization for civil administration having its headquarters in Belfast'. This was essentially home rule within home rule, but in case Carson made difficulties it was agreed to prepare an alternative draft allowing for exclusion, which would include from the start a mechanism for north–south collaboration.[120] After two meetings with Carson, Lloyd George was in buoyant mood: 'I think I am going to settle the Irish question, Pussy,' he told Frances Stevenson.[121] But to Addison's 'infinite disgust', the War Cabinet decided on 15 May not to introduce a bill after all, but to convene a convention of Irishmen in Dublin to seek an agreed solution.[122] Redmond expressed a preference for this proposal, which encouraged the government to turn its back on previous suggestions of imposing a settlement.

J. L. Garvin, editor of the *Observer*, believed Devlin at this stage to be paralysed by two factors: the impossibility of going against Dillon, and the conviction that his public concessions in 1916 could not be repeated.[123] Lloyd George announced the Convention plan on 21 May. There is much personal bitterness in Addison's two books at the rejection of his proposals, but his conclusion is correct: the proposals of Curzon, Duke, and himself 'were far less definite in their subdivision of the country and its separation from Great Britain than those which were accepted in 1921 after four years of the methods of the sword . . . Whatever might have been the consequences, they could not possibly have been more disastrous that the results that followed from the failure of the Convention onwards through the terrible years of 1919 up to 1921.'[124] There

---

117 D. Gwynn, *Redmond*, 540; Parl. Deb., H.C., xci. 424–42 (7 Mar. 1917).
118 W. A. S. Hewins, *The Apologia of an Imperialist* (London, 1929), ii. 131.
119 Addison, *Politics from Within*, ii. 180.
120 Ibid., ii, 181–2; C. Addison, *Four and a Half Years* (London, 1933), ii. 367.
121 A. J. P. Taylor (ed.), *Lloyd George: A Diary by Frances Stevenson* (London, 1971), 155–6.
122 Ibid. 157.
123 Reported by Mrs A. S. Green to Col. M. Moore, 25 Apr. 1917 (MMP 10561/17).
124 Addison, *Politics from Within*, ii. 186–7; Addison, *Four and a Half Years*, ii. 380–1.

followed a long negotiation between the government and the Irish Party on the size and make-up of the Convention. Dillon told T.P. that 'Joe is at present in a very jumpy and uncertain mood—taking different views on successive days'.[125] Another issue was the chairmanship of the Convention. Devlin had suggested Northcliffe, whom Dillon thought was 'thoroughly committed to home rule'. William Martin Murphy favoured H. E. Duke for chairman, as he was perceived to be an opponent of partition.[126] But ultimately the former Southern Unionist and agricultural reformer Sir Horace Plunkett was appointed. The Irish Party chose Redmond, Devlin, Stephen Gwynn, J. J. Clancy, and the Cookstown solicitor T. J. S. Harbison as its five nominees, Dillon having declined to serve.[127] The Catholic hierarchy's four nominees included Dr Patrick O'Donnell of Raphoe and Dr Joseph MacRory of Down and Connor.

The Convention assembled in Trinity College, Dublin, on 25 July 1917, with both the Sinn Féiners and the O'Brienites standing aloof from what they saw as a Redmond–Lloyd George conspiracy. The most hopeful sign, thought Plunkett, was that all sides realized that failure would lead to chaos and revolution (which it did!).[128] On 11 October a Committee of Nine was appointed to negotiate, comprising five nationalists (Redmond, Devlin, Bishop O'Donnell, W. M. Murphy, and the writer George Russell (AE)), three Ulster Unionists, and the Southern Unionist Lord Midleton.[129] The next evening Devlin had a private meeting with Midleton and the Church of Ireland Archbishop of Dublin, J. H. Bernard. He told them that if the Convention failed he would probably leave public life, but after two months he was becoming more hopeful. He told them that he hated Sinn Féin, 'which had no sane policy'. But, he continued, 'he was a home ruler first of all, and he would not fight on behalf of any British rule in Ireland'. Devlin had, he said, advised Lloyd George that the best way forward would be for the government of Ireland to be handed over, for the moment, to the Convention. Now was the time, he told Midleton and Bernard, for such a 'dramatic stroke'. If there was an election now, 'his Party was gone, and he cared not what became of the country'. Although 'quite frank and friendly', Bernard's note of the meeting concluded that it was 'not very satisfactory'. The impression left by Devlin on the two southern Unionists was that his prime concern was to ensure that the Irish Party did not appear to be taking any part in coercing Sinn Féiners.[130] A few days later Midleton told Bernard that 'the situation is very

---

[125] Dillon to O'Connor, n.d. [27 May 1917] (DP 6741/432).
[126] Healy to O'Brien, 11 June 1917 (NLI, OBP 8556/12).
[127] Dillon to Redmond, 21 June 1917, with note of Redmond's reply (RP 15182/24).
[128] H. Plunkett, 'Secret Report on the Irish Convention', paras. 13–14 (Irish Convention Papers, Box 1/2986).
[129] R. B. McDowell, *The Irish Convention, 1917–18* (London, 1970), 119.
[130] J. H. Bernard, Memorandum of Interview with Mr Devlin, 12 Oct. 1917 (Bernard Papers, 52782, fos. 179–81).

tangled'. There was a suspicion that 'Dillon and Devlin are canvassing against Redmond. If there is a split in that camp, it will only make matters worse.'[131]

By November things were indeed getting more awkward. The Ulster Unionists declined to come up with any scheme, and the Committee of Nine therefore reported that they had been unable to agree. Redmond's hope was that the Convention would put forward a majority report from the nationalists and Southern Unionists. He was less concerned about the question of fiscal autonomy, but Bishop O'Donnell thought that this would be essential in view of Irish public opinion: 'to water down in these circumstances, with the danger of getting left, would seem to be a crazy proceeding.'[132] Horace Plunkett confirmed that 'the difficulty with the official Nationalists is neither with Redmond nor Devlin, or I think with AE or Murphy, but with O'Donnell. I don't want to be uncharitable, but I am not sure that the RC hierarchy want a settlement.'[133] At a nationalist meeting in December O'Donnell wanted to submit an amendment to Midleton's proposal for a scheme without fiscal autonomy, but Devlin persuaded the meeting to take no action until Ulster Unionist suggestions came forward: 'Our business is to force the Ulstermen to show their hands.'[134] Over Christmas Plunkett tried to clear the ground, suggesting to Devlin that his best course of action would be for the Nationalists and the Southern Unionists to vote for Midleton's scheme, with a view to trying to sell the scheme to Ulster later. The alternative would, he thought, be chaos in Ireland, which would destroy the Irish Party in any event. It would not be saved by its having attempted, unsuccessfully, to hold out for fiscal autonomy.[135]

Devlin did not doubt that the Southern Unionist offer was genuine, but he thought that 'there could be no graver mistake' than for the Nationalists to consent to a settlement that would satisfy neither nationalist Ireland nor the Ulster Unionists. 'Frankly, my position is this: during the last five years I have been drawn, often against my own better judgment, towards proposals of settlement which turned out unsatisfying to the people of Ireland—and even then did not materialize.' What guarantee was there, he asked, that the British Government would regard it as 'substantial agreement' and implement it? He no longer had any trust in the government: 'For the past ten years, the Irish Party has been tremendously weakened and almost destroyed by the intense desire shown on their part for peace and reconciliation not only with England but with the Ulster Protestants. Each time we conceded anything our position was imperilled amongst our friends and the problem was not correspondingly brought any nearer solution.' Devlin thought that the best policy would be for

---

[131] Midleton to Bernard, 17 Oct. 1917 (Bernard Papers, 52781, fos. 49–50).

[132] O'Donnell to Redmond, 22 Nov. 1917 (RP 15217/4).

[133] Plunkett to Bernard, 18 Dec. 1917 (Bernard Papers, 52782, fos. 199–200).

[134] Devlin to Redmond, 22 Dec. 1917 (RP 15181/3); Devlin to Dillon, 20 Dec. 1917 (DP 6730/184).

[135] Plunkett to Devlin, 22 December 1917 (PF, Plunkett Papers, DEV 3).

Midleton not to submit his scheme for the moment, but to allow the Ulster Unionists to state what their position really was:

I am anxious for a settlement on the lines of a united Ireland . . . My colleagues in the Convention and I have long since ceased to care whether we are in politics or not . . . But we are . . . genuinely anxious to help in this, the latest and many think the *last* endeavour to have the Irish question settled on constitutional lines.[136]

Plunkett thought this 'one of the most helpful and elucidating letters I have received from any of the members of the Convention'. But he maintained that the situation differed from previous negotiations, for, if the Ulster Unionist representatives stood alone in not endorsing the Midleton proposals, they would be told by the government that coercion would be applied. Such an 'extraordinary concordat' would sweep English and international opinion, and even the House of Lords, into line, while Sinn Féin would be stranded. The customs issue would be 'dwarfed' by all this. Perhaps, concluded Plunkett, 'I have a little more confidence in your own powers of persuasion than you have'.[137] Devlin replied tersely that it would be better to continue the discussion when he returned to Dublin.[138]

On 1 January 1918 Midleton showed Redmond a statement in Curzon's handwriting, initiated by Lloyd George, to the effect that, if the Ulster Unionists were the only group in the Convention to oppose the Midleton scheme, Lloyd George 'will use his personal influence with his colleagues . . . to accept the proposal and give it legislative effect'.[139] O'Donnell, however, declared himself to be 'exceedingly doubtful' about even conditional acceptance of the Midleton scheme until the Ulster Unionists had shown their hand.[140] In a last effort to win him over, Midleton wrote to O'Donnell. 'You fear the country will be angry with a weak scheme—how much more angry if no scheme at all.' He concluded, 'with the utmost respect and deference'—but perhaps counter-productively—that many people were saying that the Catholic Church did not want home rule, and that, if the bishops in the Convention voted against a scheme, 'great force will be added' to such an argument.[141] As the crunch drew near, Redmond proposed an amendment to Midleton's motion that did not commit anyone to giving up customs unless the government implemented the scheme.[142] O'Donnell thought that even this was too much: 'the Nationalist who votes for it cannot stand where he stood before . . . The principle is given away.'[143] In the light

[136] Devlin to Plunkett, 26 Dec. 1917 (PF, Plunkett Papers, DEV 4/1).
[137] Plunkett to Devlin, 28 Dec. 1917 (PF, Plunkett Papers, DEV 5/1); Gwynn to Bernard, 28 Dec. 1917 (Bernard Papers, 52782, fo. 202).
[138] Devlin to Plunkett, 28 Dec. 1917 (PF, Plunkett Papers, DEV 6).
[139] D. Gwynn, *Redmond*, 579.
[140] O'Donnell to Redmond, 27 Dec. 1917 (RP 15217/4).
[141] Midleton to O'Donnell, 7 Jan. 1918, copy (BOD, Asquith Papers, 37, fo. 196).
[142] Redmond to O'Donnell, 14 Jan. 1918 (RP 15217/4).
[143] O'Donnell to Redmond, 14 Jan. 1918 (RP 15217/4).

of this exchange it is not surprising that, when the Convention met the next day, Plunkett 'had the worst shock of my public life'. Five minutes before the session opened Redmond told him that the Midleton compromise had been rejected by the bishops, and that he would not therefore move his amendment. 'Thereupon', recorded Plunkett, 'the Bishop of Down & Connor rose and made an ignorant, demagoguish, anti-English speech on Customs which he would demand, not because the British Parliament might not use the power fairly to Ireland but because it would as ever use it selfishly, cruelly for our destruction.'[144]

At the Convention on 16 January Plunkett found things 'a little better', but 'it is now quite clear that the bishops are out to wreck. They want either to avert home rule or, if this is impossible, to be in with the prevailing Sinn Féin sentiment at its initiation.' The next day Redmond recovered some fighting spirit, and made it clear that he would support Midleton.[145] But a couple of days later Plunkett heard that Devlin 'has definitely decided not to agree to the Midleton compromise unless the Government promises to coerce Ulster!'[146] Dillon warned that, if the Irish Party accepted Midleton's scheme, 'Murphy would sweep us out of public life in six weeks'. He said that Devlin 'takes a very gloomy view of the situation, and is naturally very much troubled and distressed over his differences with Redmond. Dr O'Donnell is *very* strong against Redmond's course, and rather bitter.'[147] On 23 January Midleton made 'an unwise attack' on O'Donnell, 'accusing him of bringing not peace but a sword into the Convention', but it was agreed to nominate a delegation to meet Lloyd George.[148] This proposal was seconded by the Church of Ireland Archbishop of Armagh, Dr Crozier, to the annoyance of a leading Ulster Unionist, who warned 'that he is not in possession of a sufficiently long spoon to enable him to sup safely with the Devil or the Devlin'.[149] The cabinet agreed on 13 February that there should be an all-Ireland parliament, and that the Ulstermen should be asked to say what measures they would wish for their protection. Police and taxation could not be devolved during the war, partition was also ruled out, but there should be some safeguards for Ulster relating to industry and to education. Plunkett, however, thought that 'the Bishop of Raphoe, Devlin and Murphy clearly don't mean to settle'.[150] Devlin was then struck down by influenza and laid up in London for a week. Lloyd George wrapped up this phase of the Convention by writing to Plunkett on 25 February with a number of suggestions: that customs and excise should be reserved for two years beyond the

---

[144] Plunkett Diary, 15 Jan. 1918 (PF).   [145] Ibid., 16–18 Jan. 1918 (PF).
[146] Ibid., 19–21 Jan. 1918 (PF).
[147] Dillon to O'Connor, 19/22 Jan. 1918 (DP 6742/441).
[148] Plunkett Diary, 22–4 Jan. 1918 (PF).
[149] H. de F. Montgomery to Sir James Stronge, 9 Feb. 1918 (Montgomery Papers, D627/432/7).
[150] Addison, *Politics from Within*, ii. 243–4; Addison, *Four and a Half Years*, ii. 484; McDowell, *Irish Convention*, 159–60; Plunkett Diary, 13–14 Feb. 1918 (PF).

end of the war, after which a royal commission would be appointed; that during the war all revenue raised in Ireland would be paid to the Irish Government after the deduction of the imperial contribution; that Unionists should have additional representation in the Irish Parliament; and that there should be an Ulster Committee with power to modify or veto legislative action relating to their area. The government undertook to give immediate attention to the Report from the Convention and to bring forward legislation as quickly as possible. Lloyd George's letter was read to the Convention by Plunkett and copies circulated on a supposedly confidential basis to all Convention members.[151] Plunkett thought at this stage that 'the Ulstermen know perfectly well that partition is no longer possible'.[152]

William Martin Murphy was unconvinced, calling Lloyd George's letter to the Convention 'partition in disguise'. He had little confidence in his Convention colleagues, telling Healy that, if he did not continue to attend the Convention, 'the Devlin—Raphoe lot would swallow anything'.[153] But Plunkett thought that, with Redmond dogged by ill-health, O'Donnell was 'the leader of the Nationalists' and strong enough to prevent any settlement that did not concede customs. O'Donnell had the backing of MacRory, who expected the government to attempt an imposed settlement, but thought that 'the country is in no mood to accept such a settlement as is likely to be offered'.[154] Meanwhile Plunkett was telling Lloyd George that customs must be conceded to the nationalists, while urging Bishop O'Donnell not to wreck the Convention over it. By 3 March even Plunkett, perennial optimist that he was, thought that 'the situation looks very hopeless'.[155] When the Convention reconvened on 5 March he thought that 'the end had come . . . The Bishop of Raphoe and Murphy saw their opportunity and tried to rush the Convention on to the rocks.'[156] The following morning came the news of the death of John Redmond, and the Convention adjourned until 12 March. A 'rather acrimonious debate' then took place on the proposals agreed between moderate Nationalists and Southern Unionists, which were passed by 38 to 34. The minority was an 'unholy combination of 17 extreme Nationalists led by the Bishop of Raphoe and Wm Murphy and 17 Ulster Unionists'.[157] Devlin voted with O'Donnell.

Upon Redmond's death T. P. O'Connor told Dillon that 'of course there is nobody to succeed him but yourself'.[158] William O'Brien thought that, 'if Dillon be elected leader, he will only be chief mourner at a funeral. If Devlin, he is a corner-boy who, like all bullies, is only brave when he has the mob at

[151] McDowell, *Irish Convention*, 162–4; J. McCaffery to Mgr J. Hagan, 28 Feb. 1918 (JHP, HAG1/1918/10).
[152] Plunkett to Bernard, 13 Feb. 1918 (Bernard Papers, 52783, fo. 7).
[153] Healy to O'Brien, 21 Feb. and 1 Mar. 1918 (NLI, OBP 8556/18).
[154] MacRory to O'Riordan, 7 Mar. 1918 (MOR 1918/60).
[155] Plunkett Diary, 2–3 Mar. 1918 (PF).   [156] Ibid., 10 Mar. 1918.
[157] Ibid., 12 Mar. 1918.   [158] O'Connor to Dillon, 9 Mar. 1918 (DP 6742/456).

his back.'[159] The Party met on 12 March to elect a new chairman. There are two extant eye-witness reports. One is a letter to Dillon (who was not present at the meeting) from his old ally Richard McGhee, and the other a diary account by the civil servant T. P. Gill of a conversation held a fortnight later with the Redmondite MP John Hayden. Some moderate MPs pressed Devlin to stand for the leadership but he absolutely declined to do so, and, according to Hayden, 'declared that he meant to propose Dillon, to whom he had already stated this intention'. At the meeting it was resolved to make the vote unanimous, though Hayden thought this 'a curious result seeing that not only was there a very strong minority against, but that there was a pretty general feeling in the Party that the choice would be a mistake'. Tom Condon MP told Hayden that he would vote for Dillon out of personal loyalty, but believed that Devlin—with Dillon's assent—would be a far better choice so far as both Irish and British opinion were concerned.[160] According to McGhee's account, Hayden and two colleagues sought to have the meeting hear a report from the Convention delegates before electing the chairman, with a view to influencing the new leader and the policy of the Party in the Convention. The 'temper of the meeting' was against this suggestion, and Devlin then, 'in a fine short speech', proposed Dillon. 'I confess I was never more proud of Devlin than I was while listening to his speech,' wrote McGhee. J. P. Boland then proposed Devlin, but, according to McGhee, Devlin's response was 'noble and brave . . . [and] put an end to any attempt to exploit his name as a candidate'.[161]

Thus the Irish Party, confronted by a powerful challenge from a party consisting mainly of much younger people, chose as leader a 66-year-old veteran who had been an MP for thirty-six years, while Devlin, aged just 47 and Party Secretary for the past thirteen, decided not to make a challenge. Whereas McGhee, a man of Dillon's generation, saw in this only Devlin's wisdom, courage, and loyalty to Dillon, the more critical Hayden saw a mixture of motives in Devlin's refusal:

Fear of the responsibility, distrust of himself, and a certain remorse at his desertion of Redmond for the bishops—whom by the way he is said to hate. He is a creature of moods and impulses; and the weakness to which he is occasionally liable is a handicap. A member of the Party said to me at Redmond's funeral it would be a risk having as chairman a man liable to that weakness. He probably felt this himself.[162]

What the 'weakness' was is not revealed. Probably it was over-dependence on alcohol, for which Devlin had something of a reputation. Additionally, as early as 1909 Devlin had complained to Dillon of 'a return of the nervous complaint which troubled me some time ago', which may be part of the explanation. Devlin

[159] O'Brien to Dunraven, 12 Mar. 1918 (NLI, OBP 8554/17).
[160] T. P. Gill, Memoir: note of a conversation with John Hayden MP, 28 Mar. 1918 (Gill Papers, 13478–526, Box 1916–19).
[161] McGhee to Dillon, 13 Mar. 1918 (DP 6757/1059).
[162] Gill, Memoir, 28 Mar. 1918 (Gill Papers, 13478–526, Box 1916–19).

was a brilliant but nervous speaker, while several remarks in letters to Dillon by Devlin's close friend and father-figure T. P. O'Connor tend to confirm Hayden's rather more stark picture of 'a creature of moods and impulses'. Devlin was also prone to hypochondria, his own letters frequently referring to colds and influenza. These factors may well have been psychologically important in framing Devlin's response to the vacancy. But his whole career, beginning as it had done at the time of the Parnell split, was focused on the need for unity, loyalty, and resistance to 'faction'. There can be no doubt that the final split with Redmond had distressed him—he visited Redmond almost daily at his London house during his last illness—and he would have believed strongly that solidarity was essential to the Party at such a critical moment.

In fact, just hours after the speech that had impressed McGhee so much, Devlin was taken ill once more with a severe chill, which lasted for a week. He wrote to Plunkett protesting against a vote being taken on the Ulster Unionists' exclusion motion at this stage. The Ulster Unionist Convention leader H. T. Barrie told Carson after the vote on 15 March that

Devlin has not put in an appearance since Tuesday [12 March] at the Convention, and it is not his health that is supposed to be the cause of his absence. We hear a whisper that he has not been taking good care of himself. His letter was dated last night, and alleged to have been written from a nursing home, but he was seen by one of our delegates on the street yesterday.[163]

On 22 March the deliberations of the Convention came to an end. The nationalists again split down the middle, with Devlin and the bishops and Murphy on one side and Stephen Gwynn, John Clancy, and John Fitzgibbon MPs on the other. The government had pledged to act on the findings of the Convention if there was 'substantial agreement', but there was not. The end of the Convention coincided with the great German offensive on the western front, which made military manpower once more the leading issue on the government's agenda. It was understood that the government would implement a Home Rule Bill before Irish conscription came into operation, and that the measures would be carried forward together. A cabinet committee recommended in July 1918 that the government should proceed with a Home Rule Bill on the lines of the proposals of May 1917, but in August the proposal was quietly dropped.[164]

NATIONALISTS AND SINN FÉINERS, 1918

During the tensest days of the Convention, as the Nationalist camp split, Devlin and Dillon would probably have agreed with Tim Healy that 'what really matters

163 Barrie to Carson, 15 Mar. 1918 (Carson Papers, D/1507/A/26/60).
164 Addison, *Politics from Within*, ii. 244–6.

is not the little intrigues of the Convention, but the South Armagh election', following the death of the incumbent on 14 January.[165] 'South Armagh is about the most favourable seat for us in Ireland', wrote Dillon, 'and if the Party candidate is beaten there I really do not see any reason for believing that we could hold any seat in Ireland in a general election.'[166] The Irish Party candidate won easily, with 63 per cent of the vote. In a remarkable piece of sectarianism, Griffith's *Nationality* claimed that they had won on 'Unionist' votes.[167] But a comparison of turn-outs with the previous two contests in the constituency, a Nationalist–Unionist by-election in 1909 and a Nationalist–All-for-Ireland League (AfIL) contest in December 1910, confirms the view of the Protestant Sinn Féiner Robert Barton, who campaigned in the election, that 'for the most part the Unionists abstained from voting'.[168] Then the death of John Redmond brought a by-election in the small urban constituency of Waterford City. The Party leadership was now confident enough to nominate Redmond's son William for the seat. He had been MP for East Tyrone since 1910, so success in Waterford would bring a further by-election in Ulster. Devlin took personal charge of the campaign during the final three days, and Redmond won with 62 per cent of the vote.[169] East Tyrone followed immediately. It had been held by the Nationalists since 1885 but, because Catholics and Protestants were close to an even balance, it was—like West Belfast—one of the few seats in Ireland that was always contested. The local Irish Party machine was therefore free of the rust that encrusted most of the Party's seats. As in South Armagh, Logue sought to keep his priests out of the election, but Dillon told T.P. that 'at the last moment the young priests, in spite of the Cardinal . . . put tremendous pressure on the voters' to support Sinn Féin.[170] Thomas Harbison won for the Irish Party with 60 per cent of the vote in a straight fight with Sinn Féin. Again *Nationality* played the sectarian card, suggesting that Harbison had only succeeded by attracting 700 'Unionist' votes, and that Sinn Féin had won a majority of Catholic votes. But again the low turn-out of 44 per cent in a constituency where turn-outs had previously exceeded 90 per cent indicates that the Unionists did not vote. *Nationality* suggested that Devlin, who ran the campaign, had been using anti-Catholic rhetoric and attacking the priests in order to attract 'Unionist' votes.[171] In a reversal of the standard social-class assumptions about Sinn Féin support, the Belfast Sinn Féiner Dr Russell McNabb said in a campaign speech that 'the Devlins were nothing more or less than a lot of shoeboys, stableboys and bottle-washers'.[172]

But after three successful by-elections in a row, the Irish Party's luck ran out once more. In East Cavan, Sinn Féin selected Arthur Griffith as its candidate.

[165] Healy to O'Brien, 27 Jan. 1918 (NLI, OBP 8556/17).
[166] Dillon to O'Connor, 19 Jan. 1918 (DP 6742/441).   [167] *Nationality*, 9 Feb. 1918.
[168] Laffan, *Resurrection of Ireland*, 125.   [169] Ibid., 126.
[170] Dillon to O'Connor, 6 Apr. 1918 (DP 6742/466).   [171] *Nationality*, 6 Apr. 1918.
[172] Laffan, *Resurrection of Ireland*, 128.

But then, on the night of 17–18 May, seventy-three leading Sinn Féiners were arrested, including Griffith and de Valera. A 'German plot' was allegedly suspected following the arrest of a man who had landed from a German submarine, although it probably had more to do with the recent installation of a more hard-line team in Dublin Castle. The arrests were damaging to Sinn Féin in the medium term, as they removed most of its leaders for the best part of a year, including five Belfast men who were deported to England: Seán MacEntee, Denis McCullough, Robert Haskin, Russell McNabb, and Harry Dobbyn.[173] But in the short term it gave Sinn Féin a great election boost. Dillon feared that 'the priests, who are working against us for all they're worth—in spite of the Bishop, who is a supporter of the Party—will carry the division'.[174] Devlin attacked the double jeopardy of British despotism and Sinn Féin despotism. Sinn Féin, he said, would postpone the interests of the farmer and the labourer in their pursuit of an Irish Republic. But Sinn Féin won with almost 60 per cent of the vote. Dillon thought that, had Lloyd George not raised the conscription issue, 'we had Sinn Féin absolutely beaten'.[175]

On 3 March 1918 the Soviet surrender released German forces for a major offensive on the western front. The War Cabinet was sufficiently alarmed to introduce a new Military Service Bill, which empowered the government to implement conscription in Ireland at any time. In the Irish context the timing was appalling. It coincided with the unsuccessful conclusion of the Irish Convention, and came hard on the heels of the Irish Party's run of three by-election victories. The Bill was introduced on 9 April, together with a statement by Lloyd George that it would be linked to an immediate Home Rule Bill. Devlin spoke strongly against it, and Bonar Law mistakenly took his speech to be a challenge to Dillon's leadership of the party.[176] The Irish Party angrily denounced the Bill, and Dillon led them out of the House in protest. This reflected popular opinion in Ireland. A senior *Freeman* journalist told Devlin that 'the idea that the alternative to resistance is death or mutilation . . . in Flanders . . . is universal in the simplest minds, and will stiffen the resistance of the slackest'.[177] The Irish Party then formulated with Sinn Féin a united policy against conscription and agreed that until further notice they would remain with their constituents to resist conscription. A pledge 'to resist conscription by the most effective means at our disposal' was signed by half a million people throughout Ireland, and the trade unions organized a general strike for 23 April.[178] Devlin made his way to Belfast, where he spoke at St Peter's Pro-Cathedral, declaring that 'there is no

[173] 'David Hogan', *The Four Glorious Years* (Dublin, 1953), 29; RIC County Inspectors' Reports, Belfast, May 1918 (TNA: PRO CO 904/106).
[174] Dillon to O'Connor, 17 June 1918 (DP 6742/496).
[175] *Anglo-Celt*, 22 June 1918; Dillon to O'Connor, 17 June 1918 (DP 6742/496).
[176] Thomas Jones, *Whitehall Diary* (London, 1971), iii. 2.
[177] R. Donovan to Devlin, 15 Apr. 1918 (DP 6730/193). [178] *IN*, 22 Apr. 1918.

nation in the world that has the right to conscript another nation . . . England will never get a man from Ireland while that Act is on the Statute Book'.[179] MacRory was among the most outspoken of the bishops on the matter, declaring that 'no power has any moral right to coerce young Irishmen to fight in the alleged interests of freedom until they have been allowed to enjoy freedom for themselves'.[180] The overall effect of these few weeks of nationalist unity was by-and-large beneficial to Sinn Féin, bringing it into contact with the Church in a public and cooperative way, thereby enabling it to broaden its appeal beyond the militants and the young. Its advance became irresistible, but the 'German plot' meant that most of its leaders were back behind bars for another year. The structural disunity of 1917 had been remedied, but the calibre and diverse views of the extant leadership posed problems. Tim Healy observed that the Sinn Féin executive was 'entirely at the mercy of a knot of wild men . . . The problem is a big steam-boiler over pressure with no safety valve, plus a promise by inexperienced engineers that they will bring the ship safely to port in El Dorado.'[181]

By early May it was clear that the government had no immediate intention of putting Irish conscription into effect, and a new voluntary recruiting campaign was announced. During the crisis the War Cabinet had sent the Duke of Atholl, a former soldier and Unionist MP, to report on the state of feeling in Ireland. He reported to Lloyd George that conscripts would be got only with 'the very greatest difficulty', and once enrolled would be 'more trouble than they were worth'. Neither the Catholic Church nor the Irish Party, Atholl thought, was really hostile to conscription, but unless they opposed it 'their power would be entirely gone'. Thus he argued that, 'whatever our feelings may be with regard to home rule', it should be conceded as promptly as possible. Atholl was much impressed by Devlin, believing him to be 'absolutely straight':

He did not mince his words but he almost cried over the situation. He has an intense hatred for England, and especially for the Prime Minister . . . He is strongly in favour of voluntary enlistment, but considers it absolutely impossible in the present temper of the people to even suggest it, though if home rule is passed he thinks it may be possible at a later stage . . . He states his power, which was great four years ago, is at the present moment absolutely nil. He is a nationalist because he is a Catholic, and is cold-shouldered by the Protestants in Ulster, but he is an Ulsterman at heart, and entirely for a united Ireland, and believes in the predominance of Ulster, through sheer force of character, in the councils of his nation. He believes Ulster will eventually rule Ireland in all but name. In the meantime he is having a very bad time from the relations of the men whom he got to enlist at the beginning of the war . . . I would trust Devlin absolutely if he gave his word about anything . . . He was very earnest, and—for a Nationalist—extraordinarily broad-minded.[182]

[179] Ibid.   [180] Ibid., 29 Apr. 1918.
[181] Healy to O'Brien, 18 Oct. and 4 Nov. 1918 (NLI, OBP 8556/21, 22).
[182] 'State of Ireland with regard to Conscription', 29 Apr. 1918 (LGP, F/94/3/45).

Atholl found Dillon's views very similar to Devlin's, though 'more matured', and showing 'far more education'. Dillon's hatred of England and of the Prime Minister 'was certainly more bitter . . . [but] he believes strongly that he will yet come back to power'. According to Atholl, Dillon looked upon de Valera 'more as a crank than as a rogue'.[183]

After staying away from Parliament for three months, the Irish Party returned on 23 July. Devlin now believed that nothing short of dominion home rule would be acceptable. As the new Chief Secretary Edward Shortt observed, 'he could say nothing else in a country full of republicans'.[184] On 30 July Devlin made a caustic attack on Shortt in the debate on supplementary estimates for the secret services. On 1 August he raised the question of the return of UVF weapons, and more general matters regarding self-determination. In another speech he denounced the humbug of the German plot.[185] 'Our three-week campaign in parliament has been a great success,' wrote Dillon.[186] Devlin said at Monaghan on 15 August that 'the House of Commons is the best sounding board in the world, and that from there Ireland can appeal successfully for the world's sympathy'. Unity was essential to achieve home rule, he claimed, and home rule was essential to address major social issues such as the completion of land purchase, the housing of the workers, and the question of labour and wages.[187] This echoed Devlin's emphasis on radical social reform throughout the wartime years. In October 1917 he had helped to resolve the wage dispute among the power loom tenters, whose work was crucial to aeroplane manufacture, and whose action had a knock-on effect for 12,000 other workers.[188] A few weeks later he declared that the post-war era must see the rights of labour fully recognized, including better wages, short working hours, improved housing, the elimination of child labour, and the extension of education.[189] During the spring of 1918 he unveiled a 'New Democratic Movement', advocating 'a living wage for all workers' and 'full participation in the fruits of their labour' by means of participation in control of industry and profit sharing.[190] Little more was heard of this organization, but Devlin's rhetoric continued to lean strongly towards the labour movement. He supported the strike in the Belfast flour mills for English rates of pay, and strongly endorsed the demand for an eight-hour day.[191]

In March 1918 Countess Markievicz addressed a Sinn Féin meeting in St Mary's Hall, at which two detectives were assaulted. As a result the hall was closed under the Defence of the Realm Act (DORA) until 8 October.[192] Liam

    183 'State of Ireland with regard to Conscription', 29 Apr. 1918 (LGP, F/94/3/45).
    184 Jones, *Whitehall Diary*, iii. 10.
    185 *IN*, 30 and 31 July, 2 and 6 Aug. 1918.
    186 Dillon to O'Connor, 14 Aug. 1918 (DP 6742/512).   187 *IN*, 16 Aug. 1918.
    188 Ibid., 15, 30, 31 Oct. and 10 Nov. 1917.   189 Ibid., 19 Nov. 1917.
    190 M. McDonagh, 'Sinn Fein and Labour in Ireland', *Contemporary Review*, 113 (Apr. 1918), 424–33.
    191 *IN*, 18, 20, 24 Sept. 1918.
    192 RIC County Inspectors' Reports, Belfast, Mar. 1918 (TNA: PRO CO 904/105)

Gaynor recalled that during 1918 'a watching brief' was held on the Sinn Féin organization in Belfast by the Volunteers, 'so as to prevent this body getting into undesirable hands'. Gaynor, like most of his IRB and Volunteer colleagues, was 'doubtful about the sincerity of most platform politicians'. He and some colleagues therefore took an active part in the Belfast Sinn Féin Executive, 'so as to prevent a possible clash with the policy of our armed forces'.[193] The number of Irish Volunteers in the city remained low until the conscription threat of April 1918 produced 'a big influx of recruits', although in the opinion of the Police Commissioner the movement had gained less impetus from the conscription crisis than from 'the great numbers of young men from rural districts migrating into the city, to take up the plentiful employment'.[194] In October 1918 the Belfast and East Down Volunteer battalions were consolidated into a brigade, with Cusack as Commandant and Gaynor as Communications Officer.[195] Shortly afterwards Cusack, on Collins's orders, organized the transfer to Dublin of 80,000 rounds of ammunition that had been stolen from the UVF arsenal, concealed in deliveries of oats. Only when this task was almost complete did a security leak end the operation. The corn merchant concerned, James McNabb of Queen's Bridge, Belfast, brother of Dr Russell McNabb, had to go on the run.[196] Gathering arms was a main aim of the Volunteers during this period, although Roger McCorley recalled that the results in the Belfast area 'were meagre'.[197]

THE GENERAL ELECTION OF 1918

Once the parliamentary session was over, the war approached its end, and a general election loomed, Devlin fell into depression. Dillon was meanwhile trying to develop a sense of electoral optimism. 'If Joe Devlin could be raised out of his depression and would take hold of the organization with his old spirit,' he told T.P., 'a revolution could be effected between now and Christmas... The bishops are severely frightened.' Given time, money, and 'activity and faith on our part', Dillon thought that the Irish Party could return to Parliament after the election 'with a better party than we have now, though probably considerably reduced in numbers'.[198] It was agreed to contest the election united on 'some practicable and attainable object', in contrast to the Sinn Féin policy, which was essentially a demand for an Irish Republic to be achieved by abstention, armed force, and an appeal to the peace conference. An additional hurdle for

---

[193] Gaynor, witness statement 183.
[194] McGuinness, witness statement 417: RIC County Inspectors' Reports, Belfast, Sept.–Dec. 1917 (TNA: PRO CO 904/104).
[195] Gaynor, witness statement 183.   [196] Cusack, witness statement 402.
[197] McCorley, witness statement 389.
[198] Dillon to O'Connor, 18 Aug. 1918 (DP 6742/515).

the Irish Party was the new franchise extension and redistribution of seats. Seat redistribution favoured the Protestant north, while franchise extension gave more votes to younger people, which favoured Sinn Féin. In Belfast the number of seats was raised from four to nine, but still only one had a Catholic majority. Meanwhile the franchise was extended from the male householder to include all adult males over the age of 21 and all women over the age of 30. In Ireland this increased the size of the electorate from 701,475 in 1910 to 1,936,673 in 1918, of whom about 400,000 were women. Additionally, since eight years had passed since the previous election, around 20 per cent of householder electors would have died and been replaced by younger people. Thus more than 70 per cent of Irish electors in the general election of 1918 were voting for the first time. Even had the Irish Party been in good shape, therefore, it would have needed to build new support on a large scale.

Towards the end of October 1918 Devlin's depression was exacerbated by an attack of the influenza that swept the world that winter, killing over 200,000 people in Britain alone. By 10 November he was recuperating, and on the 15th he underwent a related throat operation. Dillon told T.P. that 'Joe is still laid up and I am very much afraid that he is out of action for the election—a desperate loss'.[199] Addressing the Dublin UIL on 21 November, Dillon declared that he could see 'not the slightest prospect' of a successful electoral negotiation with Sinn Féin regarding Ulster seats. Uncharacteristically optimistic, he called for an all-Ireland seats deal, with no preconditions. Healy thought that what Dillon had said would 'drive every northern bishop and every northern Catholic to fury, and will probably decide Devlin to throw off his diplomatic influenza and separate himself from his [word illegible] leader'.[200] But Dillon found Devlin to be still 'very ill and depressed' in a Dublin nursing home, and took over his role at UIL HQ.[201] By late November Devlin was better, but Dillon thought that 'all he will be able to do is look after his own constituency', and shortly afterwards Devlin departed for Belfast. 'I suppose we shall not see him again till after the election,' wrote Dillon. He did not at any stage call the office 'to see how the fight was going'.[202] Devlin's 'disloyalty to Dillon' was even noted at a meeting of the British cabinet.[203] Dillon's impression was that 'we have infinitely more friends in the country than Joe Devlin could ever be got to admit, and that if we had a decent organization and anything like an adequate staff at headquarters we would have saved about 40 seats . . . as I warned Devlin a dozen times during the last six months'. The collapse of Devlin, he commented later, 'very largely contributed to the debacle'.[204]

---

[199] *IN*, 29 Oct., 11 and 15 Nov. 1918; Dillon to O'Connor, 18 Nov. 1918 (DP 6742/548).
[200] Healy to O'Brien, 23 Nov. 1918 (NLI, OBP 8556/22).
[201] Dillon to O'Connor, 20 Dec. 1918 (DP 6742/582).
[202] Dillon to O'Connor, 22 Nov. and n.d. [between 23 and 27 Nov. 1918] (DP 6742/552, 583).
[203] Laffan, *Resurrection of Ireland*, 156.
[204] Dillon to O'Connor, 28 Nov. and 20 Dec. 1918 (DP 6742/557, 582).

Sinn Féin was determined to maximize its support by standing in as many seats as possible, though aware of the danger of losing several Catholic-majority seats to the Unionists if there were contests between Sinn Féin and the Irish Party. But once Dillon refused to compromise on abstention, Sinn Féin declined to enter a conference.[205] The bishops of the Ulster archdiocese then wrote to the press suggesting an equal division of the winnable Ulster seats, and perhaps some outside Ulster 'where the need is similar'.[206] Dillon accepted this, attracted by the wider suggestion.[207] But Sinn Féin delayed its response, instead calling a conference of its own local representatives from eight Ulster constituencies, thus making clear its intention of restricting negotiations to those seats.[208] At this meeting it was reported that all of the five six-county bishops except Logue were on the side of Sinn Féin. These bishops advised that it would be damaging to Sinn Féin if Dillon accepted the Ulster seats compromise and it did not. Thus, on 2–3 December Dillon and Eoin MacNeill met twice.[209] They agreed on a 50:50 split of eight specified seats, but the decision as to which seats should go to which party was passed to Logue for arbitration.[210] Dillon found his meetings with MacNeill 'an absolutely sickening experience'.[211] MacNeill later recalled that 'Dillon got the better of me', by persuading him to accept Logue as arbitrator.[212] The settlement came too late to withdraw candidates, but instructions were given to voters to abide by the Cardinal's decision. Not everyone in the Irish Party approved of the compromise. Richard McGhee told Dillon that he 'had no confidence that Devlin is big enough to face the situation as a man should do. Better to go down fighting than to go down before Cardinal Logue and clerical dictation.'[213] Devlin backed the agreement, although even amongst his own friends in Belfast 'there is great feeling against the view I hold'. Without a pact, he thought, 'I cannot guarantee we will win a single seat except my own'.[214]

Adherence to the pact in all but one case makes it impossible to get a perfect measure of Ulster nationalist opinion. But an analysis of results in the seats where there was no pact indicates that the Irish Party performed better than Sinn Féin in Unionist majority seats.[215] In East Down the local Devlinites, notwithstanding interventions by Bishop MacRory and by Devlin himself, rebelled against the pact, thus allowing the Unionist minority to take the seat. Again the rebel Irish Party candidate performed better than the pact-nominated Sinn Féiner. Thus the pattern of earlier by-elections, which revealed Irish Party support to be stronger in Ulster than in the rest of the country, was continued. An important

[205] *IN*, 20 Nov. 1918.   [206] *FJ*, 28 Nov. 1918.   [207] Ibid., 29 Nov. 1918.
[208] Ibid., 30 Nov. 1918.   [209] Ibid., 3 Dec. 1918.   [210] Ibid., 4 Dec. 1918.
[211] Dillon to O'Connor, 3 Dec. 1918 (DP 6742/561).   [212] Tierney, *Eoin MacNeill*, 274.
[213] McGhee to Dillon, 28 Nov. 1918 (DP 6757/1063).
[214] Devlin to Dillon, 28 Nov. 1918 (DP 6730/201).
[215] Laffan, *Resurrection of Ireland*, 165–6.

factor in this was that the *Irish News* continued to be the main source of daily information for Catholics in Ulster at a time when the Party's Dublin paper, the *Freeman's Journal*, had long since lost its circulation contest to Murphy's *Irish Independent*.[216] This does not 'explain away' the difference but is in fact additional evidence of Catholic Ulster's difference from the rest of Catholic Ireland. As Marianne Elliott has observed, 1918 was a 'false dawn' for Sinn Féin in Ulster.[217]

In the campaign the *Irish Independent* claimed to be neutral, although its comments were more damaging to the Irish Party: 'If they are in danger of practical extinction today it is due to their inability to raise themselves above the lowest level of cowardly opportunism, and to their general attitude of contemptuous indifference to the opinion of the people whom they were elected to represent.' Sinn Féin, on the other hand, it credited with 'sincerity, earnestness and self-sacrifice . . . [although] a very large proportion of the prominent and active Sinn Féiners have committed themselves to a policy of violence'.[218] The dilapidation of the Irish Party, coupled with the age of its MPs and the fact that most of them had scarcely ever had to fight an election, meant that many sitting members decided to retire. Beset by widespread demoralization, and faced with youthful enthusiasm and more than a hint of iron fist, the Irish Party leadership struggled to find candidates. Sinn Féin won twenty-five of its seventy-three victories without a contest, including seventeen of the twenty-four seats in Munster. It won 47 per cent of the votes cast in Ireland, to which must be added the uncontested victories. The Irish Party did worse than any of its supporters—or even some of its detractors—had predicted. Apart from the four 'pact' seats, it held only Devlin's seat in the Falls and Captain Redmond's in Waterford City. In East Mayo Dillon won barely one-third of the vote in a straight fight.

In Belfast the franchise extension increased the electorate from 80,592 to 172,293, of whom 39 per cent were women. Devlin was adopted for the new Falls constituency. At no stage did his colleagues expect him to lose. Sinn Féin tended to be a little more optimistic. In any event their choice of candidate was important, as the Falls was by far the most solidly nationalist seat in the six counties, and located in the heart of the otherwise Unionist metropolis. Most of the leading Sinn Féiners were still in prison, so the likely candidates would be names on the ballot paper rather than campaigners on the street. Denis McCullough and Seán MacEntee were the senior local men, but McCullough, writing in slightly coded terms from Gloucester Prison, told his wife that MacEntee 'absolutely refused his name to go forward for the Belfast job'.[219] Winifred Carney, a Belfast Sinn Féin executive member,

[216] Maume, *Long Gestation*, 203.   [217] Elliott, *Catholics of Ulster*, 300.
[218] *Irish Independent*, 16 Nov. 1918.
[219] McCullough to Agnes McCullough, 31 Aug. 1918 (McCP P120/54/9).

then warned McCullough that there was a move to secure de Valera's candidacy. McCullough was rather bitter about this, writing to his wife Agnes on 6 September that:

Evidently Seán Mac[Entee] and myself were not good enough for Barney [Bernard Campbell] and his friends, and as he could not get it himself he saw to it that we wouldn't get the chance. We are good enough to do this kind of thing though, apparently [i.e. languish in prison]. I was feeling a bit rough and bitter about it and no wonder, though I do not think D. [de Valera] will accept the suggestion and he would be foolish if he did... If they couldn't do that much to help get me out [of prison], it is a simple proposition that they can do fairly well without me altogether. And they will![220]

Harry Boland, Sinn Féin's chief election agent, was strongly in favour of de Valera's nomination for the Falls, although Austin Stack warned him against it.[221] The Belfast police reported that a house-to-house canvass had produced discouraging results, and that 'it is doubtful if Mr de Valera will allow his name to go forward'.[222] Thus when two Belfast Sinn Féiners told the party's Standing Committee that 'on a fifty per cent canvass of the total poll of an average area they were satisfied that de Valera would win by an estimated majority of at least 552', they were being less than entirely frank. But after 'an exhaustive examination' of these figures the Standing Committee decided by majority vote that de Valera should be nominated.[223] Some weeks later Seán T. O'Kelly, who had supported the decision, visited Belfast and reported back to the Committee that de Valera 'will get a good beating'.[224] When McCullough heard that 'the W.B. [West Belfast] job has been now definitely fixed', he told Agnes that he was 'really and truly relieved... Since August 1916 my heart has not been in the work as it used to be... I have so little in common with those now in the business.'[225] McCullough was later nominated for the safe Unionist seat of South Tyrone.[226] MacRory called upon Catholic electors to vote for Sinn Féin in all the Ulster contests where there was a straight fight between Sinn Féin and Ulster Unionism, and also to vote Sinn Féin in those Belfast seats where Sinn Féin and the Belfast Labour Representation Committee were both opposing Unionism. On the Falls contest he remained silent.

Of Sinn Féin's nine Belfast candidates, only de Valera was a leader of national standing. Michael Carolan and Seamus Dobbyn were also teachers, and also interned; Dermot Barnes was a well-known local draper; Bernard Campbell

220 McCullough to Agnes McCullough, 6 Sept. 1918 (McCP P120/54/10).
221 D. Fitzpatrick, *Harry Boland's Irish Revolution* (Cork, 2003), 108.
222 RIC County Inspectors' Reports, Belfast, Sept. 1918 (TNA: PRO CO 904/107).
223 Sinn Féin Standing Committee Minutes, 10 Oct. 1918 (NLI, mic. p. 3269).
224 Ibid., 28 Nov. 1918 (NLI, mic. p. 3269).
225 McCullough to A. McCullough, 17 Oct. 1918 (McCP P120/54/9).
226 Sinn Féin Standing Committee Minutes, 10 Oct. 1918 (NLI, mic. p. 3269).

was a solicitor; Archie Savage was a long-time opponent of the Irish Party; Russell McNabb was a local physician, also interned, as was the Protestant Robert Haskin; Winifred Carney, the only female candidate in Ulster, was a Connollyite socialist. Their campaign in the Falls began quietly enough, but was soon disrupted by violence. On 19 November an open-air meeting in Albert Street, addressed by Revd Robert Fullerton and Bernard Campbell, was disrupted by 'parties of mill girls' who shouted and sang songs.[227] On the 27th they held a more successful rally at St Mary's Hall, attended by 'several thousand'.[228] On 1 December a meeting addressed by Bernard Campbell and Eileen Davitt was attacked as it passed along Catholic Divis Street. A battle ensued involving several hundred people, culminating in a police baton charge in which Archie Savage was knocked unconscious.[229] Four Sinn Féiners were charged with riot. The basis of the defence was extreme provocation by large, hostile crowds. It was said that the missiles thrown were for the most part 'cabbage stumps and condensed milk tins', but the number of minor injuries sustained was large. The jury clearly gave more weight to the allegations of baton-wielding by the four men concerned, who were convicted of riot.[230] After this incident the Sinn Féin campaign in the Falls was more subdued, though it managed to hold 'a pretty large gathering' in Clowney Street on 3 December.[231] As the campaign progressed, the clashes eased off somewhat.[232] On the 11th Bernard Campbell said that Devlin was 'the one great obstacle' to the task of bringing 'the democracy of the north into line with the democracy of the south'.[233] On the 12th Revd Michael O'Flanagan addressed 'thousands', with Revd Fullerton in the chair, and three curates on the platform.[234] When Sinn Féin's deputy director of publicity, Frank Gallagher, attempted to speak in Belfast,

the audience was a young and merry one . . . Just the material, I thought, for the new doctrine. They never heard it, for *they* had songs about their Wee Joe that they wanted to sing to *me*, and when they were done singing they had a fife and drum band which made a neat circle of marching men around my platform and smothered my eloquence in an hour of perfect bombination. Their drums never paused or halted until I had to bow gracefully and run for my train.[235]

Devlin's meetings, on the other hand, were great triumphs. In Belfast where the number of families, both Catholic and Protestant, who had members involved in the First World War was so large, the Irish Party rhetoric regarding 'the Allied cause' carried a lot more weight that it did elsewhere. 'Nothing could be more disastrous to Ireland', declared Devlin at his adoption meeting,

---

[227] *Belfast Newsletter*, 20 Nov. 1918.   [228] *Irish Independent*, 28 Nov. 1918.
[229] *IN*, 2 Dec. 1918.   [230] *Belfast Newsletter*, 21 Mar. 1919.
[231] *IN*, 4 Dec. 1918.   [232] *Irish Independent*, 10 Dec. 1918.
[233] Ibid., 12 Dec. 1918.   [234] Ibid., 13 Dec. 1918.
[235] Hogan, *Four Glorious Years*, 52.

'than to drive out of public life men who had all along supported the Allied cause and to put in their place men conspicuous by their opposition to or lack of sympathy with that cause'.[236] In his election address he adopted what the *Freeman's Journal* described as a 'socialistic' tone, calling for equal pay for women, and a redefinition of the term 'skilled worker'. 'I do not believe in class war,' said Devlin, but, 'if the intervention of the state should be necessary to compel justice for the workers, then I believe it is the duty of the state to intervene . . . limited by the right of individual liberty and by the inviolable sanctity of the home'.[237] Almost the entire election address was concerned with social problems rather than nationalism. Devlin's procession up the Falls on 29 November, which took fifty minutes to pass by, included illuminated signs proclaiming 'Labour Will Not Wait', 'Vote Devlin and an eight-hour day', and 'Devlin the friend of the workers'.[238] The rallies at St Mary's Hall on 1 and 8 December were packed out. Devlin was dismissive of Sinn Féin's policies. The abstention policy was 'humbug and tomfoolery', while an Irish Republic, he said, could be achieved only by force, which was even less likely to be successful against Britain in peacetime than it had been during the war.[239] Although in one sense Devlin was wrong about this, in another sense he was right: the policy of Sinn Féin and the IRA did not bring independence to the nationalists of six-county Ulster, but left them far worse off than before.

Devlin defeated de Valera by 8,488 votes to 3,245 on a turn-out of 74 per cent. The work of his election organizers was impressive. It was normal practice for parliamentary candidates to boost themselves by submitting several nomination papers, rather than just one containing the twelve required signatures, but the Devlin campaign turned this into a mass demonstration of support, with names and addresses of over 6,300 signatories, or three-quarters of his eventual vote, being published in the *Irish News* during the run-up to polling day. Collection of signatures took place in all streets in the constituency, and only in the few Protestant streets was the signature-rate very low. An analysis of the addresses indicates that support for Devlin was higher in the inner-city streets of the Lower Falls than in the newer and less-deprived streets of the Upper Falls. The *Newsletter* estimated that 2,000 Unionist electors in Falls did not vote, which implies a not-improbable nationalist turn-out of 85 per cent.[240] The *Irish Independent* noted that 'soldiers wore the Devlin colours', and estimated that the Sinn Féin vote in the constituency was 'almost entirely male'. The announcement of results on 30 December was a celebration of Devlin's personal triumph and a wake for the rest of the Irish Party. Devlin declared that he would set himself the task, 'not of dividing my countrymen in the south, but of uniting my countrymen in the north'. He also said that 'I never felt happier in my life'—a statement

---

[236] *The Times*, 14 Oct. 1918; *IN*, 14 Oct. 1918.   [237] *FJ*, 30 Nov. 1918.
[238] *IN*, 30 Nov. 1918.   [239] Ibid., 9 Dec. 1918.   [240] *Belfast Newsletter*, 16 Dec. 1918.

not borne out by the private correspondence of Dillon and others.[241] Richard McGhee, who had written so warmly about Devlin a few months earlier, wrote to Dillon that it was

a farce to see the congratulations to Joe Devlin over his victory in Belfast . . . I am profoundly convinced that no man in Ireland is more responsible for the debacle to the Party than Joe Devlin. I have been a quiet, but close, observer of the disintegrating character of his actions for the past four years, both in Parliament and in Ireland . . . I knew that it was eating the soul out of constitutionalism far and wide.[242]

But in the view of the *Newsletter*, Devlin's victory in the Falls was 'the death-knell of Sinn Féin in Belfast'.[243]

Sinn Féin stood in all nine constituencies, but it seemed that Devlin would be the only Nationalist candidate until at the last minute Major W. H. Davey, having been moved out of Derry City under the Pact, challenged Carson in the predominantly working-class North Belfast constituency of Duncairn. Davey, a Protestant, was editor of the Liberal weekly the *Ulster Guardian*, but he worked closely with the Irish Party, McGhee later urging Dillon to contribute £200 towards his election expenses.[244] In a constituency with a substantial Catholic minority Davey, who campaigned in British Army uniform, secured 17.1 per cent of the turn-out as against 1.9 per cent for the Sinn Féin candidate. In Pottinger, which included much of the Catholic Short Strand district, the Labour candidate obtained almost 21 per cent of the vote against 3 per cent for Sinn Féin. In Victoria the result was similar, Sinn Féin getting 3 per cent to Labour's 26 per cent. In Shankill Sinn Féin obtained just over 3 per cent of the vote against Labour's 23 per cent. The highest Sinn Féin votes outside the Falls were in St Anne's and Woodvale, where there were no Labour or other nationalist candidates. Overall it was a strong result for the Unionists, who won more than 65 per cent of the vote in the city. The four Labour candidates saved their deposits, but all the Sinn Féin candidates came bottom of the poll, with only de Valera saving his deposit. It was clear that the majority of Catholic voters outside the Falls had ignored Bishop MacRory's advice to vote Sinn Féin.

[241] *IN*, 30 Dec. 1918.　　　[242] McGhee to Dillon, 1 Jan. 1919 (DP 6757/1065).
[243] *Belfast Newsletter*, 30 Dec. 1918.
[244] McGhee to Dillon, 15 Dec. 1918 (DP 6757/1064).

8

'Bloodshed and Partition': War in Ireland, 1919–1922

Professor MacNeill's policy would . . . bring bloodshed and partition in Ireland . . . Ulster would agree if only Sinn Féin would let her.

(W. H. Davey, 1919[1])

We adopted political assassination as a principle . . . we turned the whole thoughts and passions of a generation upon blood and revenge and death . . . We derided the moral law and said there was no law but the law of force.

(P. S. O'Hegarty, 1924[2])

The 1918 election ended the influence of the Irish Party in the House of Commons. Bishop MacRory thought that the country was 'thoroughly and intelligibly tired of the Party. It was time to put an end to it.' Like many of the clergy, he was somewhat entranced by Sinn Féin. After visiting prisoners in Belfast Jail, he wrote to Rome that 'the spirit of these young Sinn Féiners is indomitable and beyond imagination. They are absolutely fearless.'[3] The Irish Party's seven MPs operated without an elected leader at Westminster, while Dillon, at home in Dublin, remained a guiding influence. During the next three years the Party, very aware that it had lost its mandate from the Irish electorate, avoided making proposals for an Irish settlement. Devlin and O'Connor, almost the only remaining speechmakers, concentrated on criticism of the Irish administration, particularly as guerrilla warfare and reprisals came to dominate events. Devlin also continued to intervene on social policies. Belfast appeared to be one of the most peaceful places in Ireland until the middle of 1920, when a combination of factors brought it into the centre of the conflict for the next two years. Devlin was very active in dealing with casework, but even after the Treaty the Provisional Government of the Free State felt committed

[1] *IN*, 27 June 1919.   [2] P. S. O'Hegarty, *The Victory of Sinn Féin* (Dublin, 1924), 91.
[3] MacRory to O'Riordan, 26 Dec. 1918 and 2 Jan. 1919 (MOR 1918/94, 1919/4).

to its own supporters in the North, and there was great reluctance to consult Devlin on policy. It was only after acute conflict came to an end, and the pattern for the future was established, that Devlin re-emerged as the leader of Northern Nationalism.

'VOICES IN THE WILDERNESS': WESTMINSTER, 1919–1920

The last few months of 1918 had been the worst of Devlin's career to date. Influenza played a big part in this, though, not for the only time, physical debilitation brought mental depression in its wake. Over Christmas Dillon thought he looked 'wretched . . . and . . . *very* poorly. In fact he is in a shattered condition . . . Unless Devlin pulls himself together and throws himself earnestly, in his old style, into an Irish movement, I do not see any possibility of keeping our friends together.' At this stage Devlin declared himself 'violently against' attending Parliament.[4] He continued for some days to adhere firmly to the view that none of the Irish Party MPs except O'Connor should take their seats. But after a few days' holiday at Portrush he began to cheer up, and told Bishop O'Donnell that he had not yet made up his mind about attending Parliament. All his 'influential constituents are in favour of my going'.[5] His parliamentary colleagues were also in favour of attendance, but he was still inclined to the view that 'so feeble a representation . . . would only advertise our own weakness', and would be characterized by Sinn Féin as an impediment to their efforts to secure admission to the Paris Peace Conference.[6] Dillon continued to be the Party's eyes and ears in Ireland. He thought that 'the extreme party have got complete control of Sinn Féin'.[7] On 21 January, at Soloheadbeg, Co. Tipperary, a group of Irish Volunteers (now renamed the Irish Republican Army) lay in wait for two policemen escorting a delivery of dynamite to a quarry, shot them dead, and made off with the dynamite. This was subsequently honoured as the first event in the War of Independence. Before he knew of this, Devlin had written to Bishop O'Donnell 'that there is about to be a serious situation in the country, which may involve bloodshed, if not worse'. He thought that 'the Sinn Féin promises' could not possibly materialize, and that in such circumstances blame would be placed upon those who had attended the British Parliament. But he then decided to consult 'a representative gathering' of his constituents, which proved to be the turning point.[8] By the end of January even the Ulster Unionists had sensed

---

[4] Dillon to O'Connor, 25 and 28–9 Dec. 1918 (DP 6742/586, 588).
[5] Devlin to Dillon, 6 Jan. 1919 (DP 6730/203); Devlin to O'Donnell, 6 Jan. 1919 (P. O'Donnell Papers, IV. 5).
[6] Devlin to O'Donnell, 22 Jan. 1919 (P. O'Donnell Papers, IV. 5).
[7] Dillon to O'Connor, 23 Jan. and 20 Feb. 1919 (DP 6742/602, 613).
[8] Devlin to O'Donnell, 22 Jan. 1919 (P. O'Donnell Papers, IV. 5).

that 'Devlin is bucking up', and they feared that he would take the credit for any settlement that might be arrived at with regard to the general strike which was tearing Belfast apart.[9] By 10 February Devlin was in London, and T.P. was 'delighted' to find him 'not only in good health but apparently in good spirits and quite ready to enter the fray'.[10]

Devlin's first impression of the new Parliament was that it was 'almost as tired an atmosphere as the old Parliament . . . They all seem to be heavily plutocratic gentlemen.'[11] 'I know', he declared in his first speech, 'that my colleagues and myself will be like voices in the wilderness in this House.' But he then weighed in with confidence on the matter of the Belfast strike. He was 'not an extremist', he said, but he did not believe that the strike in Belfast was inspired or carried on by 'Bolshevists'. It was being conducted with dignity and 'a freedom from crimes of violence unexcelled in the history of conflict in any part of the world'. People had not gone to war to restore 'sweating, low wages, long hours, lack of leisure'. While carefully disclaiming any authority to speak for Ireland, Devlin called on the government to grant Ireland self-determination. 'You will no doubt say that there is a large minority who will not accept self-government for Ireland, but you are going to force minorities in other countries in Europe . . . in Bohemia, in Poland, in Alsace-Lorraine'.[12] 'Joe was splendid,' T.P. told Dillon, 'he shamed and cowed the Orangemen.'[13] On 14 January 22,000 Belfast workers voted overwhelmingly in favour of a 44-hour week and a general strike if this was not granted. The employers' offer was rejected and the strike began on the 25th.[14] The *Irish News*—which was sympathetic to the strikers—was closed for three weeks, while the *Newsletter* and the *Northern Whig*, both hostile to the strike, struggled on. Within a week almost 40,000 workers in the city were out on strike, and another 25,000 laid off because of it. The future Unionist cabinet minister William Grant was a member of the strike committee. At the end of January Devlin called upon the Prime Minister to initiate an offer to the workers, and on 10 February the shipyard employers offered a compromise settlement. Fifty-eight per cent of strikers voted to reject the offer, ignoring the recommendation of their strike committee, but morale crumbled and by 19 February twenty out of the twenty-two unions had returned to work.[15] Once the strike was over employment was 'fairly good'. The main social problem was a serious shortage of housing. The city remained quiet during the Twelfth holiday in July.

---

[9] R. Dawson Bates to J. Craig, 31 Jan. 1919, cited in P. J. Buckland (ed.), *Irish Unionism 1885–1923: A Documentary History* (Belfast, 1973), 431.

[10] O'Connor to Dillon, 11 and 12 Feb. 1919 (DP 6742/606, 607).

[11] Devlin to Dillon, 12 and 14 Feb. 1919 (DP 6730/208, 209).

[12] Parl. Deb., HC, 5th series, cxxxxvi. 145–57 (12 Feb. 1919).

[13] O'Connor to Dillon, 15 Feb. 1919 (DP 6742/608).

[14] RIC County Inspectors' Reports, Belfast, Jan. 1919 (TNA: PRO CO904/108).

[15] *Belfast Newsletter*, 31 Jan. 1919; note of telephone message, n.d. [30–1 Jan. 1919] (LGP, F/30/3/17); O'Connor to Dillon, 12 Feb. 1919 (DP 6742/607); M. Farrell, 'The Great Belfast Strike of 1919', *NS* 3 (1971), 10–15, 18.

During 1919 and 1920 Devlin was very active in debates on social legislation. He sat on the Old Age Pensions and Proportional Representation (PR) committees.[16] He battled, with limited success, for separate treatment for Ireland on matters of health. In March 1919 he supported the Bill to implement PR for Irish local government elections.[17] With regard to the Housing of the Working Classes (Ireland) Bill, he said: 'give a man a clean, healthy and well-lighted house and you keep him in the home instead of sending him out to the meretricious attraction of a well-lighted public house.' The Belfast Corporation, he said, had built several hundred houses, but most of them were of 'very small and mean construction'.[18] In 1920 Devlin called for the extension of the Unemployment Insurance Bill to Ireland, and he opposed the Trades Union Ballot Bill of the same year as a 'Belfast-hatched plot'.[19] He also helped to defeat both the Liquor Traffic Local Veto (Ireland) Bill, which he declared was wanted only by 'temperance fanatics' in Belfast, and a private member's bill that proposed to give over the control of schools to Belfast City Council.[20] But early in 1920 the government introduced an education bill for all Ireland. Devlin forwarded to Bishop O'Donnell a letter from some Catholic National schoolteachers, urging him 'in the name of our wives and children to get the Bill passed at once. To us the Bill means a living wage . . . We fail to understand the hostile attitude of our bishops . . . Now you have to decide between Ireland's welfare and the bishops.'[21] Devlin told O'Donnell that the Bill was bound to pass, and 'we will not get twenty men to vote with us'. He therefore proposed to concentrate on securing amendments.[22] The bishops, on the other hand, thought 'that there should be neither parley nor truck with the Government'. Devlin thought O'Donnell's summary of the bishops' views 'very characteristic of the mentality of those whose mind it speaks'. In private Devlin believed that 'we have a poor case . . . I have been informed that the Catholic schools in Belfast will get whatever share of the rates raised they are entitled to'.[23] He was doubtless relieved when the Bill was withdrawn, although in 1923 the NI Government carried through a more unwelcome scheme for Northern Ireland.

In 1919–20 Devlin was for the most part back on his best form. T.P. thought that 'Joe . . . has become quite a popular favourite in the House of Commons, and everybody is delighted to hear him. I am glad to say he enjoys the work thoroughly and has not looked so well for years.'[24] But his volatile temperament continued unrestrained. The *Freeman's Journal* was in dire financial straits, and

---

[16] Devlin to Dillon, 14 May 1919 (DP 6730/223).
[17] Parl. Deb., H.C., 5th series, cxvi. 1068–70 (27 May 1919).
[18] Ibid., cxv. 1482–9 (13 May 1919).   [19] *IN*, 11 Mar. and 24 Apr. 1920.
[20] *IN*, 13 Mar. 1920; Devlin to O'Donnell, 28 Feb. 1919 (P. O'Donnell Papers, IV. 5).
[21] Devlin to O'Donnell, 13 Feb. 1920 (P. O'Donnell Papers, IV. 5).
[22] Ibid., 20 Feb. 1920 (P. O'Donnell Papers, IV. 5).
[23] Devlin to Dillon, 26 Feb. 1920 and encl.; O'Donnell to Devlin, 23 Feb. 1920 (DP 6730/252).
[24] O'Connor to Dillon, 4 Apr. 1919 (DP 6742/637).

Dillon and T.P. considered various cost-cutting measures. Devlin's criticism focused more on the paper's failure to give proper coverage to the Party's work. He declined Dillon's invitation to join the Board, and Dillon lamented that Devlin 'pours forth to all and sundry floods of abuse on the paper . . . and he offers no constructive or helpful criticism. I agree with him heartily in many of his criticisms. But his methods have not been in any degree helpful, but quite the reverse.'[25] T.P. also wanted to raise in Parliament the behaviour of Crown forces during a clash in Dublin, but Devlin was doubtful. T.P. always liked to bring Devlin with him, 'knowing his somewhat susceptible character'. He thought that Devlin's view was 'coloured by the fierce and, I might say, I think, rather factionist view he takes of the Sinn Féin movement'.[26] But T.P. was full of praise for Devlin's parliamentary work, while Dillon agreed that Devlin 'ought to give all his time to work in the House', and, if it proved possible to revive the movement in Ireland, 'a deputy should be put in full charge' of the UIL in Dublin.[27] During the autumn the government appointed a committee under Walter Long to draw up a new Home Rule Bill. Devlin was initially sceptical, taking the view that 'the whole of this business of the Long Committee is a fraud, and that the Government have no serious intention of doing anything'.[28] His mood swings, which had become a frequent subject of comment by his older colleagues since 1916, were frequent during 1919. Dillon noted in his diary that a former parliamentary colleague had seen Devlin in London, finding him 'unhappy and depressed' and eager about 'getting out of public life'. The best offer he had received was the directorship of a big whiskey firm, which in his mind contrasted with 'the depressing character of surroundings in the House of Commons'.[29] A day earlier O'Connor reported that 'Devlin is now in a much better frame of mind' and 'doing splendidly in the House'![30]

In November Dillon urged O'Connor and Devlin not to be present for the introduction of the government's proposed Irish settlement, about which the Party had not been consulted.[31] T.P. was despondent, feeling that 'the Government will have succeeded in the double purpose of making the partition of Ireland, if not permanent at least calculated to endure for a considerable period, and . . . it is no consolation to me to know that this horrible result has been produced as much by the folly of Sinn Féin as by the perfidy of the Government'.[32] Meanwhile the security situation in the South of Ireland was deteriorating rapidly. Dillon thought that 'the Church has lost all control

25 Dillon to O'Connor, 19 May 1919 (DP 6742/657).
26 O'Connor to Dillon, 14 May 1919 (DP 6742/654).
27 Dillon to O'Connor, 29 May 1919 (DP 6742/661, 663).
28 Dillon to O'Connor, 7 Nov. 1919 (DP 6742/703).
29 Dillon, 'Reflections, 1919–21', 4 Dec. 1919 (DP 6582).
30 O'Connor to Dillon, 3 Dec. 1919 (DP 6742/713).
31 Dillon to O'Connor, 21 Nov. 1919 (DP 6742/706).
32 O'Connor to Dillon, 24 Nov. 1919 (DP 6742/710, 726).

and the so-called Irish Volunteers (really the IRB) are in full control . . . The murder campaign is a widespread national movement of the most formidable character.'[33] But in Belfast during 1919 there was little indication that Sinn Féin had advanced its position. Bishop MacRory was almost an exception. Though discreet about his views at the time of the 1918 election, during the early months of 1919 he became increasingly enthusiastic. He was, however, even further off target in his predictions than Dillon and his friends, especially so far as the fate of the North was concerned. He told Michael O'Riordan naively that the young Sinn Féiners:

Are ardent patriots but they are equally ardent Catholics. Here in my diocese they are the very cream of the young men: respectable, sober, God-fearing, devoted to the Church and submissive to ecclesiastical authority. The leaders among them are well-educated . . . they have come to the conclusion that justice can never be hoped for from an English parliament. So far I quite agree with them . . . and if they continue the movement in a clean, open fashion and don't allow themselves to be goaded to desperation or driven into secret societies, they must succeed before long in winning not, probably, independence—for England will never concede that until she is beaten to the dust—but an Irish parliament with control of Irish finance . . . You will read occasionally of wild and absurd things done by individuals here, but I believe that they are done without the approval of Sinn Féin leaders.[34]

Police Commissioner T. J. Smyth, about to undergo what proved a fatal transfer to Cork, reported that Sinn Féin 'have made a serious hole in Mr Devlin's majority over them at the last election'. But in elections for the Poor Law Guardians that year the four local Sinn Féiners who stood were badly beaten by UIL candidates. By October 1919 the new Police Commissioner, J. F. Gelston, thought that Sinn Féin was 'losing ground'.[35]

The Belfast municipal elections were held in January 1920 under the single-transferable-vote system of PR. Since 1897 city elections had usually returned up to fifty-two Unionists and eight nationalists. In January 1920 the result was very different, as Table 8.1 indicates. The Unionists, still struggling after the industrial militancy of the previous year, lost a substantial slice of their majority. The Nationalists ran candidates in all nine wards, and Sinn Féin—or 'Irish Ireland' as they called themselves for this particular campaign—ran in seven wards. The distribution of anti-Unionist first-preference votes by ward is set out in Table 8.2, and compared to 1918. The overall nationalist share rose from 16 to 20 per cent, while the Nationalist Party increased its majority over Sinn Féin, partly by running more candidates. Most nationalist voters followed their party ticket or plumped for a single candidate. In some cases the Labour candidates were all elected or eliminated before Nationalist/Sinn Féin voters had exhausted their own party's

---

[33] Dillon to O'Connor 22 Dec. 1919 (DP 6742/723).
[34] MacRory to O'Riordan, 21 Mar. 1919 (MOR 1919/86).
[35] RIC County Inspectors' Reports, Belfast, June–Oct. 1919 (TNA: PRO CO904/109–110).

Table 8.1. Belfast municipal elections, 1920

Parties	Candidates	Seats won	First-preference votes	%
Unionists and allies	61	37	49,773	55.9
Labour and allies*	38	13	18,540	20.8
Nationalist Party	14	5	10,758	12.1
Sinn Féin	12	5	7,120	8.0
Independents*	17	0	2,840	3.2

*Alex Boyd, veteran of the 1907 strike, topped the poll as an Independent in St Anne's. He is here classified as a Labour ally.
Source: A. Wilson, *PR Urban Elections in Ulster, 1920* (2nd edn., London, 1971).

Table 8.2. Sinn Féin, Nationalist, and Labour voting in Belfast, 1918 and 1920

Ward	1918 general election votes (turnout 70.8%)			1920 council election first-preference votes (turnout 65.7%)		
	Sinn Féin	Nationalist	Labour	Sinn Féin	Nationalist	Labour
Cromac	6.7	—	16.8	—	13.5	19.0
Duncairn	1.9	17.1	—	5.4	8.5	11.3
Falls	27.7	72.3	—	26.1	39.7	16.8
Ormeau	2.7	—	—	—	9.2	18.4
Pottinger	3.2	—	26.1	9.2	7.4	22.3
St Anne's	10.9	—	—	8.8	4.4	31.1
Shankill	3.3	—	22.9	7.6	6.5	22.5
Victoria	4.0	—	26.0	7.5	17.1	22.3
Woodvale	9.3	—	—	7.2	3.5	23.4
Belfast	*7.4*	*9.0*	*10.6*	*8.0*	*12.1*	*20.8*

Sources: B. M. Walker (ed.), *Parliamentary Election Results in Ireland, 1801–1922* (Dublin, 1978); Wilson, *PR Urban Elections in Ulster, 1920*.

ticket. But it is possible to follow Nationalist/Sinn Féin transfers through to the end in all seven wards where they competed (Table 8.3). Although the number of Nationalist votes available for transfer was considerably greater, there is enough information to make an assessment. About 15 per cent of both Nationalists and Sinn Féiners transferred their votes to Labour rather than to their nationalist rival, but for both nationalist parties the most common choice was to transfer from one to the other. Sinn Féiners were more likely to transfer their votes to a Nationalist than vice versa, and conversely a large minority of Nationalists curtailed their selection rather than transfer their votes to Sinn Féin. Fewer than half of all Nationalist surplus votes went to Sinn Féin, and their transfers to Labour might have been larger in number had any Labour candidates in St Anne's and Shankill still been in the race. On the other hand, the overall figures are strongly influenced by what happened in the Falls. There, when the

Table 8.3. Nationalist and Sinn Féin transfers, Belfast 1920

Nationalist transfers to	Sinn Féin	Labour	Unionists/ Independents	Non-transferable papers	Total transfers
Falls	18	146	7	685	856
Pottinger	353	183	0	107	643
St Anne's	265	—	68	112	445
Shankill	453	—	25	342	820
Victoria	298	126	5	0	429
Woodvale	229	88	38	59	414
Totals	*1,616*	*543*	*143*	*1,305*	*3,607*
% distribution	44.8	15.0	4.0	36.2	—
Sinn Féin transfers to	Nationalist	Labour	Unionists/ Independents	Non-transferable papers	Total transfers
Duncairn	350	86	6	121	563
% distribution	62.2	15.3	1.0	21.5	—

Source: Wilson, *PR Urban Elections in Ulster, 1920.*

last Nationalist candidate, the trade unionist and former UIL councillor Michael McKeown, was eliminated, only a tiny number of his votes went to the remaining Sinn Féiner; far more went to the remaining Belfast Labour Party candidates, while the overwhelming majority of votes were non-transferable. This took place at the fourteenth count, so voter exhaustion may have been a factor, but it seems likely that the main explanation is that the Devlinites were still strong enough in the Falls, and sufficiently opposed to Sinn Féin, to make the difference. Outside the Falls, transfers between Nationalists and Sinn Féiners were close to parity. All this suggests that the Devlinite influence, at least so far as hostility to Sinn Féin was concerned, was predominantly a Falls phenomenon.

In June 1920 the police estimated that there were 18 UIL branches in Belfast, with a notional membership of over 6,000, 25 AOH divisions with 8,000 members, a battalion of Irish Volunteers (IRA) with 500 members and 9 Sinn Féin clubs with a total of 980 members.[36] Eoin MacNeill suggested that an active propaganda campaign in the North was needed. Northern Republicans, he wrote, 'have failed to cast off the old traditions of regarding their local opponents as the principal enemy. All these things point to the absence or weakness of the clear national ideal.'[37] This conceptualization of Ulster Catholic sectarianism as being different from Irish nationalism was shared by many Southern-based Sinn Féiners. The Belfast IRA leader Seán Cusack spoke to de Valera early in 1921 about the possibility of a more 'drastic' response by the IRA to loyalist mobs that attacked Catholic businesses, but de Valera was not in favour. 'He looked on the

[36] RIC County Inspectors' Reports, Belfast, June 1920 (TNA: PRO CO904/112).
[37] Memo by E. MacNeill, 12 Feb. 1920 (MacNeill Papers, LA1/G/179).

Unionist population in Belfast as citizens of the Republic, and the Volunteers could not be used in a sectarian issue.' This was a position that was not possible to maintain for very much longer.[38]

As the 1920 debates on the Government of Ireland Bill commenced, T. P. O'Connor itched to get involved in the fray, but again Dillon urged him to remain silent.[39] He thought it better to concentrate on the way Ireland was being governed. It would be a 'disastrous mistake' to seek to press Lloyd George into bringing forward a better measure, as 'any negotiations would be fatal'.[40] Devlin was pessimistic as he set off to London for the parliamentary session. In a prescient letter to Bishop O'Donnell he said he was practically certain that the proposed northern parliament would be for six counties rather than nine. He thought that the government would

put the Bill into operation in that part of Ireland that wants it . . . This will mean the worst form of partition and of course permanent partition. Once they have their own Parliament with all the machinery of government and administration, I am afraid anything like subsequent union will be rendered impossible. I propose if an opportunity is offered to attack the Bill, and to do so from an Ulster point of view, giving reasons why we Catholics and Nationalists could not under any circumstances consent to be placed under the domination of a parliament so skilfully established as to make it impossible for us to be ever other than a permanent minority, with all the sufferings and tyranny of the present day continued, only in a worse form.[41]

With equal perceptiveness, Stephen Gwynn pointed out in his weekly newspaper column that 'Mr de Valera is less resolute in opposition to partition than in insistence on complete freedom for so much of Ireland as desires it'.[42] Speaking at Dundee on 3 March, Devlin said that Ireland must have free elections, and a constitution of its own with safeguards for Protestants.[43] Back in August 1919, he had proposed a constituent assembly for Ireland. Dillon had not liked this, but Devlin now repeated it at Dundee, explaining afterwards that 'as a matter of fact I do not see where we stand at all as against the demand of Sinn Féin for an Irish Republic unless some such proposal as this is put forward'.[44] T.P. was quick to distance himself, telling Dillon that he had 'nothing to do with his [Devlin] putting forward his scheme of an Irish Constituent Assembly; you will know it is an old idea of his. He puts forward ideas like this somewhat impulsively. He was a little disturbed last night that you had written a letter disassociating yourself from this proposal.'[45]

[38] Cusack, witness statement 402.
[39] O'Connor to Dillon, 5 Jan. 1920, and Dillon to O'Connor, 9 Jan. 1920 (DP 6742/732, 733).
[40] Dillon to O'Connor, 14 Feb. 1920 (DP 6742/738).
[41] Devlin to O'Donnell, 13 Feb. 1920 (P. O'Donnell Papers, IV. 5).
[42] *Observer*, 15 Feb. 1920.   [43] *IN*, 4 Mar. 1920.
[44] Devlin to Dillon, 5 Mar. 1920 (DP 6730/254).
[45] O'Connor to Dillon, 10 Mar. 1920 (DP 6742/744).

During the second week of March 1920 the Ulster Unionists made clear that they would accept the six-county Parliament proposed in the Government of Ireland Bill. Stephen Gwynn regretted this, but thought that 'in any Ulster Parliament Mr Devlin will occupy a commanding position. Labour likes and trusts him.'[46] Devlin denounced the Bill as 'an outrage upon true liberty', adding that 'any safeguards asked, or any reasonable demands put forward by Ulster, I am quite sure, would be joyfully conceded by the rest of Ireland'.[47] Ulster nationalists, he told O'Donnell, 'have depended too much on the insincerity of the Government and have lulled themselves into the mistaken belief that the Government proposals will not materialize'.[48] Devlin might have included in this category Michael Collins, who told de Valera almost a year later that 'up to recently I was strongly of opinion that it was never intended to set up the Northern Parliament, but I have changed this view now'.[49] By the end of April 1920 Devlin had reached the conclusion that if nothing can be done in Parliament 'I shall not stay much longer' and 'our absence will only strengthen the hostility to the Bill'.[50]

Early in 1920 the IRA went on active service in Belfast. A year earlier the Belfast, Co. Antrim, and East Down IRA had been organized into a brigade area, with Seán Cusack in command. At the end of 1919 Cusack, who had twenty years' military experience behind him, mainly in the British Army, moved into the background as a new and more aggressive generation came forward.[51] Joe McKelvey replaced him as Brigade O/C. The IRA was developing a substantial intelligence network in Belfast, including, in Roger McCorley's recollection, 'some very important men in police headquarters'. David McGuinness's IRA intelligence unit observed its own community closely: 'In the West Belfast area we organized a series of street captains whose function was to act as observers of the conduct of the inhabitants of each particular street and make reports accordingly. These reports recorded matters such as visits by strangers, persons in uniform and all incidents which might appear suspicious.' McCorley recalled that the network covered the whole nationalist area, and 'all items of gossip in each district heard in public houses' were gathered together and analysed by McGuinness.[52] Another prominent IRA officer was Thomas Fitzpatrick, born in Co. Cavan in 1897, who had served in the British Army during the First World War, rising to the rank of Acting Major before being demobbed in February 1919. Six months later he joined the IRA's Belfast

[46] *Observer*, 14 Mar. 1920; Dillon to O'Connor, 15 Mar. 1920 (DP 6742/746).

[47] *Evening News*, 15 Mar. 1920.

[48] Devlin to O'Donnell, 2 Apr. 1920 (P. O'Donnell Papers, IV. 5).

[49] Laffan, *Resurrection of Ireland*, 334.

[50] Devlin to Dillon, 27 Apr. 1920 (DP 6730/261); Devlin to O'Donnell, 30 Apr. 1920 (P. O'Donnell Papers, IV. 5).

[51] Cusack, witness statement 402.

[52] McGuinness, witness statement 417; McCorley, witness statement 389.

Battalion, and was soon called upon to form a 2nd battalion. In January 1921 Joe McKelvey was succeeded as O/C of Belfast's 1st Battalion by Roger McCorley, born in 1901.[53] These two battalions later came to comprise the Belfast Brigade, with counties Antrim and most of Down becoming separate brigades. Early in 1921 the whole area became the 3rd Northern Division. Volunteer numbers in the divisional area were around 500 in 1920, rising to 1,200 in 1922.[54] In March 1920 the future NI cabinet minister J. M. Andrews wrote to Carson that 'recent discoveries of arms in considerable numbers in the possession of Belfast Sinn Féiners is causing a great deal of insecurity'.[55] General Sir Neville Macready, head of the British Army in Ireland, thought that a problem existed regarding 'the continued payment of unemployment pay to gentlemen belonging to the IRA who are out of civil work, but employed on their particular military duties against us'.[56] A captured IRA document signed by Joe McKelvey confirmed that paid flying columns should be set up in Belfast and Derry, as 'there are a number of good men out of work in both places'.[57]

ON THE SIDELINES: SUPER GUNMEN IN BELFAST 1920–1921

On 12 July 1920 large-scale disturbances in Belfast brought Devlin back into the forefront of politics. He delivered a withering attack on the government, on Carson, and on the 'reign of terror' in Belfast. The *Daily News* commented that absence from the Commons in recent months had not impaired his parliamentary skills.[58] On 6 August he violently denounced 'the Partition Bill', and was suspended from the House. He left the chamber amid turbulent scenes, accompanied by the remaining Irish Party members and by members of the Labour Party.[59] He spent August 1920 in a holiday home he had taken at Bangor with his friend Henry Moloney, the Dublin barrister, and his family. Earlier in the year he had raised £10,000 to convert the Grand Hotel there into a hostel to provide holidays for working women. It was opened by him on 15 April, but within weeks it became the object of a serious arson attack. It was restored, however, and offered subsidized holidays to Belfast mill

---

[53] It has been said that McCorley was the grandson of Roddy McCorley of Toome, hanged in 1798. This would have meant that McCorley's father was at least 102 at the time of his conception. McCorley may, however, have been a more distant descendant of the legendary figure.

[54] 'Special Circumstances Connected with the National Struggle in Belfast Area', n.d. [*c.*1940] (McCP, P120/26/17).

[55] Andrews to Carson, 30 Mar. 1920 (Bonar Law Papers, 98/9/8).

[56] Macready to Sir J. Anderson, 7 May 1921 (TNA: PRO CO 904/188).

[57] Memo dated 15 Feb. 1921 by J. McKelvey (BOD, Hemming Papers, MS CCC 536 Od.2.42).

[58] Cited in *IN*, 28 July 1920.   [59] Ibid., 7 Aug. 1920.

girls for many years. Horace Plunkett made a donation to Devlin's 'splendid hostelry'.[60]

As the War of Independence in the South grew in ferocity during the first half of 1920, the North-East remained mainly peaceful. But the young militants in the Belfast IRA were becoming restive.[61] Early in the year Thomas Fitzpatrick and others threw some bombs into a military vehicle store in the Markets area. This was done, according to Fitzpatrick, without any authorization from Brigade, which at that time was 'averse to activities in Belfast for fear of reprisals on the Catholic population'. Some of the younger men did not agree with this cautious policy and, led by McCorley, made vigorous protests. By Easter 1920 attitudes higher up were changing, and the burning of all but one of the government tax offices in Belfast at Easter 1920 was the beginning of a more active campaign. A few weeks later McCorley and others assisted McKelvey in an unsuccessful but bloody attack on the police barracks at Crossgar, Co. Down. Tension was further exacerbated by the murder in Cork City on 17 July of Police Commissioner Smyth, a native of Banbridge. At the main Orange parade on 12 July Carson had declared, in response to the burgeoning IRA campaign across the country, that he was 'sick of words without action'.[62] A few hours later what became known as 'the pogrom' commenced. Soon 9,000 Catholics (one-third of the minority's entire male workforce), together with many sympathetic Protestants, were expelled from their workplaces. The plans of the Belfast IRA were, according to Roger McCorley, disrupted by this development, so that its priority for the next few weeks had to become communal defence.[63] The expulsions and neighbourhood violence escalated further when the shipyards returned to work on 21 July. The military were called in, and the IRA fired on them. The number of fatalities in July was 18, with about 200 injured. Nationalist histories tend to attribute the main blame for the pogrom to Carson's speech, but Police Commissioner Gelston thought that 'the resumption of work at Queen's Island took place so shortly after the murder of Divisional Commissioner Smyth at Cork and the refusal of the railway people to carry his remains to the North', that these events acted 'as a match to the gunpowder'. By November, MacRory recorded, nearly 2,000 Catholic families had been expelled from their homes in Belfast, and 600 families in nearby Lisburn, while 40 Catholics had been killed and 200 wounded.

[60] Devlin to Moloney, 'Wed' [probably 28 July 1920] (Devlin–Moloney Letters, T/2257/6); O'Connor in *Liverpool Daily Post & Mercury*, 9 Nov. 1922; Devlin to Dillon, 2 Feb. 1920, and Plunkett to Devlin, 20 Apr. 1921 (DP 6730/249, 294).
[61] R. Lynch, *The Northern IRA and the Early Years of Partition, 1920–1922* (Dublin, 2006), provides a more detailed analysis of the Belfast IRA than is possible here.
[62] D. Macardle, *The Irish Republic* (Dublin, 1951), 356.
[63] Thomas Fitzpatrick, witness statement, 19 June 1950 (BMH, witness statement 395); Thomas Fox, witness statement, 25 Mar. 1950 (BMH, witness statement 365); McCorley, witness statement 389; McGuinness, witness statement 417.

He did not mention the Protestant figures.[64] Almost 10,000 Catholics with nearly 20,000 dependants looked to the Expelled Workers' Fund for support.[65] Michael Farrell estimates a total of 12,000 men expelled, including about 3,000 Protestants.[66]

Early in August 1920, once it became clear that the trade unions were unable to give serious assistance, MacRory initiated the Belfast Expelled Workers' Fund. Over £120,000 was soon raised.[67] But by November the calls on the fund far exceeded its capacity and MacRory sought funds from America, which supplied £5,000 per week throughout 1921. It was still necessary, however, to reduce the amount payable to a family from £1 to 15s. per week.[68] One important outcome of the visit of the AMCOMRI delegation to Belfast was that they donated £10,000 to build houses for expelled families, the most prominent outcome of which was the creation of Amcomri Street, providing 100 houses in the Upper Falls area.[69] But the split in the south of Ireland over the Treaty in the early months of 1922 brought American fund-raising to a virtual halt, for the disturbed conditions in Ireland also resulted in a split in America among people of Irish descent.[70] In September 1920 the National Club was vacated to provide temporary accommodation for some of the thousands of Catholics driven out of their homes, and Devlin's own home, at 3 College Square North, in the city centre, was surrounded by soldiers with fixed bayonets.[71] In late August the Ministry of Labour decided that the expelled workers were not eligible for unemployment benefit.[72] Devlin spent a week in London persuading the authorities to reverse this decision, securing 15s. per week for men and 12s. 6d. per week for women. It delivered about £6,000 per week into the Catholic community, but, said Devlin, 'the demands are so great that it appears small'.[73]

Serious violence erupted again on 15 August in the Short Strand. Then, on 22 August, District Inspector Swanzy—who was suspected of having been involved in the reprisal murder of Tomás MacCurtain, Lord Mayor of Cork and IRA Commandant, earlier in the year—was killed in Lisburn by an IRA unit made up of Cork and Belfast Volunteers, one of whom was Roger McCorley. The assassination was ordered directly by Michael Collins. McCorley recalled that the order had come through some time earlier, but the Belfast IRA was aware that a pogrom against Catholics was about to start, and that 'the Orange

---

[64] MacRory to Committee of Belfast Expelled Workers' Fund, 20 Nov. 1920 (MacRory Papers, XII. 11).

[65] Ibid.   [66] Farrell, 'Belfast Strike', 18.

[67] RIC County Inspectors' Reports, Belfast, Oct. 1920 (TNA: PRO CO 904/113).

[68] MacRory to M. J. O'Brien, Chairman of AMCOMRI, 1 Sept. 1921 (MacRory Papers, VII. 9).

[69] J. J. Pulleyn, President of the Emigrant Industrial Savings Bank of New York, to MacRory, 2 Dec. 1921 (MacRory Papers, VII. 9).

[70] C. J. France, Secretary of AMCOMRI, to MacRory, 31 Mar. 1922 (MacRory Papers, VII. 9).

[71] Devlin to Dillon, 13 Sept. 1920 (DP 6730/267).   [72] *IN*, 27 Aug. 1920.

[73] Devlin to Dillon, 13 Sept. 1920 (DP 6730/267).

Lodges were just awaiting an excuse to launch the attack on the nationalist areas'. They thus asked GHQ's permission to delay the assassination of Swanzy until after the troubles had started. 'When the pogrom began in July,' recalled McCorley, 'the way was clear to carry out the operation as ordered.'[74] The immediate outcome was a massive reprisal against the small Catholic population of Lisburn. Three days later the mob reprisal spread to Belfast. The main target was Catholic property in Protestant areas, with at least 22 deaths and 300 injuries occurring during the last week of August, while 'the amount of drink consumed from looting licensed premises has been enormous'. On 31 August a curfew was imposed. The Commissioner thought that, while the Orange Order, the Unionist Clubs, and the UVF had made some effort to control their followers, 'I do not think the leaders and those who figure prominently in the Unionist movement at other times have done all they might'.[75] A local IRA activist who later became a colonel in the Free State Army, Thomas McNally, admitted that the pogrom was 'aggravated' by Swanzy's murder.[76] By January 1921 the Police Commissioner believed he had detected 'marked signs that last year's bitter feeling has to a great extent disappeared'.[77] But the local IRA was in fact about to move up a gear.

After the Swanzy murder the Belfast IRA set about disarming policemen, which soon resulted in fatalities. A policeman was killed at Broadway, in the Upper Falls, in September 1920, as a result of which the first of many reprisals, undertaken by what was believed to be a 'murder gang' within the police force, took place. Five Catholics were murdered in their homes in two incidents, only two of whom were in fact IRA members.[78] The local IRA soon believed that its intelligence network had identified the members of the RIC murder gang, but Brigade staff postponed action against them, as they did not have the resources to resist further reprisals. By McCorley's account this decision 'caused very grave discontent amongst the junior officers and the rank and file of the Brigade, and caucus meetings were held with a view to trying to unseat what was called the peace party from power'.[79] McCorley 'strongly advocated that executions should take place regardless of the consequences'. As a result, he was elected O/C of the 1st Belfast Battalion, in the face of initial opposition from Brigade. Changes in Brigade organization during January 1921 enabled IRA companies in the city to carry out local missions without prior permission from higher authority. 'If this system had been adopted earlier,' recalled McCorley, 'the fighting record of the Belfast Brigade would have been much better.'[80] Between 1 January 1919 and 31 May 1921, of the 622 murders attributed to the IRA in Ireland, 50

[74] McCorley, witness statement 389.

[75] RIC County Inspectors' Reports, Belfast, Aug. 1920 (TNA: PRO CO 904/112).

[76] Witness statement by Col. Thomas McNally, 18 July 1950 (BMH, witness statement 410).

[77] RIC County Inspectors' Reports, Belfast, Jan.–Mar. 1921 (TNA: PRO CO 904/114).

[78] Fox, witness statement 365; McNally, witness statement 410.

[79] McCorley, witness statement 389.　　　　[80] Ibid.

occurred in the province of Ulster, of which 10 were in Belfast (9 policemen and 1 civilian).[81]

Around this time McCorley put forward a plan for shooting incoming RIC Auxiliary cadets. An informer within the RIC advised the IRA that Roddy's Hotel, in the city centre, was their usual staging post. McCorley and Seamus Woods, Captain of D Company, organized an attack, and three men were shot, two fatally. The victims, it turned out, were not Auxiliaries but two policemen accompanying an IRA informer to court. A few hours later a young Sinn Féiner was murdered by masked men at his home.[82] The squad that carried out the Roddy's Hotel attack became the basis for a Belfast Active Service Unit (ASU), consisting of twenty-one men employed full time on salaries, led by McCorley and Woods. Thomas McNally, Brigade Quartermaster, later recalled that McCorley and Woods were 'the super gunmen of the city'.[83] 'Certain elements on the Brigade staff' were still not in favour of such activities, but they were ignored. Using the socialist republican Danny McDevitt's tailoring premises in Rosemary Street as its regular base, the ASU sought to identify groups of Auxiliaries and Black and Tans passing through the city.[84] On 13 March three policemen were killed in the city centre. That night there were riots and the wrecking of spirit groceries in the Ballymacarrett and York Street districts. On another occasion two Auxiliaries were shot dead in the street, which led to a reprisal double murder.[85] A week or two after that the ASU killed RIC Constable Glover, whom they believed had been part of a reprisal gang.[86] One night they also attacked a police unit in Balaclava Street, in the Lower Falls, believing it to be a reprisal gang. Four policemen were killed. On another occasion they ambushed a police tender, which they believed was on a reprisal mission, in nearby Raglan Street, killing all the occupants. In McCorley's recollection the police were armed with revolvers only, which he believed to be clear evidence of their intended business. An offer of surrender was refused, and McCorley ordered that no prisoners be taken.[87] This attack, on the night of 9–10 July 1921, by twelve IRA men (though referred to in Revd John Hassan's contemporary account as 'an improvised attack by local residents') provoked large-scale loyalist reprisals.[88] Over the course of the following week 16 Catholics were killed in Belfast and 216 homes destroyed.[89]

---

[81] 'Murders by Sinn Féin, 1 Jan. 1919–31 May 1921' (BOD, Hemming Papers, MS CCC 536 Od.2.42).

[82] RIC County Inspectors' Reports, Belfast, Jan.–Mar. 1921 (TNA: PRO CO 904/114).

[83] McNally, witness statement 410.   [84] McCorley, witness statement 389.

[85] RIC County Inspectors' Reports, Belfast, Jan.–Mar. 1921 (TNA: PRO CO 904/114).

[86] McCorley, witness statement 389.

[87] Witness statement by Thomas Flynn, n.d. [late 1950] (BMH, witness statement 429); McCorley, witness statement 389.

[88] 'G. B. Kenna' (pseud.), *Facts and Figures of the Belfast Pogrom* (Belfast, 1922); A. F. Parkinson, *Belfast's Unholy War: The Troubles of the 1920s* (Dublin, 2004), 154.

[89] M. Hopkinson, *The Irish War of Independence* (Dublin, 2002), 163.

The Raglan Street ambush coincided with the Truce. Local fighting immediately died down but, McCorley recalled, 'an element of the Nationalists, under the control of the Hibernians, began looting Protestant businesses in the Falls Road'. This, he believed, was organized Hibernian 'pique' at the fact that 'our people' (that is, Sinn Féin and the IRA) had been acknowledged as the representatives of the Irish people. Several of the ring-leaders of these activities were rounded up by the IRA and given twenty-four hours to leave the city. Thomas McNally recalled that the 3rd Northern Division was always up against AOH as well as Unionist 'elements', and that 'the very large ex-British soldier family type were antagonistic and were prepared to give information to the authorities'. After a few weeks the Truce broke down in Belfast, and the Belfast ASU was recalled from camp to resume activities in the city.[90] A riot at Tyrone Street, in the Old Lodge area, on 21 August led to eight deaths and forty injuries. A local truce was agreed during the first week in September, but the second half of the month was described by the police as 'very bad', with intense sectarian bitterness 'observed among . . . a better class citizen', which had not been the case in previous riots.[91] Notwithstanding the link between IRA atrocities and Orange reaction, General Macready wrote to Dublin Castle in September 1921 regarding the Belfast crisis that 'there is no doubt about it but that the Orange mob are just as much to blame as the Sinn Féin, and we will deal with them accordingly'.[92] Another severely devastated area was that part of the Falls–Shankill interface where there was no natural barrier or neutral industrial space separating Catholic and Protestant neighbourhoods. Most notorious among these was Cupar Street, in the Clonard area. This street, one end Catholic, the other end Protestant, was divided by nineteen derelict dwellings and the skeletons of two side streets. The number of wrecked and looted houses and shops in the neighbourhood was estimated at 151.[93]

Under the terms of the Truce, IRA General Eoin O'Duffy was set up in St Mary's Hall as the IRA's Belfast Liaison Officer. The transfer of law and order powers to the NI Government on 9 November 1921 effectively rendered the Truce null and void in the six county area, 'but although the Truce was never strictly kept in the North at any time, its formal termination never took place, and Liaison Officers functioned there up to nearly March 1922'.[94] In the short run, this public profile for the IRA, and the fact that it was able to drill openly in Catholic parts of Ulster, enabled its members, in the judgement of City Police Commissioner Gelston, 'to dominate the Devlinites'.[95] O'Duffy's job was to

---

[90] McNally, witness statement 410; Flynn, witness statement 429; McCorley, witness statement 389.

[91] *Observer*, 11 Sept. 1921; RIC County Inspectors' Reports, Belfast, Sept. 1921 (TNA: PRO CO 904/116).

[92] Macready to Sir J. Anderson, 27 Sept. 1921 (TNA: PRO CO 904/188).

[93] *IN*, 30 Dec. 1921.

[94] Untitled document re IRA pension claims, n.d. (Blythe Papers, P24/554).

[95] S. G. Tallents, 'Interview with J. F. Gelston', 29 June 1922 (TNA: PRO CO 906/23).

liaise with British forces, monitor the Truce, and report incidents, but in fact 'the fighting continued practically without ceasing', by McCorley's account. He claimed that on occasion forces under the control of the British Government were effectively complicit with the IRA so far as attacks on the Specials were concerned: 'This state of affairs in which we had official relations with the RIC and British Military, and open warfare between ourselves and the Special Constabulary, continued right through the period of the Truce in Belfast.' Arms were supposed to be kept in dumps during the Truce, but this was not observed by the Belfast IRA and, in McCorley's view, could not have been safely, and 'evidently the British were satisfied that it could not be observed while armed attacks were being made on us'. This, he thought, probably accounted for the hostility that he observed between the Military and the Specials.[96] Meanwhile the Dáil discussed other means of subduing the North. Sean MacEntee said on 6 August 1920 that 'they could not reduce Belfast by force of arms, but they could bring her to reason by economic force'.[97] Two other Northerners in the Dáil cabinet, Eoin MacNeill and Ernest Blythe, opposed the proposed boycott, arguing that all it could do was make matters worse.[98] The Belfast Boycott was, nonetheless, introduced by the Dáil in January 1921, and was supported by many Ulster nationalists. It continued throughout 1921, and damaged some Belfast firms, but it did not reinstate the expelled workers, and in fact increased Belfast's dependence on British markets and added to the economic partition of Ireland.[99] The fact that Belfast's major industries, textiles and shipbuilding, depended mainly on international markets greatly limited the influence that the southern Irish market could wield.

When Parliament reassembled in autumn 1920 T. P. O'Connor urged Devlin to be present, for without him 'we know nothing . . . of the realities in Belfast'.[100] Devlin agreed that it would not be fair to leave T.P. alone, and he had no guarantee that the other five Irish Party MPs would 'turn up'. He had been excluded from Parliament since August, but on 22 October Bonar Law, as Leader of the House, introduced a motion to terminate his suspension, and the matter came to an end.[101] Devlin then made a further strong attack on the government's Irish policy and continued raising reprisals and related issues during the following weeks.[102] Immediately the session opened he and T.P. were confronted with a further painful issue, as a young Dublin IRA man, the medical student Kevin Barry, was sentenced to death for his part in a lethal raid. On 28 October Devlin spoke to Lloyd George for the first time in two years, to make a last appeal for Barry's life, after which he was 'certain that our efforts would succeed'.[103] A memo in Lloyd George's papers indicates that both the Lord Chancellor and

---

[96] McCorley, witness statement 389.   [97] Hopkinson, *Irish War of Independence*, 160.
[98] Tierney, *Eoin MacNeill*, 289.   [99] Laffan, *Resurrection of Ireland*, 231–2.
[100] O'Connor to Devlin, 11 Oct. 1920 (DP 6730/268).   [101] *IN*, 23 Oct. 1920.
[102] Ibid., 18 Oct. 1920.
[103] Devlin to H. Sheehy-Skeffington, 1 Nov. 1920 (Sheehy-Skeffington Papers, 22695/1).

the Lord Chief Justice believed that a reprieve was appropriate on the grounds
of Barry's youth, and the evidence that he had acted under duress. But the Lord
Lieutenant, Viscount French, had the prerogative, and he, along with Bonar Law
and the new Chief Secretary, Hamar Greenwood, took a hard line.[104] Barry was
hanged in Dublin on 1 November 1920. Later that day Devlin protested again
to Lloyd George regarding former soldiers from Catholic Belfast who had been
attacked by the UVF and driven from their work. 'I feel that my responsibility is
a terrible one because through me these men went out to the war, and every one
of these cases wrings my heart and makes me feel utterly ashamed that I asked
them to make such sacrifices.'[105]

On 21 November 1920—'Bloody Sunday'—fourteen newly arrived British
secret agents were murdered in Dublin in a series of skilfully executed attacks.
That afternoon the military entered Croke Park during a Gaelic football match
and fired on the crowd, killing twelve people and wounding sixty.[106] In a debate
on the matter in the Commons the following afternoon, Devlin, amidst angry
cries in the chamber of 'Sit Down!', asked why, when the murder of the agents
was being discussed in detail, no reference had been made to the second of
these 'horrible occurrences'. There were press reports that cries of 'kill him' then
came from the government benches, as a Conservative MP, 57-year old Major
John Molson, who was sitting behind Devlin, dragged him backwards over the
bench and a scuffle broke out.[107] Drink had no doubt been taken. In Canning
Town on 5 December, Devlin declared that 'he would be a Sinn Féiner with
a gun if he thought force could achieve justice for Ireland, but the odds were
too great so he wanted a settlement on constitutional lines'.[108] After this he had
one of his 'fearful colds', and was laid up for five days at T.P.'s Westminster
flat, 'as the [National Liberal] Club is not very comfortable when one is ill'.[109]
His health recovered in time for him to make a series of strong interventions
when the Government of Ireland Bill returned for its final passage through the
Commons before Christmas. It was not, he said, 'a Bill for pacification' but 'a
Bill for inflaming the worst sectarian passions'.[110] Stephen Gwynn thought that,
if the Ulster Unionists chose to use the powers granted under the Bill to create
a union in Ireland, it would bring peace, but 'unhappily there is no reason to
believe that any Ulsterman would or could at this moment put forward such
a proposal. Sinn Féin has dug the ditch too deep and filled it with too much
blood.'[111] The Government of Ireland Act, creating permanent parliaments for
six-county Northern Ireland and twenty-six county Southern Ireland, became

---

[104] File on Kevin Barry execution, Oct. 1920 (LGP, F/85/8/9).
[105] Devlin to Lloyd George, 1 Nov. 1920 (LGP, F/15/1/1).
[106] Macardle, *Irish Republic*, 398.
[107] Parl. Deb., H.C., 5th series, cxxxv (22 Nov. 1920), 39; *IN*, 23 Nov. 1920.
[108] *IN*, 6 Dec. 1920.
[109] Devlin to Moloney, 14 Dec. 1920 (Devlin–Moloney Letters, T2557/9).
[110] Parl. Deb., H.C., 5th series, cxxxvi (16 Dec. 1920), 870–8.   [111] *Observer*, 6 Feb. 1921.

law in December 1920. Meanwhile Devlin had written enigmatically to Dillon that 'I also received the attentions of the Black and Tans'.[112] What this refers to is not clear, but a couple of weeks later William Redmond warned Devlin that 'one of the most important military members of the House' had asked him to press Devlin not to go to Ireland 'as the military are determined to murder me'.[113] In fact Devlin spent Christmas at home in Belfast as usual.

As the 1921 session opened, Asquith, now Opposition leader, moved an amendment to the Address on Ireland, but Devlin was once again *hors de combat*. He 'got a frightful cold through a draft in the heated train yesterday and was not able to go down to the House today. The doctor advised me to stay in bed for a day or two, as my chest and throat are completely choked up. I am staying with T.P.' He was also diagnosed as needing a hernia operation.[114] But he recovered quickly, and made the main speech in the debate on 21 February, denouncing the reprisal policy and dismissing the new Northern Parliament as 'only for a section of the people'.[115] Dillon thought that 'the brilliant success of the work in Parliament' must make the Irish people 'realise the insane folly of wilfully throwing away the parliamentary weapon'.[116] In March Devlin was invited to lunch at Chequers, but he could not get Lloyd George to 'talk real business'. T.P. reported that after the lunch Lloyd George, 'to show you the contradictions of the man and his strange power of making himself insensible to the results of his own policy', proposed, 'with a glass of port in his hand, the toast of Ireland, to which Joe, of course, had to lift his glass'.[117] During 1921 Devlin raised hundreds of questions to do with reprisals and other violence, unemployment, and the Belfast troubles, but told his friend Henry Moloney that it was 'very unsatisfying work'.[118]

Soon after his return from America at the end of 1920, de Valera set his mind to gathering information about electoral prospects for the new Northern Parliament. Letting the elections go by default, he thought, 'would help to kill the Republican movement in the North by throwing Sinn Féiners practically into the camp of the Nationalists'. Any boycott should, therefore, be of the Parliament rather than of the elections. A contest, he thought, might in fact serve to advance Sinn Féin over the Nationalists. Thus de Valera tended towards contesting the Northern election on an abstentionist platform, with successful candidates attending Dáil Eireann instead. Abstention from the Northern Parliament he thought might also stimulate a political division between 'capital' and 'labour' among Unionist MPs.[119] But the commentator Stephen

---

112 Devlin to Dillon, 27 Nov. 1920 (DP 6730/275).
113 Devlin to Moloney, 10 Dec. 1920 (Devlin–Moloney Letters, T2257/8).
114 Devlin to Dillon, 16 Feb. 1921; O'Connor to Dillon, 18 Feb. 1921 (DP 6730/285, 6744/815).
115 *IN*, 22 Feb. 1921.   116 Dillon to O'Connor, 25 Feb. 1921 (DP 6744/817).
117 O'Connor to Dillon, 12 and 25 Mar. 1921 (DP 6744/821, 823).
118 Devlin to Moloney, 'Tuesday' [22 Feb. 1921] (Devlin–Moloney Letters, T2257/7).
119 De Valera to Collins, 13 Jan. 1921 (deVP, P150/1381).

Gwynn thought that 'no Labour candidate . . . will have a chance in the Belfast area. Resentment against Sinn Féin—against its separatist aims and its murderous methods—has driven the mass of Ulster Labour back into a purely political [i.e. Unionist] camp . . . Alliance with Mr Devlin would be a wholly different matter for Labour.'[120] De Valera had a meeting with Bishop MacRory on 2 February 1921, at which he expressed the hope that the Devlinites might not contest the election. Four days later, when de Valera met Devlin at Moloney's Dublin home, a moment's conversation convinced him that 'it was futile to hope for anything of the sort'.[121] Devlin's first suggestion was for both parties to stand aside from the elections altogether. Alternatively, he thought it worth giving serious consideration to a combined slate to secure as many seats as possible for Nationalists and Sinn Féiners. De Valera would not agree to this. A third possibility was a division of seats between Nationalists and Sinn Féin, each party to retain the right to determine whether or not to take its seats in the new parliament. But de Valera would not agree to a division of seats without a commitment to abstention, a policy that Devlin had 'always thought a fatal one'. The fourth option, which Devlin did not favour, was for Nationalists and Sinn Féiners to contest the elections quite independently, for, although he was 'quite convinced that in these six counties the overwhelming mass of the [Catholic] people do not approve of the Sinn Féin policy', he thought it vital to avoid a contest. Devlin had 'no desire to go into the Ulster Parliament nor, indeed, have I any desire to continue in Irish politics', but he felt obliged to do all he could for the people of Belfast.[122]

Devlin and de Valera then arranged for two Belfast UIL leaders and two Sinn Féiners to try to work out a common election policy. They quickly agreed on the principles of self-determination and opposition to partition, but they could not agree on the number of candidates to be entered by each party, or on abstention.[123] A month later they met again, and agreed to abstention. It was proposed that each party should put up twenty-two candidates. But at this stage the mathematician in de Valera came out. He was less than entirely happy with the briefing on PR he had received from his colleagues, concluding that 'I suppose I will have to examine it for myself'.[124] This number of candidates, he thought, could work out 'rather worse for us than for the Devlinites, for if the Devlinites put forward the full number mentioned in the schedule, the preferences will be transferred to us rather too late'. A revised draft went out from

[120] *Observer*, 6 Feb. 1921.
[121] Devlin to Moloney, 'Friday' [4 Feb. 1921] (Devlin–Moloney Letters, T/2257); de Valera to MacRory, 17 Feb. 1921 (MacRory Papers, IV. 8).
[122] Devlin to Dillon, 1 and 3 Feb. 1921, and Dillon to Devlin, 2 Feb. 1921 (DP 6730/281, 282, 283).
[123] Memo by Austin Stack, 17–18 Feb. 1921 (deVP, P150/1381).
[124] De Valera to Stack, 7 Mar. 1921 (deVP, P150/1381).

Sinn Féin proposing nineteen from each side as a maximum.[125] In the event Sinn Féin ran twenty candidates and the Nationalists twelve. On 6 April Devlin and de Valera signed the agreement. The fact that both the Nationalists and Sinn Féin opposed partition, coupled with the PR system to be adopted, made it easier for the two parties to agree than had been the case in 1918.[126] Curiously, Devlin then sought to reopen negotiations. He asked for the word 'constitutional' to be inserted into the second clause of the candidates' pledge: 'that I shall use every [constitutional] effort to defeat the policy of partition of the Irish nation.' De Valera thought such a change '*most* objectionable', 'constitutional' in his view meaning 'in accordance with the constitution set up by the Irish people'. If the matter were to be brought up publicly at this stage, warned de Valera, 'it will mean that all hope of cooperation is ended'.[127] Devlin gave way. He told Dillon that had there been no agreement it would have been impossible to get anyone to stand against Sinn Féin outside Belfast, and 'every one of our people would have been forced to go out and vote' for Sinn Féin. He thought the outcome of the elections very hard to predict, except that 'everything is all right here in Belfast' (he was in fact the only anti-partitionist candidate to win in the city!).[128] The Nationalists thus contested the elections along the lines agreed.

As the election approached, predictions began to be made. Devlin told Gwynn that the Unionists would win no more than thirty-four out of fifty-two, thus estimating the anti-partition number at eighteen. Gwynn predicted closer to thirty-eight: if Craig 'gets 40 he has won'.[129] Dillon wrote to T.P. that 'I hope Joe will come out of the Ulster fight well. It was a great risk to take. But taking all the alternatives into consideration, I think he has done the right thing to face it.'[130] As always, Devlin's campaign in West Belfast stressed non-sectarian social issues.[131] Sinn Féin also tried to link up with Labour. They funded some Labour candidates in Belfast, though William McMullen recalled that the Sinn Féin candidate Archie Savage prevented any help for Labour in East Belfast as he was afraid of losing votes.[132]

We must try [wrote de Valera to Griffith] to win the second preferences from . . . [Labour] supporters in exchange for their preferences after the Devlin group. I am against pledging our first [i.e. second] preferences to them. I think you had better handle the matter yourself. I am desperately afraid of MacEntee in any bargaining—he doesn't know where to stop.[133]

[125] De Valera to Stack, 18 Mar. 1921; Stack to O. Jamison and P. O'Kane (deVP, P150/1381).
[126] Laffan, *Resurrection of Ireland*, 336.
[127] Devlin to Stack, 29 Apr. 1921; Stack to de Valera, 5 May 1921; de Valera to Stack, 6 May 1921 (deVP, P150/1381).
[128] Devlin to Dillon, 22 Apr. 1921 (DP 6730/294).   [129] *Observer*, 15 May 1921.
[130] Dillon to O'Connor, 19 May 1921 (DP 6744/836).
[131] *Irish Bulletin*, 26 May 1921, copy (J. H. Bernard Papers, Add. MS 52783, fos. 116–18).
[132] William McMullen interview.
[133] De Valera to Griffith, 22 Apr. 1921 (deVP, P150/1381).

In the event the performance of Labour's three candidates was poor, winning only 5 per cent of the anti-partitionist vote. Sinn Féin's chief election organizer in Ulster, Eamon Donnelly, reported that 'they made no fight and were not allowed to do so. I do not see the slightest prospect of Labour ever succeeding here.'[134]

Donnelly admitted that the only effect of all the Sinn Féin literature on the Unionist population was 'to bring them out to vote against us in great numbers'. He reported to HQ that 'intimidation is wholesale. Cars were set on and drivers taken off and beaten.'[135] Many Catholics who had been driven out of the Short Strand area in September 1920 were attacked when they returned to cast their votes. Charges of gerrymandering hold some water. In Belfast, where Catholic-Nationalists numbered around one-quarter of the population, they held one Westminster seat out of four in the years before 1918 and one out of nine seats between 1919 and 1922, but in the Northern election of 1921 the four PR constituencies returned a total of sixteen members, of whom Devlin was the only non-Unionist. Although securing just over 22 per cent of the vote in the city, anti-partitionists—made up of 50.5 per Sinn Féin voters, 44.5 per cent Nationalist Party, and 5 per cent Labour—won little over 6 per cent of the seats.[136] Across the North the Nationalists and Sinn Féin each won six seats, with the Unionists taking the remaining forty. Dillon heard nothing from Devlin in the weeks immediately following the election, and on 16 June was asking T.P. 'what kind of mood is Joe in over the results . . . I think he had a great personal success.'[137] In the South, meanwhile, such was the level of IRA activity that there was serious doubt as to whether the Southern elections should be permitted to proceed. Ultimately Lloyd George was persuaded to let them go ahead. 'There is no real leadership there. Devlin told me that,' he told his cabinet on 27 April.[138] T.P. and Dillon had agreed earlier that the Nationalists should not compete with Sinn Féin for seats in the Southern Parliament 'as things stand at present'.[139] In the event Sinn Féin took all 124 territorial seats without opposition, with Unionists taking the 4 Dublin University seats. Stephen Gwynn thought that Sinn Féin has no right to complain of intimidation in the North, for 'the unanimous verdict for Sinn Féin over the rest of the country is mainly, though not solely, the effect of organized terror'.[140]

When he returned to Parliament in June, Devlin was 'in a rather bad mood' according to T.P., but he got a great reception from the Liberal and Labour benches when he rose to speak, which 'of course always cheers him up'. Dillon confirmed that Devlin was 'in a bad mood towards all his friends. He is nursing some grievance, the nature of which I do not know.'[141] The fundamental cause, T.P. concluded, was

[134] E. Donnelly to P. O'Keeffe, 24 May 1921 (deVP, P150/1381).   [135] Ibid.
[136] S. Elliott, *NI Parliamentary Election Results, 1921–1972* (Chichester, 1973).
[137] Dillon to O'Connor, 16 June 1921 (DP 6744/844).   [138] Jones, *Whitehall Diary*, iii. 60.
[139] O'Connor to Dillon, 18 Jan. 1921 (DP 6744/809).   [140] *Observer*, 29 May 1921.
[141] Dillon to O'Connor, 21 June 1921 (DP 6744/846).

a certain fatigue on account of his very exhausting labours in the election, a certain disappointment at the result, and the hopelessness of the outlook in Ireland, which means of course hopelessness with regard to his own immediate future. He is talking, I believe, to intimates of a long vacation, but I fancy this will end in mere talk. He also probably feels a sense of disillusion in coming to London and finding there is such ignorance and therefore such want of recognition of the splendid work he did in Ulster.

Devlin, however, had a 'magnificent triumph' in the Commons on 23 June. Asquith 'went out of his way to pay him a compliment', and afterwards T.P. found Devlin to be 'bubbling with delight'.[142]

Meanwhile Sinn Féin violence had forced the Irish question to the top of Lloyd George's agenda—probably its greatest achievement. His planning was complicated by uncertainties about both what Sinn Féin might accept, and what his Coalition colleagues might accept. Dillon had heard that the fighting men in Dublin were saying 'that all that is needed to secure complete victory is another six months of active operations'.[143] But by July the long-running behind-the-scenes contacts generated public communication between Lloyd George, de Valera, and Craig. There was no invitation from de Valera to Devlin. While the Sinn Féin walkover in elections to the Southern Parliament gave some justification for this, the Northern results did not. But de Valera agreed to a truce being implemented on 11 July. He held several meetings with Lloyd George in London. On at least one of these occasions Lloyd George, no doubt with some private delight, 'openly discussed matters with his private secretary Tom Jones in Welsh, in the Irish leader's presence'.[144] The Ulster question did not feature until the second of these meetings, and even then Valera thought that Lloyd George was just using it to frighten him. But James Craig, whom Lloyd George also saw, was 'quite obstinate' and thought that Lloyd George was using Sinn Féin to force concessions from Ulster. Lloyd George, confided Stevenson to her diary, was 'a little worried' that 'Ulster would again prove a stumbling block'. De Valera's first response was rejection of Lloyd George's proposals. On Ulster he stated that 'we do not contemplate the use of force. If your Government stands aside, we can effect a complete reconciliation.' But the correspondence continued throughout August and September until they at last agreed to set up a conference for the simply stated purpose of 'ascertaining how the association of Ireland with the community of nations known as the British Empire may best be reconciled with Irish national aspirations'.[145] While all this was going on Joe Devlin was taking a break. Together with his old friend Revd Frank O'Hare, PP Banbridge, he visited the Irish College in Rome. 'Be kind to them and help them to reach the main object of their visit,' wrote Bishop Mulhern to the Rector, which was probably

142 O'Connor to Dillon, 24 June 1921 (DP 6744/847).
143 Dillon to O'Connor, 21 June 1921 (DP 6744/846).
144 Morgan, 'Lloyd George and the Irish', 96.
145 *Correspondence Relating to the Proposals of His Majesty's Government for an Irish Settlement* (HC, Cmd. 1502, Cmd. 1539, 1921).

a reference to the pilgrimage to Assisi organized by the Dublin Franciscans, for the annual Feast of the Stigmata of St Francis.[146] Devlin was away for most of September. But his return home coincided with renewed rioting, and T.P. was again 'very anxious about Joe in Belfast'.[147]

In mid-October the Irish 'plenipotentiaries' arrived in London to begin negotiations with Lloyd George and his team. De Valera excluded himself from the delegation. By doing so, as Michael Hopkinson has observed, 'while strongly aware of the need to preserve unity in nationalist ranks, de Valera achieved precisely the opposite'.[148] Mulhern thought that 'the only real issue . . . is how far the delegates may go in concessions to what is called Ulster . . . I see that D. & C. [i.e. Bishop MacRory] is in London for ten days and he has not gone for a mere holiday.'[149] Devlin also arrived in London in mid-October. His view, which O'Connor agreed was the only possible one, 'is that for the moment all of us in the Constitutional Party are entirely out of it, not merely now but for some time to come'. T.P. and Devlin found it almost ludicrous that 'a gentleman named Milson' [in fact Seán Milroy] had been summoned to London to advise the Sinn Féin delegation 'with regard to the condition of the Nationalists in Ulster, while they refuse to make any approach whatever to Joe . . . Really it is one of the most comic passages of the whole business. Joe accepts the situation quite philosophically, I am glad to say.' After a long talk with Devlin, T.P. thought that Belfast 'outside the dervishes, is in a very accommodating mood'.[150] Dillon, while admitting that 'Devlin knows a great deal more about Belfast and Ulster than I do', could not accept this view. Devlin, he thought, was 'inclined to minimize . . . the risks of the Ulster situation . . . I regard the situation in Ulster as volcanic.'[151] And, indeed, Devlin was soon getting 'very pessimistic' accounts of the negotiations: 'I am quite sure Ulster will be the real issue and from that point of view the position is not reassuring.'[152] Sean T. O'Kelly, still head of the Irish delegation in Paris, told Hagan that 'our people, but in particular A.G[riffith] and C[ollins] have fallen as complete victims of Ll.G.'s machinations as ever Wilson and Clemenceau did'. Lloyd George promised to '*try* to secure the unity of Ireland (of course with a number of safeguards and guarantees for Craig & Co.) in return for a letter which A.G. has written to him (Ll.G.) undertaking to recommend the people to accept English sovereignty'. The whole thing, thought O'Kelly, was 'a betrayal of trust' by those whom he now termed 'the delegates'. O'Kelly's long and well-informed

---

[146] Mulhern to Hagan, 30 Aug.; Curran to Hagan, 14 Sept. 1921 (JHP, HAG1/1921/432, 461).

[147] O'Connor to Dillon, 28 Sept. 1921 (DP 6744/856).

[148] M. Hopkinson, *Green against Green: The Irish Civil War* (Dublin, 1988), 24.

[149] Mulhern to Hagan, 17 Oct. 1921 (JHP, HAG1/1921/527).

[150] O'Connor to Dillon, 17 Oct. 1921 (DP 6744/860).

[151] Dillon to O'Connor, 18 Oct. 1921 (DP 6744/861).

[152] Devlin to Dillon, 20 Oct. 1921 (DP 6730/297).

letter displayed far more concern over the question of sovereignty than that of unity.[153] Griffith had denounced Redmond for agreeing to partition, but in fact he and his colleagues were in practice agreeing to far more, and gaining less protection for the northern nationalist minority than the Redmond scheme would have done.

On 5 November Lloyd George thought he had persuaded Craig to agree to an all-Ireland Parliament for certain services, but Craig's Government vetoed the idea, and suggested that the proposed services should be transferred to the two parliaments separately.[154] Lloyd George replied that in this case reserved services would be transferred to Southern Ireland only, meaning in effect that Northern Ireland would not get the benefits of reduced taxation. He thought this would persuade Ulster to 'climb down', but it did not.[155] He had already conceded to Craig responsibility for security, which meant that the UVF was promptly converted into a Special Constabulary. In the Commons on 10 November Devlin asked why these powers were being transferred in the midst of the Treaty negotiations.[156] The explanation may be that the concession helped Craig with one of his internal problems: the Northern Parliament, with no nationalist opposition, was indeed divided to some extent, but not between 'Capital' and 'Labour' as the nationalists had predicted, but between Craig's Government and Unionist 'extremists', who were a combination of disappointed place-seekers and anxious Tyrone and Fermanagh Unionists.

Ulster nationalists were not much reassured by autumn developments. Dr James Gillespie, the Cookstown coroner and Sinn Féiner, wrote to de Valera that devolved government in the six counties was now 'a special problem which should be dealt with in Ulster by an organisation of *all* the Catholic people... There is *no* real leadership in Ulster, and this is a grave defect.' He proposed a group consisting of Eoin MacNeill, Devlin, and Bishops McHugh and MacRory to progress the suggestion.[157] De Valera was opposed, however, to setting up what 'would appear to be a purely Catholic combination' in the North, and also dismissed such a 'coalition' approach: 'The majority party [i.e. Sinn Féin] is strong enough of itself to give the necessary lead. The Nationalist [Party] minority can support the policy and leadership of the majority in all matters that are of common interest.'[158] This implied that de Valera believed that Sinn Féin was somehow less sectarian than the Nationalist Party, which by 1921 was a bizarre—though in the South not uncommon—point of view. Around the same time Eoin MacNeill addressed a conference of West Ulster nationalists. 'A well-organized policy of non-compliance', he advised, would

153 O'Kelly to Hagan, 4 Nov. 1921 (JHP, HAG1/1921/563).
154 Taylor (ed.), *Stevenson Diary*, 235; Craig to Lloyd George, 11 Nov. 1921 (LGP, F/11/3/20).
155 Taylor, *Lloyd George Diary*, 236.   156 *IN*, 11 Nov. 1921.
157 Gillespie to de Valera, 23 Nov. 1921 (deVP, P150/1492).
158 O'Keeffe to Gillespie, 29 Nov. 1921 (deVP, P150/1492).

reduce the Northern Government to 'a laughing stock. Nothing can make that Government a reality but the acquiescence of its opponents.'[159] Paramilitary efforts were also made to undermine the Northern regime. During the last week in November there came 'a savage outbreak' in Belfast, coinciding with the transfer of law and order powers to the NI Government. Stephen Gwynn commented that, so long as the IRA continued to arm and drill and prepare for war throughout Ireland, including the six counties, 'it is chimerical to suppose that Protestant Ulster will not do the same'.[160] In London meanwhile, the Treaty talks proceeded towards a conclusion. The story of the final days, culminating in the midnight signatures, is well known. Sean T. O'Kelly took grave exception to dominion status on Canadian lines and the oath of allegiance, but again he made no reference to Ulster.[161] In correspondence with the Vatican, Hagan expressed more concern, advising that, if the Treaty came into force in its present shape, the five Northern bishops 'will be exposed to the danger of having their dioceses cut off from the rest of the country and their people placed at the uncontrolled mercy of a bigoted and savage enemy of the Catholic Church'. Many of the bishops, Hagan continued, 'are warm personal friends and admirers of de Valera, in whom they have the highest confidence and whom they know to be a fervent Catholic, and a daily communicant'.[162] A deputation of forty-five Northerners, mainly local councillors, met de Valera and others in Dublin on 7–9 December. They included Nationalists as well as Sinn Féiners, but the five delegates from Belfast were predominantly Sinn Féin. They were briefed by MacNeill, who told them that 'the danger we are threatened with in the North—although it is a real danger—is still an artificial one. It had not got strength or permanency.' The alternative to the Treaty, he told them, 'is to go back to a state of war'.[163] The following morning MacNeill took a smaller group to meet de Valera, who told them that the purpose of the meeting was to get their views, for, 'as far as advice is concerned, that would be . . . rather difficult . . . to give you'. De Valera asked the deputation whether they objected altogether to a local parliament in the North. Many of them did not, but the general assumption was that the local parliament being talked about would be under Dublin rather than London.[164] It is apparent from the report that the deputation was not the most important matter on de Valera's agenda. The Northern deputation and, apparently, de Valera were not the only ones who thought that Northern Ireland might be devolved from Dublin rather than London. If the Dáil accepted the Treaty, wrote Stephen Gwynn, 'then it is certain that before long Ulster will fall into its normal place: will conform that is, exactly as Natal did . . . Almost

[159] Memo by E. MacNeill, 1 Dec. 1921 (deVP, P150/1492).
[160] *Observer*, 27 Nov. 1921.
[161] O'Kelly to Hagan, 7 Dec. 1921 (JHP, HAG1/1921/624).
[162] 'Memorandum', n.d. (JHP, HAG1/1921/595).
[163] 'Conference of Representatives, 7 Dec. 1921' (CHP, D/2991/13/2/4).
[164] 'Transcript of Meeting with the President', 8 Dec. 1921 (deVP, P150/1492).

certainly Ulster will end as a counterpart to Quebec within the Irish Free State.'[165]

The debate on the Treaty in the House of Commons began on 14 December. Devlin announced that he did not intend to be present for the debate.[166] Lloyd George explained that, 'although I am against the coercion of Ulster, I don't believe in Ulster coercing other units . . . [But] if you get a homogeneous area you must, however, take into account geographical and economic considerations . . . For those reasons we have recommended a Boundary Commission.'[167] Bonar Law supported the Treaty, which passed with a very large majority, but rightly asked whether anyone could say that what had happened in Ireland since 1920 'is more likely to make the people of Ulster willing to come in. Certainly not.'[168] In the Dáil the voting was much closer—64 to 57 in favour. De Valera sided with the Anti-Treaty minority and resigned the presidency. During the debate Louis J. Walsh, the Ballycastle Sinn Féiner, pointed out that Sinn Féin in the South did not prioritize the situation of Northern Catholics.[169] Patrick Baxter, a Cavan TD, said later that 'many of the southern, midland and western Deputies are not as interested in the north as they might be and should be'.[170] Sean MacEntee, himself an Anti-Treaty Republican, later wrote to his wife from prison that 'in regard to partition I am simply disgusted at the way in which the Republicans are using the plight of our people in the North as a propagandist weapon, while in their hearts they care as little about them really as the Treatyites do'.[171] At no stage had the partition issue been prioritized by the Sinn Féin leadership. It was used simply as a tactical weapon: 'stage the break' on Ulster. Michael Laffan has calculated that only 9 out of 338 pages of the public Dáil sessions were devoted to partition and, in the private sessions that were published later, only 3 out of 181 pages.[172] Half a century later Ernest Blythe, a member of the Provisional Government of the Free State, recalled that 'during the debates on the Treaty, very little thought was given by Deputies to the position of the North'.[173] MacEntee was the only speaker in the Treaty debate to place his main emphasis on partition as a reason for rejecting the Treaty, which, he declared, 'perpetuates partition . . . I would not hand over my country as a protectorate to another country without, at least, securing the right to protect my countrymen.'[174]

T. P. O'Connor's reaction to the Dáil debates was that 'I find de Valera and his associates more hopelessly stupid than my worst expectations'.[175] Dillon agreed that 'de Valera is justifying to the full the estimate of his capacity for leadership

---

[165] *Observer*, 11 Dec. 1921.   [166] *IN*, 13 Dec. 1921.

[167] Parl. Deb., H.C., 5th series, cil. 40–1 (14 Dec. 1921).   [168] Ibid., 200.

[169] J. Augustejn (ed.) *The Irish Revolution, 1913–23* (London, 2002), 129–30.

[170] Hopkinson, *Irish War of Independence*, 164.   [171] Laffan, *Resurrection of Ireland*, 232.

[172] Ibid.   [173] E. Blythe to T. Ryle Dwyer, 4 May 1970 (Blythe Papers, P24/1528).

[174] Dáil Eireann Treaty Debates (22 Dec, 1921), 152–8.

[175] O'Connor to Dillon, 14 Jan. 1922 and 30 Dec. 1921 (DP 6744/867, 865).

which I formed after my dealings with him' during the 1918 conscription crisis. 'It looks', he thought, 'as if we are in for another split quite as ferocious as the Parnellite split—with this difference, that bombs, revolvers and rifles will be substituted as arguments for the sticks and stones used in 1890'. Dillon estimated that the Irish people were 'against de Valera 20 to 1. But . . . it is quite conceivable that the 1/20 might dominate the 19/20 by the approved methods of the IRA.'[176] Devlin meanwhile was mainly at home in Belfast during the Treaty debates, with occasional trips to Dublin. Early in January he had the sad business of attending the funeral of his old Belfast colleague John T. Donovan, who died from tuberculosis at the age of 43.

WAR IN BELFAST, 1922

The Northern bishops were ambivalent in their responses to the Treaty. Mulhern could not understand why so many TDs who had already surrendered the Republic 'in fact if not in words' opposed the Treaty so bitterly. 'If any people had a right to complain,' he wrote to Hagan, 'it is we of the North East . . . That suffering will be lessened and shortened too if we have the Free State operating and helping us.'[177] But Mulhern's view of the Treaty provisions was in one respect as selfish as that of most Southerners. He thought that, if Craig chose to come into the Free State, then his diocese would be under a devolved Northern administration, whereas if Craig chose to remain outside the Free State, then there was a chance of his diocese ending up on the southern side of the boundary: 'The whole thing is funny. Collins wants Craig to come in. Many of us want him to go out, that we may get in!'[178] McHugh of Derry was more pessimistic. He did not expect that the Boundary Commission would take Derry into the Free State, and was 'very much afraid we are going to have the Belfast Convention [of June 1916] under the guidance of Messrs Redmond, Dillon and Devlin repeated . . . by Collins & Co'.[179] MacRory thought it was 'a poor settlement' for Northern Catholics in the short term, but he was satisfied that 'things will come right before many years have passed'.[180] Likewise Bishop McKenna of Clogher thought that 'the big blot on the Treaty, to which no-one in the Dáil seemed to give a thought, is the uncertainty surrounding the position of the Catholics in the North East'.[181] O'Donnell (who was not a 'Northern' bishop) told Hagan that 'the Treaty is dominion home rule . . . with one very serious blemish in the matter of "Ulster" . . . The real difficulty . . . arises from the prestige of physical

---

[176] Dillon to O'Connor, 5 Jan. 1922 (DP 6744/866).
[177] Mulhern to Hagan, 6 Jan. 1922 (JHP, HAG1/1922/15).
[178] Mulhern to Hagan, 3 Feb. 1922 (JHP, HAG1/1922/76).
[179] McHugh to Hagan, n.d. [early Feb. 1922?] (JHP, HAG1/1922/89).
[180] MacRory to Hagan, 3 Feb. 1922 (JHP, HAG1/1922/77).
[181] McKenna to Hagan, 31 Jan. 1922 (JHP, HAG1/1922/71).

force as a remedy in recent years.'[182] The Northern bishops correctly saw little to attract the Catholic North on the Anti-Treaty side. In April 1922 Mulhern told Hagan that he held de Valera, 'and him alone, responsible for the recrudescence of our troubles here'. The Anti-Treaty forces were 'a gang of murderers and robbers'.[183] Likewise Cardinal Logue commented on 'the de Valera faction' that 'English tyranny pales before the present tyranny'.[184]

Lay opinion in the Catholic North, though more divided, was not much drawn to the Anti-Treaty side. Devlin was 'very much exercised' over the situation in Ulster. But Dillon thought that 'things are shaping in his direction. The nationalists of Belfast and the six counties are very sore over the Treaty' and were therefore more likely to be drawn back to the Irish Party, which had no responsibility for it. He expressed the hope that Devlin would not attend Parliament for the present, for the boundary question had put him in 'a cruelly difficult position'. Devlin was still the only Northern-based nationalist politician of any stature. But Michael Collins told a friend of Dillon's at the end of January 1922 that 'he has been bitterly attacked by some of his own friends for meeting Joe Devlin'.[185] In fact neither side within the Sinn Féin leadership had a workable policy on Ulster. It was left to Louis J. Walsh to call in the Dáil for 'the creation of a common line of action . . . Sinn Féin, Nationalist and Labour could ask for no better advocate or more fitting leader than the Nationalist member for West Belfast, Joseph Devlin'.[186]

The worst in Belfast was yet to come. The period from February to June 1922 saw the focus of IRA activity shift to Belfast and the North, while the reaction of the police and special constabulary in general, and of the 'murder gang' that appears to have operated with them, gave what many Catholics regarded as a justification for 'defensive measures' by the IRA. Between 10 February and 21 April 1922 127 Catholics were killed and 300 wounded in Belfast.[187] Early in March 1922 Michael Collins sent Churchill a long telegram detailing recent violent incidents. He alleged that County Inspector Harrison, District Inspector Nixon, and Head Constable Giff 'were up to their knees in the crimes of 1920–21. Yet these are the men who keep the "peace" in Belfast today.'[188] Dáil Eireann's *Weekly Irish Bulletin* of 12 June 1922 gave details of troubles in the city since 1920 as 425 killed and 1,764 wounded; 8,586 Catholics expelled from work and 22,650 Catholics expelled from their homes. Of this total, 2,500 had been driven from their homes since 1 June 1922, while 36 had been killed

[182] O'Donnell to Hagan, 23 Jan. and 10 Apr. 1922 (JHP, HAG1/1922/54, 190).
[183] Mulhern to Hagan, 7 and 15 Apr. 1922 (JHP, HAG1/1922/185, 201).
[184] Logue to O'Donnell, 8 Apr. 1922 (P. O'Donnell Papers, VI. 3).
[185] Dillon to O'Connor, 27 Jan. and 7 Feb. 1922 (DP 6744/868, 872).
[186] J. McDermott, *Northern Divisions: The Old IRA and the Belfast Pogroms, 1920–1922* (Belfast, 2001), 157.
[187] Untitled document, n.d. (Blythe Papers, P24/554).
[188] Collins to Churchill, 11 Mar. 1922 (CP 22/12A).

(28 Catholics) and 115 wounded (91 Catholics) during the same period.[189]
The ratification of the Treaty had an immediate negative impact on the Belfast
situation. The Belfast IRA was informed that the British Military intended
to take over the IRA's Liaison Office at St Mary's Hall. McCorley instructed
his men to remain in occupation, but the building was left vacant one night,
and the next morning they found it had been occupied by the British, and
valuable security information on IRA activists had fallen into the hands of the NI
authorities. After this, liaison with British forces came to an end. The Northern
IRA returned to 'our normal wartime footing', which involved some aggressive
actions in Belfast and a large amount of attempted neighbourhood defence, as
the pogrom returned with renewed viciousness. The 1st Battalion, now led by
Thomas Flynn, developed a plan to burn down the Belfast Customs House,
but it was arrested on 26 March before the plan could be put into effect. As
Flynn and his colleagues were being driven to the barracks, they quietly ate their
plans.[190] Around this time, following representations from Belfast IRA officers,
the Provisional Government authorized the formation of a 'Belfast City Guard',
including the payment of £3 per week to seventy-two officers. The reason for these
payments was later said to be that the continued rioting in Belfast was making
it impossible for many Volunteers to carry on with their ordinary employment,
and the Provisional Government was anxious at this stage to prevent an exodus
of Volunteers to the South. Collins was present at the cabinet meeting when
this decision was taken. The Guard continued in existence until the end of the
fighting in Belfast and was, in McCorley's words, 'the spearhead of the offensive
campaign carried out in May/June and July 1922'.[191]

In February 1922 the Pro-Treaty GHQ in Dublin summoned a representative
IRA Convention. McCorley disliked this, as it 'seemed to me to smell of politics',
but he was selected as a Brigade representative. GHQ then decided to cancel
the event, by which time McCorley was determined to attend. Committed
Anti-Treatyites took control. There was considerable discussion of the Northern
situation, resulting in promises to make arms available. Afterwards McCorley and
his colleagues agreed that unless GHQ could match this offer they would go with
the Anti-Treaty Executive. McCorley and Fitzpatrick then saw General O'Duffy,
who said that GHQ was much better placed to supply arms to the North.
McCorley liked nothing at all about the Treaty except that it allowed the Irish
people to maintain armed forces, but O'Duffy advised him that when the Belfast
Brigade met he should seek to get everyone to agree to accept the majority
decision, whatever it might be, for 'a split was a luxury that we could not afford
in Belfast'. Accordingly, when the majority of the Belfast Brigade opted to side
with GHQ, most of those who had argued for the Anti-Treaty Executive fell
into line. The number of exceptions was 'so small that it had very little effect on

[189] Dáil Eireann, *Weekly Irish Bulletin* (Belfast Atrocities), I. iv (12 June 1922).
[190] Flynn, witness statement 429.   [191] McCorley, witness statement 389.

the fighting efficiency of the Belfast Brigade'. GHQ provided an additional 150 rifles in addition to the 300 that the Belfast Brigade already possessed, but, in McCorley's view, not nearly enough ammunition.[192] During April those officers who supported the 'Irregular' Executive were dismissed, including Joe McKelvey, commandant of the 3rd Northern. Seamus Woods returned from Dublin to replace him. The Division at this stage consisted of three brigades in eleven battalions, of which the Belfast Brigade commanded five battalions.

Devlin had intended to keep away from Parliament, but the state of Belfast in February 1922 forced him to change his mind. He made a vigorous parliamentary attack on the Ulster Unionist regime, which, according to T.P., 'was a delight to everybody . . . He is more than ever the darling of the House.'[193] Stephen Gwynn commented that 'the condition of things in Belfast is incomparably more lawless and savage than in Dublin, Cork or any other city'. Gwynn was highly critical of the Northern Government, but warned that 'the rest of Ireland cannot have it both ways . . . they are not entitled to encourage the minority in the Northern Government's area to use those means of resistance which they themselves used against the British. If they do, they are asking for a war in which the Ulster Catholics will be wiped out.'[194] On 21 March Collins complained to Churchill that 'a most reprehensible speech' by Craig in the Northern Parliament had created great alarm among Ulster Catholics.[195] But Dillon thought that the situation in the six counties was so bad 'largely because of the colossal blunder of Collins and Griffith in having put no policy before the Northern Catholics when the Treaty was signed . . . It is perfectly idle . . . to attempt to represent the present horrors in Belfast as an unprovoked pogrom against the Catholics. The Sinn Féiners, acting on a *deliberate* policy, have done everything possible to goad the Orangemen to fury . . . In private the Sinn Féiners do frankly acknowledge their policy, and are quite proud of the results. When anxiety is expressed as to the fate of the Catholics of Belfast and the six counties, the reply is that of course in great revolutionary movements there must be bloodshed and suffering.'[196]

As the three governments began to think about what could be done to ameliorate the situation, in terms of both safety and employment, Churchill sought advice from Devlin regarding financial investment in Belfast.[197] On the same day, however, the Anti-Treaty IRA leader in Co. Armagh, Frank Aiken, passed to Collins his view that 'in your future dealings with Ulster you should not recognize Joe Devlin or his clique . . . There can be no vigorous or harmonious policy on our part inside Ulster if his people occupy any position in our circle.'[198] Collins then went on to set up the North East Advisory Committee, with

[192] Ibid.   [193] O'Connor to Dillon, 4 Mar. 1922 (DP 6744/878).
[194] *Observer*, 12 and 19 Mar. 1922.   [195] Collins to Churchill, 21 Mar. 1922 (CP 22/12A).
[196] Dillon to O'Connor, 23 and 24 Mar. 1922 (DP 6744/879, 881).
[197] Churchill to Curtis, 3 Mar. 1922 (CP 22/12A/19).
[198] Mulcahy to Collins, 3 Mar. 1922, cited in T. P. Coogan, *Michael Collins* (London, 1990), 343.

no Devlinite membership. It included several cabinet ministers, together with MacRory, two other Northern bishops, and the Sinn Féiners Cahir Healy and Russell McNabb—who was described by the NI Cabinet Secretary, Wilfred Spender, as 'the representative of Mr Collins' in Belfast.[199] Thus Collins's wish or need to seek accommodation with the Anti-Treatyites at this stage overcame any instinct he might have had for building an alliance with the Devlinites in the Belfast region—which was bad news for Collins and very bad news for Ulster's Catholics.

On 23 March 1922 one of the grossest of all the Belfast atrocities occurred: the murder in their home, by a masked gang, of five male members of the McMahon family and their live-in barman. Owen McMahon was one of Belfast's leading publicans and a supporter of Joe Devlin. Immediately after this Churchill telegraphed Craig that there was an urgent need to end the bloodshed in Belfast, and invited him and Collins to a conference in London.[200] Devlin was not invited, no doubt because Collins followed Aiken's advice. The second Craig–Collins Pact, signed on 30 March by Collins, Craig, Churchill, and their senior cabinet colleagues, appeared to be a thoughtful and detailed attempt to bring an end to the immediate crises of employment and security in Belfast and to implement a formal structure for minority protection in the six counties. Collins agreed to stop IRA activity in the North and to end the economic boycott, while Craig agreed to try to do something for the expelled shipyard workers.[201] A central feature of the Pact was the appointment of various local committees in Belfast to address the problem of unemployment and the expelled workers, to resolve disputes, and to draw Catholics into the new Royal Ulster Constabulary (RUC) and, in particular, into the Special Constabulary. There were some potentially useful mechanisms here that would, had they worked, have made Northern Ireland a fairer regime in the years that followed. But efforts to implement the Pact by Craig's Government were patchy and half-hearted, while the Provisional Government regarded it less as a desirable step in itself than as an additional weapon in its campaign to undermine the Northern regime. A later document in Ernest Blythe's papers concerning IRA pension claims states that the Pact 'was never fully carried out by the Northern Government and scarcely either by our forces, and it was the last political attempt to deal with the situation'.[202] John Dillon doubted whether Collins and Griffith had 'the power to stop the atrocities of the IRA in the six counties'—although we now know that IRA activity in the North subsequent to the Pact was not just an Anti-Treaty activity, but had the active support and encouragement of Collins himself.[203]

[199] Spender to Tallents, 28 June 1922 (TNA: PRO CO 906/25).
[200] 'Minutes of Irish Cabinet Committee', 24 Mar. 1922 (LGP, F/26/1/24).
[201] Hopkinson, *Green against Green*, 82.
[202] Untitled document, n.d. (Blythe Papers, P24/554).
[203] Dillon's 'Notes on Irish Politics', 31 Mar. and 15 May 1922 (DP 6582).

The introduction of the Pact, with its famous—if tragically erroneous—first clause, drafted by Churchill, 'Peace is today declared', aroused initial enthusiasm. Devlin welcomed it as 'the foundation of . . . future peace—and I trust future unity of Ireland'.

having laboured for over twenty years to try to bring my fellow-countrymen together . . . I trust that we will now be enabled to apply ourselves to the higher and nobler task of fighting for the elevation of the poor, for the promotion of all great human causes, for the creation of better conditions for our people, and for the great purpose of joining together the democracies of these islands in all that can make for the grandeur, and power, and enduring strength of the Empire.[204]

O'Connor thought this was 'excellent . . . Joe had a great triumph. His beautiful little speech, largely impromptu, created a profound and universal impression in the House.'[205] Dillon, on the other hand, thought it 'a very foolish speech', reminding him 'painfully' of Redmond's historic speech in August 1914.[206] On reflection, T.P. thought that the Pact would be of no use unless Devlin's experience was called on. He told Dillon that Churchill had suggested to Griffith and Collins that 'they should call for counsel from some of the old politicians; but it was rejected emphatically; I think the Bishop in Belfast shares this reluctance. I am told that gentleman [MacRory] has messed things badly; and is reaping the result in great unpopularity'.[207] During the weekend immediately following the Pact the IRA carried out two operations in Belfast, including the murder of a policeman and a bomb attack that killed two children. Whether this was retaliation for the McMahon murders or a deliberate attempt to undermine the Pact is not clear, but inevitably it provoked further attacks on the Catholic community.

After a few weeks it became clear that the Pact was not working, and Stephen Tallents, a British civil servant, was sent to Belfast at the end of June to conduct a private investigation. His general comment that 'the system . . . of inviting Mr Collins virtually to act as the representative of a minority in the territory of another Government both encouraged the Catholics in the North in their policy of non-recognition of the Northern Government, and exasperated Sir James Craig's supporters'.[208] Devlin declined an invitation to join the Belfast Unemployment Relief Advisory Committee, because Collins had insisted that nationalist membership be dominated by the local committee of the Irish White Cross Association, a Sinn Féin body.[209] Devlin had also been unwell again, and O'Connor had advised him to see an abdominal surgeon, but otherwise found

[204] Parl. Deb., H.C., 5th series, clii (30 Mar. 1922), 1693–4.
[205] O'Connor to Dillon, 1 Apr. 1922 (DP 6744/884).
[206] Dillon to O'Connor, 11 Apr. 1922 (DP 6744/885).
[207] O'Connor to Dillon, 8 Apr. 1922 (DP 6744/884).
[208] D. Kennedy, 'Joint Authority was Tried and Failed in the North', *Irish Times*, 6 Dec. 1984.
[209] M. Harris, *The Catholic Church and the Foundation of the Northern Irish State* (Cork, 1993), 90, 115.

him to be 'in splendid form . . . [and] . . . apparently in very cheerful spirits'.[210] Dillon thought it wise for Devlin to remain in London, for he had 'no doubt that he would be in danger if he returned to Belfast . . . The speech he made on the McMahon murders was bound to infuriate the Specials.'[211] The shooting dead in a Belfast city-centre street of the Unionist NI MP William Twaddell on 22 May would have added to Dillon's anxiety. The McMahon murders demonstrated that a loyalist murder gang was active and not confining its activities to those it believed to be IRA activists and supporters, while the murder of Twaddell made Devlin an ideal reprisal target. 'It would be madness for him to go to Belfast under present circumstances,' wrote Dillon once again, for 'his life would not be worth a day's purchase'.[212]

After the Pact, the IRA in Belfast had been 'put entirely on the defensive'. But by mid-April 'it was obvious that the Pact Agreement would never work', and a decision was taken at a joint meeting in Dublin of GHQ and the Anti-Treaty Executive 'to resume operations in the six-county area at the first suitable opportunity'.[213] Operations began in Belfast on 22 May with an attempt to capture Musgrave Street Barracks. Twenty-two IRA men briefly gained control of the arms room, but were soon outnumbered, though they all managed to escape. One policeman was killed and another wounded. Other attacks on barracks in the city were more successful, as was the destruction of industrial concerns. Several million pounds worth of damage was caused, and the IRA inflicted 'considerable casualties during this fighting, which at times was very severe'. By McCorley's account they were able to resist any counter-attack, 'since by this time we had a well-armed, well-disciplined and well-trained brigade'.[214] The fighting continued throughout June. Both Fitzpatrick and McCorley were wounded at the end of May, the latter with a broken femur. Fitzpatrick later recalled that 'it was recognized that further fighting in the area was futile, owing to the fact that civil war had broken out in the South'. In the autumn of 1922 Fitzpatrick and McCorley both moved south, by which time the Belfast and Co. Antrim Brigades of the IRA were non-existent.[215]

On 21 May Stephen Gwynn pointed out that, while Parliament was debating the situation in the South, the North was in a worse state. He took a slightly different slant on what most nationalists regarded as an anti-Catholic pogrom:

In Belfast the tally of killings—an average of about ten a week for the past three months—far exceeds that of all the rest of Ireland . . . There is no doubt that the attacked Catholics in Belfast are retaliating by methods of senseless brutality: bombs in tram cars for instance. No doubt either, that the means are supplied largely by extremists in the south.

[210] O'Connor to Dillon, 4 May 1922 (DP 6744/886).
[211] Dillon to O'Connor, 6 May 1922 (DP 6744/887).
[212] Dillon to O'Connor, 26 May 1922 (DP 6744/889).
[213] Untitled document, n.d. (Blythe Papers, P24/554); Fitzpatrick, witness statement 395.
[214] McCorley, witness statement 389.   [215] Fitzpatrick, witness statement 395.

While leading Anti-Treaty figures such as Cathal Brugha advocated healing divisions in the South by uniting in an effort to protect the Northern Catholics, Gwynn commented that 'the result of that effort is likely to be disastrous for the protected'.[216] Dillon noted that 31 May was the worst day yet in Belfast, and 'began as usual' with an attack on two Specials.[217] As a result of this, a small group of leading Catholic businessmen from Belfast, led by the shipbroker Raymond Burke, with the support of Devlin, met Churchill on 2 June. They urged Churchill to call Craig, Collins, and Devlin to a meeting to try to end the violence in the city. Churchill agreed that 'the brushing aside of Mr Devlin had been one of the worst disasters of the situation . . . He was a better man than the present leaders in southern Ireland, a tried parliamentarian who, if given the chance, would have gone very far.'[218] At a second meeting they told Churchill that Collins's three nominees had tried to break up the police recruitment committee established under the Craig–Collins Pact, that Devlin could confirm this, and that 'Devlin's help ought to be enlisted and Collins ought to be made to face him'.[219] Burke presented a draft scheme for modifying the Craig–Collins Pact that included proposals that the police force in Belfast should be 50/50 Catholic and Protestant (as the old RIC had been), that there should be an appropriate proportion of Catholic judges on a Criminal Court of Appeal, that Catholic education should not be interfered with, that a 'Catholic' seat for Belfast in the Westminster Parliament should be assured for three years, that the cases of all internees should be heard by a balanced panel, that all houses destroyed in the troubles should be rebuilt at government expense, that the Dublin and Belfast governments should agree to a formal cooperation for a three-year period, and that all members of the Ulster Parliament should take their seats immediately.[220] Churchill's response was to set up the Tallents inquiry into the failure of the Pact.[221]

Tallents spent eleven days in Belfast in late June interviewing government ministers, prominent Catholics, and Army leaders. The only committee that really achieved anything was the one set up to advise the NI Ministry of Labour on the alleviation of unemployment, no doubt owing to the fact that it had £500,000 of Treasury funds to distribute. Figures for registered unemployment in the city in June 1922 were 22,431 men and 9,677 women, amounting to 21 per cent of the insured population, by far the highest in Ireland.[222] Tallents's assessment was that the pact had otherwise achieved very little, chiefly, he

[216] *Observer*, 21 and 28 May, and 18 June 1922.
[217] Dillon, 'Notes on Irish Politics', 16, 17, and 31 May 1922 (DP 6582).
[218] Minutes of a Meeting at the Colonial Office, 2 June 1922 (TNA: PRO, CO 906/25).
[219] Phoenix, *Northern Nationalism*, 234.
[220] 'Burke's Draft Scheme', n.d. [June 1922] (TNA: PRO CO 906/26).
[221] Churchill to Fitzalan, 15 Mar. 1922 (CP 22/13/185).
[222] P. E. Starrett, 'The ITGWU in its Industrial and Political Context, 1909–1923', D.Phil. thesis (University of Ulster, 1986), 262.

thought, 'because it dealt with minor issues before the major issues, which really govern them, were decided'. These, in his estimation, included the stability of the Provisional Government of the Free State; the fact that the Catholic minority in the North did not acknowledge the NI Government; the fact that the Boundary Commission 'still loomed'; and 'the organized conspiracy of violence to make the government of Northern Ireland impossible, which was intensified during May'. Furthermore, the approach of the Pact, in treating Collins as the representative of the Northern Catholics, encouraged Catholics in their policy of non-recognition and exasperated Craig's supporters.[223] Oswald Jamison, the Nationalist Party councillor, told Tallents that 'the great majority of Catholics' wished to recognize the Northern Government, and that not only unemployment but also a housing shortage 'runs like an accompaniment under the whole trouble'. 'The house hunger largely accounts for the expulsions', he said, 'recent burnings put out of employment more men than the employment scheme provided for.'[224] MacRory, however, told Tallents that he did not favour recognition of the Northern Government unless it would agree to cooperate in 'broad, general questions' with the Dublin Government. In mid-June MacRory met de Valera in an attempt to get him to restrain 'the violent Catholic element' in Belfast, but 'de Valera talked at great length on other subjects and left a very poor impression on his mind'.[225]

By July 1922 peace was beginning to return to the North, because of the outbreak of civil war in the South rather than any more positive reason. In Belfast there were thirty-two murders in one week in May, twenty-four in the two weeks to 24 June, four in the two weeks to 15 July, and none in the two weeks to 29 July.[226] At a conference with Northern IRA officers in Dublin on 2 August, Collins agreed that there was 'no hope of prosecuting the fight to a successful issue in the six county area'. It was decided that all IRA operations in the area should cease forthwith; that men who were unable to remain in the North should be trained at Curragh in such tactics as would be applicable to the nature of fighting in the six counties; and that they would not be asked to take part in military activities in the twenty-six counties. By Christmas there were 524 Northerners based at the Curragh, being fed, clothed, and paid 24 shilling and 6 pence per week by the Free State Army. It was intended to reopen hostilities in the North at the first opportunity, but 'subsequent developments prevented this happening'. Once this had become clear, the Curragh group began to break up: 293 joined the Free State Army, while others drifted back north or joined the Irregulars. A few remained on until cleared out of the Curragh on 31 March 1923.[227]

[223] Tallents to Masterton-Smith, 4 July 1922 (TNA: PRO CO 906/30).
[224] Tallents, 'Conversation with Cllr O. Jamison', 23 June 1922 (TNA: PRO CO 906/26).
[225] Tallents, 'Conversation with Bishop MacRory', 1 July 1922 (TNA: PRO CO 906/26).
[226] Sir W. Spender to M. Sturgis, 2 Aug. 1922 (CP 22/14/38–9).
[227] Untitled document, n.d. (Blythe Papers, P24/554).

On 22 June 1922 the NI Government's chief security adviser, Field Marshal Sir Henry Wilson, was shot dead by two IRA men, who were probably acting on their own initiative, on the doorstep of his London home.[228] This incident helped to provoke a debate in the House of Commons four days later, in which Churchill called upon the Provisional Government to act against the Anti-Treaty forces occupying the Four Courts in Dublin. On 28 June Collins's Government moved against the Four Courts, and civil war broke out in the South. In the debate Churchill said that, although the IRA had been met in 'an equally combative, bellicose sprit by the Protestant Orangemen' and that the Catholics, 'being numerically weaker, have got the worst of it', he was convinced that 'the prime and continuing cause of all the horrors which have taken place in Belfast is . . . the Irish Republican Army'. As the government's policy of equipping the NI security forces continued, Churchill said that Craig's Government 'will be able more and more to prevent and bring to an end the vile reprisals upon innocent Catholics'. Certainly Craig had less of a hand in Protestant violence in the North in 1922 than Collins had in Catholic violence in the area.[229] Devlin and T.P. did not speak or vote in the debate. T.P. told Dillon that it had been suggested to the Provisional Government by Churchill more than once that it should call in the assistance of Devlin.

Their answer was that he was an extinct volcano and could be of no use to them. Of course my feeling, and I daresay yours, is that if his counsels had been adopted with regard to Northern Ireland we should not have had the horrible debauch of murder, especially among our own people there . . . These butcheries . . . might not have occurred if it had not been for the methods of insane provocation which were adopted by some of the Sinn Féin sections.[230]

Meanwhile a general election had been held in the Free State. Military weakness caused Collins to make a pre-election pact with de Valera to avoid the election being sabotaged, but the intervention of third parties ensured that the electorate's opinion was not entirely stifled. The Pro-Treatyites won fifty-eight seats, Labour seventeen, Farmers' Party seven, and others (most of whom also took their seats) eleven. The Anti-Treaty abstentionists were reduced to thirty-five. It was a bad defeat for them, and they were lucky it was not worse: sixteen of their seats were won in uncontested constituencies and in a further four their candidates were the last to be elected, defeating only other Anti-Treatyites. Devlin had considered standing for a Dublin seat, and was convinced that he would have been successful, but O'Connor thought he 'exercised a wise discretion in remaining apart from the present conditions until they have righted themselves'.[231] In his view Devlin

---

[228] P. Hart, *The IRA at War, 1916–23* (Oxford, 2003), 194–220; K. Jeffery, *Field Marshal Sir Henry Wilson* (Oxford, 2006), 284–5.

[229] Parl. Deb., H.C., 5th series, clv. 1695–711(26 June 1922).

[230] O'Connor to Dillon, 27 June 1922 (DP 6744/890).

[231] O'Connor to Dillon, 2 Aug. 1922 (DP 6744/894).

should have gone to America on a private lecturing tour to earn some money: 'I am convinced that this is the only thing for him to do at the moment, besides keeping him away from a troubled scene in which he could as yet play no part'.[232] Dillon heard that there was 'a *very strong* movement on foot amongst the Catholics to get their representatives to enter the Ulster Parliament. But the bishops are blocking it, and a certain section of the Sinn Féin priests are *furious* at any sign of reconciliation between the Orange Party and the Catholics. It is a diabolical spirit.'[233]

A paper circulated to the Free State cabinet by Ernest Blythe on 9 August 1922 suggests a more realistic turn in thinking about the North. The Southern election result and the 'offensive against the Irregulars' gave the Provisional Government for the first time the opportunity to decide freely its North-East policy. 'There is no prospect of bringing about the unification of Ireland within any reasonable period of time by attacking the North East,' wrote Blythe. Likewise, it was 'fallacious' to think that the North's territory was too small to support a government. His conclusion was that 'the prospect of unification . . . will depend on our showing a friendly and pacific disposition towards the Northern Government and people'. Blythe argued that Catholic members of the Northern Parliament should be urged to 'take their seats and carry on a unity propaganda . . . Heretofore our Northern policy has been really, though not ostensibly, dictated by Irregulars . . . The belligerent policy has been shown to be useless for protecting the Catholics or stopping the pogroms.'[234] Within days of Blythe's memo the situation in the South was altered further by the sudden death of Arthur Griffith on 12 August and the killing of Collins in an ambush in Co. Cork ten days later. Devlin, holidaying once again with his friend Revd John McCartan in Cushendall, was amongst the many who sent messages of condolence.[235]

The changed attitudes in Dublin caused consternation among Northern IRA leaders. Seamus Woods commented to his Commander-in-Chief, General Richard Mulcahy, that 'the attitude of the present Government towards its followers in the Six Counties is not that of the late General Collins'. During the January–March 1922 period he had been satisfied that GHQ was working 'to overcome the Treaty position with regard to Ulster'. Thus when the split came he had advised his men to remain Pro-Treaty. Now the Cosgrave Government appeared to be much less supportive of the IRA.[236] Woods's view was the opposite of Blythe's, claiming that the IRA's 'campaign of burning and destruction in Belfast' was responsible for ending the Northern Government's 'terror policy', causing it to turn to 'a policy of placation towards the Catholic population'.

[232] O'Connor to Dillon, 2 Aug. 1922 (DP 6744/894).
[233] Dillon to O'Connor, 11 Aug. 1922 (DP 6744/895).
[234] 'Policy in Regard to the North East', 9 Aug. 1922 (Blythe Papers, P24/70/10–18).
[235] *IN*, 25 Aug. 1922.
[236] Woods to Mulcahy, 29 Sept. 1922, copy (MacNeill Papers, LA1/H/86/8–12).

For the moment, Woods told Mulcahy, he had issued special orders against retaliation. But recognition of the Northern Government, he claimed, would mean the break-up of his division. None of the officers could remain in Belfast 'except under war conditions', but with their departure 'it would not be possible to maintain the IRA organization . . . The breaking up of the organization is the first step to making partition permanent.'[237]

Attitudes to the Northern Parliament continued to be debated within the Provisional Government. MacNeill and one of the government's legal advisers, Kevin O'Shiel, agreed that it would be prejudicial to the Boundary Commission to advise 'the Northern TDs' to enter the Northern Parliament. O'Shiel sent an envoy, Captain E. L. MacNaghten, to meet 'a number of prominent Protestant gentlemen' and find out their reasons for not wishing Northern Ireland to join an all-Ireland Parliament.[238] MacNaghten reported that 'the principal obstacle to parliamentary union is this ferocious, fanatical and fratricidal hate moved by large bodies of the uneducated Protestant manual workers'. Another factor working against early settlement was the current unstable condition of the Free State. MacNaghten advised that abstention should end when the Boundary Commission was concluded. His suggested policy for the future, the Canada/Quebec model, was very similar to Devlin's home-rule-within-home-rule approach. 'It is not unreasonable', he concluded, 'to hope that some such scheme of arrangement may be possible in Ireland . . . Above all else, I would urge that *Festina Lente* should be our motto . . . To be impatient . . . would be folly.'[239] Likewise on the Anti-Treaty side, perceptive Northerners like Seán MacEntee realized that

the partition problem cannot be solved except with the consent of the majority of the Northern non-Catholic population. It certainly cannot be solved by their coercion . . . We are relying on England's big stick, and it will fail . . . In regard to partition we have never had a considered policy. It had always been a matter of hasty improvisations.[240]

MacEntee drafted these words to de Valera many years later, but even then the letter was not sent.

As a Westminster general election drew nearer, Devlin was aware that his days as MP for the Falls were numbered. The 1920 Government of Ireland Act cut Belfast's parliamentary representation back to four, including boundary changes that gave the restored West Belfast constituency a large Protestant majority.[241] T.P. was anxious about being left at Westminster without Devlin, but the only winnable constituency in Northern Ireland was now the two-seater of Fermanagh

[237] Woods to Mulcahy.
[238] O'Shiel to MacNeill, 13 Oct. 1922 (MacNeill Papers, LA1/H/85/1).
[239] 'Report by Capt. E. L.MacNaghten', n.d. [Oct.–Nov.1922] (MacNeill Papers, LA1/H/65/2–19).
[240] MacEntee to de Valera, 17 Feb. 1938, unsent draft (MacEntee Papers, P67/155), cited in D. Ferriter, *Judging Dev* (Dublin, 2007), 151.
[241] *IN*, 29 Apr. 1921.

and Tyrone, where the sitting Nationalist Tom Harbison had been recommended by Devlin in 1917–18. In T.P.'s view, Harbison had been a poor attender and he hoped he would resign in favour of Devlin. Dillon advised T.P. against taking such a step

> without full consultation with Joe . . . You must always keep in mind that there is a poisonously bitter faction, especially in Tyrone, who hate Devlin and whose greatest object at present is to block him in every possible way. Sinn Féin is *utterly* discredited in N.E. Ulster. But the wirepullers, including a large number of priests, are of course more bitter than ever, and they naturally look on Joe Devlin as 'the enemy'.

But Dillon thought, now that the security situation in the North was improving, that Devlin would 'before too long take the leadership of the Northern Nationalists and find the path clear to his entry into the Belfast Parliament'.[242]

Meanwhile the Northern Government was continuing to consolidate its position. Ministers were determined to reverse their local government losses of 1920. They thus passed a Local Government Bill that ended the new PR system of voting. In the last months of his office the Lord Lieutenant, Viscount Fitzalan, referred the measure to the British Government.[243] But after lengthy discussions Churchill told Collins's successor, W. T. Cosgrave, that, while he thought the Bill 'most unfortunate and ill-timed', it did fall within the delegated powers of the Northern Government and that it would be 'a very serious thing to persist in the use of the veto in these circumstances'. Cosgrave maintained that the Bill was not a domestic matter while the moment of Northern Ireland's opt-out from the Free State had technically not yet been reached and while the Boundary Commission was unimplemented, but he added that the Provisional Government was 'averse from hostile relations with the Government of the Six Counties . . . and gladly acknowledge your goodwill towards the creation of a friendly atmosphere leading to ultimate national unity'.[244] This was to become Devlin's impossible task during the last decade of his life.

---

[242] Dillon to O'Connor, 29 Sept. 1922 (DP 6744/898).

[243] Hepburn (ed.), *Conflict of Nationality*, 154–6.

[244] Churchill to Cosgrave, n.d. [*c*.31 Aug. 1922]; Cosgrave to Churchill, telegram, 8 Sept. 1922 (CP 22/14/59–60, 69).

9

The Stage Contracts: Northern Ireland, 1922–1934

We do not believe that unity can ever spring out of conflict.

(Joe Devlin, 1926[1])

Between 1919 and 1922 Devlin's circumstances and those of Catholic Belfast had diverged somewhat. Belfast was for much of the period a centre of attention, albeit it for undesirable reasons. Devlin, on the other hand, could be dismissed by Sinn Féin as an 'extinct volcano', no longer at the centre of Irish political life as he had been for the previous decade. After 1922 Devlin and his city gradually came together again as the Northern Ireland regime established itself. But the new era almost began with a further divergence, as Devlin lost his Westminster seat, briefly sought a new political career in Britain, and declined one in Dublin. The abstention from Northern politics to which he had been bound—partly at Sinn Féin's insistence, partly by the delay in implementing the Boundary Commission—kept him out of representative politics until 1925. By then both his new political stage and the prospects for Catholic Belfast into the foreseeable future were defined. The structure of party politics was determined by the Unionists, who were the beneficiaries of ethnic politics. It was not a scenario that Devlin would have chosen. The thrust of his appeal had always been to present Irish independence as the necessary partner of democratic advance and social reform. After the abolition of PR this rhetoric crumbled. Both he and his constituents rejected the Protestant socialist William McMullen, his former parliamentary colleague. A combination of circumstances forced him to follow the path of 'Catholic unity', a path that the Free State had urged and that suited the Ulster Unionists. Even this was short-lived, however, for within little over a decade after his death the party to which he had given a lifetime commitment and that he had revived after partition had ceased to exist in Belfast but lived on in rural Ulster.

[1] NI Parl. Deb., H.C., vii. 38 (9 Mar. 1926).

'A MERE ENGLISH LABOURITE WITH A BELFAST ACCENT'?

In 1918 William O'Brien MP wrote to Tim Healy that Devlin was 'sure to emerge again (in West Belfast or elsewhere) upon some flashy socialist-labour programme, but he will be a mere English Labourite with a Belfast accent'.[2] By April 1921 Devlin knew that West Belfast would be lost to the Unionists at the next election. He later declared that it would be 'futile and farcical' for him to stand again.[3] He was invited to stand in the Liverpool Exchange division, adjacent to T. P. O'Connor's constituency. The local United Irish League of Great Britain (UILGB) activists believed 'that his success is absolutely assured'. An Irish Nationalist had lost there by about 2,000 votes in 1918, when it was believed that 6,000 military votes—the great majority of which were Irish—had not been cast.[4] Liverpool had long been the largest Irish community in England, more sharply segregated than Glasgow, which from the electoral point of view was an advantage. It consistently returned T. P. O'Connor from 1885 to 1929. In 1922 the UILGB had 10,000 members in the city and twenty-three members on the city council. At an estimated 150,000 in total, the population that regarded itself as 'Irish' amounted to over 30 per cent of the city's population.[5]

On 3 November it was reported locally that 'a candidate who will unite the Nationalist and Liberal forces, as in the old days' was ready to take the field against the sitting Coalition MP, Sir Leslie Scott.[6] Then it was a 'Nomination Day Bombshell', as Devlin's papers were submitted. A somewhat anxious Scott declared that he was a supporter of the Irish Treaty, had 'always supported the Catholic schools', and was the more appropriate representative of 'this great business constituency'.[7] Devlin declared that he had been invited 'in the interests of progress and democracy . . . to fight for all the causes that concern the industrial, commercial and economic advancement of the people'. He stressed his commitment to free trade and the need for education and security of employment in order to 'prevent bolshevism' and 'avert revolution'.[8] It was 'not because I am an Irishman', declared Devlin, 'but because I stand for the people against the reactionaries that I come before you'.[9] 'We have had enough of war, except one war—the war against poverty'.[10] One howler that Devlin made was to extend his opposition to British 'colonialism' from

---

[2] O'Brien to T. M. Healy, 18 Sept. 1918 (NLI, OBP 8556/20).   [3] *IN*, 28 Oct. 1922.
[4] O'Connor to Dillon, 21 Oct. 1922 (DP 6744/900).
[5] B. O'Connell, 'Irish Nationalism in Liverpool, 1873–1923', *Eire-Ireland*, 10/1 (1975), 24.
[6] *Liverpool Daily Post & Mercury*, 3 Nov. 1922.   [7] *Liverpool Echo*, 4 Nov. 1922.
[8] *Liverpool Daily Post & Mercury*, 11 Nov. 1922.   [9] Ibid., 7 Nov. 1922.
[10] Ibid., 9 Nov. 1922.

Ireland to Palestine, where he said that the Mandate should be ended and Britain should leave. This caused something of a backlash in the local Jewish community. Scott sought to capitalize on this in a speech at the Zionist Hall, and Devlin hastily reversed his comments.[11] Lord Londonderry, now Minister of Education in the Northern Ireland Government, appeared in Exchange on behalf of Sir Leslie Scott, asking why Devlin was not 'in Belfast protecting his co-religionists'.[12]

The *Liverpool Catholic Herald* published a regular column by its group proprietor, Charles Diamond, once an Anti-Parnellite MP and now a supporter of Sinn Féin in Ireland and Labour in Britain. Diamond argued that Devlin, who 'has a good record on labour matters', should be standing as a Labour candidate. 'In the Labour ranks he would be a power, and he would assuredly be welcomed,' whereas, by joining T. P. O'Connor, 'he will plough a lonely furrow and sink into insignificance'.[13] Devlin in fact stood as an Independent, with a letter of support from the Chairman of the Parliamentary Liberal Party. At first sight it seems strange that Devlin opted for the old rather than the new. But Labour did not do well in Liverpool during these years, winning none of the city's eleven parliamentary seats in 1918 or 1922 and only one council seat in the municipal elections of 1922.[14] The approaching national collapse of the Liberal Party had not yet become fully apparent, and Devlin and O'Connor presumably thought that the 'Independent' banner would be the best means of maximizing the anti-Conservative vote. But Devlin was defeated by over 3,000 votes, winning just 45 per cent of the poll, as his predecessor had done. 'We have prevented the start of a Tammany organization,' declared Scott, and 'Liverpool does not want to be represented by a man who calls England a foreign country'.[15] Richard McGhee, now retired and living in Bolton, could not understand what had induced Devlin to stand for Exchange. He told Dillon that 'we could have got him a certainty at Bootle . . . There never was the slightest chance of Exchange Division going against Leslie Scott.'[16] The *Irish News* thought that among the reasons for Devlin's defeat were the indirect endorsement of Scott by the Catholic Archbishop of Liverpool, the under-registration of Irish voters, and the fact that the Jewish vote, 'rich and poor', went to Scott.[17] But all agreed that the key to Scott's success was his appeal to the estimated 5,000 women resident in other constituencies who could choose to cast their vote in Exchange by virtue of their husbands' business interests.[18] O'Connor lamented

[11] Ibid., 10 Nov. 1922.   [12] Ibid., 14 Nov. 1922.

[13] *Liverpool Catholic Herald*, 11 Nov. 1922.

[14] S. Davies, *Liverpool Labour: Social and Political Influences on the Development of the Labour Party in Liverpool 1900–1939* (Keele, 1996), 81, 144.

[15] *Liverpool Catholic Herald*, 25 Nov. 1922.

[16] McGhee to Dillon, 25 Nov. 1922 (DP 6757/1077).

[17] *IN*, 17 Nov. 1922; O'Connor to Dillon, 28 Nov. 1922 (DP 6744/903).

[18] *Liverpool Daily Post & Mercury*, 7 Nov. 1922.

privately that 'we were entirely misinformed as to the situation'. Some leading Liberals as well as Nationalists had said that a win was certain, 'and indeed up to the last hour the feeling was that Joe must win'. On the positive side, T.P. was pleased that the vote had 'brought our people back to unity and self-confidence . . . and we practically may regard Sinn Féin as dead among the Irish in Britain'.[19]

Although Devlin's campaign in Exchange was effective in reigniting Irish communal awareness in Liverpool, he had not been very encouraging about T.P.'s efforts to revive the UILGB. 'You know how peculiar Joe's attitude with regard to our organization in Great Britain is,' wrote T.P. to Dillon in late 1919; 'I do not look for much assistance from him'.[20] By 1921 Devlin thought that the UILGB should be wound up and future efforts invested in the Labour Party.[21] T.P. also favoured close links with Labour, but he continued to hold to the idea that the Irish in Britain still needed their own organization, 'friendly to Labour', to advance their position in British society. After the failure at Exchange he hoped that Devlin would cooperate with the Liverpool business magnate Sir Alexander Maguire to raise funds for such an organization. Maguire even suggested that Devlin be paid a salary of £1,000 a year to run this body, and T.P. thought that such a plan

would give Joe, for the interval of two or three years, which I have no doubt must elapse before he can enter on the scene of Irish politics, a work which would occupy his mind and bring out his best gifts . . . But Joe is hesitant, and raises difficulties at the idea of taking a salary as laying him open to the charge that he created the organization for the purpose of getting a salary. You know his super-sensitiveness to attack.[22]

Devlin was willing to speak at Irish conferences and meetings in Britain, but would accept no official position. By the end of 1923 the UILGB had been wound up because of lack of funds.[23]

When Parliament reopened on 20 November 1922 Devlin was absent for the first time in over twenty years. The Speaker paid tribute to his 'abilities, sincerity and worth'.[24] O'Connor increasingly felt isolated in the Commons. As well as the Donegal and Waterford seats, the Irish Party lost two of its four seats in the six counties. Only the two-seat Fermanagh and Tyrone constituency retained a nationalist majority, and one of its representatives, Cahir Healy, was a pro-Treaty Sinn Féiner who was interned until 1924. Tom Harbison was also returned again, but seldom attended. As early as April 1923 T.P. again asked Dillon if he 'could take some action . . . which would force that wretch Harbison to attend or to

---

[19] O'Connor to Dillon, 28 Nov. 1922 (DP 6744/903).
[20] O'Connor to Dillon, 24 Nov. 1919 (DP 6742/710).
[21] O'Connor to Dillon, 17 June 1921 (DP 6744/845).
[22] O'Connor to Dillon, 28 Nov. 1922 (DP 6744/903).
[23] Devlin to Dillon, 24 Dec. 1922 (DP 6730/299); O'Connor to Devlin, 28 Jan. 1924, copy (DP 6744/947).
[24] *IN*, 21 Nov. 1922.

give way to Joe?'[25] Dillon again counselled caution. T.P. acknowledged that 'the sooner Joe is able to get back to the Ulster Parliament the better; but I agree with him that as long as his hands are tied by the abstention policy of the Sinn Féiners it will be impossible for him to do so'.[26] In August 1923 Devlin was also pressed 'by an extremely influential deputation' to stand for the Dáil in Dublin North. After some thought he declined, wisely in Dillon's view.[27] In 1927 he was again pressed to stand in Dublin by his former parliamentary colleague Alfred Byrne and by former Lord Mayor Lorcan Sherlock, for 'you will be the living embodiment of the unity of Ireland'. Devlin, however, declined once more, for 'if I do that, the poor people of Belfast, who have stood by me loyally for the past thirty years and who are undergoing the tortures of the damned will, I fear, think I am taking this opportunity of slipping out of a difficult position'.[28]

The prospect of a further UK general election in December 1923 again raised T.P.'s hopes of getting Devlin back to Westminster. 'We can in no way help our people in the North of Ireland through the House of Commons without him,' he told Dillon. He reiterated his opinion that 'Harbison is useless', and sought the support of Dillon and of Devlin himself for his plan to write to the *Irish News* calling for Devlin's nomination for Fermanagh and Tyrone.[29] But Dillon still thought that a public intervention by T.P. would be 'a great mistake, and would put Joe in a very unenviable position if, as I fear might be the case, it were not followed by an invitation to stand'. The priests in the two counties, thought Dillon, 'are poisonous against the old Party, all the more bitter because they are *beginning* to realize the hideous mess into which they have helped to land the Catholics of the six counties'. Devlin himself was again laid up with one of the bad chills that increasingly pursued him in his later years.[30] His name went forward, but Dillon later reported that proceedings at the nominating convention in Omagh were 'mortifying'. Its membership, he said, was 'hand-picked by the priests'. He heard privately that, while the local Nationalists all 'recognized that Harbison was no good . . . he was the only man by whom they could keep Devlin out'.[31] Harbison and the still-interned Cahir Healy held the seats. The west Ulster nationalist press interpreted the result as a demand for the immediate establishment of the Boundary Commission, while the *Irish News* continued to argue instead for a settlement by consent.[32]

The outcome of the election was the return of a minority Labour Government, for the first time in British history. T. P. O'Connor speculated briefly about

---

[25] O'Connor to Dillon, 25 Apr. 1923 (DP 6744/927).

[26] O'Connor to Dillon, 30 Apr. 1923 (DP 6744/928).

[27] Dillon to O'Connor, 31 Aug. 1923 (DP 6744/937).

[28] Speech by Sherlock at opening of Devlin Memorial Fund, *IN* 19 Jan. 1935; *The Times*, 19 Jan. 1934.

[29] O'Connor to Dillon, 14 Nov. 1923 (DP 6744/941).

[30] Dillon to O'Connor, 16 Nov. 1923 (DP 6744/942).

[31] Dillon to O'Connor, 28 Nov.1923 (DP 6744/943).

[32] NEBB, 'Weekly Digest', 16 Dec. 1923 (Blythe Papers, P24/204/15).

being invited to join the new government and being elevated to the House of Lords, in which case he would have proposed Devlin for his Liverpool seat.[33] T.P. was in fact not offered a government position, and declined a peerage on Dillon's advice, though he later accepted a privy councillorship. A few weeks later T.P. wrote to Devlin regretting that the two of them had not joined the Labour Party 'two or three years ago . . . They always showed eagerness to have you in their ranks; and your rise to cabinet position, which would have been easily at your service, would again have been a historic memento of the final triumph of Ireland over her enemies . . . Your absence from the House . . . is a constant worry to me.'[34] In March 1924 Devlin told T.P. that if Labour were to offer him a seat,

especially in the Glasgow region, he would be willing to take it; not from any keen desire to enter British politics, but from an intense desire to have something to occupy his mind. He finds Belfast pretty intolerable at the moment and I suppose Dublin is even worse. The Labour people would be delighted to have him, but . . . their difficulty is to find a seat.[35]

But in his more reflective moments T.P. doubted whether Devlin was really interested in a new career in the British Labour Party. 'He put it quite frankly to me, saying that the one temptation to him was to escape from the want of occupation, from which he is suffering very badly. Tho' his health has enormously improved, he is very depressed. He complains that even in Belfast he is isolated.'[36]

In October 1924 there was yet another Westminster election. Harbison expressed his willingness to resign and support Devlin. T.P. thought that if Devlin 'has the tenacity he can go down to the people of Tyrone and overcome all the rascals who have intrigued him out of his place . . . You had better see Nugent, who will have the initiative which Joe lacks.'[37] But meanwhile de Valera announced that the Anti-Treaty Sinn Féin Party would contest all the NI seats.[38] Dillon predicted correctly that, 'unless Devlin has changed very much since I saw him last, he will take no risks. Of course I have all along held the view that if he had adopted a bold policy he could have overcome all opposition in Ulster. But his attitude during the last four years has taken all the fight out of his friends.' Devlin declined to stand and Dillon later thought he would have been beaten.[39] The Nationalists and Pro-Treatyites put up no candidates, even in Fermanagh and Tyrone, where Sinn Féin obtained a humiliating 13 per cent of the vote, thus handing the seats to the Unionists. This bizarre intervention by de Valera thus had the effect of minimizing the anti-partition vote on the eve of

[33] O'Connor to Dillon, 24 Dec. 1923 (DP 6744/944).
[34] O'Connor to Devlin, 28 Jan. 1924, copy (DP 6744/947).
[35] O'Connor to Dillon, 24 Mar. 1924 (DP 6744/950).
[36] O'Connor to Dillon, 7 Apr. 1924 (DP 6744/953).
[37] O'Connor to Dillon, 10 Oct. 1924 (DP 6744/966).
[38] De Valera to MacEntee, 7 and 20 Oct. 1924 (MacEntee Papers, P67/82, 85).
[39] Dillon to O'Connor, 13 Oct. and 11 Dec. 1924 (DP 6744/967, 970).

the Boundary Commission. In West Belfast, the seat that Devlin had decided not to contest in 1922, the Protestant majority ensured the return of a Unionist, but the Northern Ireland Labour Party (NILP) candidate secured more than 40 per cent of the vote against Sinn Féin's 5 per cent. Alongside the talk of his possible candidature in Fermanagh and Tyrone, a rumour appeared in *The Times* that an invitation would be made to Devlin—'who has already intimated his readiness to stand'—to run again in Liverpool Exchange. Four days later, however, it listed Devlin, as a 'Nationalist', among the withdrawals.[40] Devlin's brief appearance in Liverpool in fact gave T.P. a great deal of anxiety. The whole business was like a 'faction fight', he told Dillon, related to the battle over the municipal elections between two sets of Irish Catholics—the one standing as Nationalists, the other as Labour.[41] Devlin found this Liverpool experience 'extremely mortifying'. But Dillon thought that 'the time is quite close at hand when Joe could take over the leadership of the Nationalists of Ulster and form a powerful party in the Ulster Parliament'.[42]

THE BOUNDARY COMMISSION

On 2 January 1923 the former Southern Unionist and Lord Chancellor James Campbell, now Lord Glenavy and the elected leader of the Free State Senate, wrote a long private letter to his old parliamentary colleague James Craig. The Irregulars in the South, he said, would promptly end the civil war if the Northern Government would agree to 'come in' to the Free State. He proposed that nine-county Ulster be reconstituted, that it give up its representation at Westminster, and, instead, send representatives to the Dáil. In return, nine-county Ulster 'would be allowed to retain its own Parliament, judiciary, police and own public departments for the conduct and administration of local self-government and, most important of all', would be granted the right of absolute veto, by a vote of the majority of its representatives in the Free State Parliament, over the application to Ulster of any law passed by that Parliament for the rest of Ireland. The prospect, said Glenavy, was 'a period of unexampled prosperity', whereas the alternative was that 'not only will the North have to defend its territory with armed resistance but also I fear it will be left by England to do so with its own resources, especially if and when a Labour Government has control of that country'.[43] It was an approach that had been floated on several occasions since the days of the Irish Convention in 1917–18, but it was an interesting and provocative proposal to come from a Southern Unionist with a past reputation as a hardliner. Craig was unimpressed, however, and the letter was leaked to the

---

[40] *The Times*, 13 and 17 Oct. 1924.   [41] O'Connor to Dillon, 1 Dec. 1924 (DP 6744/969).
[42] Dillon to O'Connor, 11 Dec. 1924 (DP 6744/970).
[43] Lord Glenavy to Craig, 2 Jan. 1923 (*Irish Times*, Cabinet Papers, Supplement, 21 Apr. 1976).

press. In the opinion of Kevin O'Shiel, the Free State cabinet legal adviser, this started 'Devlin and Co. and the *Irish News* on the war path against us'. The line being developed by the *Irish News* at that time—arising from the situation of the Belfast and east Ulster nationalists—was that the Boundary Commission should be dropped and new negotiations opened. O'Shiel, a west Ulster Sinn Féiner by background, continued that, 'save for the city of Belfast', the UIL has completely disappeared. The Ancient Order of Hibernians (AOH), on the other hand, had been able to hold its 'badly shattered framework' together through its status as a friendly society. Again it was strongest in Belfast. O'Shiel thought that Devlin planned to 'raise the Catholic standard once again', and revive the constitutional movement. Having achieved this, he thought Devlin would try 'to bring off a special agreement, independent of us, with Sir James Craig in lieu of the Boundary Commission and on the basis of established partition'.[44]

The Nationalists in Belfast, who could see no prospect of saving themselves through the Boundary Commission, indeed began to regroup. In March and April 1923 Devlin held meetings with leading members of the UIL and AOH. A deputation was appointed to seek an interview with Cosgrave, but he was advised by his staff that to see a 'Hibernian deputation' from the North 'would be tantamount to admitting that Devlin has the [Free State] Government's ear, and would have a very bad effect on our own supporters'.[45] Public meetings were held around the province, organized by J. D. Nugent. Police information was that the object was to promote unity among Catholics and nationalists of all sections, 'so that they will not be hostile to the Nationalist members of the Northern Parliament taking their seats'. On the other hand, it was believed that Nationalist opinion generally, and that of Devlin in particular, was that there should be no participation unless proportional representation (PR) was retained. Bishop MacRory, it was reported, 'has decided not to interfere one way or the other'.[46] Dillon thought that 'things are shaping very well in Ulster', with the speeches of Devlin and Nugent having 'a powerful effect'.[47] However, in July the Royal Ulster Constabulary (RUC) reported that efforts to secure Catholic unity and recognition of the Northern Government had proved abortive, 'owing to the strong opposition of the extreme section'. Many Nationalists maintained that 'their failure is due in a large measure to the apathy of the Roman Catholic clergy'.[48] The Catholic bishops may have been aware of this problem, for in October they made a declaration that 'the time has come for our people to organize openly on constitutional lines'.[49]

---

[44] 'Memorandum to Executive Council of the IFS', by Kevin O'Sheil, n.d. [early 1923] (MacNeill Papers, LA1/H/94).
[45] 'Memorandum to Executive Council of the IFS', 21 Apr. 1923 (MacNeill Papers, LA1/H/92).
[46] Dist. Insp. E. Gilfillan to Minister of Home Affairs, 10 Apr. 1923 (PRONI, CAB 4).
[47] Dillon to O'Connor, 12 May 1923 (DP 6744/931).
[48] Gilfillan to Home Affairs, 5 July 1923 (PRONI, CAB 4).   [49] *IN*, 12 Oct. 1923.

When Hugh McCartan of the Free State's North Eastern Boundary Bureau reported on the situation in Belfast and Derry, he found that the prevailing feeling among the Catholic minority was that 'the Free State took no interest in their position'. He met many former Treaty supporters who had become Republicans 'on account of the Free State's apparent lack of interest in their position and the humiliations heaped upon them'. George Martin, a Belfast nationalist who advised McCartan, thought that, if the Free State Government took the initiative in forming a new Irish unity movement, the Free State Sinn Féiners ('who are a great majority in the city') would be willing to cooperate with the Devlinites, and even accept Devlin's leadership. He thought also that 'the Republicans would tend to gravitate towards such a movement'. Overall, McCartan's impression was 'that the disorganized and apathetic condition of the Catholic minority points to the need for some form of organization, based on current needs'.[50] In July and September 1923 Dáil speakers again commented that their colleagues were neglecting the interests of the Northern minority.[51] Cosgrave made a major speech on the boundary question early in August 1924, but agreed with the intervention of one TD, who commented that 'the nationalists of the six counties seemed to be only a secondary consideration with some of the deputies'.[52]

The death of Dan McCann in November 1923 hit Devlin very hard. He had been 'above all others Joe's support and stay in Ulster', wrote Richard McGhee, who told Dillon that Devlin 'looked ghastly' at the funeral, and was too unwell to go to the graveside.[53] But by March 1924 Devlin had recovered his energy, and took the opportunity of the rally held on the sixth anniversary of Redmond's death, attended by 25,000, to make a strong political speech. The Nationalist Party had, he said, for six years been silent and subject to 'outrageous calumnies', but, he said, 'we are vindicated by our calumniators . . . The time has come for the Irish people to ask themselves whether it would not have been better to have had patience for a little longer.'[54] The *Northern Whig* thought that the Catholics of the six counties now had 'no more desire to be citizens of the Free State than to become subjects of the Amir of Afghanistan'.[55] But this was a Unionist delusion. Although frequently demoralized by the apparent failure of the Free State Government to make any progress on the partition question, the border nationalists were still most anxious for action on the Boundary Commission, which many of them still saw as their salvation. The nationalists of Belfast, who had no such hope, wanted to see some revision of the Treaty proposals. Some of the bishops remained optimistic. Mulhern, for instance, thought that the Boundary Commission would soon 'create a stir', and 'if the North East is

[50] NEBB, 'Report on Visit to Belfast and Derry', 6 Nov. 1923 (Blythe Papers, P24/204).
[51] Hopkinson, *Green against Green*, 251.
[52] *IN*, cited in NEBB, 'Summary of Press Comments', 14 Aug. 1924 (Blythe Papers, P24/204/27).
[53] McGhee to Dillon, 11 Nov. 1923 (DP 6757/1079).   [54] *Irish Independent*, 10 Mar. 1924.
[55] NEBB, 'Weekly Digest', 28 July, 1924 (Blythe Papers, P24/204/120).

deprived of any of its territory it is hard to see how it can carry on'.[56] Devlin was more realistic, declaring that he could not enter the Ulster Parliament until the boundaries were finalized, 'but when they are fixed I am ready to recognize them, and would do nothing to force the Ulster State, so set up, into an Irish State against her will'.[57]

In late 1922 the security situation in the North was improving steadily, while in the South things appeared to be getting worse. Dillon told T.P. that Craig's government

have succeeded in restoring law and order, and since de Valera's gunmen [in fact also Collins's gunmen] have been withdrawn for service in the South the pogrom and murders have ceased, and I am assured by men on whom I can rely that Catholics in Belfast and throughout the six counties can go about their business in perfect safety, and can rely on impartial protection from the police. As you may remember, I frequently warned you at the time—the Belfast atrocities were to a *very extent* [*sic*] deliberately provoked for propaganda purposes... And I am convinced that if the true inner history of the Belfast disturbances could be written, it would prove to be one of the most loathsome and infamous records of the hideous movement which has reduced Ireland to a state of savagery.[58]

Referring to the later stages of the civil war and the large number of executions in the Free State, Dillon observed that 'at the moment consultation would be perfectly worthless—you might as well consult [about] how to build a skyscraper on a bottomless, shaking bog'.[59] A Free State cabinet paper took a not dissimilar view. An attempt to activate the Boundary Commission clause would not settle the civil war, for, the paper argued, those Irregulars who were driven by 'their detestation of partition do not form one per cent of the whole... As for the de Valera, or non-doctrinaire republican section, they are as strongly committed to partition as we are.' While the civil war continued, the paper maintained, there was no way that the British Government would agree to the transfer of any Northern territory to 'the chaos and disorder of the South'.[60]

The election of a minority Labour Government to power in Britain in December 1923 caused some alarm in Ulster Unionist circles, and by the summer of 1924 the MacDonald and Cosgrave governments had begun to set up the Boundary Commission. Devlin and his old colleagues were not optimistic. Dillon thought the Boundary Commission clause was one of Lloyd George's 'worst swindles', and effectively a conspiracy between Lloyd George, Griffith, and Collins 'for the purpose of humbugging the Irish people and enabling Griffith,

[56] Mulhern to Hagan, 16 Jan. 1923 (JHP, HAG1/1923/25).
[57] *Liverpool Daily Post & Mercury*, 9 Nov. 1922.
[58] Dillon to O'Connor, 8 Feb. 1923 (DP 6744/915).
[59] Dillon to O'Connor, 10 Feb. 1923 (DP 6744/916).
[60] 'Memorandum to Executive Council of the IFS', n.d. [*c.* Dec.1922] (MacNeill Papers, LA1/H/93).

Collins & Co. to assert they had not agreed to partition'.[61] In fact, Dillon pointed out, it was the Irish Party that had 'refused to consent to *any* scheme of *permanent* partition, or to the setting up of an Ulster Government'. Devlin shared Dillon's view that the setting-up of a Boundary Commission would not remedy the present situation.[62] 'It is an intolerable insult', Devlin wrote, 'that our destinies are being determined without a single representative of ours being consulted.'[63] Speaking at an AOH rally at Dundalk on 15 August, he attacked any form of boundary as 'a new pale'. He placed his emphasis on 'homes for the homeless and work for the unemployed . . . It was by working along ameliorative and constructive lines in that way that they should break down all unnatural barriers.'[64]

Meanwhile in Britain, Churchill, recently returned to the Conservative Party after twenty years as a Liberal, was working hard with his new colleagues to show that Article XII had always been intended to provide for 'adjustments' to the boundary rather than major transfers of territory. A letter from Lord Birkenhead dated January 1922 was produced, which indicated clearly that this had been the intention of the British Treaty representatives.[65] Lloyd George, at Churchill's request, publicly confirmed this interpretation, and Birkenhead's letter was published in the press on 8 September 1924.[66] In a speech at the Oxford Union, Kevin O'Higgins, a senior Free State minister, pointed out that Article XIV of the Treaty offered the Northern Government an alternative to Article XII. Under it, the territory delineated by the 1920 Act and the substantial local autonomy that it conferred could be retained if the Northern Government agreed to accept the same relationship with the Free State Government as existed with Westminster under the 1920 Act.[67] Churchill followed this up with O'Higgins, who agreed, with Free State Government approval, to a confidential meeting with Craig.[68] This was home rule within home rule again, the approach favoured by Devlin since 1913, advocated by Horace Plunkett in 1918 and again in 1920–1, and put forward by Glenavy in January 1923. The prospect of the Boundary Commission was nothing other than alarming to east Ulster Nationalists, and Devlin's Armagh friend Nugent 'startled' T. P. O'Connor by throwing out 'the suggestion that in return for leaving the six counties as they are, Craig might be ready to make . . . concessions which would safeguard the minority—a retention of proportional representation; re-arrangement of the constituencies'.[69] But this approach, let alone home rule within home rule, was not pressed by any British government during these years and—in the absence of

[61] Dillon to O'Connor, 1 Aug. 1924 (DP 6744/959).
[62] Dillon to O'Connor, 21 Aug. 1924 (DP 6744/962).   [63] *IN*, 19 June 1924.
[64] *Derry Journal*, 18 Aug. 1924.   [65] Churchill to Carson, 12 Aug. 1924 (CP 2/570/17).
[66] Churchill to Balfour and Carson, 1 Sept. 1924 (CP 2/570/98).
[67] Speech to Oxford Union, n.d. [1924], Kevin O'Higgins (CP 2/135/125).
[68] O'Higgins to Churchill, 24 Nov. 1924 (CP 2/135/176).
[69] O'Connor to Dillon, 14 Aug. 1924 (DP 6744/960).

such pressure—was clearly less attractive to the Northern Ireland Government than the status quo.

The Boundary Commission was at last constituted on 29 October 1924, with Richard Feetham, a South African judge, as the British-appointed chairman, Eoin MacNeill representing the Free State Government, and the Unionist journalist J. R. Fisher appointed by the British Government after Craig declined to nominate a representative. The North Eastern Boundary Bureau (NEBB) compiled *The Handbook of the Ulster Question* to publicize the facts of the case and to assist local witnesses in preparing their statements. The NEBB's contact with Northern nationalists was through the appointment of eight solicitors for the various districts. George Martin was appointed for Belfast. His job, as the sole agent not responsible for a 'border' district, was to prepare the case of the Belfast Catholics 'against their treatment by the Northern Government'.[70] Once the Commission was in operation, the NEBB began a series of consultations with border nationalists, mainly conducted by its secretary, E. M. Stephens, who sent a number of reports to the Free State cabinet. In Armagh City he found that 'the people were nervous of any boundary', for they feared—even though they had a small majority in the urban area—that they would be cut off from their south Armagh hinterland. In Newry, which had been the centre of Frank Aiken's Anti-Treaty activities, Stephens found most of the Sinn Féiners to be 'republican in their tendencies', which left the boundary issue more in the hands of the old Nationalist Party.[71] In Fermanagh, the nationalists were 'very sceptical about receiving fair treatment from the Boundary Commission, and fear a policy of rectification which would dismember the county . . . and leave a large portion of the nationalist majority under the jurisdiction of the Northern Parliament'. In Magherafelt, the main town in South Derry, 'the whole district was apathetic on the boundary question, as there was no chance of the area being included in the Free State'.[72]

While the Commission was sitting, in April 1925, the NI electorate went to the polls for the first time since 1921, which terminated the abstention pledge that Devlin had given to de Valera. Following the fiasco of the Westminster election of October 1924, it was the view of most on the nationalist side, including the Free State cabinet, that the election should be fought and the anti-partition vote maximized, in view of the forthcoming decision of the Boundary Commission. Devlin called for nationalist unity, and agreed to stand again. The *Irish News* reported that he could have had a Dublin seat in the Dáil for the asking, but 'his first duty and highest allegiance are to his own persecuted, victimized people'. On the same day he attended a conference of

[70] NEBB, 'Final Report, 26 February 1926' (Blythe Papers, P24/205/97–112).
[71] NEBB, 'Report of Visit to Armagh and Newry, 18 & 19 Dec. 1924' (Blythe Papers, P24/205/23–9).
[72] NEBB, 'Report of Visit to Enniskillen, 28 Apr., and to Magherafelt, 2 June 1925' (Blythe Papers, P24/205/40–3).

nationalist representatives from the six counties, at which it was agreed to present a united front.[73] In his election address he declared that 'permanent abstention means permanent disfranchisement', and that his aim was the promotion of Irish unity by conciliation and goodwill. On 29 March there was what the *News* described as 'a massive demonstration' in Celtic Park, which 'closed a bitter chapter of dissension and vision' and opened 'a new era of unity and strength for our people'. Devlin was, the paper declared, cheered in Protestant Sandy Row as 'the man for the workers'. Devlin worked in West Belfast throughout the campaign, but yet another 'chill' put an end to his outdoor meetings.[74] The cost of the £150 deposits for the Nationalist candidates was met by the Free State Government.[75]

The old Parliament of forty Unionists, six Nationalists, and six Sinn Féiners was replaced by thirty-two Unionists, five Independent Unionists, three NILP, ten Nationalists, and two Republican abstainers. This was a setback for the Unionist Party, and strengthened its resolve to abolish PR in elections to the regional Parliament, as it had already done for municipal elections. It also marked the beginning of a union between the Devlinites and the Pro-Treaty Sinn Féiners, six of the former being nominated at a convention in Belfast, and five of the latter being nominated at constituency conventions. Standing simply as 'Nationalists', they were all successful except Nugent in Armagh, who was defeated by a Republican. The combined Nationalists took 24 per cent of the province-wide poll, while the Republicans, who ran five candidates in addition to an unopposed de Valera, took 5 per cent. In West Belfast Devlin easily topped the poll with 36 per cent of first-preference votes (20 per cent in 1921), the Republican, by contrast, being eliminated with 6 per cent. Of Devlin's large surplus of 7,661 votes, 57 per cent went to the NILP candidate William McMullen, who had created quite a stir during the previous year by easily defeating a Nationalist candidate in the Board of Guardians election in Catholic Smithfield.[76] Of Devlin's surplus 19 per cent went to an Independent Unionist and 7 per cent to the Unionists, which suggests that he had attracted a significant number of Protestant votes. Only 17 per cent of his surplus went to the Republican. At his victory parade Devlin declared that 'the most blessed work to be done now would be to bury sectarian feuds and bitterness'.[77]

Two weeks after the Northern Parliament reconvened, Devlin and his Co. Antrim colleague T. S. McAlister became the first Nationalist MPs to take their seats. Immediately Devlin began to raise a series of non-sectarian social issues to do with the new Land Purchase Bill, lack of parity with British social welfare provision, workers' rights, and unemployment. As the Boundary Commission dragged slowly towards its conclusion, Devlin condemned the 'passion-provoking

[73] *IN*, 18, 21, and 23 Mar. 1925.   [74] Ibid., 25, 30, and 31 Mar., 1 and 3 Apr. 1925.
[75] Harbison to C. Healy, 12 Nov. 1927 (CHP, D2991/B/9).   [76] *IN*, 31 May 1924.
[77] Ibid., 7 Apr. 1925.

harangues of ministers'. He also raised Catholic rights issues, such as membership of the judiciary.[78] During the autumn session he made great play with the high cost of the government's plans for the proposed new parliament buildings at Stormont: 'a palace for politicians', at the expense of much-needed new housing for workers.[79] Such was Devlin's renewed energy that even the staunchly Protestant Coleraine Chamber of Commerce, incensed at what they regarded as the government's preferential treatment for Belfast business and the failure of the Co. Londonderry MPs to speak up for them, proposed asking Devlin to take up their case.[80] In a speech opposing the proposed taxation of cinemas, he declared that 'during my enforced absence from public life I frequented picture houses three or four times a week. Unfortunately I can't go there now. I come here instead.'[81] On 3 May he gave a garden party at Crawfordsburn, Co. Down, for his election workers, at which he declared that 'I have not been so happy for a quarter of a century'.[82]

Dillon thought that, if Devlin had gone into the Dáil or joined the British Labour Party in 1923, 'his whole future would have been ruined. As it is he has a very great career ahead of him . . . Cosgrave is plainly extremely anxious to cultivate friendly relations with Joe and the Northern Nationalists, whereas some time ago he was reported to me to have spoken with contempt and dislike of Joe.'[83] T.P. thought that after the election Devlin 'looked at least ten years younger'.[84] Border nationalists, on the other hand, reported E. M. Stephens to Blythe, 'tend to interpret the co-operation [by the Free State Government] with Mr Devlin for the purpose of the last election as an indication that no good result is expected from the Commission'.[85] Stephens advised Blythe that something should be done to organize Northern nationalism before the enthusiasm generated by the Boundary Commission had time to die away. But it took another year and more before all the border Nationalist representatives followed Devlin and McAlister into the Northern Parliament.[86] Meanwhile the Boundary Commission report was shelved and not officially released for forty-four years, though its recommendations were leaked in the *Morning Post* on 7 November 1925. Very minor adjustments were recommended, mainly in favour of the nationalists in South Armagh, but also in favour of unionists in East Donegal. In lieu of boundary changes, the Free State Government won no concession on Ulster nor any strengthening of Catholic and nationalist rights, but accepted a favourable modification of the Free State's financial relationship with Britain. MacNeill resigned from the Commission, and Cosgrave wrote to him to 'repeat what I said in the Dáil, that the task set the Boundary Commission

[78] *IN*, 3 and 8 Sept., 22 Oct. 1925.   [79] Ibid., 4 Nov. 1925.
[80] Ibid., 16 Jan. 1926.   [81] Ibid., 13 May 1925.
[82] Ibid., 4 May 1925.   [83] Dillon to O'Connor, 12 Apr. 1925 (DP 6744/977).
[84] O'Connor to Dillon, 10 May 1925 (DP 6744/978).
[85] NEBB, 'Report of Visit to Enniskillen, 28 Apr. 1925' (Blythe Papers, P24/205/40–3).
[86] NEBB, 'Report of Visit to Omagh, 22 June 1925' (Blythe Papers, P24/205/68–71).

was to secure Divine Solution by human agency'.[87] Half a century later Ernest Blythe recalled that

most of us felt that the broad prospect of national reunion had not been seriously injured [and] that if a wise policy were pursued, we might hope that in forty or fifty years the two parts of Ireland would be coming closer to reunion. Unfortunately the great majority of Northern Catholics, egged on from the South, clung to a policy of barren recalcitrance which kept Protestants and Catholics in separate camps and prevented all political progress.[88]

NORTHERN MINORITY LEADER

The Unionists were not happy about their losses at the 1925 election, and in March 1927 Craig announced his intention to abolish PR. Addressing the Orange Order on 12 July, he declared that 'there are certain members in our House of Commons who should never have been elected . . . Mr Devlin and his Party are the natural opposition . . . Why then should any loyalist constituency add strength to it and weaken the influence of my colleagues and myself?'[89] Devlin attacked the Bill vigorously as 'a mean, contemptible and callous attempt by the majority to rob the minority'.[90] Although it would not reduce Nationalist representation as such, it was calculated to reduce the overall size of the opposition significantly. Effectively it restored the centrality of the sectarian divide. This factor, together with the need of the Nationalists to build as much unity as they could between the various nationalist factions, led to a gradual downplaying of the rhetoric in favour of working-class unity and a greater emphasis on Catholic unity, which focused to a considerable extent on cultivating the Catholic Church. Early in 1927, for instance, the editor of the *Irish News*, Tim McCarthy, approached MacRory to secure an imprimatur for his paper. MacRory replied that, while the paper had 'done excellent work on many occasions', it was not Catholic as such, but a 'strenuous supporter of political views that command themselves to only a section of our people . . . I could not identify myself in any way with your paper without offending and disgusting many of my people.'[91] Clearly there was work to be done if the clergy were to be brought onside.

The failure of the Boundary Commission affected Northern nationalist strategy in two ways. It destroyed whatever confidence they had left in Cosgrave's government, a development encouraged by de Valera's withdrawal from Sinn Féin and his establishment of Fianna Fáil, which entered the Dáil in 1927. It also

---

[87] Cosgrave to MacNeill, 22 Dec. 1925 (MacNeill Papers, LA1/G/263).
[88] E. Blythe to T. Ryle Dwyer, 4 May 1970 (Blythe Papers, P24/1528).
[89] Copy of speech in Government Papers (PRONI, PM/9/18).
[90] NI Parl. Deb., H.C., viii. 2280 (25 Oct. 1927).
[91] MacRory to McCarthy, 15 Mar. 1927 (MacRory Papers, xiv. 6).

removed any practical reason for remaining outside the Northern Parliament. In January 1926 Devlin appealed to the nine remaining Nationalist MPs to take their seats. On 7 February Co. Down Nationalists voted for their local MP, the Devlinite Patrick O'Neill, to take his seat. The meeting was chaired by Devlin's friend and holiday companion Revd Frank O'Hare, who declared that the 'disastrous experience of the last ten years' should be a warning to Northern nationalists of 'the absolute necessity for self-reliance'.[92] A month later a conference of Derry City and County nationalists called on the Nationalist George Leeke and the former Pro-Treaty Sinn Féiner Basil McGuckin to take their seats.[93] There were also signs that popular nationalist opinion was swinging back towards the constitutional movement. Membership of the AOH, having reached a high point in 1913–14, declined gradually between 1916 and 1923. During the first six months of 1926, however, there was a substantial increase in Irish membership, mainly in the North.[94] But in Armagh and in Fermanagh and Tyrone another two sessions of Parliament were to elapse before the five remaining MPs and their constituents could agree to take their seats. Cahir Healy told William O'Brien of Cork that the struggle was essentially between the priests and the AOH Board of Erin.[95]

Reflecting on the situation at the end of 1926, Cahir Healy wrote that it was because

> we know the Northern mind much better than either Collins, Griffith or de Valera that we realized then that the big difficulty lay in Belfast and not in London. For years . . . we have had the opposite preached . . . The Free State leaders told us our anchor was Article XII: when the time of trial came they cut our cable and launched us, rudderless, into the hurricane without guarantee or security even for our ordinary civic rights.[96]

But, as 1927 progressed, the five remaining nationalists had still not taken their seats. Harbison told Healy in August 1927 that he thought 'each should decide for himself' and that 'while going to Belfast is utterly repugnant to me I am afraid we must make virtue out of necessity'.[97] Healy urged that they all act together. Alex Donnelly MP, the Omagh solicitor, was less enthusiastic, but agreed to joint action. A few days later, a Fermanagh county meeting voted that Healy and his fellow MP John McHugh should attend, which forced Donnelly to take similar action.[98] In Armagh J. H. Collins obtained support for entry from various parish meetings.[99] At last Devlin had a full group of MPs behind him in Parliament. What he did not have was an organized political party.

In September 1926 a new—though short-lived—political party, the Irish National League, was founded in the Free State by Willie Redmond, W. G. Fallon

[92] *IN*, 'Retrospect', 31 Dec. 1926.   [93] Ibid.
[94] Ibid., 16 Aug. 1926.   [95] W. O'Brien to C. Healy, 4 Mar. 1926 (CHP, D2991/A/6).
[96] Draft letter from C. Healy, n.d. [Dec. 1926] (CHP, D2991/A/1/12).
[97] Harbison to Healy, 19 Aug. 1927 (CHP, D2991/A/1/19).
[98] A. Donnelly to Healy, 10 Sept., 4 and 22 Oct. 1927 (CHP, D2991/A/1/22, 25, 39).
[99] J. H. Collins to Healy, 6 Oct. 1927 (CHP, D2991/A/130).

and several former MPs.[100] Fallon had hoped that Devlin would 'come in' once the new movement had shown 'that we mean business', but Devlin's reply was firmly negative: 'I made it clear to all concerned that I did not intend to enter southern politics, and therefore I hope you will understand that on no account can I take part in the new movement now or in the future.'[101] Thus, when Devlin and Cahir Healy at last got together in 1928 to establish the National League of the North, the common name was the only bond between the two organizations. Healy took the initiative, with Devlin as the figurehead. In January Healy drew up a draft policy. The primary aim was 'the ultimate unity of Ireland', but they sought also 'to endeavour to allay the honest fears of our fellow-countrymen in the North as to the effects of national unity by making it clear to them that we ask merely for equality of opportunity for all classes and creeds and the good of our common country'.[102] Devlin replied on 9 January that he had been 'laid up since Christmas with the worst cold I have ever had', but he approved of Healy's draft statement.[103] Healy had meanwhile obtained the support of the Fermanagh Nationalist Registration Association, and he told Devlin that 'some folks, lay and clerical, who used not to understand you, are completely changed. Unanimously they agreed that if a Party were formed you should be the pivot.'[104] Healy continued with the work, but Devlin remained sick for several weeks.

Links with the new Fianna Fáil Party were quickly established. Seán Lemass and Seán T. O'Kelly, leading members of the Party, requested a meeting with the Northern Nationalist leaders in Belfast on 10 February 1928. Healy hoped that Devlin would be able to join him, but Devlin had undergone 'another attack—this time more serious than the last—and have been in bed ever since'.[105] The meeting went ahead without him. Meanwhile Healy was much encouraged by meetings that he and his colleagues had had with bishops and other clerics, and told Devlin that 'I honestly think we have caught the tide at the flood'.[106] 'I am more sorry than I can say', replied Devlin from a Dublin nursing home, 'that my illness should have taken place at a time when all the hopes of effective work were bright. I want to thank you for your loyal co-operation and spirit of patriotism which you have so splendidly shown since you came into the Northern Parliament . . . I am sorry you cannot depend on me for any help for some some time to come.'[107] Healy replied 'that you were never so necessary to the people of Ulster as today. There is nobody to take your place.'[108] By late

[100] *IN*, 13 Sept. 1926.
[101] Fallon to Devlin, 5 Aug. 1926, and Devlin to Fallon, 7 Aug. 1926 (Fallon Papers, 22583).
[102] Healy to Devlin, 5 Jan. 1928, encl. 'Draft Policy for a Northern National Party' (CHP, D2991/A/1/59, 117).
[103] Devlin to Healy, 9 Jan. 1928 (CHP, D2991/A/1/61).
[104] Healy to Devlin, 12 Jan. 1928 (CHP, D2991/A/1/60).
[105] Devlin to Healy, 7 Feb. 1928 (CHP, D2991/A/1/70).
[106] Healy to Devlin, 8 Feb. 1928 (CHP, D2991/A/1/75).
[107] Devlin to Healy, 20 Feb. 1928 (CHP, D2991/A/1/79).
[108] Healy to Devlin, 22 Feb. 1928 (CHP, D2991/A/1/78).

March the news was better: 'Joe is improving, and will be fit in a week or so,' wrote O'Neill to Healy on 21 March. In May the National League of the North was at last launched at a Convention in Belfast, with Devlin as President. To succeed, declared Devlin, 'their organization must be such as would appeal to every section of national thought in the North'.[109]

The League held a major demonstration in West Belfast on 29 July 1928. Its approach was attacked by the radical nationalist journal *Honesty*, which declared that 'the National League will have our support as far as it can go, but the National League does not go far enough. It aims more at the reform of the Belfast Parliament than it does at the eradication of the unconscionable crime that has made this Parliament possible.'[110] During the summer of 1928 branches were formed around the province, the initiative coming from the MPs, in collaboration with priests and others.[111] But the new organization did not stir the Nationalists into contesting additional seats in the NI general election of 1929, and at the end of that year the spread of the organization across the province was still fairly patchy.[112] In October 1928 Devlin declined to accept the role of Leader of the Opposition, on the grounds that he could not be a party 'to the setting up of two rival parties in Northern Ireland, one Protestant, the other Catholic'.[113] He continued to focus on social and economic issues, and to seek to maintain his links with the NILP, though in this respect he was some way removed from his colleagues. It does not appear to have been a major cause of dispute between them, although on one occasion J. J. McCarroll, proprietor of the *Derry Journal* (who became a Nationalist MP in 1929), wrote to Cahir Healy that 'Labour appears to be making the most of Mr Devlin's appearance at their [Belfast] function a few nights ago'. McCarroll had heard from one of those present that 'Devlin would contest a seat for Labour in England. If that is so it leaves one doubting exactly where one is. There may be nothing in it, but that is what is being said. Personally I have no objection to Labour, but both here and in the Free State they do things one could not stand for.'[114] What Healy may have done about this is not known, but two days later Devlin wrote him a short letter explaining that he would not be standing for Westminster in the West Belfast constituency: 'I have just got the figures for West Belfast: total register 80,000; Protestants 50,000, Catholics 30,000. I think this shows that the prospects of winning are rather hopeless.'[115] Perhaps as a result of this, Healy stood aside in the UK general election of

[109] *IN*, 29 May 1928.

[110] *Honesty*, Aug. 1928, press cutting; Devlin to Healy, 1 Sept. 1928 (CHP, D2991/A/1/93, 102).

[111] See, e.g., McAlister to Healy, 27 Aug. 1928 (CHP, D2991/A/1/119).

[112] Healy to M. Lynch of the *Ulster Herald*, 28 Dec. 1929 (CHP, D2991/B/9).

[113] Online PRONI, introduction to Cahir Healy Papers, by E. Phoenix and A. P. W. Malcomson, Feb. 1998.

[114] McCarroll to Healy, 18 Jan. 1929 (CHP, D2991/A/1/96).

[115] Devlin to Healy, 20 Jan. 1929 (CHP, D2991/A/1/99).

30 May 1929, and Devlin was returned for Fermanagh and Tyrone, alongside Harbison, without a contest.

Thus, after a seven-year absence, Devlin re-entered Parliament, led for the second time by a minority Labour Government. In the early months of that Parliament he took up the cause of unemployment in the coal-mining industry, as he had 'for some time been interested in developing the training of miners and their families on co-operative principles'. In this connection he was in contact with Horace Plunkett, who now ran a cooperative foundation, and who congratulated Devlin on regaining his dual parliamentary position, 'which will enable you to utilise your remarkable parliamentary gifts for the good of the workers to whom your life has been devoted'.[116] Harbison died in November 1930, and, in the following Westminster election in October 1931, Devlin and Healy were returned. In his speech of thanks to electors in Dungannon, Devlin declared that 'I shall go on continuing to act as I have acted in the past, with a single purpose in view, that is to serve the lowly and the humble, common people for whom I have laboured in the past and who have given me their unchanging confidence and loyalty during the vicissitudes of the past quarter of a century'.[117]

In the NI election of 1929, fought eight days before the Westminster contest, the situation was complicated by the abolition of PR. Earlier on there had been private discussions between Devlin and Craig regarding the boundaries of the forty-eight single-member seats which replaced the eleven multi-member territorial seats (the remaining seat, Queen's University, continued to return four members by PR). Devlin kept his fellow West Belfast MP, William McMullen of the NILP, informed of his talks with Craig. If he could get Craig to agree to the creation of three non-unionist seats in Belfast, he told McMullen, he would leave one free for him, but if Craig would agree only to two, then the Nationalists would want them both. The latter was in fact the outcome, and McMullen—who, though a Protestant, was strongly identified with anti-partitionism—thereupon told Devlin that he would oppose the Nationalist in whatever constituency Devlin himself was not standing. The following Sunday, McMullen recalled, Devlin made a strong attack on McMullen, ending with 'a frankly sectarian appeal'. McMullen sought to respond by dragging in the AOH and the old row with Bishop Henry, in an attempt to suggest that Devlin was not always such a loyal spokesman for Catholicism. In the event Devlin stood in the new constituency of Belfast Central, where he took 72 per cent of the poll in a straight fight with a Unionist, while McMullen was defeated in the Falls, with 44 per cent of the vote in a straight fight with a Nationalist. McMullen also believed that this fairly bitter contest spread into the Oldpark constituency of inner north Belfast,

[116] Secretary, Plunkett Foundation, to Plunkett, 19 Sept. 1929; Plunkett to Devlin, 24 Sept. 1929; Devlin to Plunkett, 28 Sept. 1929 (PF, DEV 9, 10, 11).
[117] *Dungannon Observer*, 31 Oct. 1931.

undermining Labour support in the small Catholic neighbourhoods of Court ward and the Marrowbone, where the NILP leader Sam Kyle lost his seat to a Unionist with 49 per cent of the vote.[118] The overall outcome of the election was a net gain of five seats for the Unionists, taking two each from the Independents and the NILP. Nationalist representation fell from 12 to 11, and the Republicans lost both their seats.

The abolition of PR therefore had exactly the effect that Craig's government had sought. The Belfast Nationalists had little choice but to retreat into the cocoon of a minority sectarian party, notwithstanding the non-sectarian social radicalism that Devlin had, quite sincerely, put in the forefront of campaigns throughout his career. As well as the fact that there were a number of specifically Catholic issues that the Party needed to represent, there was a double pressure to retain unity: on the one hand, the need to resist the lurking Republican challenge; on the other, the need to sustain the hard-won territorial unity of Nationalists across the province. Both of these, in turn, implied the need to keep the full support of the Catholic Church. A continued alliance with the NILP, which would have been electorally and politically beneficial to many Belfast Nationalists, had to give way to these other concerns. The Nationalist Party was, however, active in the early years of the new Parliament, especially with regard to the 1930 Education Bill, where they secured considerably improved funding for Catholic schools. But they became frustrated at their general lack of influence or impact, and Devlin led them out of the Northern Parliament in May 1932. Other reasons for this were a wish to avoid giving added legitimacy to the formal opening of the new parliamentary buildings at Stormont, together with both a boost in morale arising from the electoral success of Fianna Fáil in the South, and anxiety at the revival of Republicanism both North and South. Devlin told the House that 'you had opponents willing to co-operate. We did not seek office, we sought service . . . You went on the old political lines . . . relying on those religious differences and difficulties so that you could remain in office forever.'[119] By this time, the National League of the North had more or less withered away.

During the early 1930s the economies of both North and South were spiralling into deeper decline. Dawson Bates, the NI Minister of Home Affairs, advised his cabinet in July 1932 that 'unless some ameliorative measures are adopted there will be a large body of the population driven to desperation by poverty and hunger'.[120] In the South de Valera was now in power, while the IRA began to pay more attention to social questions and to the border. A reorganization of the Northern IRA had been attempted in 1924. The Belfast Brigade was re-formed, but its existence remained tenuous. A mass meeting of

---

[118] William McMullen interview; *IN*, 3 May 1929.
[119] NI Parl. Deb., HC, xiv. 44–5 (8 Mar. 1932).
[120] Cabinet memorandum, 8 July 1932 (PRONI, Cab. 4/304/21).

the entire republican movement in Belfast in the late 1920s was attended by fewer than forty people.[121] In 1931 Peter Carleton and William McMullen made an attempt to start Saor Eire in Belfast, but 'it never got off the ground'.[122] The Southern-based Army Council of the IRA, in a more militant version of the rhetoric that Joe Devlin had used throughout his career, urged Northern Republicans to use social agitation to break down barriers with the Protestant working class, while—displaying a wit for which paramilitary groups are not usually renowned—also issuing an address to the Orange Order shortly before 12 July: 'Fellow Countrymen and Women . . . You celebrate the victory of the Boyne. This battle was a victory of the then Pope and William of Orange; strange alliance for you to celebrate; strange victory for Catholics to resist!'[123] The reality on the streets of Belfast, however, was an increase in sectarian tension, beginning with the establishment of the militant Ulster Protestant League in 1931 and culminating in the lethal riots of 1935. Eoin MacNeill advised Devlin around this time, repeating the views that he and de Valera had expressed a decade earlier, that it would be 'a complete mistake . . . to regard the Unionists in the North as the opposite side . . . My advice to Mr Devlin was to . . . [hold] British policy responsible all through, from the working up of sectarian bitterness in the time of the United Irishmen down to the Act of 1920.'[124] At the same time the NI cabinet minister Sir Basil Brooke—later elevated to the peerage and Northern Ireland's Prime Minister for twenty years—was telling his Fermanagh supporters that 'Roman Catholics . . . were out with all their force and might to destroy the power and constitution of Ulster . . . He would appeal to loyalists therefore, wherever possible, to employ good Protestant lads and lasses.'[125] MacNeill had clearly been away from the North too long!

The exception to this general pattern of sectarian escalation was the Outdoor Relief Riot of October 1932. It was sparked off by popular protests on both the Falls and Shankill at the Belfast Board of Guardians' policy of refusing outdoor relief to large numbers of those unemployed who were no long eligible for unemployment insurance. Even where relief payments were made, they were in return for two-and-half days per week of compulsory labour on city projects. The payments, furthermore, were considerably less than those made to claimants in Britain. This was the only major riot in Belfast's long history of rioting that saw both communities acting together. Catholics and Protestants rioted simultaneously on the Falls and the Shankill, and there was some evidence of coordination. The outcome was that the Northern Government broke with the Westminster policy and implemented a series of public works schemes. Prominent

---

[121] C. Foley, *Legion of the Rearguard: The IRA and the Modern Irish State* (London, 1992), 83.
[122] U. MacEoin, *Survivors* (Dublin, 1980), 308–9.
[123] Foley, *Legion of the Rearguard*, 112.   [124] Martin and Byrne, *Scholar Revolutionary*, 273.
[125] *Fermanagh Times*, 13 July 1933.

in the riot was Tommy Geehan, an unemployed Belfast textile worker, associated with Larkin's Irish Workers' Party in the South, who had been on a sponsored trip to the USSR in 1929.[126] George Gilmore, a Dublin IRA leader and social activist, sought to get the IRA into a position to direct events during this crisis, but was unable to do so. On receiving his advice Dave Matthews, then O/C of the Belfast Battalion, told a colleague that 'this is Communist philosophy . . . and there is as much difference between Republicanism and Communism as there is between night and day'.[127]

Eamon Donnelly, at that time a Fianna Fáil official with special responsibility for Northern liaison, conducted a long campaign to get de Valera's Party involved in the North. Donnelly retained the hostility towards Devlin that many other former Sinn Féiners had lost, and by the later 1930s he had lost faith in de Valera and Fianna Fáil as well. But in February 1933 he helped to arrange for Devlin and Cahir Healy to hold a private meeting in Dublin with de Valera and Seán T. O'Kelly. Healy later recalled to de Valera that

we had not been attending the [Stormont] Parliament here for some time . . . We came up to ask you for admission into the Dáil as an alternative to attending here, but you did not see your way to concur in our request. Neither would you give us any direction as to what we ought to do regarding attendance here. In May of that year we . . . decided to go back to the House after the summer recess, but neither to become an official Opposition nor render a day-to-day attendance.[128]

Fianna Fáil thus joined Cumann na nGaedheal in *de facto* commitment to partition.

DECLINE

By the autumn of 1933 Devlin's state of mind and health were both on the decline. He spent most of September in Italy, including another ten-day pilgrimage to Rome and a holiday on the Neapolitan peninsula. He wrote to his friend Hannah Keating from Capri in September that he 'often hoped you were here to enjoy its surpassing beauty'. He nonetheless was finding it difficult to 'shake off the depression, for every time I think of the future I feel most unhappy. I know you will say that all this is absurd, but there it is . . . If I had been in a better mood I would have regarded the holiday as glorious.' Returning via London, Devlin stayed once more with the Keatings in Cricklewood, before returning to Belfast and, later in October, to Dublin on private business.[129]

[126] Foley, *Legion of the Rearguard*, 83.
[127] MacEoin, *Survivors*, 308; Paddy Devlin, *Yes We Have No Bananas: Outdoor Relief in Belfast, 1920–39* (Belfast, 1981).
[128] Cahir Healy to de Valera, 10 June 1956 (CHP, D 2991/B/139/8).
[129] Devlin to H. Keating, 16 and 20 Sept., 28 Oct. 1933 (PRONI, T/2307).

While in Dublin he told several old colleagues that he was not going back to the Northern Parliament:

My own friends in Belfast are very disturbed about it, and I am sorry on their account, for they are very genuine and sincere. I feel with them that my not going back creates an entirely new and not very hopeful situation. But however I may regret it and feel the situation I am more than ever convinced that it was the only course for me.[130]

Nonetheless Devlin was persuaded to stand again for Belfast Central in the NI general election in November. The main reason was that IRA Republicanism, boosted by fringe movements with radical social programmes, was reviving strongly, North and South, and there was a real fear amongst Nationalists that the Republicans could win Belfast Central—as they did indeed win South Armagh—against Nationalist opposition. The main hope of opponents of the IRA was that a number of Fianna Fáil candidates, including possibly President de Valera, would agree to stand. Cahir Healy heard that Nationalists were ready to offer de Valera either the South Down or the Belfast Central seat, 'probably the latter, for it is thought that President de Valera's election to that seat would carry more weight'. De Valera would, said Healy, stand as a Fianna Fáil candidate, but would not take his seat.[131] De Valera at first declined to stand in the absence of Northern nationalist unity. But he finally agreed to stand for South Down, where he obtained over 90 per cent of the vote in a straight fight with a Republican.[132] This reintroduction of the Southern leadership into Northern politics, albeit very brief and limited, was scarcely what a fit and active Devlin would have wanted, and indeed it proved totally ineffectual. It may be that the prospect of de Valera standing in Belfast Central was what persuaded Devlin to allow his name to go forward.

Devlin meanwhile had been taken ill again while visiting friends in England, and spent much of November in a London nursing home. A Nationalist convention in St Mary's Hall on 17 November was adjourned, reported the *Irish Press* under the headline 'Puzzle of Mr Devlin's Intentions'.[133] A deputation from Belfast then met Devlin in Liverpool, and persuaded him to stand, although he was not well enough to campaign at all. The Republicans made a strong fight, with a series of processions through the constituency. Many of their leading speakers were from the South. Michael Price of Dublin, a well-known left-wing Republican, declared that 'it was a matter of deep regret that Mr Devlin was again standing in the way of resurgent Republican opinion in Belfast . . . the re-election of Mr Devlin would be considered by the Stormont Government as a mandate for its policy'.[134] The *Irish Independent*, on the other hand, reported a couple of days later that there had been 'amazing scenes' in Belfast at a pro-Devlin

---

[130] Devlin to H. Keating, 28 Oct. 1933.   [131] *Irish Independent*, 15 Nov. 1933.
[132] *IN*, 13 and 18 Nov. 1933.   [133] *Irish Press*, 18 Nov. 1933.
[134] Ibid., 23 Nov. 1933.

rally, while the *Irish News* drew attention to the fact that Devlin's Republican opponent Patrick Thornbury, a young IRA man, was no more in the constituency than Devlin was, having complied with an exclusion order and retreated to Co. Westmeath. Devlin's supporters continued to make what capital they could out of the fact that 'he was on his sick-bed tonight', and T. J. Campbell promised that 'if he had the strength he would be with us before the end of the campaign'.[135] Campbell also alleged that 'in 1920, when the Catholics of Belfast were in their agony through riots and burnings, the people who are now on the Republican platform left the city, and allowed the Catholics to continue to struggle. Those on Mr Devlin's platform never deserted the Catholics of the city.'[136] Another Devlinite, Joe Stewart, declared that it was 'a great piece of impertinence for these people to come here from Cork, Dublin and other places in the Free State and tell us we do not represent Nationalist Ireland . . . It is very easy for these men who do not know the struggle we are making here.'[137] Even the Belfast Republican and former internee Peter Carleton recalled that in the 1930s 'there was still great loyalty to Joe Devlin and the remnants of his party . . . Of course he was a great speaker.'[138] On election day Devlin sent a message regretting that he was unable to be present. He won the election easily enough, with over 61 per cent of the vote, but a vote of 4,650 for the unknown Republican Thornbury was described by the *Irish Times* as one of three 'outstanding features' of the election.[139]

Devlin returned to Belfast a few days after the election, telling Hannah Keating that supporters were saying 'if I had been here there would have been another 2,000 votes in my favour', as the Republicans would not have been able to suggest that he was an unwilling candidate. Furthermore, Devlin alleged, 'personation was carried out wholesale', while 'raids and persecution' by the authorities meant that 'the people were ready to vote for anyone who was extreme, and the more extreme the better'.[140] At this stage Devlin appears to have been more concerned about the health of one of his oldest Belfast friends, Vincent DeVoto, than about his own. DeVoto died early in January 1934, and his funeral proved to be Devlin's own last public appearance. Two days later he had another gastric attack, and was taken into St John's Nursing Home, Belfast, in a serious condition. He died on the morning of 18 January, in the arms of another old friend, the Glasgow priest George Galbraith MC, a cousin of the late Dan McCann.[141] He was buried in Belfast's Milltown Cemetery on 20 January. His funeral was an enormous event, watched or followed by an estimated 50,000 people, including leading members of both the Southern and Northern governments. Dawson Bates and two other NI cabinet ministers processed up the Falls Road alongside

---

[135] *Irish Independent* and *IN*, both 25 Nov. 1933.   [136] *IN*, 28 Nov. 1933.
[137] Ibid., 30 Nov. 1933.   [138] MacEoin, *Survivors*, 305–8.
[139] *Irish Times*, 1 Dec. 1933.
[140] Devlin to H. Keating, 13 Dec. 1933 (Keating Papers, T/2424/3).
[141] Galbraith to H. Keating, 22 Jan. 1934 (Keating Papers, D/1919/18).

W. T. Cosgrave, Seán MacEntee (now Minister of Finance in the Fianna Fáil Government), a son of de Valera, and about 200 priests, including Cardinal MacRory and two other bishops. The journalist James Kelly, who was present at the funeral, recalled at the time of the memorial service seventy years later that, having failed to unite Ireland in his lifetime, it seemed that, by his death, Devlin had at least united it for a day, 'as Dublin cabinet ministers and TDs rubbed shoulders with their Stormont counterparts in the vast procession'.[142] 'I doubt if any other person in Ireland could have drawn together so many of the outstanding figures of today,' wrote Cahir Healy.[143]

A Joseph Devlin national memorial movement was inaugurated at St Mary's Hall in January 1935, convened by Devlin's Nationalist Party successor in the Belfast Central seat, the barrister T. J. Campbell. Eamon de Valera, W. T. Cosgrave, Seán MacEntee, Eoin O'Duffy, four bishops, and Count John McCormack were among those who declared their support. A committee was established, chaired by Seán MacEntee, who declared that 'he had known Devlin since boyhood and remained a close friend until his death'. O'Duffy, who had been in charge of the IRA Liaison Office in St Mary's Hall during the period of the Truce, said that 'in the dark and evil days in the North' he had taken Devlin's counsel, 'and his advice was always safe and sound'.[144] A memorial was later erected at Devlin's grave, and on the twenty-fifth anniversary of his death, in 1959, another ceremony was organized by Devlin's first biographer, F. J. Whitford. During the years that followed the memorial fell into disrepair, and it was not until 2003 that a restoration campaign was inaugurated. The revived Ancient Order of Hibernians led the way in this endeavour, and the memorial was restored in time for a wreath-laying ceremony and memorial mass held in Devlin's honour on the seventieth anniversary of his death on 18 January 2004.[145]

---

142 *IN*, 17 Jan. 2004.
143 *IN*, brochure of inauguration of National Memorial, 17 Jan. 1935 (CHP, D 2991/E/15/1).
144 *Irish Weekly & Ulster Examiner*, 13 Apr. 1935.
145 *IN*, 30 Jan. 2003, 17 and 19 Jan. 2004.

10

Conclusion: 'The Ulster Question is a Belfast City Question'

Although I am bitter and strong in my own convictions, my whole public life has been a life of effort in the work of improving the relationship between the two countries.

(Joe Devlin, House of Commons 1920[1])

The story of Joe Devlin and the story of nationalism in the North of Ireland were closely interwoven for forty years. Even during the crucial 1919–22 period, when Devlin had very little influence or power and when the Northern IRA were active and entirely outside his orbit, this continued to be the case, for he remained in political terms the leading Northern representative. Eoin MacNeill, Ernest Blythe, and Seán MacEntee were all Northerners who took an interest in the North, but their commitment was to Southern politics, and they were in effect advisers *on* the North rather than spokesmen *for* the North. They were not personally losers, whereas both the Devlinites and the Northern-based Sinn Féiners were. This final chapter begins with a brief discussion of Devlin's personal life and qualities, and concludes with an assessment of his political career in the context of 'the Belfast city question'.

A SINGLE MAN

Joe Devlin was a short, stocky man with a large head, and a thick mane of black hair. Contemporaries recalled 'a deep, resonant Belfast voice that every man would envy'.[2] The *Times* obituarist thought that 'the accent of his native city, emphatic and harsh . . . was appropriate to his fierce style of speaking'.[3] Like one in four Irishmen of his generation, Devlin never married. Given his

---

[1] Parl. Deb., HC, 5th series, cxxvii. 1134 (30 Mar. 1920.)
[2] Recollection of Alice Clarke. Transcript of BBC NI Radio programme on Devlin, 1959 (Hanna Bell Papers, D/3358/2).
[3] *The Times*, 19 Jan. 1934.

lifestyle, this is not very surprising. Between 1902 and 1920 he was so peripatetic that he can seldom have slept in the same bed seven nights running. There is little reference to personal relationships in surviving correspondence. Richard Hazleton, his friend and fellow MP, wrote to him in 1918 that 'I have met a great many interesting people on this [American] trip, including many pretty girls, but, like you, I do not easily lose my heart'.[4] Devlin seems to have been at ease, however, in the company of women. He was the idol of the Belfast mill girls, and at least one West Belfast constituent frequently danced the Lancers with him.[5] Socially he was a courteous and much-prized guest, and seems to have found families and their children a great comfort and delight. Judge Cahir Davitt, son of Michael, recalled that, when Devlin called on Davitt's widow with friends, he was the one who 'spent a lot of time talking to us children'.[6] This is not to say that Devlin did not maintain the penchant for five-star hotels that he developed on his early fund-raising missions. At work he was widely remembered as being fastidious and something of a disciplinarian—stemming perhaps from his Christian Brothers' background. He would sharply rebuke office staff over dirty fingernails, for instance, and he gave great attention to his own personal appearance. He would hand a copy of his speeches to Unionist newspapers in advance of meetings, but not to reporters from the *Irish News*, whom he always required to attend and take verbatim notes.[7]

His friends included Belfast business families like the DeVotos and McCanns, the Moloneys in Dublin, and, in earlier years, the hotelier William McKillop (d. 1909) in Glasgow. In London he stayed frequently with Matt Keating, a Welsh-born Irishman, and his wife Hannah. Not only did Devlin find Keating a parliamentary seat, but he also introduced him to his future wife. Devlin met Hannah Sweeney in her home town of Invercargill, on the south coast of New Zealand, in 1907. He and Keating met her again in 1910, at a lunch given by Bishop O'Donnell. Three years later they married, and their house became a regular London home-from-home for Devlin in his later years. Hannah later recalled that Matt (a businessman and Irish-language enthusiast) and Joe had 'very different philosophies' but that there was an attraction of opposites and that 'my husband's friends were his friends and together they enjoyed the theatre, good music and bridge'.[8] T. P. O'Connor, who was something of a father figure, and John D. Nugent were political contacts who also became personal friends.

⁴ Hazleton to Devlin, 18 Feb. 1918 (DP 6730/190).
⁵ Recollection of Mrs Ryan, mother of Mgr Arthur Ryan. Transcript of BBC NI Radio programme on Devlin, 1959 (Hanna Bell Papers, D/3358/2).
⁶ C. Davitt to W. G. Fallon, 6 Aug. 1966 (Fallon Papers, 22589).
⁷ Interviews with W. G. Fallon, Paddy Devlin, and James Kelly.
⁸ H. Keating to F. J. Whitford, 26 Sept. 1955 (Keating Papers, T/2307).

Devlin took holidays at different times with the Keatings, the Moloneys, and the DeVotos, and frequently also with priests, including Frank O'Hare—a political associate for almost forty years—John McCartan of Cushendall, and George Galbraith of Glasgow. Bishops were another matter!

Devlin lived with his parents until he went to America in 1902. From then until he lost his Westminster seat in 1922, he lived between Belfast, Dublin, and London, with frequent tours around Britain, Ireland, and the Irish diaspora. From 1907 until 1914 his home base was in Bangor, Co. Down. He then moved to a large terrace house in College Square North, in central Belfast, where the run-down character of his constituency office was said to contrast with his private quarters upstairs.[9] For the last seven years of his life he lived at Ard Righ, a grand suburban villa on the Upper Antrim Road, formerly the home of F. J. Bigger, who had made it into a something of a cultural salon, both Gaelic and 'gay'. On Bigger's death in 1926 it was put up for auction. Yet in his will Devlin left a mere £47. He was said to be heedless with money and generous to a fault. 'You couldn't make him rich,' said T. P. O'Connor.[10] Devlin's sensitivity, however, sometimes extended to money matters, and a slight moan to Dillon in 1919 provides useful detail. He estimated that his 'entire income was about £700 per year', made up of parliamentary and UIL salaries, from which his subscriptions to bodies in Belfast and elsewhere had averaged £200 per year for the previous five years.[11] He was a director of the *Irish News* from 1906 (chairman, 1923–34), and of a large whiskey firm from 1919. In 1923 he became first chairman of the Irish Life & General Assurance Company.[12] Since 1900 he had also been accustomed to receiving testimonials, large-scale and dignified whip-rounds amongst his friends and supporters. The widow of Dan McCann, one of his richest Belfast friends, recalled that they were always trying to keep him on an even financial keel, and it seems likely that Ard Righ was bought by his friends.[13]

The Devlins were not an especially long-lived family. Devlin's mother died in 1902 followed by one of his sisters. His father died in 1906, and his brother John in 1910. Devlin was an occasionally lonely figure, prone to depression and to minor ailments from at least 1908 onwards, and more frequently from his mid-forties. Very often physical and mental problems seemed to go together. In 1909 he told Dillon that he got a bad chill and a sore throat, 'as well as the

---

[9] Paddy Devlin interview.
[10] From Devlin's mass card, Jan. 1934 (Keating Papers, D/1919/16).
[11] Devlin to Dillon, 29 Mar. 1919 (DP 6730/218).   [12] *Hibernian Journal*, Nov. 1923.
[13] Recollection of Mrs McCann. Transcript of BBC NI Radio programme on Devlin, 1959 (Hanna Bell Papers, D/3358/2).

Fig. 10.1. With members of the Keating family, *c.*1930. Devlin, with Colonel Paddy Keating-Hill and Keating children.

return of the nervous complaint which troubled me some time ago'.[14] In 1912 he was down with influenza for three weeks, and later in the year a minor car accident produced 'shock and the illness which followed it'.[15] From 1912 until 1923 no year passed without at least one reference in the Dillon–O'Connor

---

[14] Devlin to Dillon, 22 Sept. 1909 (DP 6729/144).

[15] Dillon to O'Connor, 1 Feb. 1912 (DP 6740/192); Devlin to O'Donnell, 19 Nov. 1912 (P. O'Donnell Papers, IV, V).

Fig. 10.2. Cards on the table: in the Keatings' garden, *c*.1930. Devlin, with Mrs Hannah Keating (right) and two other friends.

correspondence to Devlin's winter ailments. He was 'a tremendous smoker' of cigars, and O'Connor thought at one stage that his problem came from 'over-smoking'.[16] Richard Hazleton once told Dillon that T. P. O'Connor was 'not as bad as Joe Devlin for late hours'.[17] It seems fairly certain that Devlin struggled with a drink problem. Lord Basil Blackwood, who encountered him on recruiting missions during the early stages of the war, told his mother that, 'in spite of stories about his drunkenness, he is a rigid teetotaller', while Devlin's fellow West Belfast MP, the socialist William McMullen, recalled that he managed to cut out his drinking during the 1925 Parliament, but the 1929 campaign put him back on it.[18] The Dillon–O'Connor correspondence brings out Devlin's volatility and over-sensitivity as well as his personal charm and rhetorical brilliance. John Hayden, who was not well disposed to the Dillon–Devlin axis in the Party, may therefore have been near the mark when he described Devlin as 'a creature of moods and impulses'.[19] Both Dillon and O'Connor were occasionally on the

---

[16] *Liverpool Daily Post & Mercury*, 9 Nov. 1922; O'Connor to Dillon, 24 May 1922 (DP 6744/888).
[17] Hazleton to Dillon. 24 Oct. 1917 (DP 6755/673).
[18] J. Bardon, *A History of Ulster* ((Belfast, 1992), 450; William McMullen interview.
[19] T. P. Gill, Memoir, Mar. 1918 (Gill Papers, 13478–526). See above, p. 191.

receiving end of his impulsiveness. On one occasion, wrote T.P., he 'suddenly erupted into the debate at the wrong moment and . . . in a way that entirely upset me . . . But Joe is such a good fellow that we must put up with these little bits of characteristic waywardness.'[20] 'It is all nerves,' thought Dillon. 'He cannot restrain himself. We all have faults, and Joe's good qualities and gifts are so exceptional and splendid that one must only make the best of it when he fails.'[21]

Well into his thirties Devlin was said to have retained a youthful—or 'boyish'—appearance. Dillon thought that he had found 'that which philosophers of old sought for in vain—that is perpetual youth'.[22] Throughout his career Devlin was described as possessed of 'a modest personality which shrinks from anything devouring of notoriety or pushfulness', a man who received the plaudits of a crowd with 'becoming modesty', and who was 'shy and reserved until he stands before an audience'.[23] On a platform he 'says a thing with such vigour and vim that it is not only convincing, but poetic', wrote the Irish-American newspaperman Patrick Ford. Lloyd George thought that Devlin was 'a great orator', while the Labour minister George Barnes thought him 'one of the most charming of men . . . [and] of commanding eloquence'.[24] During the Liverpool Exchange election of 1922 a reporter commented that:

Like a great actor, he fills whatever stage he occupies . . . [His] stocky figure and strong face made one forget all that has been said and written of his height. It was his mental stature we felt, and when he rose to speak a human thrill swept through us like an electric wave, as if he had already made an appeal to our emotions before he had uttered a word. Personally I do not like the Belfast accent. Last night, as Joe Devlin spoke it, it had a quaint music which I had never heard before.[25]

T. P. O'Connor was full of praise for Devlin's parliamentary work. Other colleagues had a variety of views. Stephen Gwynn thought that Devlin as a speaker was not at his best in Parliament. The *Times* obituarist thought that 'his eloquence was rather that of the platform than of Parliament, and yet he could fill the House and hold it'.[26] But Richard Hazleton wrote in 1919 that 'Joe was admirable—and much more in the parliamentary style than he used to be. Practice has given him ease and finish.'[27] Devlin's attacks in Parliament often came with a light touch. When the Unionist Charles Craig accused him of having spoken in America in favour of total Irish independence, he wanted to know 'why the hon. gentleman is entitled to read passages from his edition

[20] O'Connor to Dillon, 18 July 1919 (DP 6742/681).
[21] Dillon to O'Connor, 20 July 1919 (DP 6742/682).   [22] *NS*, 18 July 1903.
[23] John O'Callaghan of UILUSA in *Irish People*, 31 May 1902; *The Times*, 24 Apr. 1912; MacSweeney, Memoir, ch. 10, p. 5.
[24] *Irish World*, cited in *NS*, 30 May 1903; Riddell, *More Pages*, 86; George Barnes, *From Workshop to War Cabinet* (London, 1924), 189–90.
[25] *Liverpool Echo*, 6 Nov. 1922.   [26] *The Times*, 19 Jan. 1934.
[27] Hazleton to Dillon, 4 Apr. 1919 (DP 6755/687).

of Aesop's *Fables*.[28] Walter Long responded to one of Devlin's onslaughts by saying that 'the hon. Gentleman had amused the House as he always did, and had interested them with his eloquence'.[29] Carson interrupted one of Devlin's many denunciations of the 1920 Government of Ireland Bill, saying 'you never really hate, you only pretend'. 'That is probably', Devlin replied scathingly, 'why I have less influence in public life than the Rt. Hon. Gentleman. I have nearly every disability as a politician. I cannot organize a rebellion. I cannot sit on the bench when I ought to be in the dock.'[30]

In Belfast and in the UIL Office Devlin was an effective leader. On the wider stage he was more diffident. His forceful platform manner caused some to overestimate his ambition. In 1907 Arthur Griffith's *Sinn Féin* was wildly wrong when it portrayed Redmond as a 'Merovingian princeling', in thrall to Devlin, his 'mayor of the palace'. In 1910 Cruise O'Brien thought him 'the most powerful man in Ireland'. In 1911 *The Times* thought Devlin was 'the real leader of the Nationalist party'. The Unionist MP Ian Malcolm told Bonar Law in 1913 that Devlin is 'without doubt the most powerful man in Ireland today, consumed with ambition to take Redmond's place'.[31] Louis J. Walsh was probably nearer the mark when, in assessing prospects for the O'Brienites in 1909, he wrote: 'get rid of Dillon and T.P. and there will be hope. Devlin is not personally strong.'[32] William O'Brien, perhaps more bitter than accurate, wrote in 1918 that Devlin 'is a corner-boy who, like all bullies, is only brave when he has the mob at his back'.[33] Lloyd George told Churchill and C. P. Scott in 1916 that Devlin 'had no ambition', which Scott took to mean no 'selfish ambition'.[34] As we have seen, Devlin resisted pressure to challenge Dillon for the Party leadership in March 1918. A few months later, as Dillon was about to lose his seat in Parliament, T.P. wrote to him that 'Joe is quite inevitable in the case of your own disappearance; and that is not a very hopeful prospect'.[35] In fact, the seven-man rump of the Irish Parliamentary Party never appointed a leader.

There was also criticism of Devlin at a more personal level. The socialist William McMullen, whose political career in Northern Ireland was effectively ended by Devlin's strict adherence to party lines in 1929, did not see the 'self-effacing modesty' that Devlin's colleagues knew, but thought him 'a vain little fellow' who surrounded himself with sycophants.[36] Maurice Moore wrote more perceptively in 1914 that 'one of the great difficulties in forming an opinion about Mr Devlin is to reconcile his frank, open-hearted manner with proceedings

[28] Parl. Deb., H.C., 5th series, xl. 839 (1 July 1912).
[29] Ibid., 4th series, clxxix. 209 (25 July 1907).
[30] Ibid., 5th series, cxxvii. 1134 (30 Mar. 1920).
[31] *Sinn Féin*, 14 Dec. 1907; *Leader*, 19 Feb. 1910; *The Times*, 17 Oct. 1911; Malcolm to Bonar Law, 7 Oct. 1913 (BLP 30/3/10a).
[32] L. J. Walsh to T. O'Donnell MP, 16 Nov. 1909 (T. O'Donnell Papers, 15456/7).
[33] O'Brien to Dunraven, 12 Mar. 1918 (NLI, OBP 8554/17).
[34] Wilson (ed.), *Diaries of C. P. Scott*, 220.
[35] O'Connor to Dillon, 16 Dec. 1918 (DP 6742/578).   [36] William McMullen interview.

which seem to emanate from him'. Devlin had 'apparent childlike simplicity', but Moore had been warned that he was in fact a scheming politician. 'I can form no settled opinion; he was surrounded with unreliable advisers . . . who, I am inclined to think, used him more than he used them, though this is not the common opinion. He was not a deep thinker, but he was sympathetic to the poor, generous, kindly, and yet shrewd.'[37] Unsurprisingly William Martin Murphy thought Devlin a sinister influence, who set up a job-seeking bureau and thereby lost the Party's independence. The recipient of this opinion, the Irish Attorney-General James O'Connor, replied that 'I think he is honest and sincere, and I think also if you knew him better you would agree with me. He got in with a rotten crowd in Dublin who tried to make use of him for all they were worth. And I have some reason to think he realizes that now.'[38] On the other hand, the Duke of Atholl found him 'absolutely straight', and T. P. O'Connor wrote that 'he is popular with opponents—because he is so good-humoured and so good-natured; and above all he is so straight'.[39] Overall, Devlin's image in Dublin—where radical nationalism was stronger than elsewhere, and where he was associated with 'bossism', job-seeking, the sudden growth of the AOH, and the influence of John D. Nugent—was less favourable than in Belfast, where he retained cross-class popularity, and at Westminster, where his oratory and personal charm won him so many admirers.

THE GERRY FITT OF HIS DAY?

During the Treaty negotiations, Arthur Griffith declared that 'the Ulster question is a Belfast city question. They imagine they have special interests contrary to the rest of Ireland.'[40] This was by no means entirely accurate, for Fermanagh farmers were no more likely to sell land to someone of the other persuasion than Belfast workers were to mingle across the ethnic divide. But the Belfast situation was different in several ways. The urban-industrial context made conflict sharper: human proximity meant that communal alertness was necessary to prevent erosion of the barriers by individual relationships, while, on the other hand, it was necessary to maintain and seek to extend the barriers, so that communal ground—in terms, particularly, of territory and employment—was gained rather than lost. Furthermore, while Belfast had a larger Protestant majority than elsewhere in contested Ulster, at the same time it included the largest nationalist enclave in the province. The 'Belfast question' could not be solved

---

[37] Maurice Moore, 'History of the Irish Volunteers', *Irish Press*, 8–10 Jan. 1938.
[38] J. O'Connor to W. M. Murphy, 16 Dec. 1916 (RP, cited in Whitford, 'Devlin', 126).
[39] 'Present State of Ireland', 29 Apr. 1918 (LGP, F/94/3/45)]; *Liverpool Daily Post & Mercury*, 9 Nov. 1922.
[40] Jones, *Whitehall Diary*, iii. 128.

through boundary revision nor, unless accompanied by holocaust-level violence, through population transfer. Thus nationalist politicians, even moderate figures like Devlin, came up with no compromise proposals until too late in the day.

Devlin's underlying strategy was to seek to convert the Protestant masses to home rule through advocacy of the progressive social policies that the Unionist Party opposed. This ultimately failed because the majority of the Protestant working class was in fact the group most hostile to becoming part of an independent Ireland. It was an ironic response to Devlin's 'Orange and Green democracy' rhetoric that the most visible boundary-crossers were in fact men like Lord Pirrie of Harland and Wolff, the province's greatest capitalist. Devlin, like his colleagues, was over-optimistic until too late in the day. 'Irish Protestants', he told the House of Commons in 1904, 'would not rise in revolt when Ireland received home rule, they would be the first to rush for the loaves and fishes.'[41] He was then greatly encouraged by the slippage in electoral support for the Ulster Unionists in 1906, and what he saw as a democratic shift within Orangeism.[42] Speaking on the McCann case in 1911, he declared that 'the embers of religious bigotry are dying' in Belfast.[43] In fact, *Observer* editor J. L. Garvin was closer to the truth when he told Churchill in 1912 that 'never, never have the Nationalists since Thomas Davis nearly seventy years ago faced the Ulster question'.[44] Devlin very reluctantly agreed to temporary exclusion of four counties in 1914. T.P. later told Dillon that now and then Devlin 'relapses into regrets that he ever consented to help us with regard to Ulster two years ago'.[45] But this was not his ordinary mood, and he went on to persuade six-county nationalists to agree to temporary exclusion in June 1916, although in private he was never enthusiastic about this approach. His preference throughout, once he realized that some sort of concession to 'Ulster' was required, was for some sort of home rule within home rule, whereby a portion of Ulster would have a measure of administrative devolution from a Dublin Parliament. This was never taken up by the British Government (although ministers Christopher Addison and Henry Duke both appeared to favour it), nor was it pressed by Redmond or Dillon. And it was vigorously opposed by the bishops and clergy, who were desperately anxious not to have a settlement in which 'Protestant Ulster' would control Catholic schools, and preferred temporary 'exclusion' from home rule. In fact this attitude helped to produce a much more unwelcome result, in which Protestant Ulster won, not only control of the region's administration, but a control that was both 'permanent' and devolved from London rather than Dublin.

The bishops and clergy also made misjudgements during the 1916–18 period, and carried Devlin and Dillon along with them. A detailed examination of

---

[41] *The Times*, 3 Feb. 1904.   [42] *NS*, 9 May 1908.
[43] Parl. Deb., H.C., 5th series, xxi. 172 (7 Feb. 1911).
[44] Garvin to Churchill, 24 Sept. 1912 (Randolph S. Churchill, *Winston S. Churchill*, ii. 1398).
[45] O'Connor to Dillon, 18 May 1916 (DP 6741/308).

the Irish Convention suggests that it was intended as more than just a cynical delaying exercise, and that many of those involved, including members of the government, were seriously seeking a solution. The Convention failed because of internal disagreements. As Redmond declined into terminal ill-health, it was Bishop O'Donnell, rather than Devlin, who took the lead in the nationalist camp. He and Devlin, pressed from the flank by William Martin Murphy and his newspaper, were more concerned about trying to catch up with the increasingly radical trend of Irish nationalist public opinion than they were about reaching a settlement. They thus wrecked the Convention on the question of fiscal autonomy, from which they gained nothing. Had they not done so, the available evidence suggests that the government, within which Southern Unionism as much as Ulster Unionism had influence, was ready to apply pressure to the Ulster Unionists to accept a scheme linking a Belfast administration to Dublin rather than London. After the failure of the Convention and Sinn Féin's election triumph, attitudes in London were very different.

The electoral victory of Sinn Féin meant that a conciliatory settlement—offering less independence but holding out the prospect of a less absolute partition between North and South—became impossible, and led, not just to a political frontier within Ireland, but to one that delineated two distinct sovereignties. The era of violence initiated by IRA actions greatly intensified Ulster Protestant resistance to any kind of compromise with Catholics and nationalists, either within an all-Ireland framework or even within Northern Ireland. The main victims of all this—both politically and in thousands of cases personally—were the Catholics and nationalists of six-county Ulster. The violence in the south of Ireland from 1919 to 1923 was a gift to Ulster Unionists. The southern Sinn Féin leaders during 1919–21 took the view that Northern Nationalists and Republicans needed to break out of the sectarian mentality and come to see Britain rather than Protestant Ulster as 'the enemy'. But, as the young bloods of the Belfast IRA gradually broke down the caution of their local leadership, and Protestant paramilitaries were converted into security forces, this viewpoint was stood on its head, and for some while in 1921–2 the worst violence in Ireland was that between Catholic/nationalist and Protestant/unionist in Belfast.

By 1919 Stephen Gwynn had observed that Parnell's and Redmond's aim of uniting Ireland around 'a composite nationality' was being undone by Sinn Féin. 'I heard a young clerical professor at a public meeting not long ago say that to his mind Ulster was a wen, and that what you did with wens was cut them off. That is the new nationalism . . . Sinn Féin has made Ulster's case for them as they could never have made it for themselves.'[46] A partitionist mentality among southern nationalists was in fact not uncommon, and it affected priests as much

---

[46] *Observer*, 2 Nov. 1919.

if not more than the general population. Mgr John Hagan, a Sinn Féin supporter who became Rector of the Irish College, Rome, in 1919, thought that,

were the world run by logic, it would of course be quite enough to go on repeating that Ireland is one and indivisible, and that the Orange claim is so much bluff. . . [But] just as we claim the right to determine our own lot . . . any continuous area claiming exemption should have that claim allowed, provided it can back up its claim by an *absolute majority*.

This, he thought, would reduce the excluded area, 'roughly speaking, to the diocese of Down & Connor'. Hagan believed that minority protection should be guaranteed by similar measures on both sides of the border, but that separation should 'apply in perpetuity, so that the question would not be persistently re-opened'.[47] Revd Michael O'Flanagan, Vice-President of Sinn Féin, argued for partition in a long debate in the *Leader* in 1916.[48] The Dublin lawyer and Sinn Féiner Arthur Clery argued regularly for partition in his journal writings. He distrusted Belfast Catholics and saw them as urban people, like the British working class. He thought they should be assimilated, like the Irish in British cities, just as he thought the southern Unionists should be assimilated in the other direction.[49] It was a cultural equivalent of the 'sovereignty is more important than unity' argument.

The final outcome was, of course, that 'Ulster' became, in the minds of the Sinn Féin Treaty negotiators, a ruse for 'staging the break' rather than a central issue in itself. Griffith and Collins were outmanœuvred by Lloyd George far more thoroughly than had been the case with the Irish Party in 1916. In agreeing to the Boundary Commission they agreed to permanent partition for Belfast and eastern Ulster, while the response of de Valera and the Anti-Treatyites made reconciliation even less likely. IRA activity in the North in 1922 was encouraged as much by Pro-Treaty as Anti-Treaty Southerners, for reasons that had far more to do with the situation in the South than the situation in the North. After the death of Collins, the Southern Government came to adopt a more sensible line (although its attitude to the Boundary Commission, both before and after it took place, was essentially selfish), but Republican Sinn Féin and the IRA, albeit a dwindling force, continued to stoke up Ulster Unionist intransigence. A leading Southern IRA man, Frank Ryan, speaking in Belfast in 1925, gave an indication of the lack of grasp of Northern realities, declaring with reference to Union Jacks flying over Belfast that, 'where I come from, if we can't pull them down, we shoot them down'.[50] Tom Barry displayed a similar mentality, arguing in 1938 for a military campaign in Northern Ireland rather than in Britain.[51] Its culmination was the large-scale campaign of indiscriminate car-bombing in Northern Ireland directed by the southern leadership of the IRA during the

---

[47] Mgr Hagan to 'My Dear Friend' [S. T. O'Kelly], 5 Dec. 1918 (Hagan Papers, HAG1/1918/82).
[48] Maume, *Long Gestation*, 188.   [49] Ibid. 135.   [50] MacEoin, *Survivors*, 308.
[51] Review of M. Ryan, *Tom Barry: IRA Freedom Fighter* (Cork, 2003), by Marc Mulholland, *Irish Studies Review*, 13/3 (Aug. 2005), 418.

1970s. This was a complete inversion of the idealistic rhetoric of de Valera and MacNeill in 1919–21, who blamed Northern Hibernians and Republicans for encouraging 'sectarian' animosities rather than targeting Britain as the enemy. Cahir Healy, a Sinn Féiner in 1921 but later a Devlinite, wrote that the IRA were

the real propagandists of sectarianism . . . Between themselves and the [Ulster] Protestant League lies the responsibility for most of the sectarian and political troubles in the North . . . We do not believe it [a united Ireland] can be brought about by spasmodic raids for arms, occasional shootings in an area where our opponents are all armed to the teeth, [or] by tying comrades to church doors.[52]

Attacks on Devlin for 'sectarianizing' politics through his mobilization of the AOH lack conviction. He saw the AOH as an additional organizational weapon and an important American link. His whole approach, so far as the divided North was concerned, was in fact based on working-class conciliation. It proved to be over-optimistic and ended in failure, but the 'rotten Prods' who were expelled in 1912 and 1920 and election results such as those of 1925 suggest that he did attract a certain amount of Protestant support, though not enough to achieve what he wanted. Cahir Healy objected in later years to suggestions that 'the troubles of the North have arisen by reason of Joe's identification with the AOH', referring to 'the large following he had from Protestants always'.[53] Even *The Times*, a hostile critic of Devlin's Hibernianism for many years, declared that 'in his fervid advocacy of unsectarian nationalism he was indeed a nationalist missionary among the Protestant workers of Belfast'.[54] Devlin was a wonderful speaker and a formidable organizer, and was shrewd, pragmatic, and humane. But he lacked the stability and steadiness of temperament, and perhaps the confident ambition, necessary to be a great leader.

Devlin's parliamentary work on social questions was sustained over many years. Lorcan Sherlock, former Lord Mayor of Dublin, speaking at the inauguration of the Devlin Memorial Fund in 1935, said that 'Joe Devlin was the best representative that labour has had in his country for over fifty years'.[55] Even William O'Brien's sneering comment about Devlin becoming 'an English Labourite with a Belfast accent' is some indication of his reputation. Despite the rumours, he never did stand for election under the Labour banner in Dublin or Westminster. He eventually stayed loyal to Belfast as his political base, where he could not escape being an ethnic politician. An attempt to stand on any kind of Labour ticket there could only have narrowed the base of his support. Unlike Devlin, Connolly and Larkin are the names that resonate in the history of the labour movement. Connolly is in the pantheon of martyrs. Larkin is honoured by a prominent statue in O'Connell Street, Dublin, notwithstanding his controversial and divisive career and his association with Soviet funding.

---

[52] Cahir Healy, draft letter to press, n.d. [late 1935] (CHP, D 2991/A/3/35).
[53] CHP, D 2991/B/35/16. [54] *The Times*, 19 Jan. 1934.
[55] *Irish News* brochure of event, copy (CHP, D 2991/E/15/1).

Devlin's practical contribution to the advance of working-class conditions was more substantial. What has favoured the memory of Connolly and Larkin is less their contributions to the labour movement than their association—central in Connolly's case, somewhat marginal in Larkin's—with the foundation of the independent Irish state. Like the wider history of Catholic Belfast, Devlin's personal legacy has suffered from his being on the losing side.

A tougher challenge to Devlin's reputation is the support he gave for wartime British Army recruiting. In the pre-Rising period Catholic Belfast contributed as strongly to recruiting as any Protestant area. Devlin later expressed occasional regrets about what he had done, especially as his actions did not bring the political reward that he and Redmond had projected. But the evidence suggests that Belfast recruitment patterns were very similar to those in British industrial cities, and that recruitment had far more to do with poverty and the pathetic attraction of the 'separation allowances' than with patriotism. Politicians who urged their constituents towards the carnage of the trenches do indeed have something to answer for, but in this respect Devlin should be judged in the broader context of a terrible and avoidable war rather than on national grounds. While Devlin encouraged others to serve, and parliamentary colleagues older than him did serve, he did not do so. Our only evidence on this point is Stephen Gwynn's recollection that Redmond would not let him go. *Pace* William O'Brien's 'corner-boy' characterization, Devlin does not appear to have been lacking in physical courage. When in 1921 he was caught in crossfire in Dublin while being taken to see de Valera, Seán MacEntee found him 'as cool as could be'.[56]

After 1918 Devlin had little chance to influence events. The demise of almost all his Party colleagues meant that he could no longer with any credibility take a significant part in the search for a general settlement, while the attitude of the Free State leaders in 1922 and for some years after meant that he was excluded from consultation even where his advice might have been valuable. He became increasingly isolated and sometime depressed, and his physical health deteriorated. Although he might have become a Labour politician had he decided to try to carve out a second career in British politics, he was too closely associated with the home-rule movement for that to be a serious possibility in the Belfast context. The need to maximize opposition strength and, if possible, to bring former physical-force elements into constitutional politics ensured that Catholic political unity was the priority. This was unfortunate, although it is doubtful if a different strategy, such as Devlin's old non-sectarian labour rhetoric, would have succeeded in the wake of the brutal events of 1919–23. Thus Devlin ended up leading what was in effect a Catholic-nationalist party, to which he was unable to bequeath his commitment to radical social reform.

In his book *Falls Memories* (1982), Gerry Adams speculated whimsically that many inhabitants of the Falls believe that Joe Devlin was 'reincarnated

---

[56] Draft memoir, 11 (MacEntee Papers, P67/793/2).

as Gerry Fitt'.[57] This was not intended as a compliment. Fitt, although by background a republican socialist and civil-rights activist, became during the 1970s a strong opponent of Sinn Féin and the IRA, and in 1983 lost the West Belfast parliamentary seat to Adams. Having suffered intimidation at his Belfast home, Fitt moved to England and accepted a life peerage. Devlin, on the other hand, remained a Belfast resident and elected representative until his death, and did not accept the peerage that Prime Minister Ramsay MacDonald, perhaps jokingly, was said to have offered him across the tearoom of the House of Commons.[58] But Devlin certainly shared Fitt's hostility to Sinn Féin. Devlin once famously said that Sinn Féin 'is not a policy nor even a movement; it is an emotion'.[59] This gets to the heart of it. In its style and approach, in its long endorsement of IRA violence, the popular appeal of Sinn Féin has arisen less from a belief in the wisdom of its policies than from the psychological boost it has given to an underprivileged and victimized people. It has been the 'Off Our Knees' party, in contrast to the neo-Devlinite Social Democratic and Labour Party (SDLP), which is dismissed by Republicans as the 'Stoop Down Low' party. But Sinn Féin has in fact begun to succeed in Northern Ireland since the ceasefires of the mid-1990s, as it has sought to lose its association with violence. Alongside his remarkable talents, Devlin had personal weaknesses that limited his effectiveness at key points, and his career ended in failure. But he always knew that Protestant Ulster would have to be persuaded rather than forced into an independent Ireland. This may still be a long way off, but since 1998 Sinn Féin has—to the surprise of many—made great strides in the direction of communal reconciliation at the political, if not yet the popular, level. The Gerry Adams of recent years may yet come to be regarded as a more successful reincarnation of Joe Devlin—and that *would* be a compliment!

[57] G. Adams, *Falls Memories* (Dingle, 1982), 55.
[58] Recollected by Mgr A. Ryan, who was present. Transcript of BBC NI Radio programme on Devlin, 1959 (Hanna Bell Papers, D/3358/2).
[59] Plunkett diary, 6 May 1918 (PF).

Bibliography

MANUSCRIPT COLLECTIONS

Bodleian Library, Oxford

H. H. Asquith
Augustine Birrell
F. A. Hemming
Matthew Nathan

Boole Library, University College, Cork

William O'Brien

British Library, London

John Henry Bernard
Augustine Birrell
Charles Dilke

Cardinal Tomàs Ó Fiaich Memorial Library and Archive, Armagh

Joseph Dixon
Michael Logue
Joseph MacRory
Patrick O'Donnell
William J. Walsh (Toner Copies)

Christian Brothers' Generalate, Rome

Correspondence Archive
Index of Members of the Order

Churchill College, Cambridge

Winston S. Churchill (Chartwell Papers)

Cork City & County Archives

George Berkeley

Irish National Archives, Dublin

Census of Ireland, 1901
RIC County Inspectors' Reports, 1902–8

Irish Military Archives, Dublin

Bureau of Military History, 1913–22, witness statements

Linen Hall Library, Belfast

Sean McKeown memoir
James Wood Archive

National Library of Ireland, Dublin

G. F. H. Berkeley
Edward Blake
Eamon Ceannt
W. G. Fallon
T. P. Gill
J. J. Horgan
Maurice Moore
William O'Brien of Cork
Thomas O'Donnell
John Redmond
Francis and Hannah Sheehy-Skeffington
Minutes of UIL National Directory
Minutes of Sinn Féin Standing Committee

Parliamentary Archives, Westminster

Andrew Bonar Law
David Lloyd George

Plunkett Foundation, Woodstock, Oxfordshire

Sir Horace Plunkett

Pontifical Irish College, Rome

John Hagan
Tobias Kirby
Michael Kelly
W. H. Murphy
Michael O'Riordan

Public Record Office of Northern Ireland, Belfast

Cabinet Papers
Sam Hanna Bell
Sir Edward Carson
Devlin–Moloney Letters
Cahir Healy
Keating Family
David Kennedy
Lestrange & Brett
Hugh de Fellenberg Montgomery
St Malachy's Church Parish Register, 1858

The National Archives, London
RIC County Inspectors' Reports, 1909–21

Trinity College, Dublin
Michael Davitt
John Dillon
Irish Convention, 1917–18

University College, Dublin
Ernest Blythe
Eamon de Valera
T. M. Kettle
Michael McCartan
Dennis McCullough
Seán MacEntee
Eoin MacNeill

INTERVIEWS

Patrick Darby, Portrush, Jan. 1995
Paddy Devlin, Coleraine, May 1983
Thomas Dillon, Dublin, Aug. 1966
W. G. Fallon, Dublin, Aug. 1966
James Kelly, Belfast, Jan. 2005
Alban Maginness, Belfast, Dec. 2004
William McMullen, Dublin, Dec. 1971
John O'Leary, Dublin, Dec. 1971
F. J. Whitford, Belfast, October 1970

NEWSPAPERS AND MAGAZINES

Anglo-Celt (Cavan)
An tÓglach
Belfast Evening Telegraph
Belfast Newsletter
Catholic Herald (various regional editions)
Forward
Freeman's Journal
Hibernian Journal
Irish Citizen
Irish Independent
Irish News
Irish People
Irish Volunteer

Kilkenny People
Kilkenny Journal
Leader
National Volunteer
Northern Star
Northern Whig
Observer
Reynolds' Newspaper
Sancta Maria
Shan Van Vocht
Sinn Féin
Sunday Independent (Dublin)
The Times

GOVERNMENT PUBLICATIONS

Census of Ireland, 1861–1911.
House of Commons, Parliamentary Debates.
Report of the Commissioners of Inquiry into the Origins and Character of the Riots in Belfast in July and September 1857, HC, 1857–8, xxvi.
Report of the Commissioners of Inquiry into the Belfast Riots of 1864, HC, 1865, xxviii.
Report from the Select Committee on the Belfast Corporation Bill and the Londonderry Improvement Bill. Minutes and Index. HC, 1896, viii.

CONTEMPORARY PUBLICATIONS: MEMOIRS, DOCUMENTARY COLLECTIONS, AND WORKS OF REFERENCE

ADDISON, CHRISTOPHER, *Four and a Half Years: A Personal Diary from June 1914 to January 1919* (2 vols.; London, 1933).
—— *Politics from Within, 1911–18* (2 vols.; London, 1924).
BARNES, GEORGE, *From Workshop to War Cabinet* (London, 1924).
Belfast and Province of Ulster Directory (Belfast, annual).
BIRRELL, AUGUSTINE, *Things Past Redress* (London, 1933).
BOLAND, JOHN P., *An Irishman's Day* (London, 1948).
BOWLEY, A. L., *Wages in the United Kingdom in the Nineteenth Century* (Cambridge, 1900).
BROWN, W. F., *Through Windows of Memory* (London, 1946).
BUCKLAND, PATRICK (ed.), *Irish Unionism 1885–1923: A Documentary History* (Belfast, 1973).
CAMPBELL, A. ALBERT, *Belfast Newspapers Past and Present* (Belfast, 1921).
CHAMBERLAIN, AUSTEN, *Politics from Inside: An Epistolary Chronicle, 1906–14* (London, 1936).
CHURCHILL, RANDOLPH S., *Winston S. Churchill*, ii. *Young Statesman 1901–1914*, Companion volume (London, 1967).
CLERY, ARTHUR, *The Idea of a Nation* (Dublin, 1907; new edn., 2002).
CORISH, PATRICK J. (ed.), 'Irish College, Rome: Kirby Papers, Parts 1–3', in *Archivium Hibernicum*, 30–2 (1972–4).

CRAIG, F. W. S., *British Parliamentary Election Results, 1885–1918* (London, 1974).

—— *British Parliamentary Election Results, 1918–1949* (London, 1977).

CRONIN, SEAN (ed.), *The McGarrity Papers* (Tralee, 1972).

ELLIOTT, SYDNEY, *Northern Ireland Parliamentary Election Results, 1921–1972* (Chichester, 1973).

FUNCHION, MICHAEL (ed.), *Irish-American Voluntary Organizations* (Westport, CT, 1983).

GAUGHAN, J. ANTHONY (ed.), *Memoirs of Senator Joseph Connolly* (Dublin, 1996).

GEORGE, D. LLOYD, *War Memoirs* (2 vols.; London, 1938).

GWYNN, STEPHEN, *John Redmond's Last Years* (London, 1919).

HEALY, T. M., *Letters and Leaders of my Day* (London, 1928).

HEPBURN, A. C. (ed.), *The Conflict of Nationality in Modern Ireland* (London, 1980).

—— (ed.), *Ireland 1905–25*, ii. *Documents and Analysis* (Newtownards, 1998).

HEWINS, W. A. S., *The Apologia of an Imperialist: Forty Years of Empire Policy* (London, 1929).

HOGAN, DAVID, *The Four Glorious Years* (Dublin, 1953).

HONE, J. M., 'James Larkin and the Nationalist Party', *Contemporary Review*, 104 (Dec. 1913), 786.

HORGAN, J. J., *Parnell to Pearse* (Dublin, 1948).

IRISH TRANSPORT AND GENERAL WORKERS' UNION, *The Attempt to Smash the ITGWU* (Dublin, 1924).

JESUIT FATHERS (ed.), *A Page of Irish History* (Dublin, 1930).

JONES, THOMAS, *Whitehall Diary*, iii. *Ireland, 1918–1925* (London, 1971).

KELLY, JAMES, *Bonfires on the Hillside* (Belfast, 1995).

'KENNA, G. B.' (Revd John Hassan), *Facts and Figures of the Belfast Pogrom* (Dublin, 1922; new edn., 1997).

MCCOMB, WILLIAM, *The Repealer Repulsed* (Dublin, 1841; new edn., 2003).

MCDONAGH, MICHAEL, 'Sinn Fein and Labour in Ireland', *Contemporary Review*, 113 (Apr. 1918), 424–33.

MACENTEE, SEAN, *Episode at Easter* (Dublin, 1966).

MAC EOIN, UINSEANN, *Survivors* (Dublin, 1980).

MAC GIOLLA CHOILLE, BRENDAN (ed.), *Intelligence Notes, 1913–16* (Dublin, 1966).

MCMULLEN, WILLIAM, *With James Connolly in Belfast* (n.p., n.d. [Dublin, 1951]).

MOORE, MAURICE, 'History of the Irish Volunteers' (written 1918; published in serial form in *Irish Press*, Jan.–Mar. 1938).

MORGAN, K. O. (ed.), *Lloyd George Family Letters, 1885–1936* (London, 1973).

Ó BUACHALLA, SEAMAS (ed.), *The Letters of P. H. Pearse* (Gerrards Cross, 1980).

O'BRIEN, CONOR CRUISE, *Memoir: My Life and Times* (London, 1998).

O'BRIEN, WILLIAM, *An Olive Branch in Ireland* (London, 1910).

—— *The Irish Revolution and How it Came About* (London, 1923).

O'BRIEN, WILLIAM (of Dublin), *Forth the Banners Go* (Dublin, 1969).

—— (of Dublin), and RYAN, DESMOND (eds.), *Devoy's Postbag*, ii (Dublin, 1953).

O'DEA, JOHN, *History of the Ancient Order of Hibernians and Ladies Auxiliary* (Philadelphia, 1923).

O'HANLON, Revd W. M., *Walks among the Poor of Belfast* (Belfast, 1853; new edn., Wakefield, 1971).

O'HEGARTY, P. S., *The Victory of Sinn Fein* (Dublin, 1924).

O'LAVERTY, REVD JAMES, *An Historical Account of the Diocese of Down and Connor*, v (Dublin, 1895).

RIDDELL, LORD, *Lord Riddell's War Diary* (London, 1933).

—— *More Pages from my Diary, 1908–14* (London, 1934).

STENTON, MICHAEL, and LEES, STEPHEN (eds.), *Who's Who of British Members of Parliament since 1832* (4 vols.; Hassocks, 1978).

TAYLOR, A. J. P. (ed.), *Lloyd George: A Diary by Frances Stevenson* (London, 1971).

UNITED PROTESTANT COMMITTEE, *Statistics of Protestantism and Romanism* (Belfast, 1857).

VAUGHAN, W. E., and FITZPATRICK, A. J. (eds.), *Irish Historical Statistics: Population, 1821–1971* (Dublin, 1978).

WALKER, B. M. (ed.), *Parliamentary Election Results in Ireland, 1801–1922* (Dublin, 1978).

—— (ed.), *Parliamentary Election Results in Ireland, 1918–1992* (Dublin, 1992).

WASHINGTON, BOOKER T. (ed.), *The Negro Problem: A Series of Articles by Representative Negroes of To-day* (New York, 1903).

WILSON, ALEC (ed.), *PR Urban Elections in Ulster, 1920* (2nd edn., London, 1971).

WILSON, TREVOR (ed.), *The Political Diaries of C. P. Scott, 1911–1928* (London, 1970).

WRIGHT, ARNOLD, *Disturbed Dublin* (London, 1914).

BOOKS AND ARTICLES

ADAMS, GERRY, *Falls Memories* (Dingle, 1982).

—— *Who Fears to Speak . . . ? The Story of Belfast and the 1916 Rising* (Belfast, 1991).

ALLEN, NICHOLAS, and KELLY, A. (eds.), *The Cities of Belfast* (Dublin, 2003).

AUGUSTEIJN, JOOST (ed.), *The Irish Revolution, 1913–23* (London and Basingstoke, 2002).

BARDON, JONATHAN, *A History of Ulster* (Belfast, 1992).

BEW, PAUL, *Conflict and Conciliation in Ireland: Parnellites and Radical Agrarians* (Oxford, 1987).

—— *Ideology & the Irish Question, 1912–16: Ulster Unionism & Irish Nationalism, 1912–1916* (Oxford, 1994).

—— *John Redmond* (Dundalk, 1996).

—— *Ireland: The Politics of Enmity, 1789–2006* (Oxford, 2007).

BLAKE, ROBERT, *The Unknown Prime Minister: The Life & Times of Andrew Bonar Law, 1858–1923* (London, 1955).

BOLSTER, E., *The Knights of St Columbanus* (Dublin, 1979).

BOWMAN, JOHN, *De Valera and the Ulster Question, 1917–1973* (Oxford, 1982).

BOWMAN, TIMOTHY, *Irish Regiments in the Great War* (Manchester, 2003).

BOYCE, D. GEORGE, *Nationalism in Ireland* (London, 1982; 2nd edn., 1991).

—— and O'DAY, ALAN (eds.), *The Ulster Crisis, 1885–1921* (London, 2006).

BOYD, ANDREW, *Holy War in Belfast* (1969; 3rd edn., Belfast, 1987).

BOYLE, JOHN W., *The Irish Labour Movement in the Nineteenth Century* (Washington, 1988).

BRADY, L. W., *T. P. O'Connor and the Liverpool Irish* (London, 1983).

BRITISH ACADEMY AND ROYAL IRISH ACADEMY (eds.), *Ireland after the Union* (Oxford, 1989).

BUCKLAND, PATRICK, *The Factory of Grievances: Devolved Government in Northern Ireland, 1921–39* (Dublin, 1979).

BUDGE, IAN, and O'LEARY, CORNELIUS, *Belfast: Approach to Crisis. A Study of Belfast Politics, 1613–1970* (London, 1973).

BULL, PHILIP, 'William O'Brien: Problems Reappraising his Political Career', in Oliver MacDonagh and W. F. Mandle, *Ireland & Irish-Australia: Studies in Cultural and Political History* (London, 1986), 49–63.

—— *Land, Politics & Nationalism: A Study of the Irish Land Question* (Dublin, 1996).

—— 'The Formation of the United Irish League, 1898–1900: The Dynamics of Irish Agrarian Agitation', *Irish Historical Studies*, 33 (Nov. 2003), 132.

CALLANAN, FRANK, *T. M. Healy* (Cork, 1996).

CAMPBELL, FERGUS, *Land and Revolution: Nationalist Politics in the West of Ireland, 1891–1921* (Oxford, 2005).

—— 'Who Ruled Ireland? The Irish Administration, 1879–1914', *Historical Journal*, 50/3 (2007).

CARROLL, DENIS, *They Have Fooled You Again: Michael O'Flanagan (1876–1942), Priest, Republican, Social Critic* (Dublin, 1993).

CARROLL, FRANCIS M., *The American Presence in Ulster: A Diplomatic History, 1796–1996* (Washington, 2005).

COLEMAN, MARIE, *County Longford & the Irish Revolution, 1910–23* (Dublin, 2003).

COLLINS, PETER (ed.), *Nationalism and Unionism: Conflict in Ireland, 1885–1921* (Belfast, 1994).

CONNOLLY, S. J., HOUSTON, R. A., and MORRIS, R. J. (eds.), *Conflict, Identity and Economic Development: Ireland and Scotland, 1600–1939* (Preston, 1995).

COOGAN, TIM PAT, *Michael Collins* (London, 1990).

COOTER, ROGER, *When Paddy Met Geordie: The Irish in Co. Durham & Newcastle, 1840–1880* (Sunderland, 2005).

DARBY, JOHN, DODGE, N. N., and HEPBURN, A. C. (eds.), *Political Violence: Ireland in a Comparative Perspective* (Belfast, 1990).

DAVIES, SAM, *Liverpool Labour: Social & Political Influences on the Development of the Labour Party in Liverpool 1900–1939* (Keele, 1996).

DENMAN, T., *Ireland's Unknown Soldiers: The 16th (Irish) Division in the Great War* (Dublin, 1992).

DE WIEL, JEROME AAN, *The Catholic Church in Ireland, 1914–1918* (Dublin, 2003).

DEVLIN, PADDY, *Yes We Have No Bananas: Outdoor Relief in Belfast, 1920–39* (Belfast, 1981).

ECKSTEIN, HARRY, *The English Health Service: Its Origin, Structure, and Achievements* (Cambridge, MA, 1958).

ELLIOTT, MARIANNE, *The Catholics of Ulster: A History* (London, 2000).

ENGLISH, RICHARD, *Armed Struggle: The History of the IRA* (London, 2003).

—— *Irish Freedom: The History of Nationalism in Ireland* (London, 2006).

FARRELL, MICHAEL, 'The Great Belfast Strike of 1919', *Northern Star*, 3 (Feb.–Mar. 1971).

—— *Northern Ireland: The Orange State* (London, 1976).

—— *Arming the Protestants* (London, 1983).

FARRELL, SEAN, *Rituals ands Riots: Sectarian Violence and Political Culture in Ulster, 1784–1886* (Lexington, KY, 2000).

FEENEY, BRIAN, *Sinn Féin: A Hundred Turbulent Years* (Dublin, 2002).

FERRITER, DIARMAID, *The Transformation of Ireland, 1900–2000* (London, 2004).

—— *Judging Dev: A Reassessment of the Life and Legacy of Eamon de Valera* (Dublin, 2007).

FINNAN, JOSEPH P., *John Redmond and Irish Unity, 1912–18* (Syracuse, NY, 2004).

FITZPATRICK, DAVID, *Politics & Irish Life: Provincial Experience of War and Revolution 1913–21* (Dublin,1977).

—— *The Two Irelands, 1912–1939* (Oxford, 1998).

FOLEY, CONOR, *Legion of the Rearguard: The IRA and the Modern Irish State* (London, 1992).

FOSTER, R. F., *Modern Ireland, 1600–1972* (London, 1988).

—— *The Irish Story: Telling Tales and Making it up in Ireland* (London, 2001).

GARVIN, TOM, *Nationalist Revolutionaries in Ireland, 1858–1928* (Oxford, 1987).

—— *1922: The Birth of Irish Democracy* (Dublin, 1996).

GRAY, JOHN, *City in Revolt: James Larkin & the Belfast Dock Strike of 1907* (Belfast, 1985).

GREAVES, DESMOND, *The Life & Times of James Connolly* (London, 1961).

GREGORY, ADRIAN, and PASETA, SENIA (eds.), *Ireland and the Great War: 'A War to Unite us All'?* (Manchester, 2002).

GRIFFIN, BRIAN, *The Bulkies: Police and Crime in Belfast, 1800–1865* (Dublin, 1997).

GWYNN, DENIS, *The Life of John Redmond* (London, 1932).

HANDLEY, JAMES E., *The Irish in Modern Scotland* (Cork, 1947).

HARRIS, MARY, *The Catholic Church & the Foundation of the Northern Irish State, 1912–30* (Cork, 1993).

HART, PETER, *The IRA and its Enemies: Violence and Community in Cork, 1916–1923* (Oxford, 1998).

—— *The IRA at War, 1916–23* (Oxford, 2003).

—— *Mick: The Real Michael Collins* (London, 2005).

HENNESSEY, THOMAS, *Dividing Ireland: World War One and Partition* (London, 1998).

HEPBURN, A. C. 'The Irish Council Bill and the Fall of Sir Antony MacDonnell, 1906–7', *Irish Historical Studies*, 17/68 (Sept. 1971).

—— *A Past Apart: Studies in the History of Catholic Belfast, 1850–1950* (Belfast, 1996).

—— *Contested Cities in the Modern West* (London, 2004).

HILL, JACQUELINE R., *A New History of Ireland*, vii. *1921–1984* (Oxford, 2003).

HIRST, CATHERINE, *Religion, Politics and Violence in Nineteenth-Century Belfast: The Pound and Sandy Row* (Dublin, 2002).

HOPKINSON, MICHAEL, *Green against Green: The Irish Civil War* (Dublin, 1988).

—— *The Irish War of Independence* (Dublin, 2002).

HOWE, STEPHEN, *Ireland and Empire: Colonial Legacies in Irish History and Culture* (Oxford, 2000).

JACKSON, ALVIN, *Ireland, 1798–1998: Politics and War* (Oxford, 1999).

—— *Home Rule: An Irish History, 1800–2000* (Oxford, 2003).

JALLAND, PATRICIA, *The Liberals and Ireland: The Ulster Question in British Politics to 1914* (Brighton, 1980).

JEFFERSON, HERBERT, *Viscount Pirrie of Belfast* (Belfast, 1948).

JEFFERY, KEITH, *Ireland and the Great War* (Cambridge, 2000).

—— *Field Marshal Sir Henry Wilson: A Political Soldier* (Oxford, 2006).

JOHNSTON, SHEILA T., *Alice: A Life of Alice Milligan* (Omagh, 1994).

KELLY, MATTHEW J., *The Fenian Ideal and Irish Nationalism, 1882–1916* (Woodbridge, 2006).

KEOGH, DERMOT, *The Vatican, the Bishops and Irish Politics 1919–39* (Cambridge, 1986).

KINEALY, CHRISTINE, and MACATASNEY, GERARD, *The Hidden Famine: Hunger, Poverty and Sectarianism in Belfast* (London, 2000).

KISSANE, BILL, *The Politics of the Irish Civil War* (Oxford, 2005).

LAFFAN, MICHAEL, *The Partition of Ireland, 1911–1925* (Dublin, 1983).

—— *The Resurrection of Ireland: The Sinn Féin Party, 1916–23* (Cambridge, 1999).

LARKIN, EMMET, *James Larkin: Irish Labour Leader, 1876–1947* (London, 1965).

LEE, J. J., *Ireland, 1912–85: Politics & Society* (Cambridge, 1989).

LONGLEY, EDNA, *The Living Stream: Literature and Revisionism in Ireland* (Newcastle upon Tyne, 1994).

LOUGHLIN, JAMES, *Gladstone, Home Rule and the Ulster Question, 1882–93* (Dublin, 1986).

LYNCH, DAVID, *Radical Politics in Modern Ireland: The Irish Socialist Republican Party, 1896–1904* (Dublin, 2005).

LYNCH, ROBERT, *The Northern IRA & the Early Years of Partition, 1920–22* (Dublin, 2006).

LYONS, F. S. L.,*The Irish Parliamentary Party, 1890–1910* (London, 1951).

—— *John Dillon: A Biography* (London, 1968).

—— *Ireland since the Famine* (London, 1971).

LYONS, J. B., *The Enigma of Tom Kettle* (Dublin, 1983).

MACARDLE, DOROTHY, *The Irish Republic* (Dublin, 1937; 2nd edn., 1951).

MACAULAY, AMBROSE, *Patrick Dorrian: Bishop of Down & Connor, 1865–1885* (Dublin, 1987).

—— *Patrick McAlister: Bishop of Down & Connor, 1886–1895* (Dublin, 2006).

McCONNEL, JAMES, ' "Fenians at Westminster": The Edwardian Irish Parliamentary Party and the legacy of the New Departure', *Irish Historical Studies*, 34/133 (May 2004).

McDERMOTT, Jim, *Northern Divisions: The Old IRA and the Belfast Pogroms, 1920–1922* (Belfast, 2001).

MACDONAGH, OLIVER, and MANDLE, W. F., *Ireland & Irish-Australia: Studies in Cultural and Political History* (London, 1986).

MACDONNELL, A. D., *The Life of Sir Denis Henry: Catholic Unionist* (Belfast, 2000).

McDOWELL, R. B., *The Irish Convention, 1917–18* (London, 1970).

McGEE, OWEN, *The IRB: From the Land League to Sinn Féin* (Dublin, 2005).

McHUGH, JOHN, 'The Belfast Labour Disputes and Riots of 1907', *International Review of Social History*, 22/1 (1977).

MAGEE, JACK, *Barney: Bernard Hughes of Belfast, 1808–1878* (Belfast, 2001).

MARTIN, F. X. and BYRNE, F. J. (eds.), *The Scholar Revolutionary: Eoin MacNeill, 1867–1945, and the Making of the New Ireland* (Shannon, 1973).

MATTHEWS, KEVIN, *Fatal Influence: The Impact of Ireland on British Politics, 1920–1925* (Dublin: UCD Press, 2004).

MAUME, PATRICK, *The Long Gestation: Irish Nationalist Life, 1891–1918* (Dublin, 1999).

MERCER, ERIC, 'For King, Country and a Shilling a Day: Belfast Recruiting Patterns in the Great War', *History Ireland*, 11/4 (Winter, 2003).

MILLER, D. W., *Church, State and Nation in Ireland, 1898–1921* (Dublin, 1973).

MITCHELL, ARTHUR, *Labour in Irish Politics, 1890–1930* (Dublin, 1974).

MORGAN, AUSTEN, *Labour and Partition: The Belfast Working Class, 1905–23* (London, 1991).

MORGAN, K. O., 'Lloyd George and the Irish', in British Academy and Royal Irish Academy (eds.), *Ireland after the Union* (Oxford, 1989).

MORRIS R. J., and KENNEDY, LÍAM (eds.), *Ireland and Scotland: Order and Disorder, 1600–2000* (Edinburgh, 2005).

MORRISSEY, THOMAS J., *William J. Walsh, Archbishop of Dublin, 1841–1921: No Uncertain Voice* (Dublin, 2000).

NOVICK, BEN, *Conceiving Revolution: Irish Nationalist Propaganda during the First World War* (Dublin, 2001).

Ó BROIN, LEON, *Dublin Castle & the 1916 Rising: The Story of Sir Matthew Nathan* (Dublin, 1966).

—— *The Chief Secretary: Augustine Birrell in Ireland* (London, 1969).

O'CONNELL, BERNARD, 'Irish Nationalism in Liverpool, 1873–1923', *Eire-Ireland*, 10/1 (1975).

O'CONNOR, EMMET, *A Labour History of Ireland, 1824–1960* (Cork, 1992).

O'CONNOR LYSAGHT, D. R., 'The Rhetoric of Redmondism, 1914–16', in *History Ireland*, 11/1 (Spring 2003).

O'DAY, ALAN, *Irish Home Rule, 1867–1921* (Manchester, 1998).

O'KEEFE, T. J., 'The 1898 Efforts to Celebrate the United Irishmen: The '98 Centennial', *Eire-Ireland*, 23/2 (1988).

—— 'Who Fears to Speak of '98: The Rhetoric and Rituals of the '98 Centennial, 1898', *Eire-Ireland*, 27/3 (1992).

O'LEARY, CORNELIUS, and MAUME, PATRICK, *Controversial Issues in Anglo-Irish Relations, 1910–1921* (Dublin, 2004).

O'SULLIVAN, PATRICK (ed.), *The Irish in the New Communities* (London, 1992).

PARKINSON, ALAN, *Belfast's Unholy War: The Troubles of the 1920s* (Dublin, 2004).

PASETA, SENIA, *Before the Revolution: Nationalism, Social Change & Ireland's Catholic Elite, 1879–1922* (Cork, 1999).

PATTERSON, HENRY, *Class Conflict and Sectarianism: The Protestant Working Class and the Belfast Labour Movement, 1868–1920* (Belfast, 1980).

PHOENIX, EAMON, *Northern Nationalism: Nationalist Politics, Partition & the Catholic Minority in Northern Ireland, 1890–1940* (Belfast, 1994).

—— (ed.), *A Century of Northern Life: The Irish News and 100 Years of Ulster History, 1890s–1990s* (Belfast, 1995).

POUND, REGINALD, and HARMSWORTH, G. A., *Northcliffe* (London, 1959).

REES, RUSSELL, *Ireland 1905–25*, i. *Text & Historiography* (Newtownards, 1998).

SMITH, DAVID J., and CHAMBERS, GERALD, *Inequality in Northern Ireland* (Oxford, 1991).

SMYTH, J. J., *Labour in Glasgow, 1896–1936: Socialism, Suffrage, Sectarianism* (East Lothian, 2000).

STAUNTON, ENDA, *The Nationalists of Northern Ireland, 1918–1973* (Dublin, 2001).

STEWART, A. T. Q., *The Narrow Ground: Aspects of Ulster, 1609–1969* (London, 1977).

TIERNEY, MARK, *Eoin MacNeill: Scholar and Man of Action, 1867–1945* (Oxford, 1980).

TOWNSHEND, CHARLES, *Political Violence in Ireland: Government & Resistance since 1848* (Oxford, 1983).

—— *Easter 1916: The Irish Rebellion* (London, 2005).

TRAVERS, PAURIC, 'The Priest in Politics: The Case of Conscription', in O. MacDonagh, W. F. Mandle, and P. Travers (eds.), *Irish Culture & Nationalism, 1750–1950* (London, 1983).

VAUGHAN, W. E., *A New History of Ireland*, vi. *1870–1921* (Oxford, 1996).

WARWICK-HALLER, S., *William O'Brien & the Irish Land War* (Dublin, 1990).

WHEATLEY, MICHAEL, *Nationalism and the Irish Party: Provincial Ireland, 1910–1916* (Oxford, 2005).

WHYTE, J. H., *Interpreting Northern Ireland* (Oxford, 1990).

WOODS, C. J., 'The General Election of 1892: The Catholic Clergy & the Defeat of the Parnellites', in F. S. L. Lyons and R. A. J. Hawkins (eds.), *Ireland under the Union: Varieties of Tension* (Oxford, 1980).

WRIGHT, FRANK, *Northern Ireland: A Comparative Analysis* (Dublin, 1987).

—— *Two Lands on One Soil: Ulster Politics before Home Rule* (Dublin, 1996).

YEATES, PADRAIG, *Lockout: Dublin, 1913* (Dublin, 2000).

UNPUBLISHED THESES

ALEXANDER, C. NEAL, ' "A Fount of Broken Type": Representations of Belfast in Prose', Ph.D. thesis (Queen's University of Belfast, 2004).

DOOHER, JOHN B., 'Tyrone Nationalism and the Question of Partition, 1910–25', M.Phil. thesis (University of Ulster, 1986).

FOY, MICHAEL, 'The Ancient Order of Hibernians: An Irish Political-Religious Pressure Group, 1884–1975', MA thesis (Queen's University of Belfast, 1976).

HEPBURN, A. C., 'Liberal Policies and Nationalist Politics in Ireland, 1905–10', Ph.D. thesis (University of Kent, 1968).

MARTIN, DECLAN, 'Migration within the Six Counties of NI from 1911 to 1937 with Special Reference to the City of Belfast', MA thesis (Queen's University of Belfast, 1977).

McCONNEL, J. R. R., 'The View from the Backbench: Irish Nationalist MPs and their Work, 1910–1914', Ph.D. thesis (Durham University, 2002).

SLATER, GERARD J., 'Belfast Politics, 1798–1868', D.Phil. thesis (University of Ulster, 1982).

STARRETT, PAUL E., 'The ITGWU in its Industrial and Political Context, 1909–1923', D.Phil. thesis (University of Ulster, 1986).

WHITFORD, F. J. 'Joseph Devlin: Ulsterman and Irishman', MA thesis (University of London, 1959).

Index

The letter f indicates a figure and t a table. Numbers in *italics* refer to illustrations.